MODERN SAINTS

THEIR LIVES AND FACES

The Canonization of St. Bernadette Soubirous in St. Peter's Basilica. *(Photograph courtesy of The Catholic University of America.)*

"To the honor of the Most Holy and Indivisible Trinity, for the exaltation of the Catholic Faith and for the spread of the Christian Religion, by the authority of Our Lord Jesus Christ, of the Blessed Apostles Peter and Paul and by Our own, after mature deliberation and having often implored the Divine assistance, on the advice of Our venerable brethren the Cardinals of the Holy Roman Church, the Patriarchs, Archbishops and Bishops, We define and declare the Blessed Marie-Bernarde Soubirous a Saint, and We enroll her in the catalogue of Saints, ordaining that her memory shall be piously celebrated in the Universal Church on April 16th of each year, the day of her birth in Heaven. In the name of the Father and of the Son and of the Holy Ghost."

Pope Pius XI, December 8, 1933
Feast of the Immaculate Conception

MODERN SAINTS

THEIR LIVES AND FACES

By

Ann Ball

"After this I saw a great multitude, which no man could number, of all nations, and tribes, and peoples and tongues, standing before the throne, and in sight of the Lamb, clothed with white robes, and palms in their hands: And they cried with a loud voice, saying: Salvation to our God, who sitteth upon the throne, and to the Lamb."

Apoc. 7:9-10

TAN BOOKS AND PUBLISHERS, INC.
Rockford, Illinois 61105

Nihil Obstat: Rev. Joseph Barta, C.M.
                  Censor Deputatus

Imprimatur: ✠ John L. Morkovsky, S.T.D.
                  Bishop of Galveston-Houston
                  August 6, 1980

TAN BOOKS AND PUBLISHERS, INC.
P.O. Box 424
Rockford, Illinois 61105

1983

DEDICATION

Blessed Mother of Sorrows, here at last is your book. In the midst of your sorrow at the insensitivity of the world, may you find joy in the lives of these faithful friends of your Son. This book is yours, and was written for you and for the Catholic students and educators of the United States.

DECLARATION OF OBEDIENCE

In loving obedience to the decrees of several Roman Pontiffs, in particular those of Pope Urban VIII, I declare that I in no way intend to prejudge Holy Mother Church in the matter of saints, sanctity, miracles, and so forth. Final authority in such matters rests with the See of Rome, to whose judgement I willingly submit.

—the Author

ABOUT THE AUTHOR

When she left for college in 1962 to study journalism, Ann Ball told her mother that teaching school was "the last thing I'll ever do." Since her graduation she has taught almost every grade from first through twelfth—full-time for seven years and part-time for all the other years. Her motto is "Never say 'Never.'" She studied journalism at the University of Texas at Austin, and holds a B.S. in education from the University of Houston, where she was president of the education honor society and a member of the all-school honorary.

Ann Ball is the mother of two children who attend parochial schools in Houston. She currently teaches English and agriculture at Marian Christian High School, a parent-owned and operated school, where she also supervises the school farm—vegetable garden, a burro, goats, and several breeds of rabbits and chickens. She has worked as a private investigator, and is currently the director of public relations and corporation secretary-treasurer for a private security company.

Writing is Ann Ball's hobby. She became interested in researching the lives of modern saints while teaching in California in the late 1960's. She was startled by her students' surprised reactions when she showed them a photograph of St. Therese and saw that they had not realized the saint was a real human being. Ann Ball has researched *Modern Saints* for ten years. By her desk in the family den stands a metal file cabinet which contains folder after folder of information about modern saints and candidates for canonization. The information is in a number of languages, including Chinese. Ann herself speaks only English and some Spanish, but she has been fortunate in finding translators to help her. She regrets that she was not forced to study languages more in college.

Of her active life, Ann Ball says, "Being a mother and a teacher are my vocations; security is my job. I love all three, and also my hobby of writing."

TABLE OF CONTENTS

ACKNOWLEDGEMENTS

A complete list of all those whose help and encouragement have made this book possible would fill many pages. Those persons listed on the bibliography pages under "Correspondence" have all contributed information. In order to locate these people, however, I have had recourse to many others who directed me to the proper addresses. At the beginning of my research, Miss Marie Buehrle and Sister Mary Jean Dorcy, O.P. both took pity on my inexperience in research and directed me to a number of invaluable sources. Several other authors, including Mr. Leo Knowles, have assisted me in my search for sources, as have three bishops—Most Rev. John Morkovsky, Most Rev. Bernard Ganter, and Most Rev. Raphael Ayala. My correspondence over the past ten years has been phenomenal. During one summer I received so many letters from overseas that my postman finally asked for an explanation. Told of my work, he now often greets me with a comment about the arrival of a new saint.

Postulators and Vice Postulators of individual causes and of entire orders have been generous in taking time to answer questions and make suggestions. Some letters have sadly reported an inability to help, but all have encouraged me in this project. Never has anyone refused my requests for help. From the archivist of the Sacred Congregation for the Causes of Saints to the neighbors on my street who have given rough translations of letters in foreign languages, from bishop to postulant, the response has always been positive and helpful. I am most grateful to all who sent the pictures which have made this book possible.

In particular, I wish to thank Mr. Doug Descant and Mr. Jim Cirincione for their help in copying some of the photographs used in this book; St. Mary's Seminary, for the use of the seminary library; Miss Anna Bobak for her translations from Polish; Mr. Gene Decker of the University of Houston, for his translations from French; and Rev. Stephen Mandry for his translations from Italian, Latin, and several other languages, as well as for his advice on theological matters and canonical regulations.

Special thanks go to my relatives and my friends, and particularly to my family who put up with my research and enthusiasm. And to all those not specifically named, I leave your reward and thanks in the hands of Our Blessed Mother.

AUTHOR'S PREFACE

The idea for this book was conceived because of the reactions of a group of my students to a photograph of St. Therese of Lisieux. After making many references throughout the year to her and to her "little way," I brought to class a photo of St. Therese in her wheelchair. Comments ranged from "Where are the roses?" to "You mean she was real?"

I had been speaking of Therese Martin, a real person, but the children had visualized only a statue of a nun holding a bunch of roses. After questioning them, I discovered that these otherwise intelligent students had no concept of what sanctity was. And how could I expect them to be interested in or to imitate a plaster statue?

Immediately, I began to search for more photographs to "prove" that the saints were real. Much to my sorrow, I discovered that too many biographers had chosen to illustrate their books with artistic representations rather than true portraits. And artists, like some enthusiastic biographers, often tended to exaggerate the saints' good points and ignore their faults to the point where often a painting bore little resemblance to the person. I believe most of these artists chose this method of illustration in a misguided attempt to show the inner beauty of the servants of God. However, sometimes this very act of loving respect had the effect of performing a disservice to the saint portrayed.

A halo and pink cheeks and lips were added to the only known photograph of St. Gabriel Possenti. Perhaps this improved his pious expression, but looking at that picture it is hard to see a young man brave enough to disarm several drunken soldiers who had been looting and burning buildings, and run them out of town at gunpoint. Other photographs in this book have been altered to include a halo or flowers. In some cases, oil colors were added, distorting the original.

But instead of romanticized portraits of the saints, what we really need is the assurance that there have been and always will be real, warm, flesh and blood people who have lived the sort of lives that made them fit candidates for canonization. We need to know that we, too, have the opportunity to become saints.

xiii

Fortunately, many of the photographs in this book are true and unretouched. The photograph of St. John Bosco, for example, shows the whiskers which he probably did not have time to shave off.

For some saints, there is simply no photograph in existence. Both Maria Goretti and Dominic Savio were poor, and both died young; in their day photography was neither as cheap nor as popular as it is today. The representation of Dominic in this book is said to resemble him closely, and the painting of Maria was approved by both her mother and the Postulator of her cause as actually looking like her. The photo believed to be of Maria as a small child came to light only a few years ago, and is quite poor in quality. When an artistic representation instead of a photo is used in this book, it is considered to be a close likeness of the person. ˙

The first successful photographs were made around 1826 by a French inventor named Joseph Niepce. In 1829 he became a partner of L. J. M. Daguerre. In 1837, Daguerre brought out his own finished pictures which he called "daguerreotypes." There was no shutter on his camera, and the subject had to sit still for a long exposure—from fifteen minutes to an hour. Often he sat in a special chair equipped with clamps to hold his head and hands in place. Early pictures of this sort often show the pained expression caused by this forced immobility. The pictures seem stiff and solemn. This was the most popular type of photography until the late 1860's.

Next came the famous and very popular tintypes. These were actually printed on thin sheets of metal.

In 1886, George Eastman introduced the first Kodak camera. Thus with the development of a simple camera and of an easy method of making pictures, good photographs became widely available.

INTRODUCTION

What Is A Saint? A saint is any person who has died and gone to Heaven. All such persons, both known and unknown, are venerated on All Saints Day, November 1. But usually the word "saint" is used in reference to a Catholic who has lived a life of such exemplary holiness that the Church has officially proclaimed him a saint. This official declaration is called "canonization."

In the title of this book, the word "saints" is used loosely. In the case of those who have not been canonized, the word is to be taken simply as a description, rather than as an official title.

It is permissible to pray to and request the intercession of anyone believed to be in Heaven. However, official public honor in the liturgy is reserved for those whom the Church has recognized.

Who Can Become A Saint? Any Catholic who sincerely desires it can become a saint. God calls all the faithful to sanctity, and gives His grace to each one. The essence of holiness is the carrying out of God's Will each day through the practice of the virtues—especially faith, hope and charity—to an heroic degree. Extraordinary deeds and mystical graces are not necessary. Contemplative prayer is a very great help in bringing about deep love of God, though it is not absolutely necessary. All have an obligation to pray, and if a person perseveres in meditation and practice of the virtues, it is not unlikely that God will grant the gift of contemplative prayer, even to an "ordinary" person.

There is a great variety of personalities among the saints. Some have been witty and entertaining; others have been quiet by nature. Some have been rich, some poor, some beautiful, and some homely.

There are saints from countries not mentioned in this book. Those from countries which are today controlled by Communist or other anti-religious governments are not represented here in the numbers in which they surely exist. Information on these is very scanty. There are, however, no geographic boundaries to holiness; saints can come from any place in the world.

Can Only Priests And Nuns Become Saints? Definitely not!

Although the majority of the people in this book were priests or members of religious orders, all should strive for sanctity.

One reason there are so many religious in this book is that their orders were most helpful in supplying the information. In addition, the process of canonization is long and involved, and the members of religious orders have often been the ones to keep the causes of their deceased members progressing on the road to canonization; this involves much collecting and compiling of information and records. But there are also canonized saints like Gemma Galgani, who was refused admittance to the convent, or Maria Goretti, who preferred to die at an early age rather than commit a mortal sin. Many of the martyrs of all centuries were lay people. Not one of the twenty-two martyrs of Uganda was a priest or member of a religious order.

Do Catholics Adore Saints? No. God alone is worthy of adoration. Catholics venerate, or honor, the saints; the saints are accorded a veneration technically called *dulia*. To Our Lady is given a higher form of veneration called *hyperdulia,* but to God alone is reserved the supreme form of veneration known as *latria,* or adoration. God is glorified in His saints; the last of the Divine Praises is "Blessed be God in His angels and in His saints."

Why Does The Catholic Church Canonize Saints? Saints are canonized to honor them, to implore their intercession (prayers to God for men), and to give an example of holiness for imitation by the faithful. Canonization does not *make* anyone a saint; it is an official declaration by the Church that a person *is* a saint.

The Mystical Body of Christ is composed of the saints in Heaven who form the Church Triumphant, of the faithful on earth who form the Church Militant, and of the souls in Purgatory who form the Church Suffering. The saints intercede for the faithful on earth and for the souls in Purgatory; the faithful on earth honor the saints in Heaven, ask for their intercession, and imitate their virtues.

Some saints, of course, did things which one ordinarily could not or should not attempt to imitate. For example, Padre Pio received the stigmata, the wounds of Our Lord. This is not something which a person should ask to imitate; certainly, however, a Christian should follow Padre Pio's example of devotion to Our Lord. Imitating the saints will not make anyone into a carbon copy of anyone else. Even though each virtue—humility, for example—is essentially the same from saint to saint, it will take on a somewhat different form in each individual, depending on God's will in each life.

A priest in Houston once remarked that saints often "come in clumps." As the reader will discover, many of the saints in this book did indeed know and influence each other.

Are Saints A Modern Idea? No. From early Christian times a special honor was paid to the martyrs, and intercessory prayer has a biblical basis. As early as the fourth century, exemplary Christians who were not martyrs were also being honored. The early Christians believed that those who had died for the Faith must be especially close to God, and priests began to offer Mass by the tombs of the martyrs. Later, the remains were removed from tombs to altars in churches named in honor of these martyrs. From this grew the term "raised to the honors of the altar."

At first, there was no official canonization procedure. Those who had died a martyr's death, or who had defended the Faith (confessors), or who had led an outstanding Christian life excelling especially in penance, teaching the Faith, or great charity, became revered as saints by popular acclaim. Local Christian communities spontaneously began to venerate these people. Even in the earliest days the bishops attempted to put some form of official order into this veneration, but inevitably abuses arose. The need for a definite standard of spiritual perfection was felt.

Up to the end of the first thousand years of Christian history, the Apostolic See gave its consent to the veneration of saints only tacitly, and no formal act is preserved in which the pope recommends or prescribes the veneration of any particular saint. In 993, Pope John XV undertook what can technically be called the first canonization, declaring by papal bull that Bishop Ulric of Augsburg was a saint. The first laws concerning papal dominion in the cases of canonization were promulgated by Innocent III (1199-1216) but a brief of Urban VIII in 1634 unequivocally reserved all matters pertaining to the saints to the Roman See. The provisions of this papal brief were further developed by successive popes and were codified in 1918 in the Code of Canon Law. Alexander VII instituted the solemn consummation of the process of beatification through the ceremony in St. Peter's. Francis de Sales was the first to receive this honor, which was conferred in 1662.

How Does The Church Canonize Saints? The process of canonization by which Holy Mother Church declares a person a saint is long and involved. The procedure is the most careful and thorough investigative process to be found anywhere in the world. Until the 1969 reforms of Pope Paul VI, which consolidated a number of the steps, the canonization procedure involved twenty separate and well documented steps. Even after these reforms the procedure is still long and complicated. Following is a brief sketch.

If a person has lived a most exemplary life, or died a martyr, his cause may be begun. The cause may be requested by the faithful or may be begun by the local bishop or by Rome. There are a series of investigations and trials in the diocese; this is known as the Ordinary Process. If the Congregation for the Causes of Saints (formerly called the Congregation of Rites) decides that the person truly died a martyr's death or that he practiced virtue to an heroic degree, a detailed examination of his life, writings, reputation, and at least two miracles attributed to his intercession is made. This is called the Apostolic Process, or Papal Process, and it signals the Introduction of the cause for beatification. The Servant of God is declared Venerable, and study continues. Martyrs do not need the same proof of miracles in this part of the process as do non-martyrs.

In order to insure accuracy and fairness, a Promoter of the Faith, popularly called the "Devil's Advocate," is appointed to raise any objections to the cause. If the Congregation's findings are positive, the person is beatified, that is, he is declared Blessed. Persons who have been declared Blessed, known as "Beati," are honored locally or in specific religious communities or dioceses.

After beatification, the process continues. There is a re-examination of the evidence, and there must be proof of two new miracles through the intercession of the Beatus. From earliest times, miracles have been considered proof of God's approval of the life of a candidate for canonization. There are numerous and specific regulations dealing with miracles. Usually the cures accepted as proofs of sanctity must be of an organic nature and must be instantaneous. Although in most cases two miracles are required for beatification and two for canonization, as many as four may be required for each step in some cases where eyewitness testimony to sanctity is not available.

If this part of the process is carried out successfully, the Beatus (or Beata) is canonized. In a magnificent solemn ceremony in

St. Peter's Basilica, the Pope declares to all the Church that this person is a saint in Heaven. The saint's veneration is extended to the entire Church. He may be named in the public prayers of the Church, including the Mass and Divine Office, and churches may be dedicated to him. His feast is incorporated into the liturgical calendar, usually on the day of his death, which is his birthday into Heaven.

The type of canonization outlined above is known as "ordinary," or "non-cultus." Most canonizations are carried out in this manner according to the ideas outlined by Pope Urban. In some cases, known as "extraordinary," the purpose of the Church's investigation is to prove that there is a long-standing history of veneration of a certain person. In this form of canonization, the requirement of miracles as proofs of the person's sanctity is dispensed with. The person's heroic virtue must be credible in light of what is known about him. In such cases, the pope may dispense with the solemn canonization, and instead, after due investigation, he will "confirm the cult." This is called an "equivalent" canonization. Such was the case with the beatification of Kateri Tekakwitha, the first American lay person to be beatified.

How Many Saints Are There? Of all the holy persons who have ever lived—the sanctity of many of whom may never even have been suspected—only a few begin the long canonization process, much less complete it. Many Christian martyrs throughout history were not even buried with the information of their names. Many causes are dropped before completion. Most of the saints are known to God alone.

The revision of the Church calendar after Vatican II led to much speculation that some saints had been "demoted." This is inaccurate. No canonized saint has ever suffered a loss of status. Many of the saints removed from the calendar had never been formally canonized to begin with, but even these may still be honored privately, and in some areas, publicly.

Although one unofficial listing of recognized saints shows 2,565 entries, it is not possible to compute the exact number of saints acclaimed locally before the year 1000. Some estimates range to over 4,000. Between the year 1000 and August of 1980, only four hundred twenty-three persons were officially canonized by Rome. (Up to 1634, only one hundred twenty-five had been canonized.) When you consider that this small number includes several groups of martyrs such as the Twenty-two Martyrs of Uganda and the Forty English and Welsh Martyrs, it is obvious that the Church has canonized only a few saints. Between 1665 and August of 1980, the Church declared 1,224 persons Blessed, and causes for about 1,000 other Servants of God are currently under investigation in Rome. Hopefully the reforms made in the process by Pope Paul VI will help to speed up the procedure so that the Church may soon have saintly examples from all states of life and all parts of the world.

Explanation Of The Information In The Chapter Headings

The title of the chapter is the name by which the person is commonly known. The first of the two names in smaller type is the person's complete name and current title, and the second name is his baptismal name. In a few chapters there is only one name in smaller type; this is the baptismal name. In these cases the popular name and the complete name are the same.

The letters after some of the names indicate a particular religious order. For example, the letters S.J. after Father Miguel Pro's name indicate that he was a member of the Society of Jesus, a Jesuit. The dates given are the years of the saint's birth and death. The country is the country where the saint was born; if a second country is listed, it is the country in which he died. Finally, the saint's age at the time of his death is given.

In the preparation of this book I have made every effort to be accurate, especially with regard to the status of each cause. Any error of fact in the text is my own, and unintentional.

ANN BALL

— 1 —

SAINT JULIE BILLIART

Saint Julie Billiart, S.N.D. de N.
Marie Rose Julie Billiart
1751 - 1816
France - Belgium
Died Age 64

As a child, playing "school" was Julie Billiart's favorite game. Usually, Julie had the role of teacher, by the wish of the other children. When she went to work as a field laborer at the age of sixteen to help support her family, she began to teach "for real." She sat on a haystack during the noon recess and told the biblical parables to the workers. Julie carried on this mission of teaching throughout her life, and the congregation she founded continues her work.

Jule was the fifth of seven children. Her parents at one time had been well-to-do, but at the time of Julie's birth they lived on the proceeds of a small linen draper's shop. She attended a little one room school in Cuvilly to learn to read and write. Julie enjoyed all her studies, but she was particularly attracted to the religion lessons taught by the parish priest. This priest recognized something "different" and special in his young pupil. He allowed her secretly to make her First Communion at the age of nine when the normal age at that time in France was thirteen. In addition to her catechism lessons, the priest taught Julie how to make short mental prayers, to control her fiery temper, and to develop a great love of Jesus in the Eucharist.

In a mixture of innocence and wisdom beyond her age, Julie said, "I ought to die of shame to think I have not already died of gratitude to my good God." "The good God" is a typically French expression, and it was Julie's favorite. With her, however, this was not just a pious national comment. Each time Julie spoke the words, "the good God," she meant them with all the sincerity of her heart.

At home, Julie had plenty of practice in controlling her temper.

Her younger brother constantly teased and played tricks on her. He was, in short, a pest. Julie tried not to react in anger, and she played with him frequently. Her older sister was blind for many years, and Julie, with her warm and loving heart, spent long hours reading to her and helping to cheer her life.

Debts and poor investments reduced Julie's family to poverty. In an attempt to help support her family, Julie overworked. A murder attempt on her father shocked her nervous system badly. A period of extremely poor health for Julie began, and was to last for thirty years. For twenty-two of these years, she was a completely paralyzed invalid, unable to move about even with the aid of crutches. All of her sufferings and pain she offered up to her "good God." Visitors were so impressed with her cheerful acceptance of these trials that her reputation for sanctity began to spread over the countryside. Many came to her bedside to hear her talk about the lives of the saints, the catechism, the parables, and "the good God."

When the French Revolution broke out, Julie offered her home as a hiding place for loyal priests. Rumors of the aid Julie gave to these faithful sons of the Church reached the ears of the revolutionaries, and Julie became hunted prey.

Once while she was staying at the home of friends, an angry mob arrived. They planned to burn the hated "devotee" on a huge bonfire made of church furnishings. Hastily, Julie was hidden on the bottom of a rude cart and covered with hay. While a servant distracted the mob's attention, she was smuggled to safety. Five times in three years Julie was forced to flee in secret to avoid compromising her friends. Each move troubled her health more and more. At last, more dead than alive, she almost completely lost the power of speech. During this time, sixteen of Julie's Carmelite friends were led to the guillotine.

In desperately poor health and without the consolation of priestly care, Julie was privileged to receive an astounding vision at this time. She saw her crucified Lord surrounded by a large group of religious women dressed in a habit she had never seen before. An inner voice told her that these would be her daughters and that she would begin an institute devoted to the Christian education of young girls. How impossible this project must have seemed to the poor invalid! Nevertheless, she accepted this revelation with the faith that if God had chosen her for the work, it would be accomplished.

In 1794, Julie met the Baroness de Bourdon, a rich young woman who had cheated the guillotine only through the death of Robespierre. Together these two women founded the Sisters of Notre Dame de Namur.

At Amiens, the two women and a few companions began living a religious life in 1803. In 1804, Julie met the missionary priest, Enfantin. Recognizing a favored soul in Julie, he secretly resolved to obtain her cure. He asked her to begin a novena to the Sacred Heart with him for a special intention, not telling her what the intention was. On the fifth day when he visited her, he found her seated alone in the garden. Abruptly he said, "Mother, if you have any faith, take one step in honor of the Sacred Heart."

Julie arose and put her foot to the ground for the first time in twenty-two years! After a few steps, the priest made her promise not to mention what had happened. On the ninth day of the novena, he removed the obligation of secrecy, and Julie walked to the dining room where the rest of her sisters were.

The stunned sisters clearly heard her first words to them, "Te Deum Laudamus." Immediately after her thanksgiving, Julie began to help some missionaries by traveling to neighboring towns to give instructions. Some of her friends who knew how recently she had been an invalid begged her to stay off her feet and rest. Laughingly she replied, "Since the good God gave me back my legs, surely He intended that I should use them."

In 1805, Julie and three companions made their profession and took their final vows. She was elected as Mother General of the young congregation. Less than a year later, there were eighteen sisters. Soon schools and houses were beginning to grow in several dioceses.

No lasting success is reached except through the cross. For the Sisters of Notre Dame, the cross took the form of misunderstandings with the bishop and some members of the clergy. In 1809, the bishop wrote to Mother Julie that she was free to retire to any diocese she chose, but the houses given to her order would be used to train "true Sisters of Notre Dame." Calmly and with no bitterness, Mother Julie prepared her sisters for this terrible blow. She never failed in her charity and did not entreat her sisters to follow her. Unanimously they chose to go with her to Namur where they had been offered a home.

From 1808, Mother Julie had been given a gift of healing. Once, upon returning from a trip, she found twenty-three of her sisters in the infirmary with typhoid fever. She addressed them with these words: "My children, if you have any faith, arise!" All but four immediately arose, cured. These four left the order after a long illness. Julie also cured a young girl suffering from bad eyes by praying with her and making the Sign of the Cross on her eyes. Both of these miracles, along with several others, were examined and approved during the canonical inquiry into Mother Julie's life.

In 1812, when the same priest who had had Mother Julie sent from the diocese of Amiens recalled her and publicly repented of his actions, she treated him with humility and charity, rather than adopting an attitude of triumph.

In 1815, Mother Julie taxed her ever poor health by nursing the wounded and feeding the starving left from the battle of Waterloo. For the last three months of her life, she again suffered much. She died peacefully on April 8, 1816. Julie was beatified on May 13, 1906, and was canonized by Pope Paul VI in 1969.

St. Julie Billiart, who cured 19 out of 23 nuns of typhoid fever with the words, "My children, if you have any faith, arise!" This picture was probably painted from memory by one of her sisters after her death.

BLESSED PHILIPPINE DUCHESNE

Blessed Philippine Duchesne, R.S.C.J.
Rose Philippine Duchesne
1769 - 1852
France - United States
Died Age 83

The name of Rose Philippine Duchesne is the first inscribed on the Pioneer Roll of Fame in the Jefferson Memorial Building in St. Louis, Missouri. After coming to America at the age of forty-nine, she worked thirty-four years in the mission fields of the Society of the Sacred Heart, bringing education and love to the people of the area.

Philippine was born in Grenoble, France on August 29, 1769. As a child, she often accompanied her mother on visits to the sick poor. To the children of these homes, she gave many of her toys and other small possessions. When beggars came to her own door, she gave them her spending money. When her parents protested that they gave her these things for her pleasure, Philippine rather tartly replied, "This *is* my pleasure."

At the age of twelve, Philippine was sent to a boarding school run by the Visitation Sisters. Here she developed a deep devotion to the Sacred Heart, and determined to become a sister herself. Although she did not speak of this vocation, her father suspected that she was inclining in this direction. He was a liberal and somewhat anticlerical, and so he removed her from this school. He sent her to dancing school and had her tutored, along with her cousins.

When Philippine was eighteen, her father introduced her to a young man whom he intended her to marry. She informed her father that although the young man was most pleasant, she had decided to become a sister. Somewhat to her surprise, she got away with this statement, although her father refused to discuss the possibility of her entering a novitiate.

One day on a visit with her aunt to the convent of Ste. Marie,

6

Philippine simply stayed, leaving her poor aunt to go and face her father's wrath. A day or so later, she thrashed the matter out with her family through the protective grill and finally won her father's grudging consent to stay. She thought she was settled for life, but the French Revolution broke out and her father forbad her to make her vows and removed her from the convent. She went in obedience and silence, hoping one day to bring her father back to the Church. During this trial, as in all others she was to endure in her long life, she went for consolation to the one Heart that would never fail her.

In the years of the Revolution, Philippine was saddened by the loss of her beloved mother. Her father, who had become a lawyer in the Revolution, was the cause of much heartbreak to her on account of his actions and views.

For eleven years, Philippine worked for her family at home and performed works of mercy for political prisoners, the poor, and the sick. When someone was dying, Philippine would bring a priest to administer the Last Sacraments. At Grenoble she often risked imprisonment for her charitable ministrations to the victims of the Terror awaiting the guillotine. Her former convent had been turned into a prison for political prisoners, and she helped them in any way she could.

Driven by the desire to spread the news of Christ and His Kingdom, Philippine rounded up a group of street urchins and began to teach them catechism in her home.

At last the Revolution was over. Although it was still not entirely safe to resume the religious habit, Philippine bought her old convent from the government and invited her former superior and sisters to join her there. The superior was over eighty years old, and could not regain a firm control. The life was very austere, and one by one the sisters left, leaving only Philippine. Philippine was saddened by this, but she accepted the failure as God's Will. A priest friend suggested that she offer both herself and the monastery to Madame Madeleine Sophie Barat and her newly founded Society of the Sacred Heart. The offer was accepted, and Philippine became a member of the new society.

For twelve years, Sister Philippine lived under the direction of this gentle and saintly foundress. Mother Barat helped her control her impetuous nature and bend it to the Will of God.

In 1818, after many years of pleading with her superior, Sister Philippine and four other sisters left France for the mission fields of

America. At this time, she was already forty-nine years old.

In America, these sisters literally carved their foundations out of the wilderness, in spite of intense poverty and freezing weather. At times it was so cold that the milk froze in the bucket from the barn to the house. The sisters faced misunderstanding, language difficulties, and disease. Through it all, Mother Philippine and the sisters held to their goals of bringing Christian education to the pioneer children and spreading devotion to the Sacred Heart.

A letter from the bishop who invited the sisters to America shows the spirit in which the pioneer sisters were to work. "You have come, you say, seeking the Cross. Well, you have taken exactly the right road to find it. A thousand unforeseen difficulties may arise. Your establishment may grow slowly at first. Physical privations may be added, and those more keenly felt, such as lack of spiritual help under particular circumstances. Be ready for all . . . One must plow before one raises a crop. You and I shall spend our lives in this thankless task; our successors will reap the harvest in this world— let us be content to reap it in the next." This letter was to prove prophetic. Many hardships and trials did attend the foundations in America. In spite of all difficulties, however, Mother Philippine and the sisters kept their hope in the Sacred Heart, and their work slowly but surely began to prosper.

Once, in the early days of one of the foundations where the sisters were desperately poor, Mother Philippine's brother offered to pay her return fare to France. She wrote to her sister, "Tell him to use the money to pay the passage of two more nuns coming to America."

The Jesuits of the Missouri mission field claim a special debt to Mother Philippine. Their novitiate was moved to a log cabin at Florissant in 1823. A sturdy band of twelve Jesuits arrived to prepare for a lifelong mission to the Indians. Toward this little group, which included the missionary Father de Smet, apostle of Kansas, Mother Philippine showed the greatest charity.

Father William Robinson, S.J., said of Mother Philippine Duchesne, "She saved the struggling Missouri mission and prevented it from failing through absolute lack of resources." She cooked, sewed, and deprived herself to share the little she had. In addition, Mother Philippine considered it a great joy to be able to help these Fathers with their schools for Indian children.

For many years, she had dreamed of being a missionary to the American Indians. At last, when she was seventy-two, Mother

Philippine and three other sisters went to the Potawatomi at Sugar Creek, Kansas, to establish a school for the young Indian girls. Here the sisters were greeted by a group of Indians in festive dress on horses decked out with plumes. After a welcoming speech by the chief, several hundred braves and squaws filed past to shake hands. As their house was not ready, the sisters stayed in a vermin infested cabin belonging to a member of the tribe. There was a complete lack of privacy, as the cabin was always filled with visitors. Some of them brought the sisters gifts of human scalps as a mark of their esteem.

To her great sorrow, Mother Philippine could not learn the difficult language of these Indians, and so could not teach them. The priest at this mission had known Mother Philippine before she came. Though he recognized the drawbacks of her mission plans—her age, and the probability that she would not be able to speak the language—he nevertheless wrote, "Let her come. If she can't work she will obtain the success of the mission by her prayers."

Although they could not communicate with her verbally, the Indians loved Mother Philippine. They named her "The Woman Who Prays Always," for she spent much of her time praying in front of the Blessed Sacrament for the success of their mission.

Mother Philippine was recalled to St. Charles after only a year. Although she went willingly, in obedience to her superiors, she felt the loss of her Indian children keenly. In a letter to a priest friend she wrote, "I live in solitude and am able to employ all my time in going over the past and in preparing for death; but I cannot put away the thought of the Indians, and in my ambition I fly to the Rockies."

During the last ten years of her life, Philippine spent most of her time praying in front of the Blessed Sacrament for the Church, her society, and its missions. She died peacefully on November 18, 1852. Many years before, she and Father de Smet had made a pact that the first of them to die would obtain a particular favor for the other. Immediately after her death, Father de Smet received the favor.

Mother Philippine's love of prayer and the constancy of her devotion to the mission fields had impressed all who met her. Her funeral was attended not only by a great number of religious, but also by many lay persons, among them a number of Protestants.

Three years after her burial, the superiors decided to transfer the remains to a different burial place on the grounds. During this ex-

humation, the body of Philippine Duchesne was found to be incorrupt, although following the laws of nature it has since been reduced
to bones and ashes. (The only true photograph of her was made at
the time of this first exhumation.) Today, her relics remain at the
shrine dedicated to her honor in St. Charles, Missouri. Philippine
was beatified by Pope Pius XII in 1940.

Blessed Philippine Duchesne, who secretly aided prisoners awaiting the guillotine during the French Revolution, then crossed the ocean at age 49 to spend the rest of her life as a missionary in the American wilderness. This is a painting of Blessed Philippine.

3

SAINT JOAQUINA

Saint Joaquina de Vedruna de Mas, Ca. Ch.
Joaquina de Vedruna
1783 - 1854
Spain
Died Age 71

The handsome and aristocratic young lawyer, Don Teodore de Mas, had paid a visit to the home of Don Lorenzo de Vedruna, bringing a gift of candy for the daughters of the house. Joaquina de Vedruna, one of Don Lorenzo's charming daughters, loved sweets, and was quick to tell the young man so. Soon Don Teodore was back to ask for the young lady's hand in marriage. This was a fortunate match, and Don Lorenzo was quick to give his blessing. Following the custom of the time, Joaquina was hardly consulted, and on March 24, 1799, she obediently married the young lawyer who was ten years her senior.

A few days after the wedding, Teodore noticed that his young bride seemed depressed. Gently he questioned her as to the reason for her sadness. In his arms she sobbed out the fact that she had always intended to become a nun in a strictly cloistered order, and she was worried for fear she was being untrue to a God given vocation. Teodore told her that he, too, had felt the call to the religious life, but being the eldest son, he had acceded to his family's wishes that he marry and beget heirs to the family titles. Later, telling her children this story, Joaquina said, "We comforted one another."

Joaquina had been born in Barcelona, Spain, on April 16 of 1783. Her parents were well-to-do, although not rich, and she had the company of seven brothers and sisters. Her mother departed from the normal custom of having children educated by governesses; instead, she taught her children herself, being especially certain to give them a good Catholic background.

A happy, outgoing child, Joaquina attempted to see God in every part of her everyday life. She was especially devoted to Our Lord's

Passion, and told her mother that everything around her reminded her of this event. Her lace-making needle reminded her of the crown of thorns, and the thread recalled the ropes that bound Christ to the pillar. Even the weeds in the garden reminded Joaquina of her own faults, which she must weed out.

At age twelve, Joaquina once went to the Carmelite convent in Barcelona and gravely requested an interview with the superior. When the prioress came in response to the call, Joaquina begged for admission into the order. Fighting a natural tendency to smile at the childish request, the prioress tactfully told her that she was much too young, but that she was certain that if Joaquina had a vocation she could call again in a few years. Joaquina accepted the refusal gracefully and returned home. All assumed the incident had been forgotten, for Joaquina participated in all the customary activities of a girl of her day and class.

After their marriage, Joaquina and Teodore settled into a routine and began an ideally happy married life. Although the Vedrunas were an excellent family, and Joaquina was pretty, devout, and well-mannered, Teodore's family did not care for her. They felt she was too young, and that Teodore had married beneath himself.

Conflicts with her in-laws made Joaquina sad, but she and Teodore loved each other very much. Their love of God also strengthened the marriage. The couple began each day with Mass, and ended it by saying the Rosary. Soon the arrival of the longed-for children added to their happiness.

Four children had already been born to the couple when the Napoleonic wars forced the family's evacuation to Vich where they took up residence in the family mansion, the Manso Escorial. Teodore joined the army. A short while later, Joaquina and her children had to flee one night; one servant accompanied them. Joaquina's courage carried the little group to safety in Monteseny. Here, her third daughter was born, though the infant died within a few weeks. A son, Francis, also died quite suddenly.

In 1810, when it was safe to do so, the family returned to Vich. Teodore's military service had been distinguished, but his health had been seriously undermined. Three more children were born, but Joaquina realized that her husband had only a few more years to live. The quarrel with Teodore's family grew even more bitter. His sisters and brothers made constant financial demands, as he had inherited the bulk of the family fortune.

Joaquina's beloved Teodore died while she was confined to bed in another room of the house. The thirty-three-year-old widow was left to bring up her six children alone.

Joaquina's most important task at this time was the education of her children. In addition, she increased the fervor of her religious devotions. In solitude she practiced severe penances and mortifications.

After a period of mourning that lasted two years, Joaquina began wearing the habit of the Third Order of St. Francis—a light brown sack, tied with string. She continued to wear this costume for the next eight years, and began working at several charities such as nursing patients in the local hospital. Public opinion acclaimed her mad. Both her own relatives and those of Teodore were horrified at the sight of Lady de Mas going about in a rough sack! They even appealed to the bishop to make her stop wearing the strange garb. Joaquina, however, calmly followed her generous and loving heart, continuing to teach her children and practice her works of charity.

One day in 1820, Joaquina mounted her donkey to ride to the Carmelite church were she customarily attended Mass. With the perverseness of his breed, the stubborn little animal instead stopped at the Capuchin church, where Joaquina met a Father Stephen de Olot. Father Stephen had received an inspiration in a vision, and he directed Joaquina to found a group of nuns who would combine the contemplative life with the active apostolates of teaching and nursing. Joaquina could only stammer, "But where shall I find the nuns?" The priest replied simply, "They will come."

Although her older children were beginning to be settled in life, her youngest daughters still needed her, so for a time Joaquina continued her previous life of prayer, penance, and charity.

Because of the agitation of the anti-clericals, civil unrest broke out. Father Stephen was arrested and later exiled to France. Joaquina, too, was forced to flee to France, taking her three youngest daughters with her. Here she and Father Stephen began to draw up the plans for the future foundation.

Eventually, back in Spain, Joaquina made arrangements for the care of her three youngest daughters. She entrusted them to her son and his wife and to her brother. Although there is no record of the mother's sorrow at the time of parting, the many tender letters Joaquina wrote prove that her love stayed with her children.

In 1826, in the private chapel of the bishop, Joaquina made her vows. The new institute was to be called the Carmelite Sisters of Charity and would adopt the Carmelite habit, though in black instead of brown. With a small group of women directed to this work by Father Stephen, Joaquina began her religious life. As in her marriage she had been mother to her children, here she became "Madre" to the sisters. Through all the difficulties common to the founding of a new order in the Church, Joaquina held fast to her love of God. She said, "The more we love God, the more we will want to love Him."

The life of the young congregation was hard, and some of the original members did not stay. One night at supper, one of those who eventually left stood and announced her disapproval of the meal, which consisted of a single egg. In her humility, Mother Joaquina knelt at the feet of the sister and begged her pardon.

Civil unrest between the anti-clericals and the Carlists again broke out in 1835. Joaquina's son Joseph was well known as a Carlist and a bitter enemy of the anti-clericals, and the latter took their hatred of Joseph out on his mother. On February 7, nine men appeared at the Manso Escorial, which served as the motherhouse of the community, and arrested Mother Joaquina.

They dragged her through the streets to the municipal prison. Once inside, one of the soldiers struck her with the butt of his rifle. For five days, Mother Joaquina was held at the prison; throughout this time she made no complaint. Finally, she was simply released, and no charges were made.

Although she returned home briefly, she first fled to one of the other houses of the order, and then back again to France. Here she was concerned about the young congregation and her own family. Placing complete trust in God, she prayed for their safety. At last she was able to return.

In 1844, the members of the community at Vich were at last allowed to make their vows in public. Through a number of further trials, the small community began to grow steadily.

In 1849, Mother Joaquina suffered the first of a series of strokes that left her totally paralyzed for the last five years of her life. Although for some time she had also been bereft of the power of speech, she received the Last Sacraments with touching devotion, and quietly died in Barcelona on August 28, 1854.

Mother Joaquina bequeathed to her community an example of heroic love of God. Twenty-five of her sisters were killed during the

Spanish Civil War of 1936 - 1939. Joaquina was beatified in 1940, and canonized in 1959.

St. Joaquina—wife, mother of nine children, and foundress of the Carmelites of Charity. This is a painting of St. Joaquina.

4

SAINT DOMINIC SAVIO

Dominic Savio
1842 - 1857
Italy
Died Age 14

Dominic Savio had decided to become a saint. Immediately he went to the chapel to pray. He refused to play any games with the other boys, and put on a long, serious face. For two days Dominic remained in this sober attitude. Finally, Don Bosco, his teacher, called him and asked if he were sick. No, Dominic assured him that he felt particularly well and happy. Then why, asked Don Bosco, had Dominic refused to play his customary games, and why the sober expression?

When Dominic explained his great desire to become a saint, Don Bosco praised his decision, but counseled him to be cheerful, and not to worry; serving God is the way to true happiness.

Dominic was born on April 2, 1842, the son of a very poor blacksmith. He went to school near his home for as long as possible. Later, he walked a six-mile round trip to attend a school in a nearby town. One day, while the teacher was out of the room, two boys brought in a lot of snow and trash and stuffed it into the only iron stove which was heating the room. When the teacher returned, he was so angry that the two guilty boys claimed that Dominic had done it. The teacher gave Dominic a severe scolding, telling him that were this not his first offense, he would have been immediately expelled. Dominic said not one word in his own defense, but stood in front of the class and hung his head while the teacher scolded. The next day some of the other boys probably tattled. At any rate, the teacher learned the truth of the matter. He went immediately to Dominic and asked why he had not answered the charges made against him. Dominic said that he knew the teacher would have expelled the other boys, and he wanted them to have another chance.

17

"Besides," said Dominic, "I remembered that Our Lord was unjustly accused and He said nothing."

Even at this early age, Dominic had begun the practice of the virtue which was later declared heroic at his beatification. From the time he was a small child, he had been very religious. He pleaded to help the priest at Mass when he was only five. But more than simply observing religious customs and practices, Dominic lived his religion for the entire span of his brief life.

In 1854, he went to Turin and became a pupil at Don Bosco's Oratory. Here he worked, studied, played, and prayed for three years before his final illness forced him to return home.

During Dominic's brief time at the Oratory, he gained the love and respect of all the boys and the priests. He was not pushy and would not interrupt to state his own views, but he was not afraid to oppose wrong and could always give reasons why he thought a certain action was wrong.

Once Dominic overheard two boys planning a rock fight. They had become very angry with each other and were going to fight it out. Dominic tried his best to talk them out of this idea which was quite dangerous, but nothing would sway their determination. He could have told the teacher, but he felt this would only have served to postpone the fight. Finally, he made the boys agree to one secret condition which he would tell them about just before the fight. The morning of the fight, Dominic went with the boys and helped them make their preparations by piling up rocks. When the boys were ready to begin, Dominic held up a small crucifix and reminded them that Christ died forgiving sins, but that they were going to fight a dangerous fight to get even for a minor slight. "Now," said Dominic, "throw your first rock at me. That is my condition."

At this demand, one of the boys said, "But Dominic, you have never hurt me or done anything to me, and you are my friend."

"You will not hurt me, a poor human, but will you, by your actions, hurt Jesus Christ who is also God?" asked Dominic.

The boys hung their heads in shame and dropped their stones. Dominic never mentioned this incident, and we would have no record of it had not the two combatants told all their friends.

Dominic had a great love for the Mother of God, and organized a club to honor her. His stories of the Blessed Mother were a favorite entertainment with the younger boys.

Dominic lived before the reforms of St. Pius X. Not only were children obliged to wait until they were eleven or twelve to receive First Communion, but afterwards Communion was received comparatively rarely. A good Catholic usually only received three or four times a year. Because Dominic seemed to understand his religion and his catechism very well, his priest allowed him to make his First Communion at the age of seven. Afterwards, he received monthly until he came to the Oratory where he was encouraged to do so more often.

Before his First Communion, Dominic made four promises and wrote them in a little book which he often reread. He wrote:

1. I will go often to confession and I will go to Holy Communion as often as I am allowed.

2. I will try to give Sundays and holy days completely to God.

3. My best friends will be Jesus and Mary.

4. Death, but not sin.

The fourth promise was to be Dominic's motto for the rest of his life. Time and again, he asked God to let him die before offending Him by committing a mortal sin. Dominic knew some pretty rough boys and was often in a bad part of town. However, to the end of his life he never committed a mortal sin. In fact, he led a saintly life.

Never in robust health, Dominic became quite ill in March of 1857 with what the doctors diagnosed as an inflammation of the lungs. The treatment in those days consisted of bloodletting, or slitting a vein and letting "excess" blood drain out. In the space of four days, the doctor cut Dominic's arm ten times. Far from helping, this probably hastened his death. He died quietly in his home on March 9, 1857. His last words were, "What a beautiful thing I see."

Don Bosco and the boys at the Oratory had been anxiously awaiting word of Dominic. His father's letter arrived; it began, "With my heart full of grief I send you this sad news. Dominic, my dear son and your child in God gave his soul to God on March 9th after having received with the greatest devotion the Last Sacraments and the papal blessing."

Dominic's friends were the first to realize his sanctity. They began praying to him, and soon reports of a cured toothache or a passing mark on an exam were brought to Don Bosco. In 1876, Dominic appeared to Don Bosco in one of the saint's vivid dreams. At this time he made several predictions, and when asked, told Don Bosco that he was in Heaven. Dominic himself was beautiful and glorious, and he appeared in the company of many other blessed souls. He gave Don Bosco three slips of paper; in one the priest saw the faces of Oratory boys who were living in their baptismal innocence. In the second he saw those who had fallen but were trying to rise from their sin. When he opened the third paper (boys living in mortal sin), it gave off such a disgusting and nauseating stench that Don Bosco abruptly awoke; he found that the disgusting odor still clung to his clothes.

"The Oratory has had many saintly boys, some of whom have practiced virtue as heroically as St. Aloysius." These words of Don Bosco were proven in the case of Dominic Savio. Dominic's cause was officially opened in 1908. He was beatified in 1950, and canonized in 1954.

St. Pius X called Dominic a true model for the youth of our times. Dominic lived the type of life that can be imitated by teenagers all over the world. It is fitting that the two miracles accepted for his beatification involved teenagers.

St. Dominic Savio, whose motto was, "Death, but not sin." No photograph of St. Dominic Savio exists; this painting is the best likeness of him.

5

SAINT JOHN NEUMANN

Saint John Neumann, C.Ss.R.
John Nepomucene Neumann
1811 - 1860
Bohemia (Czechoslovakia) - United States
Died Age 48

If you have ever attended a Catholic elementary school or participated in the Forty Hours devotion in a Catholic parish in America, then you have felt the effects of the work of a shy immigrant priest, John Nepomucene Neumann. He came to America as a penniless seminarian in 1836, and died only twenty-four years later, after accomplishing more than many men accomplish in twice that period. At the time of his death he was the fourth bishop of Philadelphia. The life of this saint is the perfect demonstration that sanctity is open to all. There were no miraculous events during his lifetime. Instead, he took the ordinary path of simply following his vocation with all his heart and strength and with perfect constancy.

John was born March 28, 1811, in the village of Prachatitz in Bohemia (now Czechoslovakia). His father was a Bavarian who owned a small stocking weaving business, and his mother was a native of the village where John was born.

John was a quiet boy, the bookworm type. His hobbies were botany and astronomy, and as a young child he thought often of becoming a scientist. At twenty, when a choice of life had to be made, he was torn between the desire to be a doctor and the thought that he should become a priest.

The priesthood seemed almost unattainable. The seminary would accept only twenty of the ninety applicants, and John had no influential friends. After John talked it over with his parents, his mother told him, "Well, John, if you really are thinking of the priesthood, it's only fair to yourself to try."

Without much hope, John made application to the seminary, and to his surprise was accepted. He studied hard and made a good scholastic record there, learning to speak six languages and becoming familiar with two others. John's linguistic skills would be one of his greatest assets in life.

Because of this, John was offered an excellent government post. Neither the seminary rector nor the two dignitaries who had come to offer the job could understand his quiet refusal. John had seen where he thought he was needed—in pioneer America where the European immigrant Catholics needed a priest who could speak their languages and hear their confessions. The three men found it hard to accept the fact that John would willingly give up the life of luxury and honor they offered and choose instead to travel to the difficult life in America.

As John had completed his studies, he waited anxiously for ordination. The bishop was ill, and the date was put off indefinitely. Thinking that perhaps an American bishop would ordain him, he wrote several letters offering to come and serve in America. He did not receive a single reply. John determined on a bold course. He would make his appeal to an American bishop in person.

John packed a small bag and made his way, largely on foot, to the port of Havre, where he embarked in the spring of 1836. After forty days at sea, he arrived at the docks in Manhattan. In an interview with Bishop Jean Dubois, he learned that an invitation to him had been mailed, but he had left before its arrival. The bishop ordained John on June 25, 1836, and sent him to a parish of nine hundred square miles near Buffalo. In this mosquito infested swamp land, there were about four hundred widely scattered Catholic families— German, French, Irish, and Indian. Later asked what he had done in Buffalo, John smilingly replied, "Walk." He walked throughout his large parish, sometimes ten to twenty miles a day, carrying his Mass kit in a pack on his back.

Father Neumann had a special love for the children, and he kept his pockets filled with rock candy as an inducement for them to learn their catechism. Many of the children whom he met were growing up speaking a hopeless mixture of German and English and had no opportunity for any form of education. This need inspired John to begin one of his favorite projects—his schools.

John's parish work, though not easy, gradually took on a bit of routine. Still there were exciting moments, for example, the time he was caught and nearly hanged by masked bandits—or the time he was almost shot in the back by a drunken mule skinner.

Fatigue at last caught up with the young priest. On one of his trips, Father Neumann passed out in the woods, where he was found by some Indians and carried back to his hut. This incident prompted a friend to offer a horse for the longer journeys. Father Neumann was short and had to coax the beast close to a stump or fence in order to mount it. On one occasion, he mistakenly put the wrong foot into the stirrup. The horse started off and the little priest hastily flung himself into the saddle. Imagine his chagrin when he realized that the horse's tail was in the place where his head ought to be. Luckily two nearby workmen were able to halt the steed and return Father to a more conventional position.

Although Father Neumann recognized that his work on the frontier was needed, he found there was something lacking in his own spiritual life. He felt he needed the company and advice of other priests, and determined to join a religious order. He had met a Redemptorist, and was impressed by what he had learned of this order. With the grudging permission of his bishop, who hated to lose such a good priest, John left by stagecoach to join the Redemptorists where they were still struggling in Pittsburgh to make their first permanent foundation in America. Here he was received as a novice, and made his vows in 1842.

During his first years as a Redemptorist, Father Neumann was stationed in a number of places. At the age of thirty-five he was appointed superior general of the order in America. John was not popular in this post for a number of reasons. He was young, and relatively new to the order. His personality was unobtrusive. Most of all, his policy of using all his available personnel to staff existing foundations, instead of splintering the group and making new foundations, was not what the eager members of the order wanted. John's sensitive soul smarted under the criticism, and he humbly begged his superiors to relieve him of this post. At last, after two years, he was allowed to resign and become a simple religious again. His days "back in the ranks" did not last long, however, for in January of 1851 he was again made a superior; he was chosen to head the group of Redemptorists at St. Alphonsus in Baltimore.

No one knows how the rumor started, but soon people were whispering that John was to be named bishop. He was confessor to the Archbishop of Baltimore, and one day the archbishop jokingly remarked how nice John would look dressed as a bishop. John was stunned; he did not want to be appointed to an office which he feared would keep him from his people. He asked his friends to pray that he not be made a bishop, and also went so far as to ask his superiors to plead for this. One of the Redemptorists, a friend of the pope, was told, "The Holy Father has his own reasons."

One afternoon, upon entering his room, John noticed something lying on an open book—a bishop's ring and pectoral cross. When he asked who had been to his room, he was told the archbishop had come to see him while he was out. John was consecrated a bishop on his forty-first birthday.

Father Neumann was named Bishop of Philadelphia. He chose as his motto, "Passion of Christ, strengthen me," for he had no illusions as to the type of work needed in this still largely mission area. Within weeks of his arrival, he had visited every church and religious establishment in the city, and when the spring thaws opened the back roads, he set off for visitation in the country.

Even as a bishop, John was extraordinarily active and accessible. Although at first his new diocese looked askance at his frayed collars and high country boots, they soon grew to love him for his kindness and simplicity. Probably one of the main reasons Rome had chosen John was his language skill, so needed in this diocese thronged with immigrants. By this time, he spoke twelve languages fluently.

The story is told of an old Irish grandmother who went to Bishop Neumann for confession. In fast Gaelic she rattled off her sins. Then, after listening to the bishop's wise advice, she left the confessional exclaiming in Gaelic, "Thanks be to God we finally have an Irish bishop!"

In his eight years as bishop, John gave his diocese eighty new churches, and at the first national council of the American bishops he helped map out a plan of Catholic education for the whole United States. In his diocese he set the goal of a Catholic school for every parish. At his installation in 1852, Philadelphia had only two Catholic grammar schools; eight years later, it had one hundred. Bishop Neumann brought several religious orders to the diocese to help in the work of education which he considered so vital.

John wanted to begin the Forty Hours devotion in his diocese, but there were objections to this plan. No American diocese had begun this devotion, for the presence of the violently anti-Catholic Know-Nothings meant a constant danger of sacrilege. At last, following an interior guidance, Bishop Neumann did begin the devotion. The faithful came in droves, and there was no notice by the Know-Nothings. Other dioceses quickly followed.

After becoming a bishop, John was not obligated to observe the vow of poverty made as a Redemptorist. However, his love for religious poverty was so strong that he observed it to the end of his life. What little money and material things he could claim as his own, he gave away to any beggar who asked. What he kept for himself became little better than rags. One day, a fellow priest chided him, "Bishop, you look shabby. Today is Sunday. Have the goodness to change your clothes."

He replied, "What do you want me to do? I have no others."

Since New Year's Day of 1860, the bishop had been feeling a little weak and dizzy, but he told no one. On the fifth, when he went down to dinner, he had trouble recognizing an old friend who was there. When asked how he felt, he admitted that he felt a little odd, but that a walk in the fresh air would do him good. Then he added a rather strange remark: "A man must always be ready, for death comes when and where God wills it."

Bishop John Neumann collapsed in the street that afternoon after suffering a stroke. Loving hands carried him into a nearby house, but he was dead before the arrival of the priest so quickly summoned.

Before his funeral, the largest one Philadelphia had ever seen, thousands filed past Bishop Neumann's open coffin. Many wept openly. Some, however, had to smile. They had never before seen their bishop resting—and he was dressed in new clothes!

At rest—but still working—Bishop Neumann was scarcely placed in his tomb before many were flocking there to ask his intercession. Reports of prayers answered began to accumulate, and a canonical investigation of his virtue was begun twenty-six years after his death. He was beatified by Pope John XXIII in 1963, and canonized by Pope Paul VI in 1977.

This miniature shows St. John Neumann as a child. Miniaturists were careful artists who usually tried to make a portrait exactly resemble the subject.

The mitre and crozier have been added to this old photograph of St. John Neumann. Bishop Neumann gave the diocese of Philadelphia 80 new churches in only eight years, and began the Catholic school system and the Forty Hours Devotion in the United States.

28

6

SAINT GABRIEL POSSENTI

Saint Gabriel of the Sorrowful Mother, C.P.
Francis Possenti
1838 - 1862
Italy
Died Age 24

As a youth, Francis Possenti greatly enjoyed the pleasures of the world. Then, guided by Our Lady, he entered the Passionist order and became an apostle of the Sorrowful Mother. There was nothing outwardly extraordinary about his daily life, and his sanctity consisted in his love and faithfulness to prayer and sacrifice, and was reflected in his joyful spirit. Although no miracles or supernatural events occurred during his lifetime, after his edifying death his tomb became a place of pilgrimage where many prayers were answered. At his canonization in 1920, Pope Benedict XV named St. Gabriel the new Patron of Catholic Youth.

Francis Possenti was born in 1838 in Assisi, Italy, the eleventh of thirteen children of a wealthy government official. When he was four, his mother died of meningitis. Each of the children was with her at her death, and gave her a parting embrace. When Francis' turn came, he approached to kiss his mother goodbye. She whispered, "May Mary keep you, my Checchino!" The following day, as Francis cried for his mother, his older sister Maria Louise gathered him in her arms and promised to care for him in their mother's place. This sister kept her promise, and helped her father manage the large household and see to the religious education of the family until her own early death of cholera in 1855. More than anything else, the death of this beloved and devoted sister made Francis realize the purpose of man's life on earth. After this event, he remembered an early promise to become a priest, and asked for the guidance of his Heavenly Mother in choosing the particular manner of following this vocation.

In an effort to enlist heavenly aid in ending the cholera epidemic

of 1855, the people of Spoleto asked the archbishop to bless them
with a centuries-old Byzantine icon of Our Lady, claimed by tradition to have been painted by St. Luke. During the blessing, the
archbishop promised that the people of Spoleto would make an annual procession if the epidemic were ended. From the time of this
blessing, no more deaths or new cases of cholera were reported.
During the promised procession the following year, Francis knelt
with the crowd in honor of Our Lady. As the procession passed him,
he heard in the depths of his soul a voice which said, "Francis, why
do you remain in the world? It is not for you. Follow your vocation!"

At this time, Francis was a senior at the Jesuit college. When he
requested his father's permission to join the Passionists, his father
refused, as he had done previously. After further discussion, his
father appeared to give in to his son's wishes, but in reality he continued to attempt to make Francis change his mind, enlisting the aid
of various relatives to dissuade the boy from his plan.

When Francis had spoken of his wish to join the Passionists the
year before, his father's flat refusal had ended the matter temporarily. Because of his love and respect for his father, Francis had
let the matter drop, and finished the year of schooling left. At this
time, seven of the thirteen children of the Possenti family had died.
Of the remaining six, one was a priest, one was married, and two
were away at school. Francis' father, now in his mid-sixties, wished
to keep the remaining two at home as long as possible. Because of
Francis' outgoing personality and intelligence, his father had many
plans for him. In addition, he felt that the life of a Passionist was far
too severe for his son, who enjoyed so much the things of the world.
The Passionist order, which combines the life of the strictest contemplative orders with a missionary apostolate, appeared to be one
in which Francis would have to sacrifice all the things he had previously enjoyed.

After this first request, Francis continued the same life he had
been living. A good student, he was chosen to give the commence-
ment address. He liked to hunt and was an expert marksman. He enjoyed riding and dancing. He liked the girls, and tried to dance with
as many as possible. Noticing this last trait, his friends nicknamed
him "Il Ballerino"—"the dancer." Sometimes they also called him
"Il Damerino"—"the dude"—for he enjoyed dressing in the latest
styles, and was always immaculately groomed.

A bit of a clown, Francis found it easy to keep his friends in fits of laughter. Because of this trait, he had many friends. With them, he enjoyed attending the theatre, opera, and writing poetry.

As a younger student, Francis got into his share of scrapes and harum-scarum activities. In one scuffle, his brother broke his nose. With a group of his friends who termed themselves the "Lords of Spoleto," Francis was in the middle of many youthful stunts. One of the most boisterous of these occurred when several of the group raced their horses through town, eventually rearing their mounts in an attempt to get them to pound some householders' doors with their hooves. With these friends he smoked in secret and played chess and cards, often making small side bets to enliven the game.

In the matter of romance, Francis did not single out any particular girl. The daughter of family friends, Maria Pannechetti, was very fond of Francis. Her parents, and his father, indeed, considered the young couple practically engaged, but there was no such agreement on the part of Francis and Maria.

After his second request to his father, Francis wrote to the Passionists requesting admission. When a letter of acceptance came, his father hid it. After waiting some time for a reply, Francis determined to journey to the Passionist novitiate at Morrovale and request admission in person.

After enlisting the aid of two of Francis' brothers in attempting to dissuade him, his father finally agreed to let him go to the monastery, accompanied by his brother. Friends and relatives would be told that the brothers were going to visit relatives so that if Francis changed his mind he could come home without embarrassment. His father sent letters to several of the relatives the brothers planned to visit on the way to the monastery, asking them to try to talk the boy out of becoming a Passionist. But by controlling his temper and making honest and firm replies to all the questions and objections to his vocation, Francis won over all—except his father.

Finally nearing the monastery, Francis became overwhelmed with worry that after all he might not be accepted. On his arrival, he was stunned to hear the words of the novice master, "We had practically given up hope of seeing you, Francis."

He and his brother, a Dominican priest, then realized that their father must have hidden the letter of acceptance. Although Father Aloysius was sad at leaving his younger brother, feeling that he might never see him again, he was proud of Francis' determination to journey to the monastery not even knowing whether or not he would be accepted as a member of the order.

In a dramatic ritual which symbolized the life of self-denial asked of each Passionist, Francis received a cross to remind him of the cross of Christ, along with a crown of thorns and the exhortation to "humble thyself and be subject to everyone for His sake." In addition, he received the name Confrater Gabriel of the Sorrowful Virgin. "Confrater" is a Latin word which means "associate brother"; it is applied to all Passionist clerical novices and students to distinguish them from the "fraters" or lay brothers. Gabriel did not, however, live to see his ordination.

Gabriel's novice master wisely helped him realize that the spirit in which he did anything was far more important than what he actually accomplished. He therefore meditated on the significance and meaning of humility, and attempted to practice that virtue in many little ways. In a spirit of sacrifice and self-denial, he completed his novitiate, attempting to be faithful to the rule of his order at all times. In his notebook, he wrote, "I will attempt day by day to break my will into little pieces. I want to do God's Holy Will, not my own!" Deliberately he accepted extra tasks, controlled his impetuous nature, and denied himself many small pleasures. Was there a feeling of martyrdom in these efforts? In a letter to his father, Gabriel wrote, "My life is one of unending joy." Perhaps the only true sadness of this time for the young man who was so attached to his family lay in the fact that his father refused to attend his profession.

Like many saints, Gabriel did experience some periods of spiritual aridity when he felt that he had been abandoned by God, or when he was subjected to temptations and trials. At these times, with God's grace and by a supreme effort of will, he remained faithful to his prayers and his rule.

After hearing of the death of one of the young Passionist students at a nearby monastery, Gabriel went to the chapel and prayed for the grace of an early death. When he told his novice master what he had prayed for, the horrified master forbad him ever to make such an imprudent prayer again. Possibly, however, God chose to accept this willing sacrifice, for from about this time, Confrater Gabriel's health began to fail. He developed a suspicious cough and later was diagnosed as having tuberculosis.

After completion of his novitiate, Gabriel was sent—along with several other clerical students—to the monastery at Isola, high in the mountains. There was a great deal of political turmoil in the country, and it was felt that this monastery would be the safest place for the continuation of their studies. The dissolution of the Papal States had begun.

At the monastery, Gabriel and the others continued their preparation for the priesthood. One day, while cleaning a storeroom, Gabriel found a statue of Our Lady which was chipped and discolored. After asking permission to work on it, Gabriel repaired and repainted it. He dressed it in fabric clothing, and when he was finished, it was so beautiful that the rector had a special place prepared for it over the tabernacle in the monastery chapel.

During these days of study, Gabriel's devotion to Our Lady continued to increase. Whenever he found a reference to her he copied it into his notebook. From these references he composed his "Simbolo Mariano," a document containing fifty-two propositions regarding Mary. A measure of his devotion to the Mother of God can be found in a letter to his brother Michael. He wrote, "Love Mary! . . . She is loveable, faithful, constant. She will never let herself be outdone in love, but will ever remain supreme. If you are in danger, she will hasten to free you. If you are troubled, she will console you. If you are sick, she will bring you relief. If you are in need, she will help you. She does not look to see what kind of person you have been. She simply comes to a heart that wants to love her. She comes quickly and opens her merciful heart to you, embraces you and consoles and serves you. She will even be at hand to accompany you on the trip to eternity."

In Gabriel's love and devotion for the Blessed Mother there was nothing of the falsely pious or foolishly sentimental. He understood, however, how she could aid souls on their path to God.

Slowly, the war came closer. In 1859, the Piedmontese King, Victor Emmanuel, joined forces with Garibaldi. Forces of the Piedmontese army were entering even small towns to loot, confiscate, rape, and burn. A frightening rumor circulated that a band of marauders was coming toward Isola, and many families rushed in panic into the backwoods, leaving few in the town.

The rector of the monastery hid the valuables and locked himself in his room, after directing the students to take refuge in the sanctuary to pray that the town would be spared. For the few who remained in Isola, the next few hours were a nightmare. The soldiers looted without opposition, running off the local militia who were hopelessly outnumbered. At the thought of the injustice, anger flared in Gabriel, dispelling any fear he might have felt. After requesting permission to see if he could help, he ran toward the town.

About twenty men were ransacking the town. They were drunk and abusive, and had begun to burn some of the houses.

A soldier, dragging an unwilling girl, saw Gabriel and stepped into the road directly into his path with a sneering remark about such a young monk being all alone. Quickly, Gabriel took the man's pistol out of his holster and threatened to shoot if the man moved or failed to release the girl. Seeing a second soldier, Gabriel shouted a command for him to drop his gun, which the surprised soldier did. Well armed, all of Gabriel's hunting training came back to him. The shouts of his captives had brought the rest of the company to the scene, although seeing an armed monk, they slowed to a walk in their approach. When all were gathered, Gabriel demanded their disarmament.

Their leader, a sergeant, made a sarcastic comment about a single little monk thinking he could stop a whole company. Just then, a lizard darted into the street and paused a moment. Gabriel barely took aim before he fired, and the lizard flopped over dead.

Pointing the second revolver at the sergeant, Gabriel repeated his command for the company to drop their arms. His display of marksmanship had impressed the cowardly crew, and they disarmed immediately. Gabriel made them empty their pockets and drop the loot they had collected. Holding their sergeant hostage, he forced them to put out three fires they had started. Finally, marching the whole company ahead of him, he made them leave the town. Outside the city, the soldiers took to their heels.

A few of the townsfolk who had remained in town had followed the courageous young monk. In a triumphant procession, they accompanied him back to the monastery.

Gabriel's health continued to decline. In hopes that fresh air would be beneficial, he was sometimes sent to assist the shepherds in the field and to teach the children in neighboring towns. Gabriel enjoyed this work, and the peasants became very fond of him.

After a long, exhausting trip to Penne by mule to receive tonsure and the four minor orders, Gabriel became much worse, coughing up blood and continually wracked with pain. Dizzy spells became frequent, and he suffered violent headaches. During this time, his interior union with God made his life a continual prayer.

When the townspeople of Isola noticed that Gabriel was not at his accustomed place in church, they asked about him. Hearing that he was sick, they brought offerings of butter, cream, eggs, and meat. He had protected them in their need and they wished to repay him in any way they could.

In his final letter to his brother, Gabriel asked that his brother give his love to all of the family. He continued, "Assure them, too, that I have always been content here . . . I would rather by the divine mercy be the least among the Passionists than be the son of the king and heir to the kingdom!"

During his final illness, his classmates and some of his brothers in religion never suspected the intensity of his suffering. Gabriel remained cheerful and smiling, and for each visitor he had a joke or a funny story to tell.

When one of the students was assigned to sit up with him at night, Gabriel apologized for his coughing which might keep him awake, and asked the superiors to let the student sleep late the next day.

On February 27, 1862, holding a picture of Our Lady, Gabriel attempted to follow the prayers for the dying. Softly murmuring the words "Jesus, Mary, and Joseph," he closed his eyes for the last time.

In 1891, the official investigation into his life and virtues was opened by the ecclesiastical authorities at Terni. Gabriel was beatified in 1908, and canonized in 1920. The original canonization date of 1913 had to be postponed because of political upheaval.

At Gabriel's canonization there were forty-five cardinals, two hundred eighty bishops, and sixty-one thousand visitors present. His brother Michael, Maria Pannechetti, and his nurse during his last illness were also there.

St. Gabriel Possenti, the monk who single-handedly marched 20 drunken, looting soldiers out of town at gunpoint. This is the most accurate likeness of St. Gabriel; it was made by painting over an old tintype.

7

SAINT BENILDUS

Saint Benildus, F.S.C.
Pierre Romancon
1805 - 1862
France
Died Age 57

If you have ever been called a "shrimp" or a "pipsqueak," then you have something in common with little Pierre Romancon. The insults received because of his small physical stature did not stop when he was a child, but continued well into his adult life.

When Pierre's father went to register his son's birth, several family friends went along to testify, because Mr. Romancon could not even write his own name. Both of Pierre's parents were illiterate, but they wanted their son to have some education. They made provision for him to leave some of his work on the family farm in order to attend school.

Although both his parents were uneducated, hard-working country folk, they were very religious. Though too busy to attend daily Mass, Pierre's mother slipped into the church for a brief visit to the Blessed Sacrament each morning after completing her early chores. Later in life, the saint said his earliest memories were of these visits, as he accompanied his mother from about the age of four. He credited these visits with contributing greatly to his vocation.

When Pierre was thirteen, his teacher appointed him to help teach a group of unruly seven-year-olds which the old teacher himself could not handle. The degree of success he had with the class amazed all—especially the teacher who had appointed him. Pierre had discovered what was to be part of his life's work—teaching.

Walking through the village one day with his mother, Pierre noticed a pair of strangely garbed men. Each held a rosary in his hand and wore a tricornered hat. At this time, France was just struggling back from the bloody, anticlerical French Revolution, and many religious orders had still not resumed their habits. Pierre, who had probably never seen many, if any, garbed religious, asked his mother who these strange men were. She replied, "Those are the brothers, men who teach school for the love of God."

Pierre later decided that he, too, would like to be a teaching brother. This posed quite a problem in his family. His mother felt he should at least be allowed to try this vocation, but his father wanted Pierre to become a lay teacher so that he could always stay close to home. Besides, argued his father, at his young age he was not ready to make an important decision about his future. His parents compromised by allowing him to board with relatives and attend the brothers' school in Riom. His stay only strengthened his resolve to become a brother.

Yet another obstacle had to be overcome. When Pierre first applied to the novitiate, he was turned down on the grounds that he would be much too small to handle the disciplinary aspect of teaching. But this obstacle gave way after he was allowed to teach the younger children for a few days. His manner with them was so good that the superiors decided to allow him to at least try his vocation. His father consented, while secretly hoping that Pierre would find the life much too hard.

In 1820, Pierre received the habit of the Brothers of the Christian Schools, and a new name—Brother Benildus. His father made one more try to change his mind. He paid a visit to the young novice and said, "Pierre, I want you to come home with me." After recovering from the shock of realizing that his father was still against his vocation, Brother Benildus answered, "If I had to live here on nothing but potato skins, I would not leave this house." His eyes blurred with tears as he watched his father walk sadly down the path. He shut the door and went immediately to the chapel to pour his sadness out to God in the Blessed Sacrament.

In 1821, Brother Benildus began his teaching career. In 1839, he was sent to direct one of the brothers' schools. Two years later he was appointed director of a new school at Saugues.

As a teacher and director, Brother Benildus exacted obedience and sometimes inspired fear. He was known to use the strap, though with much less severity than was common at that time in France. He punished justly and never gave way to whims or partialities. Brother Benildus treated rich and poor alike, and left each of his students feeling like the "teacher's pet." Under his direction, the school became popular and truancy all but died out.

Controlling his temper and being a fair and just teacher did not come easy. The boys in his schools often came to the school rowdy and undisciplined. Brother Benildus once mentioned that he felt it was only with the help of the Blessed Virgin that he was able to keep from murdering some of his most unruly students. "I imagine that the angels themselves, if they came down as schoolmasters, would find it hard to control their anger."

When Brother Benildus first went to Saugues to set up and direct the new school there, there were murmurs of anger and disappointment from the parents there. They felt that no man as small as Brother Benildus would be able to control their rough sons, who far preferred playing truant to going to school.

At first, the classroom was a battleground. On one side stood large rowdy country boys. On the other was a very small brother, determined to carry out his mission of love and education.

One ten-year-old threw his shoe at Brother Benildus while he was writing on the chalk board. Rather than lose his temper or administer a well-deserved beating, Brother quietly told the boy to stay after class for a conference with his parents to decide on a proper and just punishment. He was guided in his restraint by the words of the saintly teacher and founder of his order, St. John Baptist de la Salle. This saint had counseled his brothers that as teachers they served as substitutes for their students' parents, and should maintain the gentleness of a mother as well as the firmness of a father.

No teacher can inspire respect and love if all he does is administer punishment, although many of the teachers in the France of this time were unduly harsh and severe with their pupils. Brother Benildus set up teams for competition, and used kind words and other rewards. He recognized the needs of the individual, and always treated his students with respect, no matter how poor they were. Not only did he recognize the need for a team spirit, but he also instituted a plan of giving cardboard tokens to individuals as rewards. The tokens could later be exchanged for small prizes. These teaching methods which Brother Benildus was using in his classrooms in the middle of the nineteenth century are the same ones that many psychologists and educators have hailed as new discoveries! The methods of individual attention and immediate positive reinforcement were used so well by Brother Benildus that soon his rugged country boys were coming to school because they wanted to come, not because they were forced to do so.

The parents were amazed at the changes in their sons, and began to have a greater respect for the value of education. A group of parents came to Brother to ask him to give them lessons at night so that they might at least learn to write their own names. Brother Benildus instituted an adult night school, and for over two years gave the instructions himself.

Although Brother Benildus was a strict disciplinarian, he was also noted for his cheerfulness. He enjoyed recreation with the other brothers and with his students. Once, he taught his students how to make wooden whistles and other primitive musical instruments. Unfortunately, the parents were not impressed when the boys played them at home, so Brother good-naturedly held an auction and bought up all the offending instruments.

Brother's love and concern extended to all, not just his regular pupils. Once an eighteen-year-old illiterate boy who was almost totally deaf asked Brother how he could learn enough to make his First Holy Communion. Brother Benildus went to the trouble to learn sign language in order to instruct the boy. Another time, the brothers surprised a thief in the act of stealing from their house. Benildus refused to allow them to call the police, and then he talked to the young man. Discovering that he had a family to care for, Brother helped him get immediate aid and figure a better plan for improving his financial situation.

In his daily life, Brother Benildus tried to follow the rule of his order to the letter, and was a model for his brothers. When he became superior of the house, it was his duty to impose penances for infractions of the rules. A common punishment was to make the Stations of the Cross. It was not unusual for the superior who had assigned this penance to slip in and join the penitent.

Brother Benildus was a good teacher and a model religious. But what did he do that was really outstanding or remarkable? Unless you consider the great number of vocations he inspired, you will have to answer that question by saying, "He did nothing very exciting."

There is no record of any miraculous occurrences, special visions, or other favors during Brother Benildus' lifetime. But saints are never canonized simply for glorious deeds which they have performed. Rather, they are recognized for what they have been. Pope Pius XI called Brother Benildus the "Saint of the Daily Grind," and reminded us that Brother's sanctity lies in his doing usual things unusually well—for the love of God.

Brother Benildus died quietly at Saugues on August 13, 1862. His final words reflect the joyful spirit which had completely filled his life in religion: "How happy one is to die in our holy state."

How did the true sanctity of this quiet saint come to light? A cheap brass crucifix belonging to Brother Benildus was given by the brothers to the carpenter who made his coffin. The carpenter's wife loaned this relic to many who needed divine assistance. A man who was dying refused to receive the Sacraments. After being touched with the crucifix, he asked for a priest. Other miraculous occurrences began to be attributed to this relic. Both of the cures documented and accepted as proofs for Brother Benildus' canonization involved persons who had been diagnosed as having incurable cancer.

In the Collect prayer at Brother Benildus' beatification, the faithful prayed that God would allow them to follow his example of being true to the little things in life, in order to attain the great and everlasting rewards of Heaven.

In October of 1967, Brother Benildus was canonized by Pope Paul VI.

St. Benildus, of the Brothers of the Christian Schools, who once admitted that it was only with the help of the Blessed Virgin that he was able to keep from murdering some of his most unruly pupils. Pope Pius XI called him the "Saint of the Daily Grind." St. Benildus was never photographed; this pencil sketch is the best likeness of him.

8

HENRIETTE DELILLE

Henriette Delille
1813 - 1862
United States
Died Age 49

To be free, educated, and beautiful was to have the highest status possible for a black woman in a slave state before the Civil War. Henriette Delille possessed all these advantages, but for the love of God, she chose to exchange a life of relative ease and wealth for one of poverty. She gave up the possibilities of life with a wealthy man for a life of dedicated chastity, and resolved to use her talents and education for the good of her race. She even chose the more difficult course of remaining in the United States to establish an order of black nuns, rather than choosing the easier option of going to France where she would have been welcomed by an existing integrated order. Remembering the example of Our Lord, who was Himself a member of a despised and oppressed race, Henriette decided to become a servant to the slaves.

To understand the magnitude of the choices made by this free woman of African descent, it is necessary to understand a little about the social structure of the South at this time, as well as of the particular city in which Henriette lived—New Orleans.

Black people in the South were usually slaves. They were considered property, not persons, and it was forbidden by law to educate them or to do anything which would cause sympathy for them. Since they were not considered persons, there seemed no necessity for formal marriages (these were actually forbidden), and families were often split up by the sale of one or more of the family members. These conditions prevailed in all the slave states. There were, of course, many kind and generous masters who tried to keep families together. Many of these slaveholders freed their slaves shortly before or during the Civil War. Many of these masters thought of the slaves as children, and considered their responsibilities toward them in this light. But whatever the attitude of the masters, the fact remains that a slave was simply that, a slave, and his future and fortune depended upon his owner.

The New Orleans of this time was unlike any other city, even others where slavery existed. The city was much influenced by the French background of many of its earliest settlers, and had developed a strict social structure uniquely its own.

In New Orleans there were, in addition to the slaves, numerous free blacks. First, of course, there were the former slaves who had been freed by their masters. The second group of free blacks consisted of the children and descendents of mixed marriages. Although they were still denied many things, such as the vote, these people could be educated and were considered free by virtue of the fact that their white fathers were free men. Even when the union between a white man and a black woman was not sanctioned by law or the Church, the offspring were considered "natural" children, and as such, free.

A whole social structure, complete with its own vocabulary, sprang up with regard to this intermingling of the races. A second generation child was known as a "quadroon," and the third generation was called "octoroon." According to the traditions of the quadroon society, the young women were eager to establish an alliance with a white man, usually one of wealth and often from a high family background. Their eagerness for this life is primarily explained by their wish that their children be free. Also, the life was a comfortable one. Annual quadroon balls were held where these young ladies dressed in their finest to meet the available young men. "Available" was not necessarily synonymous with "single," as many of these men had legitimate wives and families in addition to their quadroon concubines, although some were very faithful, refusing to marry a white woman and sometimes even going through some form of marriage ceremony with their quadroon "wife."

To begin to list all the laws, rules, and regulations governing this society would take pages. This brief introduction serves, however, to illustrate the uniqueness of the choices of the remarkable young woman who chose to remain within the confines of this society in order to work for the slaves and poor blacks of the city. Today the sisters founded by Henriette Delille continue to work for their race in several states and in South America.

Henriette was born early in 1813. She was a descendant of some of the oldest free colored families of New Orleans; both her mother and her grandmother were natural daughters of aristocratic men.

Henriette was the youngest of three children. Her sister, Cecilia, was six years older than she, and her brother, Jean, was three years older. The family lived in a comfortable Spanish style cottage. Henriette was two when the Battle of New Orleans was fought, and she grew up hearing about her relatives and the other free blacks who had played such an important part in this battle.

Her training in the cultural traditions of her class began early in her life. Henriette was educated to converse intelligently about French literature, to have a refined taste in music, and to dance gracefully. At home she was taught poise, how to dress well, and other social graces. Her mother also taught her nursing skills—both how to prepare and administer medicines, and a great sympathy for the sick.

In 1824, Cecilia met and contracted a liaison with a wealthy Austrian merchant. This same year, Henriette met someone who was to introduce her to what would eventually lead to her own contract of love, a contract between herself and God. She was introduced to Sister St. Marthe Fontier, a French nun whose words of faith and acts of charity to her black neighbors greatly impressed Henriette and introduced her to a new dimension of love—vowed celibacy.

Sister St. Marthe, a Dame Hospitalier, ran a school for young girls of the free black class, and the school became the nucleus for missionary activities among the Negroes, both free and slave. In addition to the other subjects, she taught religion to her students, and at night gave instructions to adults.

Most of the blacks who had been born Catholic, as well as many of the white Catholics, knew little about their religion, due to a shortage of qualified priests and catechists. Sister St. Marthe began to instruct her students on how to teach religion to the slaves whose masters allowed them to have these classes. By the time Henriette was fourteen, she had become an enthusiastic lay catechist. At sixteen, unlike most of her friends who were dancing and dreaming of the ball and the men in their lives, Henriette was deeply involved in visiting and aiding the sick and the aged, as well as in her catechetical activities among the poor blacks and slaves. Most importantly, she and a group of friends began to develop a rich prayer life, both silent and in common, at the Ursuline chapel.

In all their work, which could be both dangerous and frustrating, Henriette and her friends faced the handicap of working within a system of myriad laws regarding the association and education of slaves and free blacks.

To combat a shortage of personnel, Sister St. Marthe attempted to found an integrated order of nuns for this work; this was done with the enthusiastic approval of the bishop. Although the attempt failed, Henriette was inspired by the idea of an order of nuns of African descent working with the members of her race there in the slave mart of the country. A black nun in a slave community was a novelty. The idea of a quadroon becoming a nun was revolutionary!

Trying to pass for white was a common practice for free blacks (people of mixed descent were considered black), because of the advantages of being white. Henriette's family, especially her brother and sister, were most interested in doing this. They were not happy that Henriette, by her constant association with the colored school, constantly proclaimed that she was in fact black.

At this time, Henriette's sister Cecilia introduced Henriette to many wealthy and influential white people who later would become staunch supporters in her works of charity.

In 1830, Henriette not only refused to deny her racial heritage, but she was also in open rebellion against the traditions of the quadroon class. Henriette and a few of her friends boldly refused to go to even a single ball, or to seek the love and financial security offered by a white man. Other than dependence upon a man, the only self-supporting activity open to a respectable woman was teaching or running an elite school. Henriette's mother worried that her daughter would squander her inheritance on the poor, refusing to teach the rich, and that she would wind up in poverty. Henriette's mother suffered a nervous breakdown at this time. An executor was appointed, and he finally declared Henriette of age in 1835.

In 1836, Henriette sold all her property and, with nine companions, again attempted to form a religious community. Miss Marie Aliquot, a French woman who after a dramatic rescue from drowning by a black man had determined to devote her life and fortune to the betterment of this race, was the leader of the little group. But after only about a year, this second attempt also quietly failed.

This time, the failure was primarily due to the fact that Miss Aliquot was white and the others were black; such a community life was a high misdemeanor according to an 1830 revision of an act of the legislature. Of the members of the little group, some went to France to become nuns, some may have been accepted by the Sisters of Charity—perhaps passing for white—and Miss Aliquot continued her life of service to the black race on the plantations in rural Louisiana. Henriette and her friend Juliette Gaudine, another free black woman, remained to storm the gates of Heaven with their prayers and their dream of a black order of nuns in New Orleans.

Their prayers were answered through Father Etienne Rousselon, a recent immigrant from France. It was his counsel that directed Miss Aliquot to the plantations. To Henriette and Juliette he gave encouragement and advised patience, trust, and waiting. Because of conflicts between the Church and civil authorities, he felt the time was not yet ripe for the foundation of a religious order.

During this wait, Henriette lived for a time with her sister, caring for her in her last illness. In addition, she and Juliette continued their numerous works of charity. One of their primary jobs was to instill a respect for God's laws and to improve the moral condition of the members of their race. Although it was highly illegal, they encouraged the women and men to have their marriages ratified by the Church, often obtaining permission for this from the owners, if the couple were slaves. Although such ceremonies were not valid according to civil law (since slaves were considered to be property rather than human beings), the two women felt that this was the Will of God, in order to keep the couples from living in sin. Their motto became: "It is better to please God than man."

In 1838, Father Rousselon quietly asked permission of the bishop for the establishment of a community of Negro nuns under the leadership of Henriette Delille. The order would be attached to the new church which Father Rousselon would serve as pastor, and would continue its charitable works among the black people of the city. The permission was granted, and Henriette joyfully helped to raise funds for the building of the new church and to found a house for the sisters' residence.

On November 21, 1842, the Sisters of the Holy Family were officially formed, the only members being Henriette and Juliette. Within a year, however, their friend Josephine Charles joined them. After Henriette's death, Josephine became the second leader of the community.

During these first years, in spite of ridicule, poverty, and hard work, the members of the little community went placidly about their work of teaching the poor slave children and performing other works of charity. By 1847, the sisters were still only three in number, but during that year, a group of lay people called the Association of the Holy Family was formed. This group of free colored men and women allied themselves with the nuns and gave them the moral and financial support needed for their work to grow. In 1849, largely through the efforts of this association, the Hospice of the Holy Family was dedicated. This home was the sisters' first convent and was also for the use of the sick, aged, and poor who had no other place to go. At last, new candidates began to come to join the sisters in their work.

All arrangements for the foundations had to be made by word of mouth, and prior to the Civil War, the sisters wore no habit or uniform. In 1852, the Madames of the Sacred Heart graciously agreed to train Sister Henriette and Sister Josephine and allow them to make a novitiate with their own sisters. At last, on October 15, 1852, Sister Henriette, Sister Juliette and Sister Josephine pronounced their vows publicly in St. Augustine's Church.

In spite of the fact that Henriette had been in poor health throughout her life, no amount of pleading by her sisters could prevent her from not only directing, but also participating in all the works of charity carried on by the Sisters of the Holy Family. Under her direction, the group began to build orphanages and schools, in addition to their home for the aged. At last, completely worn out by her work, Henriette died on November 17, 1862. She had suffered a long and painful illness with great resignation. In her obituary it was noted that Henriette Delille "for the love of Jesus Christ made herself the humble and devoted servant of the slaves." A cause for her canonization is contemplated.

Henriette Delille, a beautiful young free black woman, rejected the future prescribed by the South (become a concubine or teach school) in order to found an order of black nuns in the slave market of the United States, New Orleans.

Henriette Delille, foundress of the Sisters of the Holy Family.

9

FRANCIS SEELOS

Servant of God Francis X. Seelos, C.Ss.R.
Francis Xavier Seelos
1819 - 1867
Bavaria - United States
Died Age 48

Once upon a time in the United States of America, two saints lived at the same rectory in Pittsburgh, Pennsylvania. An unlikely story? The Catholic Church has already canonized the pastor of St. Philomena's parish, Father John Neumann. Father Seelos was his assistant.

Francis Xavier Seelos was born January 11, 1819 in Fussen, Germany. His family were devout Catholics who enjoyed a moderately good standard of living from their father's labor as a tailor. Francis is remembered as a happy, gentle, and devout child. In addition, he enjoyed playing pranks on family and friends alike.

On carnival days in Fussen, the children wore masks and paraded through the village, playing tricks on the townspeople. On one occasion, young Francis donned his father's best frock coat and hat and joined in the fun amid the laughter of his friends at the sight of the little boy in the big clothes. The children laughed so hard that Francis' father came to investigate—and rescued his wedding clothes.

Francis attended six years of grammar school in his home town and later attended St. Stephen's Academy in Augsburg and the University of Munich. From his early teens, he wanted to become a priest, and the pastor of his local parish was helpful in getting benefactors and a scholarship to help him with the cost of his education.

All his life, three words could describe the constant personality of Father Seelos—cheerful, gentle, and charitable. He once gave the following words of advice to a young priest—advice which he himself followed faithfully. He said, "The priest who is rough with the people does injury both to himself and to others. Thousands reject the Church and perish in eternity simply because they have been badly treated by a priest."

In 1842, Francis read a plea for help for the Germans in the United States. He applied for admission to the Redemptorist order, was accepted, and was sent to Baltimore.

Throughout his life, Francis was a loving person. In return, he was well-loved by his family, his friends, and all who came under his influence. When he was planning to leave for America in 1843, he realized how painful it would be to say good-bye to his family. Instead of going home to bid farewell, he wrote them a tender and touching letter that they did not receive until after his departure.

In America, Francis was first sent to St. James parish in Baltimore to make his novitiate. He made his profession on May 16, 1844, and was ordained in December of that year. In August of 1845 he was given his first official assignment—to St. Philomena's in Pittsburgh.

At St. Philomena's, Francis' pastor was Father John Neumann. During the years they worked together there, the saintly pastor gave the young priest a good example of all the things a good parish priest and pastor should be and do.

At first, Father Seelos had a good bit of difficulty preaching in English. After one of his first sermons, an old woman remarked that she had understood very little of what he said, but added that it did her good to see him struggle so hard. Later, his preaching became so outstanding that people would walk miles to hear a mission preached by him.

In Pittsburgh there was much anti-Catholic feeling. The fires of distrust were fanned by such radical groups as the Know-Nothing party. On one occasion, a non-Catholic lured Father Seelos to his house by telling him that his Catholic wife was very ill. When the unsuspecting priest arrived in the house, the man beat him almost unconscious. Later, some staunch Catholics heard of the attack, although Father Seelos had not mentioned it. They wanted to have the man arrested, but Father Seelos would not allow it.

In 1851 Father Seelos was designated pastor. His example of faithfulness to his duties and his loving nature endeared him to all who knew him, and inspired them to live better lives. He was available to all his parishioners for help and he took special delight in visiting with the school children. His reputation for sanctity began to be spoken about, and his wise counsel was particularly noticed.

One day in the confessional, Father Seelos heard a strange request. An anxious penitent who had just finished her confession asked, "Father Seelos, will you please pray that my child will die?"

Father Seelos asked the tearful woman, "But why should she die; what is wrong with her?" After the woman talked for a few minutes, Father Seelos said, "That is epilepsy." When he asked why the woman had not told him this, she replied that the doctors had told her to keep the young girl's malady a secret and not to send her to school. Father Seelos then requested that the little girl be brought to him. After talking to her a while, he took the girl and her mother to the altar of the Blessed Virgin where he placed his hands on her head and prayed over her. Afterwards, he told her mother that the child had been cured by God, and to keep silent about the whole affair but to send her to school to continue her education.

Another time, a crippled man came to the rectory and asked Father Seelos to cure him. "My good man, I'm no doctor—I cannot cure you," replied the priest. The man answered, "I'm not leaving until you cure me," and with that he threw his crutches out the window. Impressed by the man's faith, Father Seelos read to him from the Bible and blessed him. When the man was able to stand alone, Father Seelos again gave complete credit to God.

A Redemptorist seminarian had been tempted and had doubts and anxieties regarding his vocation. He went to Father Seelos who prayed over him and then told him, "Look, little one, these temptations have been very good for you. Later on, when you will be hearing confessions, you will have learned how to have compassion on fearful souls who need consolation."

After nine years in Pittsburgh, Father Seelos was transferred and appointed pastor of St. Alphonsus parish in Baltimore. Later he was a pastor in Cumberland, Maryland, and a director of the Redemptorist seminary. His final pastorate was at Annapolis, Maryland. In 1863, he began working in the most characteristic apostolate of the Redemptorists—conducting "missions." For three years he held missions in over a dozen states. He served briefly in a Redemptorist parish in Detroit in 1865, and his last assignment, in 1866, was to New Orleans. Everywhere, Father Seelos was remembered for his brilliant sermons, but the true proof of his sanctity was found in the confessional. Hundreds later recalled his ability to impart great consolation, and his extreme love and zeal for souls.

Nothing seemed to bother him in his quest to save another soul for God.

Once, in Baltimore, Father Seelos was called late at night to the deathbed of a young woman. Only when he reached the second floor of the house did he discover that it was a house of prostitution. Nevertheless, he heard the young woman's confession and prepared her for death. Somehow an anti-Catholic newspaper found out about the call and featured a story about a midnight visit of a distinguished clergyman to a bawdy house. When some of his co-workers showed him the insinuating report, he replied only, "Well, I saved a soul."

At one time, serious thought was given to making Father Seelos a bishop. In his humility, he wrote the pope a letter, begging him not to do this. Father Seelos was happy to remain a simple priest.

In New Orleans, he spent most of his time working with the German-speaking people at St. Mary's. Outbreaks of yellow fever were frequent in this city, and in September of 1867 the disease struck again. Father Seelos worked tirelessly among the sick and dying until he himself was stricken with the disease. During the month before his death, Father Seelos remained often in prayer, never complaining and completely at peace. He died quietly on October 4, 1867.

Father Seelos' mission of healing did not end with his death. Many people, convinced of his sanctity, asked his help and intercession in prayer, and reports of favors granted began to be spread about in all the dioceses where he had served. Five years after his death, a dying baby was cured after his grandmother prayed for Father Seelos' aid. The baby was suffering from pneumonia and meningitis. A sixteen-year-old girl was cured of smallpox, and in 1938 a six-year-old boy made an apparently miraculous recovery from polio. Two of the Redemptorists who had known Father Seelos began to collect all reports of favors attributed to him, and to request that an investigation be opened. At last, by request of the Redemptorist superiors in Rome, the ordinary process was begun in 1900. In 1903, the transcripts were taken to Rome. The cause of Father Seelos currently awaits further action by the Congregation for the Causes of Saints.

Father Francis Seelos, saintly Redemptorist priest. A crippled man once came to the rectory, threw his crutches out the window and refused to leave without a cure. Father Seelos blessed him and read to him from the Bible. When the man was able to stand alone, Father Seelos gave complete credit to God.

Hundreds attest to Father Seelos' great zeal for souls in the confessional. He died of yellow fever caring for the sick and dying during an epidemic in New Orleans in 1867.

10

SAINT PETER JULIAN EYMARD

Saint Peter Julian Eymard, S.S.S.
Peter Julian Eymard
1811 - 1869
France
Died Age 57

One day when Peter Julian Eymard was five years old, his sister found him in church, perched on a stepladder behind the main altar, with his ear pressed to the tabernacle. When she asked him what he was doing, he told her that he was praying close to the Blessed Sacrament so that he could better hear "Him." With the simplicity of childhood, Peter had realized the truth that was to become the center of his life—the Real Presence of Jesus in the Most Blessed Sacrament of the Altar.

Today, the reception of frequent and even daily Communion is not an unusual idea. In fact, it is encouraged. In Peter Julian's day, however, the remnants of a great heresy called Jansenism were still being felt all over Europe. Among other things, this heresy taught that Holy Communion was such a privilege, and the laity were so often unworthy, that monthly or even yearly Communion was acceptable. Anything more frequent was considered a sign of vanity on the part of the recipient. In a day when Scriptural studies were somewhat dormant, Peter Julian saw that the presence of God over the Ark of the Covenant in the Old Testament was a *type* of the Eucharistic Presence of Christ to the Christians of the New Testament. His thoughts on Holy Communion were expressed before the pronouncements of St. Pius X, the great "Pope of the Eucharist." Peter Julian's practical advice about the reception of the Eucharist is as current today as it was when he wrote it over a hundred years ago. In Pope John XXIII's homily on the occasion of Peter Julian Eymard's canonization, he honored this saint as a perfect adorer of the Blessed Sacrament, and enjoined the faithful, "After his example, always place at the center of your thoughts, of your affections, of the undertakings of your zeal this incomparable source of all grace, the Mystery of Faith which hides under its veils the Author Himself of grace, Jesus, the Incarnate Word."

The life of Peter Julian Eymard exemplifies the truth that the Catholic home is the cradle of sanctity. His father, Julian, had worked hard at a variety of jobs to bring his family out of poverty, and at the time of Peter's birth he was a moderately successful owner of an oil press and cutlery shop. His first wife had died after bearing him five girls. Four of them went to live with relatives, but one, Marie-Anne, came to live with Julian and his second wife, Peter Julian's mother. Both his mother and this half-sister were very devout. From the time he was a baby, they took Peter Julian with them on their daily visits to the Blessed Sacrament. Some of his first memories were of being in front of the golden monstrance. Although for many years M. Eymard vigorously opposed Peter Julian's vocation, he finally allowed his son to follow what he felt to be God's Will. The early refusal is explainable, in part, by the fact that Peter Julian was an only son, and the only survivor of the four children by Julian's second wife. His opposition cannot be taken as an indication that he was not a good Catholic, and before his death he completely changed his views and no longer offered any opposition.

Although Peter Julian as a child was what would be referred to today as a "good" boy, he was certainly not the plaster saint type of person who is rarely believable. He lived the life of a normal boy. Though not proficient at games, he still enjoyed playing with his friends. In spite of a frail constitution, he particularly liked playing in the snow. He was sometimes disobedient, often curious, and on one occasion his vanity led him into trouble.

Napoleon Bonaparte had recently marched through town at the head of his army. The little boys immediately began to play at being soldiers. The better equipped you were, the higher your rank in this miniature army. Peter Julian spied a real military plume in a variety shop and temptation overcame him. He stole the plume and sneaked out of the shop. Before he had gotten very far, however, and before the plume was even missed, remorse overcame him. He sneaked back into the shop, replaced the plume, and ran away as fast as his small feet would carry him. He remembered this incident with sadness all his life, and even made reference to it a few days before his death.

Peter once heard a visiting Carmelite mention in conversation that friends never pass one another without speaking. At this point, Peter realized how unfriendly it must be to pass the Eucharist without visiting and speaking with Christ. His practical reaction to religious indifference was simple and logical: "Jesus is there; everybody [go] to Him."

Peter Julian longed to make his First Communion. He already felt the stirrings of his vocation, for he asked Marie-Anne to go to Communion for him to ask that he might become a priest.

He began serving Mass on Sundays and weekdays. It was the custom for boys who wanted to serve Mass to go through the streets fifteen minutes before Mass ringing a bell to summon the people. Peter loved doing this so much that he sometimes took the bell home the night before.

Peter had gotten as much education as was common for boys of his class, so his father brought him home to work with him on the oil press. Realizing that he needed to learn Latin, Peter began to study it on his own. He got some seminarians to show him how to do the declensions, and studied from an old Latin grammar book he had bought.

One night when Peter was seventeen, he overheard his parents discussing a marriage for him. Entering the room, he told them that his decision to become a priest was final and that nothing could change his mind. His father recognized defeat and allowed Peter the freedom to resume his studies; he refused, however, to assist him financially.

Hearing of a priest at Grenoble who was willing to teach Latin in exchange for help at the rectory, Peter left for the position, hopeful that at last he would be able to learn the necessary language. When he arrived, he found that the priest was chaplain to a lunatic asylum next door to the rectory. The people in this bedlam (as such institutions were then called) were mainly of the lowest classes. Many were there with social diseases which had affected their minds. The priest was not good about fulfilling his promise to teach, and Peter Julian was expected to do a great deal of work. He was often left alone with the patients with no thought of the dangers to which he was exposed.

At the end of the first quarter, in a chance conversation with the director of the asylum, the man casually mentioned that it was sad for Peter to be left without a mother. No one had even told the young man of her death. Although he hurried home, he was too late for the funeral. His father's tears kept him at home for a brief time. Later the saint was to remember, "In my mother's death, my father found a new weapon against my vocation."

In 1829, some mission priests came to preach a mission. They were Oblates of Mary, members of a new society formed to preach in the vernacular. They attempted to help the people to understand their religion better. The preacher so impressed M. Eymard that he allowed his son to leave to become a novice in that order.

But Peter's deficiency in Latin was to prove his undoing. He had to study so hard to overcome this that he ruined his health and was sent home dying. His condition was so poor that the priest was sent for, to give the Last Rites, but Peter Julian prayed to be allowed to offer at least one Mass before accepting his death. This prayer must have pleased God, for Peter soon recovered his health.

After his convalescence, and through the help of the founder of the Oblates, Peter was admitted to the diocesan seminary and was finally able to complete his studies and be ordained. There was no work open, and he again applied for admittance to the Oblates, but was turned down because they felt his health would not stand the strain of their missionary apostolate. He was given a parish where the parishioners remember him as a good and dedicated priest who spent a great deal of time in the presence of the Blessed Sacrament. One mentioned that he spent as much time in the church as in the rectory.

Father Eymard met some members of another new order, the Marist priests. Because of his devotion to the Blessed Mother, he wanted to join this group. Though reluctant to lose such a good parish priest, the bishop consented, and Peter remained with the Marists for seventeen years.

After this time, he came to realize that every mystery of the Faith had a religious order dedicated to it—except the mystery of the Real Presence. He received the inspiration to establish a community of religious whose major purpose would be to dedicate their lives to the adoration of the Blessed Sacrament. He wanted it to be a part of the Marists, but the superiors felt they could not undertake this work. Instead, they willingly released Father Eymard to follow what he believed to be his calling. He appealed to the pope, who granted him permission to found the congregation.

The young congregation was beset by a number of problems. Money was a scarce commodity. In the first house, the altar was of plain wood. On one occasion, Father Eymard was happy to report,

"Today we covered the altar with calico, which cost us eight cents a yard. It looks much better." He always wanted his altars to be beautiful thrones for the King.

Father Eymard also wrote a number of books on all aspects of devotion to the Most Blessed Sacrament. As Cardinal Gibbons has stated, Peter Julian Eymard looked at the world only through the "divine prism of the mystery of the Eucharist."

At first there was a lack of vocations. Some of the young men who came decided to leave. The foundation met opposition from anticlerical civil authorities and from the religious authorities. In spite of these difficulties, Father Eymard retained a simple trust that since God wanted the work, it would be done. At last he received the important approval from Rome, and the young community began to flourish.

At one time, a young sculptor who had entered the order after an emotional time in his life was introduced to Father Eymard. After some talk, Father Eymard said, "I hope God will forgive me the sin of vanity if you find your true vocation here." The young sculptor said earnestly, "I will try."

When the priest questioned him about his art, he mentioned that he intended to give it up completely.

"There is no hurry, Brother Augustin. You will find your vocation here or not, as it pleases God. However, one should not enter our order as an escape but as a fulfillment."

Later the saint counseled the young man to leave the order to resume his art. He led him to the realization that art, rather than the life of a religious order, was to be the young man's life work. A bronze bust of St. Peter Julian Eymard, sculpted by this artist, Auguste Rodin, is considered to be one of his finest works.

In addition to the congregation of male religious, Father Eymard also began the People's Eucharistic League for the laity, an order of contemplative nuns, and the Priests' Eucharistic League for parish priests. When Miss Marguerite Guillot consulted the Cure of Ars concerning Father Eymard's plan to appoint her as the first superior of the new society for women, he advised her to place herself in his care without reservation.

"He is a great saint," St. John Vianney told her. "When you see him, tell him for me all that friends tell each other when they meet, and that we shall all meet in Heaven."

Worn out by fatigue and penance, Father Eymard left Paris in

July of 1868 for a rest at LaMure, to recover his strength. On the way, he took an outside seat in the coach, giving the better, inside seat to another passenger. The intense heat of the broiling sun brought on a paralytic stroke. Once at LaMure, Father Eymard's health was too poor for him to rally against a number of complications, and he died peacefully on August 1. The documents carefully assembled immediately after the death of Father Eymard testify that many of his first associates believed they had lived in the company of a saint.

War broke out in 1870, and in 1880, the congregation was expelled from France. The members fled to Belgium for refuge. Few thought the order would survive, but within a few years a new house was opened in Rome, and the members of the order continued to carry out the mission of their saintly founder. The inquiry into the virtue of Peter Julian Eymard was begun in 1899.

Cardinal Gibbons wrote of him: "We know of no apostle of modern times who has so thoroughly imbibed the Eucharistic spirit as Venerable Pere Eymard." Peter Julian Eymard was beatified in 1925 and canonized on December 9, 1962.

St. Peter Julian Eymard, founder of the Blessed Sacrament Fathers, was a close friend of the Cure of Ars, who said of him, "He is a great saint."

11

SAINT ANTHONY MARY CLARET

Anthony Claret
1807 - 1870
Spain - France
Died Age 62

From weaver to priest to archbishop, Anthony Claret spent his days in the full service of his Lord and his Mother Mary. The author of one hundred forty-four books, founder of three religious orders, a proponent of land reforms, and a builder and organizer of many projects dealing with youth, Anthony spent his last years fleeing from persecution and political calumny. At his death in 1870, the famous lament of St. Gregory was carved on his tombstone: "I have loved justice and hated iniquity, therefore I die in exile."

Anthony was born on Christmas Eve in 1807—a Christmas present for his parents, Juan and Josephina Claret. Anthony was the fifth of eleven children. His father owned a small textile mill in Catalonia.

Anthony learned to read early, and religion and mathematics were his favorite subjects in school. He was popular with his classmates, and when his presence was missed for a game, they knew where to find him—in the church making a visit.

From the time he was a young child, Anthony wanted to become a priest. His father, however, noticed his mechanical aptitude and skill in design, and wanted Anthony to follow him in the trade of weaving.

Anthony was impulsive by nature, but with great effort, he gained such complete self-control that few who knew him even suspected what this cost him. In deference to his father's wishes, he studied to become a weaver, and worked so well that he was soon made head of the shop.

Once Anthony gained the confidence of the workers, he invited them to pray the Rosary with him daily and to attend Mass often. He did not dock their pay for the time spent in these devotions, and under his direction the shop began to prosper. Even in his teens, he understood that happy workers would be more productive.

At age eighteen, Anthony asked his father to allow him to go to a trade school in Barcelona to learn more advanced methods. Here he studied hard and worked in a factory to support himself. Although he enjoyed the work and made many friends, he began again to think of his vocation to the priesthood, and went to the Oratorian Fathers for advice. They encouraged him to begin a study of Latin. At twenty-one, Anthony realized that he did, indeed, have a priestly vocation, and under the patronage of the Bishop of Vich, he began seminary studies.

Throughout his life, Anthony had a great devotion to Our Lady. He wrote, "Our Blessed Lady is my Mother, my Patroness, my Mistress, my Directress, and—after Jesus—my All!" Such devotion would not be unrewarded. Throughout his life, Anthony was privileged to see the Blessed Mother in several visions, and she often gave him help. Anthony himself added the name of his Heavenly Mother to his own name.

Anthony was finally ordained at the age of twenty-eight. In Spain he served first as a parish priest and later as a pastor. In 1839, seeing that Spain had many priests, he went to Rome to ask to be sent as a missionary to foreign lands. He met the Jesuits and for a time thought he should join them, but in the novitiate he developed a strange paralysis of the leg which made it impossible for him to continue. As soon as he left, his leg was immediately cured, and Anthony took this as a sign that this was not the work to which Our Lady wished to direct him. Later he went as a missionary to the Canary Islands at the invitation of the bishop, and after a fruitful apostolate there, he returned again to Spain. During his time in Spain, thousands were converted through his zeal for souls. It is estimated that during his lifetime he preached over 25,000 sermons.

Back in Spain, Father Claret took a special interest in the catechetical instruction of both children and adults. His belief in the value of this apostolate led him to open several centers dedicated to instruction in Christian doctrine. He composed four books on the subject, graded as to age level, and introduced the novelty of illustrations for the books. At the numerous missions he preached, he would gather the children and adults around him to explain some point of doctrine that he would later reinforce in his sermons. He recruited helpers if the number was too great, usually saving the smallest children or the slowest adults for his own group. Anthony wanted these children of God to understand their religion completely, and because of his work, the Catechetical Congress of Valladolid later gave him the title of "Most Outstanding Catechist of the Nineteenth Century."

On July 16, 1849, Father Claret met with five young clerics at the seminary at Vich. He had seen a tremendous need for missioners, and decided to form a congregation of missionary priests dedicated to the Immaculate Heart of Mary. After he outlined his ideas for the congregation, one of the seminarians objected that they were young and few in number. With confidence and conviction Anthony replied that through the power of God this congregation would flourish; he predicted that it would spread worldwide. This prediction has come true.

As to the specific apostolate for this group of missionary priests, Father Claret listed some types of work including teaching Christian doctrine and the establishment of the apostolate of the press. He closed his remarks, however, by telling these young men to "make use of all possible means to save souls."

On a visit to Cuba, Father Claret became convinced of the need for a new order of sisters for teaching Catholic girls, and in collaboration with Antonia Paris he formed the Teaching Sisters of Mary Immaculate. He also aided Doctor Masmitja in the foundation of the Immaculate Heart Sisters. Father Claret realized that many young women with a call to serve God were prohibited for various reasons from entering a religious order, so he established a sodality to meet this need.

Over his own objections, Anthony was named Archbishop of Cuba in 1849. One look at his diocese convinced him, however, that this land was a true field for a missionary. The major seminary had ordained no priest in thirty years. Under his influence there were soon over two hundred seminarians in residence. As archbishop, he immediately began to visit each city and town, regularizing marriages, administering Confirmation, and establishing Christian solutions to every problem he saw. During his time in Cuba, he confirmed 100,000 people and rectified 9,000 marriages.

This new archbishop so completely won the confidence of his people that during a revolution at Port Principe, he was asked to be a mediator.

Favored by God with the gift of prophecy, he foresaw both an earthquake and an epidemic of cholera. When both of these unfortunate predictions came true, he personally went to every part of his diocese to give aid and comfort to the victims.

Archbishop Claret introduced a system of teaching modern methods of agriculture to the farmers through a network of organizations. In order to provide for a large number of homeless boys, he established a modern ranch. The ranch was self-supporting through sale of the crops raised, and the boys were given a good education at a school on the ranch which had, in addition to classrooms, a library, science laboratories, and a botanical garden.

Because change is always resented by some, there were a few who saw a threat in this saintly archbishop. Once, an assassin succeeded in getting close enough to slash at him with a knife. Fortunately the wounds were not serious, although he was cut in several places.

In 1856, Queen Isabella II recalled the archbishop to Spain, wishing him to be her personal confessor. The thought of a life at court was repugnant to him, but at the express wish of Pope Pius IX he went. Back in Spain, in addition to his duties at court, Anthony continued writing, preaching, and teaching. As in any court, there were many intrigues. Anthony was offered bribes and other inducements to use his influence with the queen. All attempts failed, and he let it be known that he refused to mix in politics in any way. Thwarted, some liberal politicians began to slander him, and several attempts were made on his life. Fortunately, through his gift of foreknowledge he was sometimes able to see in advance the designs of the would-be assassins. In fact, more than one of these actually became his converts. In 1865, when the queen recognized the new kingdom of Italy in opposition to papal right, Archbishop Claret wished to resign. But again following the instructions of the pope, he continued at the court until he was exiled to France during the Spanish Revolution of 1869.

During his time at court, in addition to his other activities, Anthony had organized the Academy of St. Michael, a group of writers and artists; he organized numerous clubs for all classes of people, established credit unions in parishes, and was designated president of the Escorial, a large educational institution. Pius XI called him "Apostle of the Press" because of his ministry of the written word. His theory here was, "Since we cannot send missionaries everywhere, let us send good books which can do as much good as the missionaries themselves."

During his exile, he traveled to Rome for the Vatican Council. The main concern of this council was the doctrine of papal infallibility, a doctrine that has always been misunderstood and misinterpreted by many. Anthony asked to be allowed to speak, and with simple eloquence he pointed out the roots of this doctrine in Scripture and Tradition. There is reason to believe that his remarks and his already acknowledged reputation for sanctity exercised a crucial influence in the deliberations.

Anthony Claret was not born a saint. Throughout his life he had a constant struggle against defects in his own nature. In his attempt to fulfill the purpose of his existence, he spent his life trying to serve and love God as perfectly as possible. In his last days, because of political persecution, he was forced to flee from place to place, finding sanctuary at last in the Cistercian monastery at Fontfroide. He died there on October 24, 1870, exiled from his beloved Spain but united with his two greatest loves—the Sacred Heart of Jesus and the Immaculate Heart of Mary.

Anthony Mary Claret was beatified in 1934 and canonized in 1950.

In his seven years as Archbishop of Cuba, St. Anthony Mary Claret confirmed 100,000 people and rectified 9,000 marriages. During his life he preached over 25,000 sermons, wrote 144 books and founded three religious orders. He died in exile.

St. Anthony Mary Claret saw the Blessed Mother several times during his life; he added her name to his own.

12

SAINT BERNADETTE SOUBIROUS

Bernadette Soubirous
1844 - 1879
France
Died Age 35

Many Catholic families are familiar with the story of the miraculous apparitions of Our Lady at Lourdes. Most know that she appeared to a little French girl, Bernadette Soubirous, who is now known as Saint Bernadette. Was she canonized simply because she was privileged to see the Blessed Mother? No, although this is certainly an important part of her story. The Church canonized not only the visionary of Lourdes, but also the nun of Nevers. Living with extreme ill health and spiritual sufferings, Bernadette remained kind and humble, as she offered herself as a victim to Our Lord.

Bernadette was the oldest of the four surviving children of nine born to a poor miller and his wife in the Lapaca quarter of Lourdes, France. Five children had died in infancy. When Bernadette was about twelve, Francois lost his mill through poor management, and the family moved from one room to another, finally arriving in a single room in an old building which was loaned to them by a cousin.

Even at no charge, the room was not much of a bargain. The building had originally been a jail, and the family's room on the first floor overlooked a dung heap and a stableyard. The room next to theirs was occupied by their cousin's livestock. The building was of stone and very damp, which contributed to an odor which was less than pleasant, to say the least. The room was only large enough to hold a cupboard and the family's three beds, with a fireplace for cooking. Both parents worked at odd jobs when they were available, but could not seem to get ahead.

A typical breakfast for the family consisted of slices of a rough maize bread, similar to cornbread, rubbed with garlic and sprinkled with salt. In spite of the poverty of her home, and despite asthma which kept her in poor health, Bernadette was always very neat and clean. She was a good needlewoman and her mending jobs were so neatly done that friends remarked that they looked like embroidery.

In 1857, the family was in such a desperate situation that they were happy to agree when Bernadette's "foster mother," Marie Lagues, asked to take Bernadette home to Bartres with her. Madame Lagues promised to send Bernadette to school, and to teach her catechism. Instead, she sent her out in the fields to watch her sheep. Here Bernadette spent her time playing with the sheep and praying the Rosary.

In spite of the type of existence her family was forced into because of finances, Bernadette was a cheerful child, warm and loving. Although Madame Lagues used her to watch the sheep instead of sending her to school as she had promised, there was much affection between the two. At night, Madame would get out the catechism and try to teach Bernadette. Tired and puzzled by the difficult French (Bernadette spoke a dialect of the district) in which she had to memorize the sentences without being able to read the words, Bernadette seemed a very poor pupil.

After two years, Bernadette realized that she would be unable to learn her catechism at Bartres, and she wanted to make her First Holy Communion. At her request she returned to her family in Lourdes.

On February 11, 1858, the fourteen-year-old Bernadette and two friends went to gather firewood. They stopped near the Gave River to remove their shoes and wade across the small stream. They were near a natural grotto at a place called Massabielle. The other children waded into the icy stream and ran ahead, but Bernadette hesitated for fear that the cold water might bring on another asthma attack. Suddenly, she heard the sound of rushing wind and saw a bright light near the grotto. In this light appeared a lady whom Bernadette later described as being "so beautiful that to see her again one would be willing to die." Bernadette felt inspired to pray the Rosary, and slipped the well-worn beads out of her pocket. The lady seemed to smile, and she joined in the "Glory Be to the Father" prayers.

At a subsequent apparition, the lady asked Bernadette to return each day for fifteen days, which the young girl promised to do. During the apparitions, the lady gave Bernadette a number of messages. The main purpose of most of her requests was to ask people to do penance for their sins. The lady gave Bernadette some messages for herself which she never revealed. She also asked for a chapel to be built at the grotto, and for processions. During one of the apparitions, she asked Bernadette to drink from the spring; Bernadette, not knowing of a spring, turned and began walking toward the Gave, but the lady called her back. She indicated a spot on the ground, and Bernadette obediently dug into the earth. The people watching were astounded to see the little visionary apparently eating mud or dirt. From this spot, an underground spring welled up which today provides water for the pilgrims at Lourdes.

One of the beautiful lady's remarks was prophetic of Bernadette's life: "I do not promise you happiness in this world, but in the next."

During the time of the apparitions, word began to get around and large crowds of people began coming to the grotto to watch Bernadette. Praying there, Bernadette would enter a state of ecstasy, and observers say her expression was radiant. On two occasions, the lady did not appear, and Bernadette was led away weeping.

Bernadette was investigated by the police and by the local religious authorities. She never wavered in her story, and she insisted that the lady had asked for a chapel. The parish priest told Bernadette to ask the lady her name; at the last apparition, the lady folded her hands and said, "I am the Immaculate Conception." On previous occasions, the lady had spoken with Bernadette in her native *patois,* or dialect, but when asked her name, she replied in proper French. Bernadette did not understand the words, and had to keep repeating them to herself as she went to tell the priest. She asked him what the words meant, as she had never heard them, in spite of the fact that Pope Pius IX had proclaimed the dogma of the Immaculate Conception of the Blessed Virgin Mary just four years previously, in 1854.

People began to think of Bernadette as someone special, and they wanted to give her things such as food and money. It is a mark in her favor that Bernadette would not accept these gifts, and was determined that she and her family would not profit in this way from the apparitions. She felt that to do so would be stealing.

In June of the year of the apparitions, Bernadette made her First Holy Communion, at the age of fourteen. Later she was asked which gave her more pleasure—the sight of Our Lady or the reception of Our Lord. She was unable to reply, saying only that both were the most joyous occasions of her life.

Eight more years passed for Bernadette at Lourdes. During part of the time, she attended school with the Sisters of Charity and Christian Instruction of Nevers at their hospice there. They had a school which they allowed her to attend without paying tuition. During this time, she learned to speak French, to read and to write and spell somewhat. Although she was a bright girl, school was difficult for Bernadette, and she was never a strong student.

When Bernadette was sixteen, the local priest arranged for her to live with the nuns because of her poor health. Another reason was that many people came to see and talk to her, providing constant interruptions at home. For her protection, while she was with the sisters, a nun always accompanied her to the parlor when there were visitors.

In 1866, Msgr. Fourcade came to the hospice to ask Bernadette what she intended to do with her life. He explained that she could not stay with the sisters indefinitely as she was not a nun.

When he brought up the idea that she might like to become a nun, Bernadette answered, "It is impossible, Monsignor. You know very well that I am poor. I haven't got the necessary dowry."

The priest explained that sometimes convents accepted poor girls if they were convinced that the girls had a true vocation. He concluded the interview by recommending that Bernadette pray to Our Lady for guidance.

In April of 1866, Bernadette made formal application to join the sisters who had been her teachers—the Congregation of the Sisters of Charity of Nevers—and in July she left for the novitiate in Nevers. Her name as a religious was Sister Marie Bernarde.

Once at the motherhouse, Bernadette was treated with extremes for the rest of her life. Many people, including some of the sisters, treated her as a saint; this was a danger to humility. Others, especially her lawful superiors in the order, treated her as nothing. The mistress of novices was very severe with her. Although Bernadette herself said that she was nothing, she had a sensitive nature, and each rebuff must have hurt. However, she accepted everything with humility, never considering herself to be someone extraordinary. She fit into the convent life just like the other sisters. Yet for all her humility, upon her deathbed, when asking forgiveness for her faults, Bernadette asked pardon particularly for faults of pride.

Bernadette thoroughly enjoyed the periods of recreation with her sisters. She told funny stories and sang gentle songs in her native dialect, although she often made the sisters laugh by saying that when she sang, everybody ran away. She had a natural gift of mimicry, and provoked much laughter with her imitations of people's mannerisms.

As a treatment for her asthma, Bernadette had been told to take snuff. On one occasion, just as she took a pinch, one of the sisters cried out that Bernadette would never be canonized. When Bernadette asked why, the sister replied, "Because you take snuff. They nearly didn't canonize St. Vincent de Paul just because of that." Smiling, Bernadette asked, "Well, does that mean that because you don't take snuff you will be canonized?"

Bernadette had her own distinctive and sometimes humorous way of saying things. She described an agitated sister as "wriggling like a cut worm." After a meal of roast fowl, Bernadette became sick to her stomach. To make discussion a bit more delicate, she requested a basin with the explanation, "My little bird is flying away."

In the kitchen, when some milk boiled over, the cook cried out, "Here's my milk running away!" Bernadette gaily advised her to "go quickly and fetch a policeman."

Sometimes even Bernadette's advice or rebukes were tinged with humor. When one of her sisters complained that it was difficult to make a proper thanksgiving after Communion, Bernadette told her, "You must receive God well; give Him a loving welcome, for then He has to pay us the rent."

It was often Bernadette's job to assist in the infirmary. The sisters who were ill reported that she was a loving and tender nurse, concerned for their feelings as well as for their physical health. Yet she could be firm.

On one occasion when Bernadette held the post of head infirmarian, she found that a novice whom she had instructed to stay in bed had arisen and gone to Mass. Bernadette chided her for her disobedience, telling her that obedience was "the whole duty of the religious life." She told the novice to go back to bed and also told her not to read. The novice obeyed for a while, but then became bored and began reading a religious book. When Bernadette returned and found her again disobedient, she took the book away. Then when the novice had recovered and was allowed to leave the infirmary, she asked for her book. Bernadette told her she would have to go ask the Mistress of Novices for it.

Bernadette practiced this same firmness with herself. She took advantage of the many opportunities offered by her illnesses and by the observance of the rule in order to practice obedience and mortification. In a poem to Our Lord, she wrote: "Have pity on your little servant, who despite all would like to become one of your greatest lovers."

The suffering of frequent illness was Bernadette's cross for the rest of her life. Being sick and feeling useless were particularly difficult for her to bear, since her enthusiastic nature urged her on to activity. She always prayed for patience in suffering, and often stated that her job was to be ill. She wrote: "I do not beg you, my God, not to afflict me, but that you abandon me not in my affliction . . ." Bernadette learned to love suffering as the way to God, and the last entry in her notebook reads, "The more I am crucified, the more I rejoice." She suffered the terrible desolation of the "dark night of the soul"; in fear for her eternal salvation, she prayed fervently to St. Joseph, whom she considered her "father."

Bernadette's deep love for the members of her family is shown in her letters to them. In a letter to her brother and godson, Pierre, who had been only seven years old when Bernadette left home, she counseled him either to become a priest, if that was God's Will for him, or to learn a trade, but not on any account to become a priest simply for a worldly position. She wrote, "I would rather you became a ragpicker." Bernadette ended the letter with the words, "Good-bye, dear godson; I end by embracing you most affectionately. Your very devoted sister and godmother, Sister Marie-Bernarde Soubirous."

On All Saints Day, one of the sisters heard that Bernadette was ill; she sent her a little bouquet of flowers with the message that they were sent because, being All Saints Day, it was Bernadette's feast day. The answer came back: "Since it is my feast day, [it is] also yours. Please accept half of my cakes" (a special treat allowed to patients in the infirmary).

When one of the sisters brought up the topic of the apparitions, Bernadette calmly asked her what she did with a broom when she was finished with it. She continued, "You put it behind a door, and that is what the Virgin has done with me. While I was useful, she used me, and now she has put me behind the door."

Bernadette was deeply devoted to the Blessed Mother for the rest of her life. One sister recalled that when praying the Hail

Mary, "Bernadette's dark, deep-set sparkling eyes became heavenly. She was seeing Our Lady in spirit, and looked as though she were in ecstasy." Bernadette longed to see her Heavenly Mother again. She advised a sister to take a rosary to bed and pray it until she fell asleep: "Do the same as little children who fall asleep saying 'Mamma, Mamma.' "

Bernadette was very fond of a statue of the Blessed Mother at the convent, but she felt that most statues did not portray Our Lady accurately. She said that the sculptors of such images would be startled, in Heaven, to see what the Blessed Virgin really looked like.

It has been recorded that several cures were brought about by Bernadette during her life. On one occasion, a woman brought to the convent her little boy who was unable to walk, hoping that Bernadette would touch him. The Mother Superior called Bernadette and told her to take the child to the garden while she spoke with the woman. One of the sisters reported later that Bernadette "had a great love for children. She took him in her arms, then finding him too heavy, put him on the ground. The little fellow ran off gaily to his mother."

Bernadette's final illness lasted about four months. Her right leg caused her intense suffering both from a tumor and from a disease of the bone. Her racking cough shook her whole body, increasing the pain of her leg. When nearing death she kept murmuring, "Heaven, heaven . . ." She also suffered terrible temptations from the devil. Groaning, she seemed to feel him to be near. She cried out: "Go from me, Satan, go!" Later Bernadette became calm. Before she died, on April 16, 1879, Bernadette whispered, "Holy Mary, Mother of God! Holy Mary, Mother of God! Pray for me . . . poor sinner . . . poor sinner . . ."

Bernadette was buried on the convent grounds behind the motherhouse in Nevers. Her reputation for sanctity spread rapidly, and her cause for beatification was introduced. When the ritual exhumation took place, thirty years after her death, her body was found to be incorrupt.

Bernadette was canonized on December 8, 1933. Today, lightly coated with wax, her lovely features can still be seen where she rests in a beautiful reliquary coffin in the chapel dedicated to her at the motherhouse of her order in Nevers.

Bernadette was photographed often and her pictures were sold everywhere; she joked, "I am on sale for [ten cents] at every street corner!" This is a retouched photograph.

At age 14, St. Bernadette Soubirous, the visionary of Lourdes, saw the Blessed Virgin Mary in several miraculous apparitions. Our Lady asked for penance in reparation for sin.

Left: St. Bernadette as a nun, Sister Marie Bernarde. This photograph was probably taken when she was 24 years old. Bernadette's life was filled with suffering, in fulfillment of Our Lady's prophetic words: "I do not promise you happiness in this world, but in the next."

Right: The body of St. Bernadette, lightly coated with wax, remains miraculously incorrupt. This photograph was taken many years after her death.

13

SAINT MARY MAZZARELLO

Saint Mary Domenica Mazzarello, F.M.A.
Mary Domenica Mazzarello
1837 - 1881
Italy
Died Age 44

An illiterate peasant woman from the Piedmont region of Italy, Mary Mazzarello founded one of the world's largest religious orders for women, an order dedicated to the education and care of the young. Her sturdy hands, trained for the planting and picking of grapes, were used instead to help poor and orphaned girls of her native land. The order has spread throughout the world.

Mary Mazzarello was the daughter of an Italian peasant couple who earned their living working in the vineyards of wealthy landowners. She was born on May 9, 1837, in the town of Mornese. Mary was the oldest of seven children. Highly competitive, she worked in the fields with her family, often challenging others to match her labor. She had a keen sense of humor and was physically attractive. In her teen years, more than one young man spoke seriously of marriage, but Mary gracefully declined. She seemed to feel that although the position of a Christian wife and mother was an exalted one, she did not wish to be restricted to such a small circle of people to care for.

Peasant women of this time were uneducated; schools for girls were unheard of. Some girls, including Mary, managed to learn to read a little, but none could write. Mary was intelligent and had a keen mind. She was especially clever at working with figures in her head, and soon learned to help her father with keeping accounts.

Mary grew up near a small church dedicated to Mary, Help of Christians. Here she learned her catechism, often taking top honors in contests conducted by the parish priest. A Child of Mary, she was one of the first members of the sodality of the Daughters of Mary Immaculate formed of outstanding young ladies of the parish by the local parish priest. To this confessor, Mary turned for advice as to her future vocation. He counseled prayer and waiting.

When Mary was twenty-three, an epidemic of typhoid struck the city, taking a grim toll in lives. When an entire family of her cousins was stricken with the disease, she generously went to care for them. She nursed the adults who were all sick, and cared for the children as though she were their mother. Because of the heavy responsibility placed on her, she had little time to sleep or even rest, and as the family members regained their strength, Mary came down with the disease. Although she eventually recovered, the typhoid robbed her of much of her former vitality, leaving her in a frail condition that lasted the rest of her life.

Shortly after this illness, Mary was taking a long walk prescribed to help her regain her strength. Topping a hill, she noticed a large building on a field below. A group of religious sisters were playing with the village girls. Mary blinked and the scene disappeared, leaving only the empty field. Not the type of person given to visions or imaginative fancies, she thought deeply about the meaning of this strange occurrence.

In Turin, the saintly priest Don Bosco also had a vision. He saw himself in the center of a large square of the town, surrounded by ragged, unkempt girls. A group of them, standing to one side, seemed to say to him, "Can't you see, no one cares for us." Some of the girls began tugging at his clothes. Then a beautiful woman appeared. She said, "These are my children too—take care of them!"

During the fall of 1864, Don Bosco took a group of his boys from Turin on a camping trip to Mornese. He had already heard of the little group of fifteen women who formed the Daughters of Mary Immaculate. Here Don Bosco met Mary Mazzarello.

The fifteen young women had already begun to live a religious life. Their work was the care and training of the local village girls. They taught the girls sewing and other domestic skills and gave them religious instruction. In 1867, Don Bosco brought the women a rule, and the Congregation of the Daughters of Mary Help of Christians was begun. Now thirty-four years old, Mary was elected acting superior.

Under the direction of the local priest, Father Pestarino, the people of the town had built a new school for the boys of the area. Don Bosco instructed Father Pestarino to turn the building over to the Daughters for use as a school for girls. The townspeople were shocked at the idea of education for girls, but their priest insisted. Since Don Bosco already enjoyed a saintly reputation, the people at last agreed.

On July 31, 1872, this group of dedicated women received their habits, sewn by themselves, in a clothing ceremony where they also received their official title. Since there was no official superior, Don Bosco asked Mary to continue to lead the group. She objected, saying that her "ignorance" would be an impediment. He insisted, however, telling her it would be only a "temporary" assignment.

After reluctantly accepting, Mary confidently laid the keys of the house at the foot of Our Lady's statue with the words, "Our Lady is the superior of this house." For this reason, she asked to be called the vicar, rather than the superior.

After two years, Sister Mary Mazzarello was formally elected superior general of the congregation. There was only one negative vote in the election—her own. She held the office for the remainder of her life.

Under the wise guidance of Mother Mazzarello, the little congregation prospered and grew at a phenomenal rate. Two years after its founding, the second house was opened. Within five years, the first band of missionaries left for the fertile mission field of South America. Vocations came so quickly that the townspeople laughingly referred to the house as a "factory for making nuns." In sending the first group of missionaries to Uruguay, Mother Mazzarello wrote, "If we can do nothing more than save one soul for God we shall be more than repaid for any sacrifice that we make."

The sisters who were fortunate to live with her testified to her humility and her motherly attitude toward them all. She kept the idea that all sisters in the order, no matter what office they held or what job they performed, were equal. She took a profound interest in them, and no problem was too small for her attention.

Mother Mary advised her sisters, "Speak little to creatures, but speak much with God. He will make you truly wise." At the age of thirty-five, she began to learn to read and write. Her letters to her sisters and others attest to the fact that she was successful in the enterprise.

Mary never forgot her humble background, and her simplicity and humility added greatly to her personal charm. In addition, she kept a good sense of humor all her life, joking about almost anything. She told her sisters, "Be cheerful always; never be sad. Sadness is the mother of tepidity."

On one occasion, Sister Petronilla, a close friend who had grown up with Mary Mazzarello, expressed her worry that the institute's rapid growth might lead to problems. She mentioned the large number of intelligent, well-educated young women who were rapidly swelling the ranks. "Shh!" interrupted Mother Mazzarello in a stage whisper. With mock seriousness she continued, "If they find out how much we don't know, they'll never let us stay!"

Prayer was an integral part of Mother Mazzarello's life. She cautioned her sisters to be constantly armed against evil. "Let prayer be the weapon which you always have at hand."

On a trip to Genoa to accompany a group of sisters leaving for the South American missions, Mother contracted pleurisy and a severe respiratory infection. She continued on to France for a visit to the sisters in Nice. Here Don Bosco paid his final visit to his co-founder.

In her customary manner, and knowing of Don Bosco's uncanny ability to predict future events, Mother Mary asked him if she would recover and be able to continue her work. By means of a parable, he informed her that she was not destined to live much longer. Back home, she at first seemed to have improved, but within a few days she collapsed. She had suffered from a fresh onslaught of pleurisy.

From her sickbed, Mother Mazzarello continued to advise the sisters and the leaders of the congregation. In the evenings, the sisters came to her room to pray and sing the Marian hymns she so loved. She asked to be allowed to receive the Last Sacraments, and after the ceremony jokingly asked the priest, "Father, now that I've got my passport, have I permission to leave?"

For another three weeks she lingered painfully. In her last few days, she gave much good advice to those who would follow her in leadership, particularly stressing the need for obedience, and reminding the sisters that Our Lady alone was to continue as superior of the order. She cautioned them against petty jealousy, and instructed them to keep God first in their affections. Her final words were of Our Lady, the Mother who had led her throughout her lifetime.

The cause for Mary Mazzarello was begun in 1911. Speaking in 1936 about her virtues, Pope Pius XI said, "Here is a woman of simplicity—extreme simplicity, a simplicity as pure as that of the

simple elements, as simple and unmixed as gold without alloy."
Mother Mary Domenica Mazzarello was beatified in 1938, and
canonized by Pope Pius XII in 1951.

At age 34, St. Mary Mazzarello collaborated with St. John Bosco to found a religious order to care for and educate young girls. At age 35, Mary Mazzarello began to learn to read and write. This painting is a close likeness of her.

14

SAINT CHARLES LWANGA
AND COMPANIONS

The Twenty-Two Martyrs of Uganda
British East Africa
Died 1885 - 1887

Never in the history of the Church has a group of Christians lived, suffered, and died in so close an imitation of the apostles and early Roman martyrs as have the martyrs of Uganda. St. Bruno Serunkuma, on his way to death, told his brother, "A fountain fed from many springs will never dry up. When we are gone, others will rise in our place." The fountain of blood shed by these twenty-two Catholics has watered the seeds of the Faith in Africa.

In July of 1885, the White Fathers, Catholic missionaries, were invited to return to the kingdom of Buganda (now part of Uganda) from which they had been expelled three years previously. Upon the death of his father, the young King Mwanga invited the "praying ones" to return, and gave them some land. His invitation was prompted partly by a request of Joseph Mukasa, his major-domo, who was a leader in the Christian community.

When they returned, the missionaries were pleased to find that the Christians had faithfully followed their recommendations and had continued to catechize. Apostles in the true sense of the word, they prayed and read their catechism daily, then taught their relatives, friends, and servants. They lived as Christians, although the prevalent pagan religion was an animistic spirit worship, and polygamy, slavery, pillage and massacre in war, drunkenness and many forms of debauchery were acceptable. The Christians remained faithful to a single wife, did much of their own work themselves rather than delegating it to servants or slaves, and refused to indulge in excesses. They were peaceful. Remaining loyal to the king in all things that did not conflict with God's law, they continued their regular jobs while carrying out many Christian acts of mercy.

During the three-year absence of the missionaries, a plague struck the country; the Christians valiantly went out and nursed the sick with no thought for themselves. John Mary Muzeyi reported that during the epidemic, the Christians had baptized all the Christian catechumens who died. The Fathers were happy to see that during their absence the Christian community had grown from a small handful to several hundred at court and the surrounding area. These came for Baptism as soon as the priests came back.

Shortly after he ascended the throne, Mwanga became convinced of his absolute power, and began to reign as despotically as had his father. Much of his power was based on his subjects' fear. Because the peaceful Christians did not seem afraid of him, he began to worry about his retention of power should his country become Christian. In addition, the king's top advisor, the chiefs, the queen mother, and the witch doctors all feared and hated the Christians; they attempted to influence the king against them. In the king's court as his personal servants, there were about four hundred royal pages, chosen from among the best youth in the country. In order to preserve their own purity, the Christians among the pages refused to indulge in despotic excesses with the king, and it was over them that the major storm of persecution broke.

In November of 1885, the Anglican missionaries announced that Bishop James Hannington, the first bishop of East Equatorial Africa, and six other missionaries planned to enter the country in an attempt to open a short route to the Lake Victoria area. The Anglicans were particularly feared because they were English, and the king gave the order for their massacre. Joseph Mukasa Balikuddembe, his major-domo, courageously spoke up and asked the king simply to forbid them entry, but the king would not change his mind, and the Anglicans were killed. At this point, the king and his advisors began to think of getting rid of Joseph, who was one of the leading catechists for the Christians.

In addition to being the leader of the Catholic Christians, Joseph, in his position as major-domo, had carefully watched over the Christian pages. When the king sent for one of them, Joseph would hide him in his own house or send him out of the way, knowing that he was thereby placing himself in great danger. Finally, the king found an excuse to get rid of the troublesome Joseph. Joseph gave the king an opium pill when the king felt ill, and although this was a customary medicine, the king stated that it was an attempt to poison him. He gave the order for Joseph to be burned alive.

The executioner, along with most of the other members of the court, liked Joseph, and at first delayed in carrying out the order, thinking the king would change his mind. When the king sent a messenger to check to see if his orders had been carried out, the executioner, out of pity, had Joseph beheaded before burning his body.

Joseph walked to his death unbound. "Why should you bind me? From whom should I escape? From God?" Then, in keeping with true Christian heroism, he sent a last message to the king: "Tell Mwanga that I forgive him for putting me to death without a reason, but let him repent. Otherwise, I shall accuse him in God's court." Joseph, the model for the young Christian community, was its first Catholic martyr, at the age of twenty-six.

Charles Lwanga and several of the other catechumens working in the court realized that they, too, would probably be executed, so they went to the mission for Baptism.

Joseph's death dismayed but did not discourage the Christians. Realizing the danger to those who worked close to the king, the missionaries were hesitant about sending the guards back to court. Smilingly, the newly baptized group asked the priests, "Is it bad to go to Heaven?" Both the Catholic and the Anglican missionaries believed that they, too, would be killed, and began to prepare for martyrdom.

Although the king announced that he planned to kill all "those who pray," the Christians remained resolute. Charles Lwanga took Joseph's place, and he, too, guarded the purity of the Christian pages by hiding them. The missionaries spent their time preparing the Christians for death and comforting them.

King Mwanga had been greatly frightened by Joseph's last words. In addition, there was a shower of shooting stars twelve days after Joseph's death, as well as a number of fires in the compound, and then lightning struck one of the huts. To the King's superstitious mind, this meant a curse. He realized that his plan to frighten the Christians by Joseph's death had not worked. Christmas came and went with no further action on the king's part. Near Easter, the priests received word that a plan to massacre all the Christians was underway, and they sent word for them not to come to the mission, hoping to avoid further conflict.

In order to get his sister, Clara Nalumansi, out of the way, the king assigned her to guard the royal tombs. A Christian, she burned the fetishes at the tombs and sent away the witch doctors. This made her brother furious, but he was afraid to have her executed.

Returning unexpectedly from an unsuccessful hunt, the king found all the Christian pages missing. When one of them returned, he confessed that he had been with Denis Ssebuggwawo, who had been teaching him a religion lesson. Furiously, the king sent for the sixteen-year-old Denis, and taking a lance, thrust it into his body, later commanding the boy to be taken away and finished off.

The pagan pages advised all the Christians to flee, but the Christian pages refused. Since they were in the king's personal service, an attempt to hide would have been seen as a revolt. Although several of the youngest did hide for a brief time at the home of the armorer, an Anglican, they returned, and all the Christian pages prepared to die for their religion.

The king shut the gates of the compound, called all the chiefs and executioners, and had the drums beaten all night.

Under the direction of Charles Lwanga, all the Christian pages assembled and spent the night in prayer. The youngest page, Kizito, had been begging for Baptism, but his request had been denied up to this time because the Fathers felt he had not studied the Faith long enough. Charles baptized him and four others, although the Christian names they received are not known. He then encouraged the entire group to confess their Faith boldly and to continue to pray. He comforted little Kizito by telling him that if they were sentenced to death, he would hold his hand, and together they would die for Christ.

When all the chiefs and executioners were assembled, the order was given for the pages to appear. Then the king issued a single sharp order: "Let all those who pray go over there." Taking Kizito's hand, Charles Lwanga stood up and walked to the spot indicated. The others followed his lead, including the Anglicans. One witness later reported that "their faces were a picture of joy."

Bruno Serunkuma, one of the king's bodyguards, silently left his place and joined the pages. Mugagga, a page who was about sixteen, also joined the group. Other than the Christians, no one had known he had secretly been taking instructions at night. In addition, the adopted son of the chief executioner was a part of the group. His father ordered him to hide, and when the boy did not move, one of the other executioners told him to obey his father. He answered,

"My Father whom I must obey is in Heaven."

During the ritual sentencing, Father Lourdel had been waiting outside the gate where he was prevented by the guards from entering. As the bound prisoners left, he watched them walk by. He noticed that Kizito was laughing as if it were a game. He blessed them for the last time, and then went to the king to plead for their lives. Finally, he begged, "At least send me where you have sent my children," but the king refused. Several others who had been imprisoned for different reasons joined the death march, preceded by the chief executioner, beating his drum. The group, which included about thirty Anglican and Catholic Christians, was marched to a site at Namugongo, about sixteen miles from the king's compound, where a large pyre of wood could be built on top of a hill. Along the road, the prisoners had to pass through several villages.

When the group passed the village of Andrew Kaggwa, the chief musician for the king, the king's advisor demanded that Andrew be executed. Andrew had been expecting this, and had sent his family to safety. He was praying in his hut when he was dragged out to the group. Andrew, thirty years of age, was one of the main Christian leaders of Buganda. He had been a major catechist during the absence of the missionaries. The king and Andrew were friends, and the king did not want to kill him. The envious prime minister, however, had his way. Andrew's arm was cut off with a knife, and then he was beheaded and further dismembered on May 26, 1886.

Pontian Ngondwe, a member of the king's bodyguard who had been imprisoned with the pages, said at Mengo, "I have told you I am a Christian, so kill me here." In his words, he did not want to "carry death about the roads." He was stabbed to death on May 26. As a pagan, St. Pontian had been inclined to hatred and violence, but after his conversion he had proven a model in forgiving those who wronged him. He was between thirty-five and forty years old.

Gonzaga Gonza, about twenty-four years old, was a model of compassion and pity. The chains on his feet cut so deeply into his flesh that he became unable to walk further, and was speared to death on the march on May 27. The executioners admired his courage, and said, "This young man was so resolute that he died without even a groan." His body was thrown onto an ant hill.

By custom, at each crossroad the executioners would kill a prisoner to frighten passers-by. At the next crossroad, Athanasius Bazzekuketta, age twenty, volunteered. He was beheaded and dismembered on May 27. Athanasius had been loved and respected by everyone at court, and after his death the others encouraged each other by recalling his courage.

During the march, the group passed through the home village of Bruno Serunkuma. He had been beaten and was suffering from a fever, but remembering the example of Christ on the cross, refused a drink of banana wine from one of his brothers.

The death of St. Matthias Mulumba, who at about fifty years of age was the oldest of the martyrs, was the cruelest. He was dragged before the prime minister, who accused him of doing things unworthy of a chief. He mentioned that Matthias did his own cooking, to which Matthias smilingly replied, "Am I on trial for my thinness or my religion?" In a rage, the prime minister ordered that Matthias be made to suffer more than the others, and taunted him by asking, "Will your God save you?" Matthias quietly replied, "He will rescue my soul, but you will not see." Both Matthias and Luke Banabakintu joined the march, but Matthias was killed before reaching Namugongo. His arms and legs were hacked off, and pieces of his flesh were burned in front of him.

To prolong his death agony, his arteries and veins were tied off, and he was left, mutilated, to die in the broiling sun. Two days later some slaves coming to cut reeds heard him cry out for water, but ran off terrified because of the rule that anyone helping a condemned man was made to share the same punishment.

At the village of Mityana, the leading catechist, Noah Mawaggali, had sent all the Christians into hiding, though he himself refused to leave. Previously he had told his sister—who later became the first native nun—"I know there is another life, and for that reason I am not afraid of losing this one." The thirty-five-year-old Noah turned his face to avoid looking at his murderers. He was speared and tied to a tree where he was cut to make the blood flow in order to attract wild dogs. He died on May 30, after several hours of agony.

Matilda Munaku, Noah's sister, courageously gave herself up to the executioners, but she was simply imprisoned. Noah's wife was taken before the prime minister and cruelly beaten.

At Namugongo, the execution village, the prisoners were left bound, and were thrown into huts to await execution. Much of the story of their martyrdom came later from Denis Kamyuka, whose life was spared. He said that the older ones encouraged the younger men. They prayed constantly, and even the very youngest member of the group, Kizito, did not seem sad or worried.

In addition to the Catholics and Anglicans, there were seven or eight non-Christians who were in prison. The Christians began to instruct them, and all but two began praying with the Christians. The next morning, two of the Anglicans spoke with the executioners, telling them it was not right to burn those who did not pray, so the pagan page Aliwali and the Moslem Adudala were taken back safely. From this time, the group was unanimous in constant prayer, and no one testified to a single lament.

The prisoners were kept for several days. Mbaga Tuzinde, the adopted son of the chief executioner, had been kept separate from the others in an attempt to persuade him to recant.

The prisoners were lined up to be marched to the pyre. One of the executioners passed down the line with a long reed lighted at the tip, tapping the head of each prisoner in a pagan ritual to prevent the spirits of the condemned from returning to bother the king. If a prisoner failed to receive the tap, he knew he was reprieved. Reaching Charles Lwanga, the executioner said, "This one's for me," indicating that his suffering would be greater. Calmly, the young man told the others, "My friends, goodbye. We'll meet again in Heaven." He was tied to a low stake and burned. Although his eyes blinked incessantly with the pain, Charles continued to pray, and thought first of his executioner's soul. Quietly, he told Senkole, "How happy I should be if you, too, were to embrace my religion." Although Senkole simply snickered, he later became a catechumen.

At the execution platform, the executioners, dressed in animal skins with their faces painted with red paint and soot, began chanting in order to frighten the prisoners. Their cruel chant, translated, was "Today, the parents of these children are going to weep." Neither the sight of the platform or of the executioners apparently frightened any of the group. The prisoners were rolled in reed mats and tightly bound, and three of the reprieved pages were set aside. St. Bruno sadly told these three, "It would have been better for us all to die together. The king will make you give up religion, my children." These three protested, but were ignored. They wanted to be executed with the others.

Denis recalled later that one of the martyrs called out, "Tell Mapera [the native name for the priest] that we have been faithful!"

The chief executioner then made a final appeal to his son to recant. He had him unbound and made him kneel before him. The young man bravely refused, so his father ordered his neck to be broken with a club before he was put on the fire. Two of the Anglicans were also accorded the same privilege.

With burning torches, the platform was immediately set afire. Denis remembered hearing an intense murmur, the prayers of the dying invoking God. St. Bruno called out, "You kill the body only; the soul belongs to God," and then resumed his praying. Denis recalled that on the way back, one of the executioners said, "We have killed many men, but never such as these. The others did nothing but moan and weep, but these prayed right to the end."

The last of the twenty-two Catholic martyrs was John Mary Muzeyi. He was a kind and respected counsellor who had often assisted Joseph Mukasa as a catechist at court. A generous man, he often used his modest savings to ransom young slaves whom he then took to the mission. During the persecution, he hid for a time, upon the advice of the missionaries, but later appeared openly. He was beheaded on January 27, 1887, and his body was thrown into a pond.

With pain and with pride, the White Fathers learned the news of the heroic deaths of the martyrs. The faithfulness of the other Christians, who nightly came to the mission for the Sacraments, consoled them. Because of the martyrs' example, the Christians were so unafraid of the persecutions that the Fathers had a difficult time persuading them not to give themselves up for execution. The priests counseled them to return to their villages and become true apostles by teaching others about the true religion.

The Ugandan Martyrs have given Catholic parents of African descent many new choices of saints' names for their children. The names of the Ugandan martyrs are the following:

St. Charles Lwanga	St. Luke Banabakintu
St. Joseph Mukasa	St. James Buzabaliawo
St. Matthias Mulumba	St. Bruno Serunkuma
St. Denis Ssebuggwawo	St. Mugagga
St. Andrew Kaggwa	St. Kizito
St. Pontian Ngondwe	St. Mukasa Kiriwawanvu
St. Athanasius Bazzekuketta	St. Gyavira
St. Mbaga Tuzinde	St. Adolph Ludigo
St. Gonzaga Gonza	St. Anatole Kiriggwajjo
St. Noah Mawaggali	St. Ambrose Kibuka
St. John Mary Muzeyi	St. Achilles Kiwanuka

In 1887, there were five hundred Christians and about a thousand catechumens in Uganda. By 1964, the number had swelled to two million Catholics. Native priests, brothers, and sisters were dedicating themselves to evangelizing their country.

The lives of the martyred saints serve as a sterling example of Catholic Faith. Pope Paul VI canonized the Twenty-Two Martyrs of Uganda in 1964.

Left: Father Lourdel, one of the White Fathers who instructed the Ugandans in the Faith. He was not allowed to go with the martyrs to their execution.
Right: A painting of St. Charles Lwanga.

The 22 Martyrs of Uganda are shown here grouped around Joseph Mukasa, the Protomartyr of Bantu Africa. In the right-hand panels, grouped around Charles Lwanga, are the martyrs who were burned alive at Namugongo. To the left, grouped around Matthias Mulumba, are the martyrs who were speared to death. Note the symbolism of swords and flames; the Christian names are in Latin. This painting was done in 1962 by the Swiss artist, Albert Wider.

— 15 —

SAINT SOLEDAD

Saint Maria Soledad Torres Acosta, S.M.
Vibiana Antonia Torres y Acosta
1826 - 1887
Spain
Died Age 60

Father Michael Martinez and some friends were taking a walk one fine spring day in 1851. During the course of their conversation, one of the friends commented that he felt it strange that the Daughters of St. Vincent de Paul, who were in charge of the city's hospital, could not make an exception to their rule and send a nursing sister to the governor's home to nurse his daughter. This chance remark was to be the seed from which a new and different congregation of religious women was to grow—the Congregation of the Sisters, Servants of Mary. Father Michael, pastor of one of the poorer suburbs of Madrid, was aware of the problem of the poor and abandoned sick who often could not afford hospitalization. Suddenly he had an idea; he would begin an order which would exist to provide nurses to go to the homes of the sick. If the patients could not pay, God would provide.

Immediately, Father Michael set about getting the necessary permission and recruiting the young women he felt would be good candidates for his new foundation. Because of his special devotion to Our Lady of the Seven Sorrows, he wanted to begin with seven "servants" of Mary. The seventh applicant he accepted was little Vibiana Torres. She was so slight, and looked to be of such frail stuff, that he hesitated to accept her.

Vibiana was born December 2, 1826, the second of five children of a dairyman. Although her family was not extremely poor, they lived in a poor neighborhood. Even as a child, Vibiana was aware of the problems of the sick poor who could not afford to go to the hospital for treatment.

Although she was a rather mischievous child, Vibiana's mother taught her a great love of God and of Our Lady. Vibiana loved to gather the children of the neighborhood and have childish processions in honor of Our Lady. Later, she began to visit the sick of the neighborhood and to perform small penances for the souls of others. She was an ordinary looking person, and few guessed the depth of her spiritual maturity, although many predicted that she would eventually become a nun.

In spite of her kindness and outgoing nature, Vibiana secretly longed for the contemplative life. To the surprise of many of her friends, she applied for admittance to the Dominicans as a lay sister. They accepted her conditionally. There were only a certain number of places in the convent, and it was already full. Vibiana would have to wait for a vacancy. Several months passed, and she had received no word, so she began to pray, telling God that if the delay was to prove her constancy she would gladly accept it. However, if He had other plans for her, she prayed that He would make them known.

Vibiana heard of Father Michael's plan. She realized that chances for an opening with the Dominicans were slim, and began to wonder if this new order were not her vocation. Although she longed for contemplation, she realized that in the sickroom at night there would be many hours when the world was sleeping and she could make the sickroom her cloister. In addition, she would be serving God actively by her care of His sick.

Vibiana requested an interview with Father Michael. He was immediately convinced of her sincerity and her piety, but he was worried because she seemed so small and frail. He wondered if she could stand up to the difficult strain of a nursing apostolate. Reluctantly, he accepted her. Neither he nor Vibiana could have imagined that of the original seven, only Vibiana would stand up to the rigors and hardships of the early days of the foundation.

On August 15 of 1851, the twenty-four-year-old Vibiana and six others took the three religious vows of poverty, chastity and obedience, received the habit of the new congregation, and changed their names. Vibiana became Sister Maria Soledad.

Wholeheartedly, Sister Soledad began her service of God through His sick. She visited the homes of the wealthy and the miserable shacks of the poor. Always, she attempted to bring God's love with her nursing skills. Being human, at first some of the outward manifestations of the diseases of her patients revolted her. In addition, she was terrified of dead bodies. Later in life, she would often talk to the novices about their fears, to encourage them with the thought that they were natural.

Sister Soledad triumphed over her fears and revulsions through heroic self-control. She saw Christ in each of her suffering and sick brothers.

Many problems beset the young congregation. The first superior left the congregation and tried to undo all its works. The sisters were very poor—at times their supper consisted of only garlic soup and bread. In 1856 there was a revolution brewing in Spain, and the governor of Madrid ordered the sisters to dress in secular attire. This was equivalent to dissolving the congregation. The governor, however, contracted cholera during an epidemic, and he asked for a Servant of Mary to nurse him. After experiencing for himself the sister's untiring charity, he retracted the order to assume secular dress.

In 1856, following what he believed to be an inspiration, Father Michael left for the mission territory. When he left, Sister Soledad begged to be one of the sisters who would accompany him. He refused, saying, "Remain here, Soledad, because if you go, the congregation will perish." He appointed her superior general of the community.

Through many hardships, Mother Soledad persevered in charity, humility, and in her wise guidance. The poverty of the young community was often extreme. Mother Soledad told the sisters, "Do not be so anxious about a house on earth when we have such a beautiful one in Heaven. We are poor, but charity compels us. We must share what God gives us among His poor."

Mother Soledad spent many hours praying for more sisters. She prayed, "May God give me fervent Servants, and they will be apostles in their attendance upon the sick." She encouraged her sisters as to the meaning of their apostolate: "My daughters, work with enthusiasm for the glory of God and the salvation of souls."

At this time, her title was Mother General, but the title of Servant would have been more apt. Mother Soledad did all the chores the other sisters did, and did not seek the top position in anything. Weekly, the sisters would go to the river to do their wash. Finally, the sisters convinced Mother Soledad that she should not join in the washing, telling her it was unseemly for the head of the congregation to do so. Instead, Mother Soledad quietly stayed behind, gathered firewood, and cooked dinner for the sisters.

The young community faced so many problems that the young spiritual director hesitated to help them write a rule, fearing they would eventually die out. After praying to know God's Will, he had a vision in which he was rebuked for his hesitation. Mother Soledad had the joy of living to see her congregation given full papal approval in 1876.

From the beginning, Mother Soledad had placed her community under the protection of Mary, Health of the Sick. This tradition is continued today by all her spiritual daughters.

Through revolutions and epidemics, the sisters persevered and the community grew. First, establishments were made in other cities in Spain. In 1875, a first group of sisters left for overseas missions in Cuba. Today, the Servants of Mary serve the sick in twenty-one countries around the world.

Mother Soledad contracted pneumonia in 1887. She died quietly at the motherhouse after receiving the Last Sacraments. She was originally buried in the sisters' plot at the cemetery, but on January 18 of 1893, her remains were exhumed and transferred to the motherhouse. The sisters were overjoyed to discover that her body was intact. It exuded a bloody liquid, and a sweet odor was noticed by all present. A few years later, only the bones remained.

Mother Soledad was beatified in 1950 by Pope Pius XII, and canonized by Pope Paul VI in 1970.

Above: St. Soledad, foundress of the Servants of Mary, sisters who nurse the sick in their own homes. St. Soledad realized that there would often be hours available for prayer during the night when the sick were asleep; she made the sickroom her cloister.

Preceding page: At the first exhumation, St. Soledad's body was found to be incorrupt; however, a few years later only the bones remained. Her relics are venerated in this beautiful reliquary in Madrid.

16

SAINT JOHN BOSCO

John Melchior Bosco
1815 - 1888
Italy
Died Age 72

A story is told about two of Don Bosco's friends who were worried about his sanity. He had spoken with such confidence of the things he had seen in his "dreams," that they were afraid he was losing his mind. They asked him to take a ride in their carriage, planning to trick him into seeing a doctor to check his mental stability.

Don Bosco readily accepted the offer of a drive in the country. When the coach drew up at the door, he politely insisted that the other two get in first, while he held the door. Instead of climbing in after them, he slammed the door shut and called to the coachman, "To the lunatic asylum, quick!" The coachman set off at a lively pace.

It was only with the greatest difficulty that the two clerics persuaded the doctors at the asylum that the wrong persons had been brought. After this incident, they did not badger Don Bosco about his "dreams" again.

Throughout his life, Father Bosco, or Don Bosco, was guided by these strangely vivid dreams. Through them, he learned what to do about his life's work—boys. He founded an order dedicated to helping the poor boys of Italy, and later, boys all over the world.

In addition to his dreams, so many miraculous occurrences happened to and around Don Bosco that Pope Pius XI said of his life, "The supernatural almost became natural, and the extraordinary, ordinary." Through Don Bosco's blessing, many people were cured of dread diseases. He had the gift of prophecy, and could read hearts. In addition, his sanctity seemed to encourage sanctity in others. Several of the candidates for canonization in this book, as well as two canonized saints treated herein, were directly influenced by Don Bosco.

When he was growing up, John Bosco worked hard on the family farm at the foot of the Italian Alps. The greatest influence on him was his devout mother, Margarita Bosco. Later in life, she came to help in the care of his students. Margarita made many sacrifices for her children, including allowing John to go to school in Castelnuovo at the age of nine, and board with a good family she knew. After school, he worked at odd jobs to support himself and send some money to his mother and the two brothers left at home.

John had an excellent sense of humor, and more than once played tricks on his unsuspecting friends. At one house where he boarded while attending school, he played so many tricks on his host that the poor man began to suspect that John was in cahoots with the devil, and complained to a local canon. The canon called John in to answer the charges. Very politely, John asked the canon the time. When the man felt for his watch, he found that it had disappeared, along with his purse. When John explained where the items had gone, and how he had done the tricks, the interview ended with much laughter.

As a child, John Bosco learned to be an expert juggler and acrobat. He put on little shows for the children and adults of the neighborhood. In payment for his performance, John asked his audience to say a few prayers with him, or to attend Mass. Later, when he was a priest, one of Don Bosco's favorite maxims was: "Enjoy yourself as much as you like—if only you keep from sin."

Once, during a mission, John and some friends found a professional juggler setting up his stall outside the church. He planned to perform during Mass. John challenged him to a wager on a test of skill—and won. Rather than take the man's money, John asked him to promise not to perform until the Mass was over.

After a vision of Our Lord and Our Lady when he was nine, John had determined to become a priest to fulfill the vocation they had shown him—a vocation of love and help for poor street boys. Although he started his studies late, John was so diligent that he completed the necessary work and was ordained in 1841, at the age of twenty-six.

At this time in Italy, there was no protection for juveniles. Boys of twelve and thirteen were often sentenced to prison for small breaches of the law. Once in prison, there was seldom hope for them to be out again for long, as they seemed to get into trouble again and again. Don Bosco believed that these boys would not be where they were if they had someone to love and care for them.

Child labor was prevalent all over Europe, and from the age of about seven on up, young boys were sent to work in the factories. These boys worked long, hard hours and were not allowed to spend a carefree childhood.

After work, the boys might stop in the local cafe for a glass of wine if they had the money. Some of these boys had homes, but many were orphans who slept in empty houses or on the streets. Some came from large families and others worked to support widowed mothers or disabled fathers. One thing they all had in common: they were poor.

One night Don Bosco discovered the sexton of his church scolding a young boy who had crept into the sacristy for warmth. "You don't know how to serve Mass! Then what are you doing here? Leave at once!"

Don Bosco called the boy back and talked to him kindly. He offered to teach the boy his prayers, and invited him to come back the next Sunday with his friends. The boy showed up the next week with four other ragged street boys. All looked as if they needed a meal. Don Bosco recognized in these children the boys Our Lady had shown him in his vision, and soon there was a group of thirty boys coming to talk to the friendly priest. The group became known as the Oratory, and it grew so large that it had to meet in the country because the neighbors began to complain about the noisy games.

Don Bosco recognized the need for a permanent place for his boys. He realized that some of them had no homes, and needed food and shelter. He rented a house and brought his mother to help care for the little group. Besides feeding and clothing them, Don Bosco helped the boys to find jobs, taught them catechism, and began night schools to teach them to read and write. Later he began trade schools to teach them a good, and honest, way to make a living.

Don Bosco's motto was, "Give me souls; take away the rest." He told the boys of the Oratory to do three things to stay on the path to Heaven: "Go to confession regularly, receive Communion often, and choose a regular confessor to whom you can unburden your heart."

Don Bosco sometimes saw in dreams the state of soul of boys at the Oratory. In one dream he saw some of them shining with light, and looking so handsome that they no longer seemed to be his boys. He saw others with eyes, ears and tongue covered with sores, their mouths filled with dirt, giving off a foul odor, and their bodies a deathly color. Others appeared in the dream with their hearts eaten through with maggots or filled with snakes, that is, mortal sins. Don Bosco was in agony over their terrible state, and longed to bring them back to spiritual health.

Don Bosco described this dream to the boys, without mentioning specific names, and urged them to examine their consciences and cleanse their souls in confession. He was bombarded with questions, but he answered, "Come to my room one by one and I'll answer your questions." All day long, boys visited Don Bosco to speak of their souls. One boy later related that Don Bosco knew, without being told, of a sin he had withheld in confession to another priest. When Don Bosco brought it up, the boy began to weep, but then literally ran back to make a sincere confession. In his dream Don Bosco had also seen hearts filled with flowers, or virtues, and most of the boys jumped with joy when Don Bosco told them of the rewards of a good life.

In another dream, Don Bosco saw three boys on whose shoulders sat ugly monkeys with long sharp claws. These were sinners against purity, and the monkeys kept them from confession. Don Bosco told the assembled boys of this dream and promised to tell more to anyone in private. To many who presented themselves, he answered, "No, it's not you," but he was frank with the three when he did speak with them. One of these later admitted that Don Bosco had truly seen the state of his soul.

Don Bosco was poor all of his life. Often there was no money to pay the rent or the workmen on the churches which he built. He placed his entire trust in God, and God took care of this remarkable man. Before his death, he had spent millions on his boys, building large schools, a basilica to Our Lady in Turin and one to the Sacred Heart in Rome, and financing mission expeditions. Whenever he was directed to a work through one of his dreams, he began it immediately, whether or not funds to finance it were available. God always provided.

At one time, an intensely anti-Catholic group known as the Waldensians made several attempts on Don Bosco's life. He was shot at more than once, and often, on his travels through the city of Turin late at night after hearing a dying person's confession, ruffians would set upon him to beat him up. Mysteriously, a large gray hound dog that Don Bosco called "Grigio" would appear to make his rounds with him and protect him from attackers. Although the dog was several times seen returning home with him, it never stayed around, disappearing as silently and mysteriously as it had appeared.

Miracles, small and large, were everyday occurrences around this saintly priest. Once, when Don Bosco was halfway through saying Mass, the sexton realized that he had forgotten to put the extra ciborium in place for the consecration. A large crowd was there and the sexton was worried about how unhappy the priest would be when he ran out of Hosts.

Don Bosco's dismay was evident as he looked at the small number of Hosts in the ciborium. With a quick prayer to Heaven, he began to distribute Communion. When he had given Communion to the large crowd, he returned to the altar. There was still one Host left— as well as a greatly astonished sexton.

Italy at this time was unsuited to the formation of any new religious order. Those already in existence were being harassed and sometimes disbanded by the anticlerical government. Yet, it was a liberal politician who suggested the idea of a new congregation to Don Bosco. When the saint smilingly told the man that he felt it would be foolish to start a new order only to have the politician immediately suppress it, the man said, "No, you work for the poor. No one will resent what you do. We will not touch you."

Guided by Our Lady, Don Bosco looked first to his own students in forming his new order. In 1859, the Congregation of St. Francis de Sales—the Salesians—was born, and it received papal approval by 1869. In 1875, after seeing a vision of starving, unwashed, poorly clothed girls who pleaded for help, Don Bosco and St. Mary Mazzarello founded the Salesian sisters, whom Don Bosco called the Daughters of Mary Help of Christians. The third part of his religious family was a group of lay people known as Salesian Cooperators; the Cooperators pledge themselves to work with and help the Salesian priests, brothers and sisters in the salvation of young people. These all use the preventive system, working to help boys and girls learn to be good before they get into trouble.

In one vision, Don Bosco saw a horde of savages who were massacring some white men. A group of missionaries dressed as Salesians came through the jungle, and the savages dropped their weapons and bent their heads in prayer. This vision became a reality when in 1875, at the request of Argentina and the Holy See, the first

Salesian missionaries left for South America. Soon their missions extended throughout the Latin world.

"First tell the devil to rest, and then I'll rest too," Don Bosco used to reply to those who urged him, later in life, to slow down in his vigorous activity. Toward the end of his life, he was afflicted with the loss of vision in one eye, a weak back, and painfully swollen legs. Still he would not rest. "While I have time, I must work."

One special helper of Don Bosco was Dominic Savio, a former pupil. Dominic died at the age of fifteen after promising to send help from Heaven. In 1876, Don Bosco had a dream in which he saw Dominic in glory. And indeed, Dominic was declared a saint in 1954.

Happily, Don Bosco was able to live to see the spread and early growth of his congregation, which is now one of the largest orders in the world.

This man who lived poor, also died poor. On the day of his death in 1888, his fellow religious were obliged to beg the baker for bread on credit.

Pope Pius XI said of Don Bosco, "God gave him magnanimity of heart as the sand on the sea-shore." Don Bosco was beatified in 1929, to the great joy of a large and tumultuously happy crowd. He was canonized just a few years later, on Easter Sunday of 1934.

Upper: As a boy, St. John Bosco often entertained people with his acrobatic feats; as payment for the show, John would ask his audience to say a few prayers with him or to attend Mass.

Lower: St. John Bosco grew up on a farm at the foot of the Italian Alps.

Left: Don (Father) Bosco's motto was, "Give me souls; take away the rest." He laid great stress on the Sacrament of Confession as a means to holiness. Here Don Bosco is shown hearing the confession of Paul Albera, who later became the third superior of the Salesians.

Right: Don Bosco wanted the boys of the Oratory to be saints—happy saints, not "long-faced saints."

In addition to his prophetic dreams, so many miraculous occurrences happened to and around Don Bosco that Pope Pius XI said of his life, "The supernatural almost became natural, and the extraordinary ordinary." This unretouched photograph of St. John Bosco shows the stubble of his beard which he rarely found time to shave adequately.

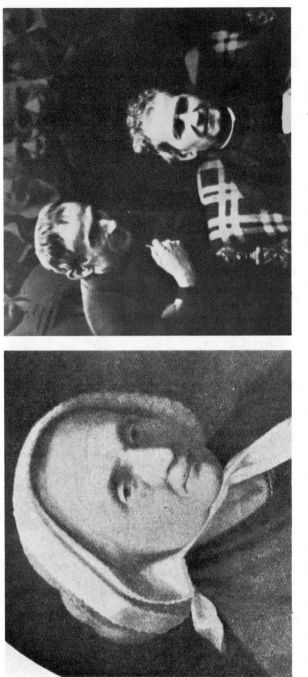

Left: "Mama Margarita," John Bosco's mother, was a strong influence in his life and a great help in his work as a priest. She became the "mother" of his homeless boys, though she almost packed up and went home on one occasion when the boys had been causing more trouble than she could bear. This picture is probably taken from a painted miniature.

Right: Don Bosco as a feeble old man toward the end of his life. Behind him is his former student and successor, Blessed Michael Rua.

17

VENERABLE FATHER DAMIEN

Venerable Damien de Veuster, SS.CC.
Joseph de Veuster
1840 - 1889
Belgium - Hawaii
Died Age 49

When Brother Damien set sail in 1863 for the kingdom of Hawaii, did he realize to what lengths his health and faith would be tried in the mission land he was so eager to enter? Years later, in the face of all obstacles and privations, he still remained eager to say "Yes" to all that he felt God asked of him.

Jef, as his family called him, was the son of Flemish grain merchants. He was born in a hamlet which is today the town of Tremeloo, Belgium. He attended a Flemish school until he was thirteen, and then went to work with his father and two of his brothers in farming the family land.

When Jef was eighteen, his father decided that Jef should go into the grain trading part of the business. His parents realized that he did not have enough education, and needed to be able to speak French, so he was sent as a boarder to a Walloon school. Here he seems to have felt the first stirrings of a religious vocation, but there were many obstacles to following it.

Jef was already behind in his studies. In addition, three of his eight brothers and sisters had already become religious, and he knew his family was counting on him to go into the grain business. For several months, the idea of his vocation lay dormant. Finally, he spoke to his parents, and they agreed to allow him to follow what he believed to be God's Will for him. His brother Pamphile talked him into entering the Sacred Hearts congregation where he himself was already a novice.

Had it not been for the support of Pamphile, it is doubtful if the superiors of the order would have accepted Jef at that time. Jef had no knowledge of Latin and did not speak French well. As it was, he was accepted as a novice for the brotherhood instead of as the candidate for the priesthood which he wished to be. He did not give up his hopes of the priesthood, but began to study Latin, Greek, and philosophy. The name which he adopted as a member of the order was Damien.

This large, healthy Flemish peasant lad was full of good humor, a humor which remained for his whole life. His confreres and professors nicknamed him "Le bon gros Damien" (big, good-natured Damien).

In 1863, the congregation decided to send missionary reinforcements to the Hawaiian Islands, and Pamphile was chosen to go as one of the group. Shortly before the ship was to sail, Pamphile came down with typhus and had to give up the idea of leaving for the missions. Damien wrote to the Father General and begged to be allowed to go in his brother's place. His request was granted, and he rushed to say good-bye to his family before embarking on a four and a half month ocean crossing.

In Hawaii, Damien attended the College of Ahumanu, Oahu, to finish his studies for the priesthood. By diligent application, he crowded into four years the amount of study that would normally have taken ten years to complete.

Hawaii was not a part of the United States at this time. It was a kingdom, and a ripe field for Christian missionaries. The kingdom was comprised of several islands, which in turn were broken down into districts, each with a missionary priest. Father Damien spent his first eight months in the district of Puna, and then he was given the double district of Kohala and Mamakue. This district was so large that it took six weeks to cover by canoe and horseback. Here Father Damien spent eight years converting the Hawaiians, attending to the Christians, learning Spanish, Portuguese and Hawaiian, and building chapels. In the beginning, he had difficulty with the Hawaiian language. He was a constant source of amusement to the Hawaiians, for when he could not think of the correct words, he would smile, whip out his handkerchief, and vigorously blow his nose to have time to think.

Damien felt that because the Hawaiians loved pomp and ceremony, they should have many chapels, beautifully made and ornamented. But as always in mission lands, money was scarce. Father Damien used the money he could obtain to buy materials, and with the help of native workers, built the chapels himself.

In the 1860's, an epidemic of leprosy (Hansen's disease), aggravated by smallpox, swept through the Hawaiian Islands. Perhaps no disease in history has inspired more dread and been more misunderstood than leprosy. Today, only one of the four major types of leprosy is thought to be incurable, and this type affects only a small percentage of leprosy victims. Even this type can be cured or arrested in its early stages by the use of sulfone drugs. The cost is only about one dollar per patient per year. In 1970, a new treatment was found to be effective in curing the disease.

In the 1800's, however, there was no accurate information about leprosy. With no treatment, it ravaged the bodies of its victims, causing acute pain and extreme disfiguration. There were many theories as to how the disease was spread—including the idea that it was transmitted with syphilis and tuberculosis. Amost all theories agreed that it was contagious. We know today that it is contagious, but it takes from three to thirty years of constant association to catch leprosy, and even then some people never become infected. Because of the lack of knowledge and the fear of the disease, King Kamehameha V ruled that all lepers were to be sent to a leper settlement on the island of Molokai.

In spite of the example of people who understood the reason for the exile, many families refused to hand over their afflicted members. The police were instructed to hunt them down.

The settlement at Molokai quickly got the reputation of being a graveyard and a lawless place. Newcomers were greeted with the cry, "In this place there is no law."

Children were abandoned by their parents, and "adopted" on Molokai to become virtual slaves. Women and young girls were forced into a life of prostitution in order to have friends to help take care of them. When they became too disfigured, they were chased away. Stealing, drunkenness, and quarrels were common.

On the island, there were no police to keep civil order, no priests to bring the Sacraments and to better the moral atmosphere, and no doctors and nurses to offer medical care. Although the government did supply some food and clothing, it was not sufficient.

There was, however, a small group of dedicated Catholics on the island. They pleaded with the bishop to send them a priest to administer the Sacraments. These people raised the money for materials for a chapel, and a brother was sent to help them build it. When the brother returned to the bishop, he took their request for a priest who would live there with them. Finally, the bishop agreed; Father Damien and three of his fellow priests were chosen to serve on a rotation basis. Each priest was to stay three months on Molokai, and to spend the rest of the year in his own district. Damien became the first to go.

Molokai was not a pretty place, and the young priest was not immune to the horrors of the settlement. The rotting flesh of the people gave off a smell like that of an open grave. Time and again, Damien reminded himself of the funeral pall he had lain under during his profession, when he promised to die to the world and to live in Christ. He remembered the words of Our Lord, "Amen I say to you, as long as you did it to one of these my least brethren, you did it to me."

Upon his arrival on Molokai, Father Damien soon realized that something must be done to supply for the temporal needs of the people in order to make them more receptive to help for their spiritual condition. He set to work with characteristic vigor.

The board of health was made up primarily of people who were opposed to the Catholic religion. Because of public opinion, they could not force Father Damien to leave. However, they hit on the plan of forbidding him to travel back and forth to and from the settlement, to prevent the spread of the disease. He must choose either to leave immediately, or to become a virtual prisoner. They thought he would leave of his own accord.

But Father Damien refused to leave; he would stay as long as God willed it. And stay he did—for sixteen years, until he himself died of leprosy.

One of Father Damien's hardest crosses was the fact that since he had no priestly assistant, he himself could not receive the Sacrament of Penance. It is said that he once rowed out to harbor to a supply ship which had another priest on board. He asked that the priest be allowed to land so as to hear his confession. When this request was denied, he asked to receive the Sacrament right there, and called out his confession in a loud voice to the priest on board.

Father Damien built churches and houses at the Molokai settlement. He sought funds from other Christians, both Catholic and Protestant, and distributed food and clothing to all. He dressed the lepers' wounds, tried out new treatments, and built orphanages for the boys and girls. In order to give the patients something to do, Damien organized bands and confraternities. When his people died,

Father Damien not only said the prayers over their bodies, but often also built the coffins that held them.

Because of his impetuous nature and rough manner, and because of jealousy on the part of some non-Catholics, as well as a lack of communication, Father Damien had many critics as well as admirers, especially in his later years. These critics were to be found even in the ranks of his own congregation. Damien suffered more on this account than he did from the leprosy he at last contracted.

A dedicated layman from the United States, Ira B. "Brother Joseph" Dutton, came to assist Father Damien in 1886, and stayed on Molokai for forty-four years. Brother Joseph had served in the Union army. He had sowed a lot of wild oats, and wanted to help Father Damien in reparation for his sinful early life. Another helper was an Irishman, "Brother" James Sinnot, a nurse who came and stayed for the last eight months of Father Damien's life.

In 1888, Father Lambert Conrardy came to stay at Molokai. After Father Damien's death, Father Conrardy went on to become a doctor, and traveled to China to work in a leper colony there.

Perhaps one of the greatest consolations of Father Damien's last months was the arrival of three Franciscan sisters in 1888 to take over the care of the orphan children. At the time of Father Damien's death, plans were already made for a new home for the girls, and one of Father Damien's last requests was to ask the sisters to take care of his boys.

After his death, nothing about Father Damien's life was spared from attack. After one particularly brutal attack on his mode of life, the famous author Robert Louis Stevenson, himself a Calvinist, wrote a long and moving defense of Father Damien.

Father Damien accomplished many things for the lepers at Molokai, but all the lepers in the world are to some extent in his debt. By his heroic example, he focused attention on these suffering people and inspired many others to follow his example.

Father Damien's cause was officially introduced in Rome in 1955. In 1977, the Sacred Congregation for the Causes of Saints declared him Venerable.

Venerable Father Damien at age 33, the year he volunteered to remain with the lepers at the Molokai mission. He is wearing the habit of the Fathers of the Sacred Hearts of Jesus and Mary.

Father Damien eventually contracted leprosy himself. This picture was taken two months before his death.

Father Damien with a girls' choir he established for the lepers at Molokai.

Father Damien with his leper boys, two months before his death.

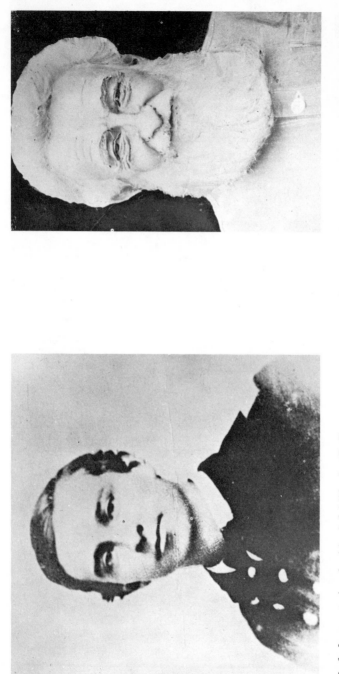

Left: In reparation for his sinful life, Ira B. Dutton came to Molokai at age 43 to help Father Damien. He stayed for 44 years. At the time of this picture he was a 20-year-old lieutenant in the 13th Wisconsin Volunteers during the Civil War. *Right:* Vermont-born Ira B. Dutton, lay missionary. He worked at Molokai from 1886 to 1930, and died in 1931.

18

VEN. AUGUSTUS CZARTORYSKI

Venerable Augustus Czartoryski, S.D.B.
Augustus Czartoryski
1858 - 1893
France - Italy
Died Age 35

"Presenting His Highness, Prince Augustus Czartoryski, legitimate heir to the Polish nobility, nephew to the reigning Queen of Spain." The prince had been educated in the best European schools, was heir to a fortune, and was the obvious leader for the national movement in exile, which longed for the freedom of Poland from the Russian occupation. The year was 1883; the place, a church in Paris. The handsome, twenty-five-year-old prince approached the visiting Italian priest for whom he was to serve Mass. The two had never met. The priest spoke: "It has been quite a long time, my prince, that I have wanted to make your acquaintance." Stunned, the young man wondered how the priest could have heard about him.

The priest was Don Bosco. Don Bosco had a gift of prophecy, and he had foreseen this meeting in a vision. He knew even before their first meeting that Augustus would become a Salesian, although he was to spend the next four years testing the prince's vocation.

Prince Augustus Czartoryski was the oldest child of Prince Ladislas of Poland and Princess Amparo, the daughter of Queen Maria Christina of Spain. Born in Paris in 1858, while still a baby he suffered from a severe case of pneumonia that undermined his health for the rest of his life. His mother, the Princess Amparo, died of tuberculosis when Augustus was only four. His contact with the disease at this early age may have affected him, for the same killer ended his own life at the early age of thirty-five.

Augustus' parents had been living in exile in Paris since the Russian occupation of Poland in 1795, although for much of the young prince's early childhood they traveled frequently throughout

Europe, in particular being welcome guests at the court of Spain. Throughout his education, Augustus' purity, piety, and in particular, his spirit of recollection while at prayer were noted by his teachers and counsellors. The constant brilliant social whirl to which he was subjected wearied him; instead, he preferred quiet and prayerful solitude.

As he grew older, the prince had to disappoint his father in his dreams of military might for his son. He told his father that he wanted to become a Salesian priest. To give up the title to the properties of the royal Czartoryski family? To reject an inheritance from his grandmother, Queen Maria Christina of Spain? To turn away from years of culture and training in all the social graces? And most impossible of all, to accept a life of poverty and hard work in the service of poor and uncultured youth? The answer was a definite "Yes."

Augustus traveled to Turin to visit the saintly Don Bosco on May 24, 1884, in order to request admission to the Salesians. The answer was a definite "No." Shocked and bewildered, the young prince questioned the verdict. Don Bosco encouraged him in his decision to become a priest, and urged him to try his vocation with the scholarly Jesuits, or the Carmelites, but the Salesian vocation was too austere. With the Salesians his work would be among the poor and the uncultured classes—no place for a prince.

Again and again for four successive years the prince renewed his appeal. Again and again the saint denied it. At last, when Augustus was twenty-nine, Don Bosco suggested recourse to the wisdom of Pope Leo XIII. The princely supplicant traveled to Rome and arranged for an audience with the vicar of Christ. Explaining the problem and asking for advice, he left with the pope's written instructions that he be admitted to the Salesian society.

After reading the directives of the pope, Don Bosco said, "You may join us, Augustus, and I desire that you remain a Salesian until death. Don Bosco will die within a very short time. If, after I pass away, my successor should desire to send you away for any reason whatsoever, it will be enough for you to tell him that Don Bosco wants you to stay. He will not disturb you, I assure you. I have wished to test your constancy. Now I am glad to tell you that you will be ours, even until death."

Joyfully, Augustus entered the novitiate in 1887. On November 24, he received the habit from the hands of Don Bosco in the most brilliant and crowded ceremony held up to that time in the Basilica of Mary Help of Christians. The royalty among the congregation included many of Augustus' relatives—princes and princesses, dukes and duchesses from Spain, Poland, France and Germany. During the last solemn Benediction the saintly founder was to pronounce, Augustus was blessed without recognition of his class status, so important in the nineteenth century, but rather as a soul redeemed by the Precious Blood of Jesus Christ.

Opposition to Augustus' vocation did not end with his acceptance by the Salesians. This nephew of Isabella, the reigning queen of Spain, was well-loved and greatly missed by his family. In the following six years, his father, step-mother, and aunt raised every possible objection. Time after time, appeals were sent to Salesian headquarters in Turin and to Rome. "His health is too poor to stand the austerity of such a life. He was coerced and unduly influenced. He did not reflect enough—take time about his decision. He has acted impulsively." To every single letter of appeal, the reply came, "With proper dispensations, the prince is *free* to return home, if he himself requests it." He never made this request.

Augustus' vocation to the Salesian order was somewhat unusual. Although piety has never acknowledged class boundaries, few of the rich, much less members of the royalty, had dedicated their lives to the particular apostolate of the Salesians—an apostolate aimed primarily at the poor and uneducated. Though he was an aristocrat, Augustus chose to live his life with the common people. Wealthier than the highest dreams of most men, he joyfully embraced a life that was dedicated to poverty. Perhaps in no other order of the times, except the Franciscan order, would he have found such a sharing of poverty with the people who were served. Augustus gave up a life spent in the castles and luxurious surroundings all over Europe in order to accept humble lodgings and simple discussions. And although equal in religion, as a novice he was far older than his fellows. For someone with the background of this young man, the adjustments to his chosen life could not have been easy. But because of his desire to do the Will of God, he was able to pass every test. Augustus persevered in his vocation with a thirst for sanctity at any cost, and was ordained on April 2, 1892.

Unfortunately, Father Augustus' steadily weakening health did not permit him to share fully in the Salesian religious life and active apostolate. He spent most of the next year in battle with the final stages of tuberculosis. As readily as he had accepted his call to join the Salesian order, he accepted the disappointment of realizing that he would not have a long priestly life. He offered his prayers and his sufferings for the salvation of souls. Don Bosco had promised that Salesians would eventually work in Augustus' homeland, Poland. The young Salesian's courage and perseverance inspired such a generous response that by the year of his death, over a hundred Polish-speaking aspirants from all parts of Europe had followed his example and joined the order.

Father Augustus Czartoryski died barely a year after his ordination. On April 8, 1893, he passed to his eternal reward murmuring the words, "Jesus Christ, my Master."

In 1898, Don Bosco's successor, Father Michael Rua, accepted the invitation to send members of the order to a small shrine in Oswiecim, more commonly known by its German name, Auschwitz. Here and in other parts of Poland, the Salesians have borne the cross of Church persecution by a hostile state. Pope John Paul II studied with them in an underground seminary in the Salesian parish in Debniki, a suburb of Krakow. Don Bosco has not forgotten his promise.

Augustus' cause was introduced in 1941, and in 1979, Pope John Paul II issued a decree formally acknowledging his heroic virtue. This decree initiates the Vatican process which eventually may lead to the beatification of Father Augustus Czartoryski.

Venerable Augustus Czartoryski, the saintly Polish prince. To test his constancy, St. John Bosco repeatedly refused to admit Augustus Czartoryski to the Salesians. After four years of refusals, and then mutual recourse to Pope Leo XIII, Don Bosco told the prince, "You may join us, Augustus, and I desire that you remain a Salesian until death."

125

19

BL. AGOSTINA PIETRANTONI

Blessed Agostina Pietrantoni, S.C.S.J.A.
Livia Pietrantoni
1864 - 1894
Italy
Died Age 30

Sister Agostina was beatified not simply because of her violent death, but because of her peaceful life of charity in the service of the sick poor. Although acclaimed by the press as a "martyr to Christian charity," she was declared Blessed under the title of "Virgin," rather than "Martyr."

Livia Pietrantoni was born in 1864, the second of ten children born to a Catholic family of average means for that area. Her grandfather, who lived with them, had an unquestioned authority. Faith was for this family a living reality. In the evenings, Livia's father led the family Rosary, and they continued with hymns or discussions of a religious nature. Often the neighbors joined in.

As a child, Livia earned the nickname of "the professor." She was a good student at school, although she was often reprimanded for unexcused absences. But though marked "unexcused," Livia's absences were caused by her having to help her mother with a chronically ill father, almost crippled with arthritis, and with the younger children. From the age of seven, Livia also had to work to help with the family finances.

Although Livia was a shy, quiet girl, she attracted many friends and playmates. She had a natural ascendancy over them, and they often sought her advice on even the most trivial matters. With her brothers and sisters, too, Livia proved a good "little mother." One of her brothers tells us, "At home I never remember Livia slapping or vexing any of us."

Livia learned to work hard at a very early age. At home she helped with the children, tended the cattle, worked in the fields, and even became fairly proficient at making shoes. At times, she and her friends went to Tivoli to help with the olive harvest, a difficult job requiring both hard labor and patience. Her friends' parents were glad for their daughters to go with Livia, as she was known as a girl who was sensible and could be trusted. For four years she labored carrying sand and gravel to help build the main road, Orvinio— Poggio Maiano. Although she received very little pay for this back-breaking job, no one remembers ever hearing her complain.

Livia grew into a lovely, healthy young woman who attracted more than one suitor. One of these suitors tells us, "I had courted her for a few months. Although I had no hope, I decided to make my official declaration of love . . . It was not easy to be alone with her . . . One evening I overtook her on the road, just by chance. She was reading. She stopped, bewildered. Then she pulled out of the book a [holy card picture of Christ]. Showing it to me, she said, 'Here is the one I will marry.' I answered, 'I knew it—and you are worthy of Him.' "

Although her mother tried to induce Livia to marry and remain close to home, she remained true to her dream of becoming a sister. At the age of twenty-one, she confided this dream to a maternal uncle, a religious brother. He offered to provide her dowry when he was convinced of her vocation. Although her friends tried every way to convince Livia that her decision was wrong, she applied to the Sisters of Charity of St. Joan Antida in 1886. She was refused admission at first, but the sisters reconsidered this decision and Livia was allowed to enter the novitiate in Rome. She kissed her brothers and sisters good-bye and knelt to receive the blessing of her parents and her grandfather. As she closed the door, she turned back and kissed it, tracing a large Sign of the Cross on it. Wiping the tears from her eyes, she ran to the carriage and happily left for her new life.

The director of the postulants remembers Livia as always smiling, always obedient, and always happy to serve the Lord. The novice mistress once asked her what her most difficult task was. Livia replied, "All is too little for the Lord. I am ready to do anything for Him."

After the end of her novitiate, and after receiving the name of Sister Agostina, she was sent to work as a nurse at the Hospital of Santo Spirito. Although this hospital had a glorious history and had felt the footprints of many saints, in Sister Agostina's time secularization had attempted to strip it of any religious character.

The anticlericals had removed the crucifixes from the wards and burdened the sisters with many regulations, including a prohibition against speaking of God to their patients. Sister Agostina did not need words to speak of God; her actions spoke clearly of her love for Him, and everybody seemed to understand.

After a brief time, Sister Agostina contracted tuberculosis, but after receiving Viaticum, she recovered. She then asked to be allowed to work in the tubercular ward, so that none of the other sisters would contract this disease.

The conduct of the men in this ward was terrible; blasphemy and vulgarity were dominant. The police were often called in to intervene. Sister Agostina's patients would sometimes spit on her, they insulted her, and once she was badly beaten. But she was not frightened by her work, and even defended the patients, saying, "They are not bad, but they are ill and one must pity them. You must rather help me to pray for them." At all times, she was patient and cheerful, even when her patients were their rudest.

For help with the unruly patients, Sister Agostina turned to Our Lady. She wrote notes to the Blessed Mother and "mailed" them behind a picture in a small shelter near her ward. One of these messages read, "Most Holy Lady, convert that wretched man whose obstinate heart I am not able to change and I promise to do two or three extra night duties in your honor."

Sister Agostina had a great devotion to Our Lady, and her favorite prayer was the Rosary, which she recited each day. She prayed a great deal. For her, prayer was not a duty, but rather a fact of life such as breathing. She credited her prayer life with enabling her to stand the duty of the "impossible" ward.

Although Sister Agostina worked very hard, often replacing one of the other sisters who was tired or ill, she did, of course, have moments of rest. Once she accompanied one of the sisters to the motherhouse, saying she would wait for her in the chapel. When the sister returned at the end of the day, Sister Agostina told her, "I have had a nice rest in front of Jesus."

Sister Agostina preferred to work, rather than to rest. Prophetically, the evening before her death she told her sisters, "We will lie down for such a long time after death that it is worthwhile to keep standing while we are alive. Let us work now; one day we will rest."

Sister Agostina made her solemn profession on September 23,

1893. Then she returned to her work in the "terrible" ward. Many of the patients in this ward had come directly from prison. One of the leaders of the most restless group was Giuseppe Romanelli, a man who had already been condemned four times. When his mother and sister visited, Sister Agostina was extremely kind to them, sometimes even giving them alms. When Giuseppe was dismissed for his misbehavior, he blamed Sister Agostina, although she had had nothing to do with the matter. He wrote her several threatening notes. Although she realized that he was a dangerous man, she remained serenely at her job.

Tuesday morning, November 13, 1894, Sister Agostina was at work in the ward. Accompanied by a patient to whom she had promised a special treat, she left the ward and descended the steps to a narrow hallway.

Suddenly she found herself faced by Romanelli. He had with him a large, sharp knife with which he began viciously to stab her. The patient with sister finally began to yell for help. As patients and nurses began to arrive, the murderer escaped. Sister Agostina had fallen to the floor with her final words, "Blessed Mother, help me."

One of the sisters, aided by some hospital attendants, carried her to a bed. The superior shook her gently and asked her if she forgave her murderer. Although she could not speak, Sister Agostina nodded her head and smiled. After only a few moments, she died.

Immediately the hospital was invaded by newsmen, photographers, and others who shouted, "We want to see the martyr!" One of the sisters, seeing that she could not move the body, placed a lily in Sister Agostina's hands and a crown of white roses on her head. After an autopsy the next day, the funeral was held on the 15th. The impressive crowd was composed of representatives from all the political parties, the hospitals of the city, and the religious orders. Most of all, the crowd included hundreds of common people, honoring the sister who had become a martyr of charity.

Romanelli was arrested on the day of Sister Agostina's funeral after a knife fight with the police. In spite of Sister's family's pleas for mercy, he was given a life sentence. He died in prison less than a year later, after being reconciled to Christ and receiving the Last Sacraments.

The informative process for Sister Agostina was begun in 1936, and the decree for the introduction of her cause was published in 1945. She was proclaimed Blessed by Pope Paul VI in 1972.

Blessed Agostina Pietrantoni, of the Sisters of Charity of St. Joan Antida. Hers was the difficult apostolate of nursing patients in the tubercular ward of a hospital, where the prevalent conduct was terrible and the police were often called in to intervene. She was sustained by constant prayer. This picture is a close likeness of Sister Agostina.

This photograph of Blessed Agostina was made shortly after she was murdered by a hospital patient. One of the sisters hastily placed a lily in her hands and white roses on her head just before newsmen and photographers rushed in and began taking pictures.

20

VEN. ANDREW BELTRAMI

Venerable Andrew Beltrami, S.D.B.
Andrew Beltrami
1870 - 1897
Italy
Died Age 27

Intelligent and physically attractive, Andrew Beltrami had cause for pride and hope for a brilliant career in any one of a number of fields. How did he himself view his pride and his dreams? He considered his dreams "vainglorious," and of his pride he wrote, "I see that my chief obstacle to holiness is pride. I *will* overcome it!" Faced with the challenge of worldly vs. religious values, Andrew spent months of agonized soul searching, armed only with an intense spirit of prayer. Eventually he concluded that his talents and abilities could best be put to God's service in the service of the poor, in the newly founded Salesian society. On a worldly level, membership with this group had little to offer other than extreme poverty and a life as an almost unnoticed elementary or secondary school teacher. But on the religious level, he felt it offered him a chance for sanctity. His stated ambition was "to become a saint, and that quickly."

Andrew was born in a small town near the beautiful Lake of Orta, on June 24, 1870. He first attended a regular school in the village, and later followed a commercial course at the Conti Institute at Omegna. Although he made excellent grades, commerce had no real attraction for him.

As a boy, Andrew was already generous. He was also assertive and strong willed; with his quick temper, he was easily roused to anger. But under the influence of the Salesian teachers, he exerted great energy to attain complete self-control. Gradually, through his piety and a great love for Our Lady, a deep spirit of obedience and patience took the place of his faults of earlier days. At college, Andrew was first in his class. His natural leadership abilities made him a model and an indisputable authority to the other students.

At sixteen, Andrew decided to become a priest and a Salesian. He wrote, "It is my ambition to concentrate my care and affection on the poorest boys among the poor, on the most uncultured, the most disliked." On November 4, 1886, Andrew was one of the one hundred novices clothed in what was to be the last such ceremony the saintly Don Bosco would preside over. The aged priest reminded each novice, as he helped him into the religious habit, "Take off the old man and put on the new."

Andrew did not lay down his spiritual struggles at the door of the novitiate. Here, too, he had to continue his battle to clean his heart of worldly desires in order to concentrate solely on God. In his notebook he wrote his resolutions. "I will never speak of myself . . . I will refrain from asserting my opinion . . . I will say nothing when I am humiliated . . . I will ask my superiors to correct me, even in public, without pity . . ." I will. I will. I will. Andrew's positive attitude became the hallmark of his life.

Of his novitiate, his novice master writes, "His humility was manly. He accused himself of his faults with frankness and without self-pity. The Lord has let Andrew go through many severe trials. From them he has suffered and still suffers a great deal, but with the assistance of divine grace he has overcome them all and still keeps fighting his battles with unflinching courage."

Inspired with an intense thirst for knowledge, Andrew began his secondary studies and theological training. His rich background in the study of the classics made a good basis for his study in philosophy and the humanities. For two years he studied intensely, and he distinguished himself as a brilliant student of "belles lettres" at the University of Turin. While still in school he was assigned to coach the slower students in literature and philosophy. Later he taught philosophy at Valsalice, and Latin and Italian at the novitiate at Foglizzo. He loved his work, but he threw himself so completely into it and into his studies that he was forced to take a summer rest at the Salesian school in Lanzo.

During this vacation in 1888, Andrew became acquainted with a slightly older Salesian seminarian whose exemplary sanctity greatly influenced him. Andrew and Augustus Czartoryski, of the Polish royalty, became good friends, with a type of spiritual friendship that transcends ordinary human relationships. Augustus had been diagnosed as having tuberculosis, and it is probable that Andrew contracted the disease through his association with Augustus.

In 1891, Andrew suffered from pulmonary hemorrhage, but he completed his theological studies. Although he was well aware of the nature of his illness, he simply refused to lie down to die, preferring to keep active as long as possible. Realizing that the young man did not have much longer to live, the Salesian superiors requested and obtained a special dispensation to allow his early ordination. He was ordained January 8, 1893, in Turin in the private chapel where Don Bosco had said his daily Mass during his last illness.

The joy Father Beltrami experienced on his ordination carried through the last four years of his life to such an extent that it was communicated to all those around him. In spite of his gradually deteriorating health, he continued to say his daily Mass and to complete all the other daily religious exercises common to his order. In addition, he spent long hours of adoration before the Blessed Sacrament, offering himself as a martyr of suffering for the salvation of the souls of sinners. He tried, as far as possible, to conceal the fact that his terrible wracking coughing spells brought with them a great deal of pain.

In addition to his religious works, Father Beltrami continued an apostolate of writing, especially the lives of the saints. Particularly outstanding are his biographies of St. Margaret Mary Alacoque, St. John Baptist de la Salle, and St. Stanislaus Kostka. His book entitled *Dawning of the Stars* was a collection of biographies of the boyhood lives of thirty-three saintly heroes. His biography of Napoleon, published after his death, became a standard on high school reading lists. At the time of his death, he had begun work on a critique of the complete works of St. Francis de Sales.

Several hemorrhages in late December forewarned the young priest that death was near. In his notebook, the following record of one of his last days was found: "For five hours I have been pleading before the tabernacle for the conversion of sinners and of all pagans. I have been in spirit on bloodstained Golgotha, pleading that out of Our Redeemer's wounds five rivers of mercy should issue to flood the five continents!"

In the early hours of December 30, 1897, death from a heart attack came quickly and quietly to Father Andrew Beltrami.

The diocesan process was instituted in 1911, and in 1939 the Salesian society made formal application for the introduction of his cause. Father Andrew Beltrami was declared Venerable on December 15, 1966.

Venerable Andrew Beltrami in his priestly garb. At an early age, he wrote, "I see that my chief obstacle to holiness is pride. I *will* overcome it."

21

SAINT CHARBEL

Saint Charbel Makhlouf
Abdullah Youssef Makhlouf
1828 - 1898
Lebanon
Died Age 70

On December 5, 1965, the Lebanese hermit Charbel Makhlouf was beatified in the presence of many of his fellow countrymen and numerous cardinals and prelates of the entire Church who were present in Rome for the closing of Vatican Council II. Charbel was the first confessor of the East elevated to this honor according to the formal procedure of the Catholic Church. He was canonized in 1977.

Youssef was born May 8, 1828, in a small Lebanese mountain village called Beqa'Kafra. He was the fifth child of a modest farming family. His family was a close one; they were good Christians who left Youssef with a solid faith.

Youssef attended the village school which was attached to and supported by the parish church. In his village he was noted for being pious, honest, simple, and sincere. Prayer was a large part of his life, and he had a special devotion to Our Lady. As a young man, he prayed to the Blessed Virgin to help him become a monk. Two of his maternal uncles were monks, and he wished to follow their example.

When Youssef spoke of his wish to become a monk, his family attempted to change the subject, or did not pay much attention. His family and a young lady of the area had marriage in mind for him. So, without giving any advance notice, he left in 1851 for the Monastery of Our Lady of Mayfoug of the Lebanese Maronite order. At age twenty-three he began his first year of novitiate, choosing the name of Charbel, an early martyr. For the second year he was sent to the Monastery of St. Maron at Annaya. Here he made his monastic profession and took the solemn vows of poverty, chastity, and obedience in 1853 at the age of twenty-five.

After his profession, Charbel was sent to the Monastery of St. Cyprian at Kfifane. This monastery served as the scholasticate of the Lebanese order. Here Charbel studied for the priesthood. A good student, he was consistently among the top students in his class. He was ordained to the priesthood on July 23, 1858, at the Maronite patriarchal residence, Bkerke. After this, he returned to the Monastery of St. Maron, where he spent sixteen years of monastic life before withdrawing to a hermitage.

When Charbel entered the monastery he was already known as a mature young man, a man of prayer, and in his monastic life he continued to grow in virtue. All the testimony collected for his cause points especially to an almost legendary obedience. "Pray without ceasing" was his precept, and hour after hour he knelt in adoration before the Blessed Sacrament.

In his monastic work, Charbel consistently chose those tasks that were the hardest or the lowliest. He respected all his brother monks, and to them he became a model of the monastic life. He often fasted and performed acts of mortification. His daily union with God was apparent to those who lived with him.

Father Charbel felt called to the life of a hermit. According to the Eastern monastic tradition, monasticism reaches its fullness in the solitary life. Many times, Father Charbel asked to be allowed to retreat to the hermitage which was connected to the monastery at Annaya. This hermitage had room for three monks, and three were already there. In spite of the fact that the hermitage was already fully occupied, the superiors acceded to Father Charbel's request in 1875; permission was granted after a lamp in his cell remained lit for several hours despite the fact that it contained no oil.

Father Charbel spent the remaining twenty-three years of his life in the peace of the hermitage. His life there was most austere. He practiced severe mortifications, slept on the hard ground, and ate only one meager meal a day. He usually offered Mass about noon in order to spend the entire morning in preparation and the rest of the day in thanksgiving.

At eleven o'clock, on the morning of December 16, 1898, Father Charbel was saying Mass in the chapel when he suffered a paralytic stroke just at the moment of the Major Elevation. After an agony of eight days, he surrendered his soul to God on Christmas eve, at the age of seventy.

Even before his death, Father Charbel had been considered by many to be a saint. On the day of his burial, the superior of the monastery made the following unique notation in the monastery journal: "On December 24, 1898, Father Charbel of Beqa'Kafra, a hermit, struck with paralysis, died after receiving the sacraments. He was called to the bosom of God at the age of seventy. *Because of that which he will do after his death,* I need not give any details of his life. Faithful to his vows, and of exemplary obedience, his conduct was more angelic than human."

In spite of this unique testimony to the feeling of his brother monks that they had lived with a saint, it is very likely that Father Charbel would have simply rested quietly in his grave were it not for the fact that an extremely bright light shone around the grave for forty-five nights after his burial. Because of the enthusiasm of those who witnessed this phenomenon, the superiors of the monastery requested permission to exhume the body. At this exhumation, four months after Father Charbel's death, his body was found to be perfectly incorrupt, in a lifelike flexible state, although in accord with the tradition of the community he had been buried with no coffin. In addition, the ground was wet from recent rains. After being cleaned and reclothed in fresh garments, the body was placed in a wooden coffin in the private chapel of the monastery.

Several other strange phenomena accompanied the preservation of the body in such a lifelike state. One that deserves mention is that the body continued to exude a liquid that was a combination of perspiration and blood. The postulator for Father Charbel's cause, Father Joseph Mahfouz, writes, "I have personally touched the body in August 1952. It seemed that the body was both living and dead. It is not a rare phenomenon that a cadaver will remain preserved, but that the mortal remains continue to be flexible, soft, pliable and that there is constant perspiration is extraordinary and unique. This is the case of our Saint whose body remained preserved and perspired until the day of his beatification. We can say that his body, which is now simply decomposed, was without alteration in 1965. After opening his tomb, one does not smell the odor of corpse. Rather, there is an aromatic odor."

The body was re-sealed after the beatification, as it had been several times before. Father Mahfouz writes of the last exhumation: "His tomb was recently opened (1976) and I was present. His body was completely decomposed and all that remained was a skeleton." God apparently allowed the incorruptibility to last until the sanctity of His servant Charbel was recognized by the Church.

In 1950, Charbel's monastery began keeping records of the miracles reported at his tomb. Within a two-year period, over twelve hundred reports had been collected.

Many of the miracles reported at the tomb have involved miraculous recoveries from disease or deformity. One outstanding cure involved a seamstress who had had a hunchback and certain other deformities since childhood. She visited Charbel's tomb to pray for her relatives, not for herself. After the cure, her physician testified that he had examined her many times. Her figure became the normal figure of a woman who was not deformed by a hunchback. The cures accepted for Charbel's beatification and canonization include the cure of an extremely severe stomach ulcer, the restoration to sight of a man with a torn retina, and the cure of a throat cancer.

Charbel was canonized on October 9, 1977. Pope Paul VI said of him, "He helps us to understand in a world very often fascinated with riches and comfort, the irreplaceable value of poverty, of penance, and of asceticism in freeing the soul in its ascent to God."

St. Charbel Makhlouf, the Lebanese hermit whose body remained incorrupt from his death in 1898 until 1965.

22

BL. MARIA DROSTE ZU VISCHERING

Blessed Maria Droste zu Vischering, R.G.S.
Maria Droste zu Vischering
1863 - 1899
Germany - Portugal
Died Age 35

For Maria Droste zu Vischering, love of the Sacred Heart of Jesus was not a vague emotion or a sentimental devotion. For her, it was the reality she lived, and she desired to lead the world to this Source of Love. Three years before her death, in an extraordinary divine communication, Our Lord made known to her that He wanted the entire universe consecrated to His Heart, and that she was to request this of the Holy Father. In obedience to His divine Will, she petitioned Pope Leo XIII for this in June of 1898. On Our Lord's further insistence, she again petitioned the pope in January of 1899. "My mission on earth will be completed as soon as the consecration is accomplished," she confided to her confessor.

Maria was born September 8, 1863 in Munster, Germany. Her father was Count Clement Droste zu Vischering, and her mother the Countess Helen von Galen Droste zu Vischering. Both were descended from a long line of devoted Catholics noted for their heroic loyalty to the Church. One of seven children, Maria had a will of iron.

In spite of her somewhat explosive character, Maria had a sensitive heart and was generous with a deep feeling for others.

Maria was raised amid wealth at the family home, Darfield castle. There was an enormous contrast between the elegant furnishings of her study and rooms at Darfield, and the stark simplicity of the room she later occupied in the Convent of the Good Shepherd in Munster. Willingly, she exchanged her early life of luxury for a life of simplicity and hard work.

At fifteen, Maria began attending the boarding school of the Sisters of the Sacred Heart in Riedenburg. Later, she said of her time there, "I began to understand that the love of the Sacred Heart without a spirit of sacrifice is but empty illusion."

From the time of her Confirmation at the age of twelve, Maria had felt drawn to the religious life. After leaving school in 1881, poor health prevented her entering any religious order. Instead, she privately made a vow of virginity and lived a life of solitude and prayer at home with her family.

In 1888 her health improved and she began to think seriously of joining a religious order. Shortly after she befriended an unhappy girl in a nearby hospital, Maria felt called to the Sisters of Charity of the Good Shepherd. She later wrote, "This thought—you must enter the Good Shepherd—was so clear to me that from this moment I was convinced and determined."

The primary apostolate of the Good Shepherd sisters is directed toward the care and help of those who because of character, family, social or behavior problems, need special care and love. Their work is one of prevention, rehabilitation, and protection. They attempt to give each of those they serve a greater sense of self-worth and dignity as a child of God.

Maria began her novitiate on January 10, 1889 and received the name Maria of the Divine Heart. She made her perpetual vows on January 29, 1891, at the age of twenty-seven. As a youth worker, Sister Maria's firmness, combined with kindness and a spirit of happiness, helped her with the girls. She attributed all her success in her apostolate to the Heart of Our Lord. "Only the Heart of Jesus is responsible for the success I always had with the girls, and often when I was confronted with an especially desperate case He would level all difficulties. When you are appealing to His Divine Heart for a soul, He will never refuse you, although sometimes He demands much prayer, sacrifice, and suffering."

In 1894, Sister Maria was assigned to Lisbon, Portugal. She was homesick and missed those in Munster, but from her notes of that time we realize that she went to God for consolation: "Lord, I have left all, yes all, that I might love You until the last moment of my life and that with all my energy I might spread devotion to Your Sacred Heart."

Sister Maria was appointed superior of the Convent of the Good Shepherd in Oporto, Portugal, in May of 1894. This convent was in drastic need of good and capable administration. Without thinking of herself, Maria prayed, trusted, and triumphed. A Benedictine abbot who knew her recalls, "I was astonished by the leadership exercised by this very young superior." Her wise administration made the convent a center of spiritual radiation.

In 1896, barely two years after coming to Portugal, Sister Maria became afflicted with a spinal disease that brought with it tremendous pain and progressive paralysis. In spite of her pain, she continued her administrative work as superior. It was at this time that Our Lord made known to her His wish for the consecration of the world to His Sacred Heart, and directed her appeals to Pope Leo XIII. In May of 1899, Pope Leo wrote the encyclical "Annum Sacrum," which contained the decree for the consecration of the world. Sister Maria had predicted that she would die as soon as the consecration was accomplished. On June 8, 1899, two copies of the encyclical were personally delivered to her, and at 3:05 p.m. she quietly gave back her soul to God. On June 11, 1899, Pope Leo XIII consecrated the entire human race to the Heart of Jesus.

The informative process for the cause of Maria Droste zu Vischering was opened in 1921, and the apostolic process was begun in 1942. At the ritual exhumation in 1944, Maria's body was found to be intact. She was declared Venerable in 1964, and beatified by Pope Paul VI in 1975.

Above: Blessed Maria Droste zu Vischering had several visions in which Our Lord requested and insisted that she petition the Pope to consecrate the entire universe to His Sacred Heart. This she did. Sister Maria's body was found incorrupt 45 years after her death.

Opposite: Maria at four years of age and at 14. Maria had a will of iron and an explosive temper, but also a sensitive and generous heart. She grew up amid luxury at her family home, Darfield Castle.

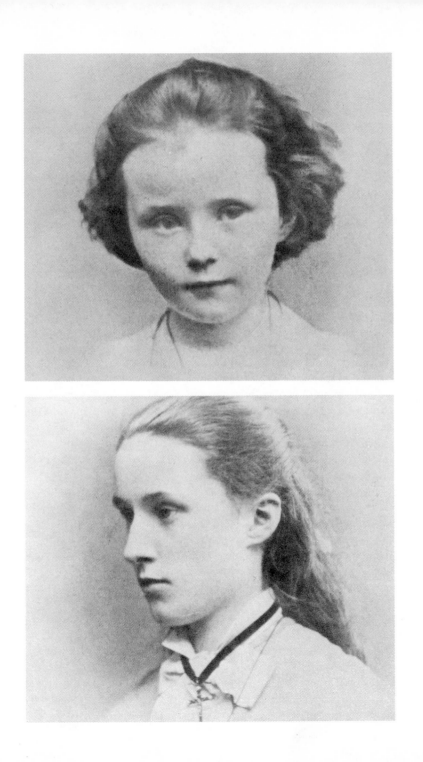

23

MOTHER ANGELA TRUSZKOWSKA

Servant of God Mother Angela Truszkowska, C.S.S.F.
Zophia Kamilla Truszkowska
1825 - 1899
Poland
Died Age 74

Mother Angela quickly answered the frantic pounding on the convent door. Opening the door, she saw a terrified young soldier. "Hide me, Sister," the young man pleaded in terror. There was no time to get the young man to safety in the special niche in the cellar wall, as Mother Angela could hear the rough boots of the police coming quickly down the street.

"Follow me," she ordered tersely. Stopping before some large garbage cans, she commanded the young soldier to climb into the largest. Speedily and efficiently she piled heaps of used, bloody bandages from another can on top of the terrified man, who promptly fainted under the refuse of the day's work in the hospital of the Felician sisters.

At the second knock, Mother Angela unhurriedly opened the door. Several rough policemen pushed past her and began searching, silently and efficiently. One angrily jerked the lid off the garbage can with its unconscious contents. He plunged his hand inside, but noticed almost immediately that the can was filled with bandages full of blood and pus. Quickly, he removed his hand in disgust and revulsion. After a fruitless search, the police left. The young soldier escaped, thanks to Mother Angela's quick thinking.

Mother Mary Angela Truszkowska, foundress of the Polish Felician sisters—a branch of the large Franciscan family—lived, worked, and died during one of the saddest periods of Polish history. From 1795 to 1918, the country of Poland did not exist politically, and was removed from the maps of Europe. For one hundred twenty-three years, the Polish people suffered untold national agony as their country was partitioned between Russia, Prussia, and

Austria. In 1830, the Poles revolted against the Russian government; this revolt brought severe reprisals. The landed estates were confiscated, the nobility were deported, the Ruthenian Catholics were persecuted, and there was an attempt at Russification of the entire Polish people. The second revolt, in 1863, brought even more and greater reprisals, including the suppression of religious communities. But in spite of troubles and persecution, the Felician sisters persevered and grew, under the direction of Mother Angela. In 1874, the sisters came to the United States and remain today a large, strong congregation.

Zophia Kamilla Truszkowska was born on May 16 of 1825, in Kalisz, Poland. She was the oldest of the four children of Joseph and Josepha Truszkowska. The family were members of the Polish nobility and were staunch Catholics. Joseph was a lawyer, assistant procurator at the juvenile court in Kalisz. Joseph and Josepha's daughter was born prematurely; the little girl was tiny and weak, and was immediately baptized at home as the doctors had little hope for her survival. Determined to keep her child alive, Zophia's mother devised an incubator, and with her husband began to storm Our Lady of Czestochowa with petitions for the baby's life.

The motherly heart of Mary could not resist such faith, and Zophia lived. In gratitude, Josepha imparted to Zophia a love of Our Lady that grew and matured with the years.

Zophia was a bright child, constantly asking questions about anything and everything. Her parents hired a governess to teach her, and this woman exerted a strong influence on her religious outlook as well as on her studies. Often their long walks would end at one church or another for a visit to the Blessed Sacrament.

From her earliest years, Zophia seemed to be aware of and compassionate toward misery and suffering of any kind. When walking with her governess, she would take the pennies she had been given for little treats and happily give them to any beggars or other unfortunates they passed on the way.

At the age of twelve, Zophia moved with her family to Warsaw and attended a private boarding school. Here she excelled in her studies and in deportment, and one of her teachers openly called her "little pet," a source of embarrassment to the shy girl.

At sixteen, Zophia contracted tuberculosis, but fortunately the disease was diagnosed in its early stage. Her parents sent her to Switzerland with her governess in an effort to improve her health.

The beauty of the mountains impressed Zophia with the wonders of God's creation, and she realized that she wished to become a nun. Back home in Warsaw, her parents opposed the idea of her entering a convent, so for a time she lived quietly at home, continuing her studies and praying.

Study and prayer did not, of course, occupy all her hours. She helped her parents in the supervision of the younger children, and tutored them in their studies. Unknowingly, she was preparing for her vocation as teacher and mother to countless orphans.

Zophia made a youthful resolve to be the first worshiper each morning at Mass in a nearby church. In company with her younger sister Valerie, she would sneak out of the house early each morning for several weeks. Often the girls had to stand for some time in the bitter cold and snow before the sacristan arrived to open the door. Their lofty ambitions came to a speedy halt one morning when they were accosted by the family caretaker who had been given strict orders by their father that the girls were not to leave the house before five a.m.

Valerie's early death at sixteen made a profound impression on her sister. Meditating by Valerie's coffin, Zophia reflected on the brevity of earthly life and the length of the life of the soul thereafter. She later talked with her confessor and decided to enter a life of contemplation with the Visitandine nuns, but her mother met her request with tears and her father with a flat refusal. About this time, her father became dangerously ill, and Zophia became his dedicated nurse. Feeling that her wish to become a nun disturbed him, she promised to give up the idea of her vocation until after his death. She accompanied him to Germany for a cure at the mineral springs in Salzbrunn, and later visited the major cities of Germany. At the great cathedral in Cologne, Zophia became aware that God was not calling her to the cloister of the Visitandines, and although still uncertain as to His Will for her, she later said she was filled with peace and resignation.

Back home in Warsaw, Joseph Truszkowska began to plan to introduce Zophia into society, in hopes of arranging a good marriage for her. She remained obedient to her parents' wishes, and attended parties and cultural events. As she was naturally shy and retiring, these large functions were a trial for Zophia. At many of the large balls, she would search out her friend and cousin, Clothilde Ciechanowski, and the two girls would retire to the quietest spot available to discuss their mutual interests. Clothilde, too, felt drawn to the cloister, and was also experiencing family opposition to her vocation.

In the summer, after the busy whirl of the winter social season, Zophia and Clothilde spent their vacation at Clothilde's family's summer estate in Grojec. Here the two girls occupied themselves teaching catechism to the village children and sewing vestments for the poor village parish church. At night, when the other occupants of the house were asleep, Zophia at last had time for the prayer she longed for, and kept a nightly prayer vigil. Her former governess, who had remained with the family, accidentally discovered Zophia's attraction to self-denial when she found her asleep on the floor early one morning. In imitation of St. Francis of Assisi, Zophia refused to sleep in the large comfortable bed. Realizing Zophia's religious nature and the fact that her parents would probably object strenuously to this type of mortification, the governess kept her discovery to herself. Sleeping on the floor was not the only mortification Zophia practiced in her effort to overcome her own will, but all were done quietly and without attracting attention.

One night as Zophia was meditating in front of the picture of Our Lady of Czestochowa in her room, a candle somehow caught her dress and the picture frame on fire. When her governess smelled smoke, she went to investigate; noticing Zophia and the picture burning, she began to scream for help, bringing the other occupants of the house on the run. Zophia was either asleep or in such deep prayer that she had not noticed the fire. When the flames were extinguished, the family members were amazed that neither Zophia nor the picture had been harmed, although her dress and the frame were ruined. This event was unanimously regarded as unusual, and the picture was given a special veneration by the family from that time on.

Since Zophia no longer mentioned leaving for a convent, her father allowed her to care for the poor in the slums of Warsaw, and generously contributed to the support of two orphans she took charge of. Later, their number grew to six, and Zophia and Clothilde became two of the first members of the newly organized Society of St. Vincent de Paul. At the suggestion of her confessor, Zophia also became a Franciscan tertiary at the age of twenty-nine, and took the name Angela. With financial assistance from her father and donations she had solicited, she and Clothilde established an institute for the care of orphans and the shelter of homeless and abandoned women. On November 21, 1855, she and Clothilde solemnly promised to consecrate themselves to the service of Our Lady according to the Will of her Son, Jesus Christ.

The example of service given by these two attracted many other young women from the finest families in Warsaw. Since they all became Franciscan tertiaries and began living a community life, their advisor decided to give them a religious habit; in 1857, ten of the group were clothed as Franciscans. The young sisters often took their orphan charges to a nearby Capuchin church dedicated to St. Felix of Cantalice, and the townspeople soon began to call the orphans the children of St. Felix. When the sisters began wearing the habit, the people referred to them as the Felicians, a name that stuck. In 1860, the congregation was registered at the Vatican, and Pope Pius IX gave his blessing to the new convent. Angela was designated as superior of the group.

At the convent, Mother Angela was both a mother and a teacher to the orphans in her care. She was a friend, nurse, and comforter to the elderly women the sisters cared for. In addition, she found time to visit with the poor in their homes in the slums, bringing financial help as well as spiritual comfort to them.

Soon, so many applicants came to join the sisters that Mother Angela began to spend more and more time directing the new religious order. Within a mere four years, the sisters had begun teaching in twenty-seven village schools in the Russian sector of Poland. During the day, the children had classes in the schools, and at night the adults gathered for religious instruction.

All the original sisters who knew and lived with Mother Angela testified that she was exacting in her demands on them, but was able to give each the individual spiritual guidance and direction that put their vocations on a solid basis. In 1860, a contemplative branch of the Felicians was established. Twelve of the sisters were cloistered to pray in reparation and for the work of the community, while the active sisters continued their apostolate. Mother Angela was one of the original twelve contemplatives, but after three years, her role as superior of both groups made it mandatory for her to rejoin the active sisters.

In 1863, a military insurrection against Russia arose. The Felicians took care of wounded Polish soldiers, and later, when the insurrection collapsed, they hid political refugees. One wall in the cellar of one of their hospitals had special removable bricks over a niche large enough to hide a man.

Mother Angela's letters to her sisters at this time contained words of comfort, encouragement, and the recommendation to "help all without discrimination, friend and foe alike . . . Everyone is our neighbor."

Because the Russians felt that the Felicians had participated in the insurrection, the czar disbanded them along with many other religious orders. Police entered the convent and at gunpoint ordered the sisters to assume secular dress and leave the convent within three days. The cloistered sisters were allowed to go to a convent of Bernardines at Lowics, and Mother Angela went with this group. Before leaving Warsaw, she made certain that each of the sisters had a place to stay with relatives or friends.

For a time, no one was allowed to give money to the sisters living at the Bernardine convent. Police guards were stationed at the doors to see that no one brought the sisters food or other supplies. One night the two groups of sisters came down to dinner to find that the only items on the neatly set table were large pitchers of water. With startled, then resigned glances back and forth, Mother Angela and her sisters began to laugh. After all had released their tensions with a hearty laugh, Mother Angela began to lead the Magnificat and the Te Deum, and all joined in the thanks before settling down to their dinner of water.

The plight of the dispersed sisters who could only work as a sort of religious underground was a constant source of suffering to Mother Angela. At last, in 1865, she received permission from the Emperor Franz Josef allowing the sisters to stay in the Austrian sector of Poland. She sent joyful word to the sisters to gather in Krakow, where she joined them in May of 1866.

Although she resumed the responsibility of the government of the congregation, Mother Angela's health began to fail and she became increasingly weak and nearly deaf. In 1869 she resigned her office as superior, and took charge of the convent garden.

In 1873, Mother Angela initiated a new ministry for the order— work among the students of the large university in Krakow. A soup kitchen was established, and the sisters fed the poorer students and helped them to find books and clothing in order to continue their studies. Mother Angela had a strong devotion to St. Anthony, but rather than quietly folding her hands to pray to him, she spent long periods conversing in front of his picture in the convent. Some who happened to overhear her said it seemed as if she were carrying on a conversation with a person in the same room. Once she was observed pacing back and forth in front of the picture shaking her finger at it and admonishing St. Anthony for his lack of help for a particular young student. The boy needed a new suit to wear for his examination before his teachers. No suit, no exam. As she paced, the doorbell rang. There stood a man with a fine new suit. "Sister, the stupid tailor has made my new clothes too small. Do you have any use for them?"

In 1874, a number of requests came from America for sisters to work with Polish immigrants in the United States. Mother Angela considered it a great happiness to bless the first group of five who left for this mission field on October 24.

In 1899, Mother Angela developed stomach cancer, and for the last few weeks of her life she was unable to eat. Her heroic patience and uncomplaining attitude were noticed by her doctor, who remarked, "Only saints know how to suffer like that." She died quietly on October 10, and was buried in the chapel adjoining the motherhouse in Krakow.

After Mother Angela's death, many people visited her tomb seeking her intercession. So many favors were reported that her cause for beatification was initiated in 1949. The Apostolic Process was opened in 1967 by the Archbishop of Krakow, Karol Cardinal Wojtyla, who is now Pope John Paul II.

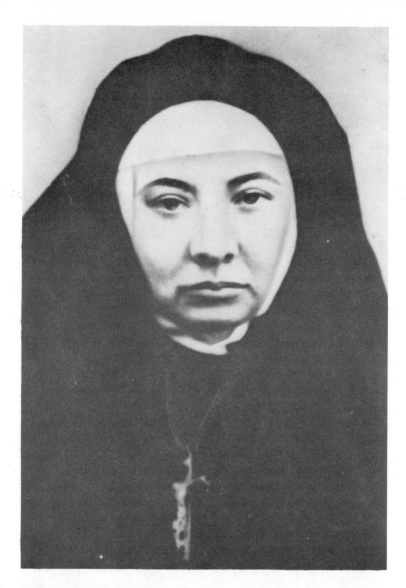

Mother Angela Truszkowska. When she was born, the doctors had little hope for her survival. However, her mother devised a homemade incubator and both of her parents begged Our Lady of Czestochowa to let their baby live. Their prayer was answered. Mother Angela died at age 74 of stomach cancer. Her doctor's comment on her heroic patience was, "Only saints know how to suffer like that."

Mother Angela Truszkowska, foundress of the Felician sisters, lived in Poland during a time of political chaos, military turmoil, and religious persecution.

24

BLESSED GREGORY
AND COMPANIONS

The Twenty-Nine Martyrs of China,
including the Seven Protomartyrs of
the Franciscan Missionaries of Mary.
Died in China
Died 1900

In 1900, during the Boxer Revolution in China, it is estimated that over 20,000 Christians of all denominations were put to death for refusal to deny their Faith. The names of most of these courageous men and women are known to God alone. In 1926, the cause for beatification of 2,416 of the Catholic martyrs was begun. These had suffered and died in the vicariates confided to the Order of Friars Minor in China. The vicariates presented the necessary information to the Sacred Congregation of Rites.

In order to avoid lengthy delays, twenty-nine of these martyrs were chosen as the first to be beatified. The representative group includes bishops, priests, brothers, sisters, seminarians, and members of the third order.

In particular, the Seven Protomartyrs of the Franciscan Missionaries of Mary are numbered among the members of the group—all of whom are in some way affiliated with the Franciscans.

The persons mainly responsible for the massacre of 1900 were the Empress Tsou-Hi and the Viceroy of Shansi. The empress had dethroned her grandson when she found him too favorable to modern ways, and it was on the Christians that she vented her fury at the presence of foreigners in China. She did this by making use of the Boxers, a secret society of armed fanatics who brought death to everyone who got in their way. Christians were told to give up their Faith; those who would not, and who did not escape from the country, were massacred.

After a series of threats, twenty-six of the twenty-nine martyrs of this group were imprisoned in an old Chinese house. They were kept there under house arrest for four days. Ironically, the house was called the Inn of the Celestial Peace.

Every morning, the bishops and priests celebrated Mass. All remained calm and serene. The seminarians went so far as to play games in the courtyard. When they were admonished by one of the priests to spend their time preparing to die rather than playing, the youngest answered, "If we die martyrs we will all surely go to Heaven. We do not have to worry."

On the afternoon of July 9, 1900, a messenger from the Viceroy demanded the presence of three of the group at a tribunal. An hour later, the Boxers invaded the house and seized the others. Bishop Grassi gave final absolution before they were taken before the tribunal.

As they were being dragged to the tribunal, their hands were tied and their captors began beating the bishops on the head, making the blood flow. The sisters sang the Te Deum, according to the testimony of an eyewitness.

More than 3,000 Boxers were assembled at the tribunal. The Viceroy himself struck Bishop Fogolla on the chest and shouted the execution order, "Kill! Kill!" The executioners rushed forward and began striking right and left, cutting off heads, arms, and legs, mutilating corpses and firing off guns to scare away evil spirits.

The Seven Protomartyrs

Thirty-four-year-old Marie Hermine of Jesus was superior of the little group of Franciscan Missionaries of Mary. A native of France, she had joined this order because of her love for the missions. Both courage and gentleness were outstanding characteristics of this superior. Bishop Grassi had invited her to leave China before the danger came too close to her mission, but she refused, humbly begging him not to deny her or her sisters the grace of martyrdom, if that became necessary.

Blessed Mary of Peace, an Italian orphan, was the youngest of the sisters. She was twenty-four at her death. Although of a delicate nature, sensitive, timid and silent, she never wavered in her decision to accept martyrdom.

Blessed Maria Chiara is said to have been the first of the sisters to be attacked. She was the tallest of the group, and because of her outgoing nature, probably appeared to her executioners to be the leader. Prophetically, before leaving for the China missions she had told a friend, "If you want to join me in China, hurry, for I will soon have my head cut off for Jesus." Those who knew her say she was always ready for any sacrifice for the salvation of souls. Her life was her final, great sacrifice.

Blessed Mary of St. Nathalie went to the missions hoping for a life of hard work in order to save souls. Once there, however, she was stricken with a chronic illness, and found an apostolate of suffering to prepare her for her later martyrdom. In spite of constant pain, this young Frenchwoman was always amiable and smiling. She once said, "If I had nothing to suffer, I would think God did not love me." She accepted both her illness and her martyrdom willingly for the sake of others.

Blessed Mary of St. Just was multi-talented and an expert at many kinds of work. She was particularly skilled at gardening, weaving, and typesetting, and could profitably have remained off the mission and out of danger, using her talents for God in another place. Instead, she received the palm of martyrdom. She said, "I attach myself to the Will of God as the anchor of my salvation."

Blessed Mary Adolphine, born in the Netherlands, was questioned as to her reasons for entering the order. Smiling, she replied that her motive was "the desire to suffer for Our Lord." A humble person, she quietly reserved for herself the most difficult tasks. Before leaving for China, she was warned of the danger, as were all her sisters. She gladly accepted the danger in her willingness to serve God and convert souls.

Blessed Mary Amandine, a native of Belgium, was a living personification of the spirit of Franciscan joy. Her perpetual smile and constant good humor were much remarked on by her Chinese patients at the mission hospital. After the persecutions began, she said, "I pray God to fortify the martyrs, but I do not ask Him to preserve them." Like the early Christians, she knew that "The blood of martyrs is the seed of Christians." The Franciscan Missionaries of Mary continued to go to China as missionaries. Their sister, Bl. Mary Assunta, died there in 1905 and has been beatified.

The twenty-nine martyrs of China are known as "Blessed Gregory and Companions." They were beatified by Pope Pius XII on November 24, 1946.

Following is a list of the names of the Seven Protomartyrs of the Franciscan Missionaries of Mary:

Blessed Marie Hermine of Jesus
(Irma Grivot)
Born April 28, 1866, in Beaune, France. Died at age 34.

Blessed Mary of Peace
(Mariana Giuliana)
Born December 13, 1875, in Aquila, Italy. Died at age 24.

Blessed Maria Chiara
(Clilia Nanetti)
Born January 9, 1872, at Ponte San a Maria Maddaiena, Italy.
Died at age 28.

Blessed Mary of Saint Nathalie
(Jeanne-Marie Guerquin)
Born May 5, 1864, at Belle-Isle-en-Terre, France. Died at age 36.

Blessed Mary of Saint Just
(Anne-Francoise Moreau)
Born April 9, 1866, at Faye, France. Died at age 34.

Blessed Mary Adolphine
(Anna Catherina Dierks)
Born March 8, 1866, at Ossendrecht, Netherlands. Died at age 34.

Blessed Mary Amandine
(Pauline Jeuris)
Born December 28, 1872, at Herck-la-Ville, Belgium.
Died at age 27.

Upper: Blessed Gregory and some of his companions in the martyrdom of 1900 in China. Thousands of Catholics were martyred.
Lower: Blessed Marie Hermine of Jesus, the superior of this group of Franciscan Missionaries of Mary. She desired the grace of martyrdom. These seven nuns are the Protomartyrs of the Franciscan Missionaries of Mary.

159

Upper: Blessed Maria Chiara foresaw that she would be called upon to die for Christ. Before leaving for the missions, she told a friend, "If you want to join me in China, hurry, for I will soon have my head cut off for Jesus."
Lower: Blessed Mary of St. Nathalie went to the missions to work for souls, but she was stricken with a chronic illness and so embraced an apostolate of suffering.

160

Upper: Blessed Mary Adolphine said that her motive for joining the Franciscans was "the desire to suffer for Our Lord."
Lower: Blessed Mary of Peace—sensitive, timid, and silent—never wavered in her decision to accept martyrdom.

Upper: Blessed Mary of St. Just had many talents. She said, "I attach myself to the Will of God as the anchor of my salvation."
Lower: Blessed Mary Amandine was a living example of Franciscan joy. After the persecutions began, she said, "I pray God to fortify the martyrs, but I do not ask Him to preserve them."

25

SAINT MARIA GORETTI

Maria Teresa Goretti
1890 - 1902
Italy
Died Age 11

To many, the story of Maria Goretti is already familiar as the story of a young girl who refused to acquiesce in a grave sin against chastity. Few realize that before the final dramatic refusal, Maria had also resisted blandishments and threats. The canonization of Maria Goretti was not based on a single moment's struggle against sin, but upon her practice of heroic virtue through her entire short life. To die rather than to sin was a far more natural choice for Maria than was the alternative—to sin in order to avoid death.

Maria's story begins with her home, where the moral basis of her heroic choice was nurtured. Her mother, Assunta, was an orphan who had never learned to read or write. Maria's father finished his military duty, returned to his home town of Corinaldo, married Assunta, and began to farm for a living. This couple had little to sustain them other than their love for God, Our Lady, and each other.

Although Assunta had never been to school for any formal lessons, she learned from the Church about the love of God, and transmitted this great love, by words and actions, to her family. Luigi, her husband, also had a deep love and devotion to God. Rather than feel bitter about their poverty and way of life, this valiant couple accepted all as God's Will, and greeted the birth of each of their children as a great gift from God. The lesson of love was imparted to each child. After the death of their first son as an infant, Luigi and Assunta had another boy, and on October 16, 1890, a girl was born.

In thanksgiving, the child was named Maria, after Our Lady, and Teresa, after the great saint of Carmel. She was baptized the day after her birth. This was not because of any near danger of death, but simply because Maria's mother had such a great hatred of original sin that she wished to lose no time in freeing her child from it at the first possible moment. Maria and her brother were also confirmed in Corinaldo according to the custom of the time.

The family grew to four children, and the poverty that had never been absent became much more acute. In Corinaldo, the family had a small house and plot of land. Although Luigi managed the land well, it simply was not large enough to raise an adequate supply of food. The family had few possessions, and a small image of Our Lady was considered their greatest treasure. The children had no toys, so an apple or rock often took the place of the ball another child might have played with. Maria never had a single doll. Because of their poverty, the children never attended school. But in spite of this type of life, the entire family was happy, until the food shortage became so critical that something had to be done.

Luigi and Assunta loved their small home in this beautiful part of Italy. To better their fortune, however, they decided to become tenant farmers, in a different part of the country. They realized that the needs of the children might be better met by this move. As Luigi explained it, "We must not think of ourselves; but they [the children] are gifts from the Good God and we must show our gratitude by taking care of them."

And what of Maria? At the age of six, her father credited her mother with having taught her to be obedient, to pray well, and to love God and His Blessed Mother. Like other six-year-old children, she played, running through the grass and picking flowers, laughing and smiling. Her mother tells us that even by this age Maria seemed to have an understanding beyond her years. Maria was obedient, but rather than waiting to be asked to help, she begged to be allowed this privilege. She enjoyed playing, but most often she played with her younger brothers to amuse them and keep them from troubling their mother. Cheerfulness is the one thing that all who knew her mentioned when giving testimony for her beatification.

When Maria was eight, the family moved to the Pontine Marshes. Although much of this land has now been reclaimed through reforms, in Maria's day it was one of the grimmest parts of Italy. Because of the swamps, disease was rampant—especially those diseases carried by mosquitoes. Even the air there was said to be unhealthful. Maria's father, along with his partner, Signor Serenelli, and Signor Serenelli's sixteen-year-old son, Alessandro, became tenant farmers to Conte Mazzoleni.

At Ferriere di Conca, the Goretti's and the Serenelli's moved into housing above an old dairy barn. Previously, when the Goretti's had discussed the move to this area, the worst part of the Pontine Marshes, Luigi had expressed concern as to what effect the atmosphere would have on the children. Assunta had predicted that Maria would be their joy wherever she was. True to the prediction, Maria remained a happy, helpful child. Because of her exceptional goodness, Marietta, as she was called, was loved by all who knew her. She was a pretty child with long, light chestnut hair. Although she was always clean and neat, vanity had no part in her personality.

Many of Maria's friends and playmates wore roses in their hair for decoration in the absence of jewelry or lace. The first landowner for whom Luigi worked in the Pontine Marshes was on a tour of inspection and noticed this young girl who wore no flower in her hair. He asked his foreman to introduce her, and after a few remarks, Maria was sent back to her play with the other children. The foreman told him, "Everyone loves Marietta. She is as good as she is lovely, and has the intelligence of a grown girl." The landowner realized that Maria's beauty needed no roses to enhance it.

By the time Maria was nine, she was sent to do the family marketing. She always took time to be friendly, but did her errands and returned home where she was needed as soon as possible. Even in these brief contacts in town, the tradespeople recognized something special about this child sent to do a woman's chore. They often gave her small gifts, for which Maria thanked them warmly.

One day in the grocery store, Maria had completed her small purchases. The grocer, Giovanni, said, "Here, little one, I have a nice red apple for you." Enthusiastically, Maria thanked him and slipped the apple into her bag of groceries. In surprise, the grocer asked her what she intended to do with it. Maria cheerfully replied that she would give it to her brother Alessandrino, as he was particularly fond of apples.

Hearing this, the grocer then gave her a sugar cookie. Again, Maria thanked him warmly, but made no move to eat the cookie. The grocer asked, "Marietta, what are you going to do with that cookie?" Almost apologetically, Maria explained that she would take the cookie home to her little sister, Ersilia. She thanked the grocer for being so good to her family and turned to go. The grocer, however, was determined to do something for Maria, so he told her that he would be very hurt if she did not accept a little gift from him.

He handed her another cookie and said that this one must be for Maria herself. Not wishing to displease him, Maria ate the cookie there and thanked the grocer again.

Because of Maria's outstanding qualities—kindness, cheerfulness, obedience, friendliness—many of the people in the area began to notice and comment on her. Maria was totally unaware of these comments, but her mother heard them. She would answer by saying, "She is only doing her duty," although from time to time she felt that Maria was truly a special child. Long after Maria's death, her mother was to state that she could never remember Maria voluntarily displeasing or disobeying her.

Financially, the Goretti family did not seem to prosper, even working in partnership with the Serenelli's. Luigi, tired and run-down from overwork, fell a victim to the familiar multiple diseases of the marsh—typhus, malaria, meningitis, and pneumonia. During the ten days preceding his death, Assunta stayed by his bedside. Ten-year-old Maria did all the cooking, ran the errands, and kept the children quiet. Constantly, too, Maria prayed. She often wore her rosary around her wrist so it would be at hand in the odd moments she could find for its use. Before his death in May of 1900, Luigi begged Assunta to take the children and return to Corinaldo.

Luigi's death forced Assunta to take upon herself the man's job of laborer in the fields. She felt it would not be possible to move, so the family continued to live in the Pontine Marshes. Maria assumed the position of "mother," doing the household chores necessary for the Goretti family and also for the Serenelli's. Maria was not a good cook, but when rebuked for this fault she simply begged pardon for not being able to cook as well as her mother. Unfortunately, the family seemed to descend into even deeper poverty, largely due to the stinginess of Signor Serenelli. At one point he locked up the cupboard to keep the children from using any food other than that which he allotted for meals. Assunta had to resort to going to the landlord in order to straighten out this problem, a move which served as one more count against her in the eyes of Serenelli.

One of the duties that Maria assumed at this time was that of teaching the children as she herself had been taught. She taught them their prayers and told them stories. Although she had had no formal education, Maria would come home from church and repeat practically word for word the Bible stories she had learned there.

Testimony from people who knew the family at this time contains many references to the fact that after her father's death, Maria accepted all her responsibilities and carried them out not only efficiently but with joy and cheerfulness. She never appeared tired. When Maria played now, it was never to amuse herself, but only to please the younger children. A friend who had brought a pot of soup as a gift for the family noted that Maria served all the others first and kept very little for herself. When questioned about this, Maria gave the excuse that her mother and older brother had to do heavy work and needed the nourishment, and the younger children were only babies and deserved the treat. In addition, Maria often comforted and cheered her mother, counseling total dependence on God and His Blessed Mother to provide and protect. The death of her father called forth reserves of strength from Maria.

Besides the loss of her father, the only other sadness which Maria mentioned was the long wait to receive First Communion. In Assunta's great respect for this Sacrament, she told Maria that because of her inability to read, and because the family had no money for the proper clothes, she was afraid that Maria would have to wait. Maria's reply was, "You'll see, Mama; God will provide."

Maria herself thought of a person who would teach her Christian doctrine, and she promised to discharge all her household duties before walking into Conca to these lessons. Throughout the spring of 1902, the eleven-year-old Maria seemed to grow spiritually as she prepared to receive her Lord. This love of God was translated into an even greater willingness to do her daily tasks lovingly for those around her.

In May, the local priest examined Maria and found her well prepared for the Sacrament. A white dress, lace, and pearls were not possible for Maria. Instead, on the morning of May 29, 1902, she arose and dressed in the gifts which the poor of the neighborhood had provided, gifts which the donors felt it a privilege to bring. Assunta had provided the dress, a wine-colored dress with tiny white dots. One friend had brought a pair of new shoes, another a veil, a third a candle. Another friend had woven a wreath of real flowers. At the last minute, Assunta took the two treasures her husband had given her—a coral necklace and a pair of gold earrings—and put them on her child.

Maria's sensitive conscience led her to make one final preparation. She went around the house and begged pardon of her family members and the Serenelli's for any wrong she might have done them. Then the entire family, for once, began the walk to Conca for the ceremony.

The message the archpriest gave these first communicants was "purity at all costs." How well Maria had absorbed this lesson was shown less than two months later.

During the month of June, Maria received Communion four more times. Also during this month, Alessandro Serenelli twice made advances to her. On both occasions he had managed to be alone with her in the house. This young man, nearly twenty, had been accepted by Maria as another brother. But suddenly, he was paying her compliments and attempting to come close and touch her. Instinctively, Maria recognized something of his intentions, and the purity of her soul was revolted. On both occasions he threatened to kill her if she mentioned the matter to anyone.

Maria did keep silent, but not through fear of harm to herself. Rather, she realized that exposing Alessandro would bring worry and grief to her mother and financial ruin to their family. During this month, she attempted to keep as far away from Alessandro as possible and to be in the company of her mother whenever she had to be in his presence. She hoped by this to avoid any further occasions for confrontations.

And what of Alessandro, this brutal murderer and would-be rapist? Psychologists would be interested to know that he was brought up by a stern and harsh father after the early death of his mother. During part of his teenage years he had lived alone, doing work on the docks, and had been exposed to all sorts of vices. He had some education, although his family had lived most of the time in the same poverty as that of the Goretti's. Alessandro was quiet and fairly shy, and Assunta later testified that he usually kept the door to his room closed at all times. In his room he read all sorts of violent newspapers. Some biographers mention that he read a great deal of pornography, although in the strict sense this material was more sensational than sexually oriented, with news reports of brutality and murders. At any rate, it was unhealthy reading material.

On the other hand, from the time he and his father began living with the Goretti family, Alessandro exhibited many traits of goodness. He attended Mass and often joined in the saying of the family Rosary with the Goretti's. He was a hard worker in the fields, and from time to time actually defended one or the other of the Goretti's against the verbal abuses of his father.

By his own testimony, Alessandro first noticed how beautiful Maria was while praying the family Rosary. He also noticed that when praying, this girl really prayed, and did not simply mouth the words.

On Saturday morning, July 5, 1902, the Goretti's and the Serenelli's were working in the field about one hundred thirty yards away from the house. After the noon meal, Signor Serenelli fell asleep under the stairs and the others returned to the field. Maria sat on the landing with her mending, watching over her sleeping baby sister. The other Goretti children were riding in the noisy threshing wagons with their mother.

Alessandro exchanged his place behind the lead oxen with Assunta and returned to the house. He brushed past Maria, went to his room, then came past her again carrying a handkerchief and went to the storeroom downstairs. Later, it was learned that he had sharpened and tapered a nine-and-a-half-inch pointed blade. He returned again to the house, and called Maria to come to him. When she called out to ask why, he repeated his demand. She told him she would not come unless she knew why she was needed. Alessandro came out to the landing and dragged her into the house. Any cry she made was drowned out by the steady hum of the thresher going round and round in the blazing sun. According to Alessandro, Maria's words were, "No! No! No! What are you doing? Do not touch me! It is a sin—you will go to Hell!" More than instinctively fighting to preserve her honor, Maria thought even at this time of the sin which would condemn Alessandro to Hell. Although she fought with all her strength, she could hardly expect to hold out long against the husky young man. He pushed a gagging handkerchief into her mouth, but confronted with a will stronger than his own, he could not touch her.

At this point, Alessandro picked up the knife and began stabbing Maria. Reports as to the number of wounds vary, but fourteen major ones were treated at the hospital. Because of the threshing, those in the field did not hear Maria's cries for help. The baby on the landing awakened at the noise and began to cry; the baby's cries awakened Alessandro's father at the foot of the stairs, and Assunta, glancing up, noticed that the baby was unattended and in danger of falling off the landing. Signor Serenelli and Assunta ran toward the house, where they discovered Maria who had begun to drag herself toward the door. When questioned, she answered in her direct way that

Alessandro had stabbed her. "He wanted to make me do wrong and I would not."

The local doctor arrived, and as he was binding her wounds, Maria did not cry out with pain. From time to time, however, she spoke: "Oh, Alessandro, how unhappy you are! You will go to Hell!"

By the time the ambulance arrived, a crowd had gathered. Some dragged Alessandro from his room where he had shut himself up, and would have harmed him if the local police had not taken him away. Many of the others followed the ambulance, on foot, to the hospital.

During the trip to the hospital and the twenty hours of agony she spent before her death, Maria was conscious much of the time. She did not complain, and rarely even moaned with the pain. After asking twice for a drink of water (which was refused because her injuries were internal and water would have caused further damage), Maria gave up this comfort without complaint, as well as the comfort of having her mother beside her at night. The hospital had a rule that no visitors could stay overnight, and Assunta was forced to sleep in the back of the ambulance.

The priest was called soon after Maria's arrival at the hospital. Although the doctors performed surgery, none of the three doctors on the case had much hope for success. As the priest arrived, Dr. Bartoli assured him, "Father, you will have little to do. We are leaving a dying girl but you are finding an angel."

The same priest who had given Maria her First Communion came to bring her the last. Before he gave her Viaticum, he asked her if she forgave her murderer with all her heart. Maria replied with no hesitation, "Yes, I too, for the love of Jesus, forgive him . . . and I want him to be with me in Paradise . . . May God forgive him, because I already have forgiven him." Maria died shortly after three o'clock.

Alessandro's trial began on Maria's birthday, October 16, 1902. In spite of the defense plea of insanity, Alessandro was found guilty. Because he was a minor, his sentence was thirty years in prison. He was sent to a prison in Sicily where he spent the first eight years with no sign of remorse or regret for his crime. But one night, after living with a dead soul for all those years, Alessandro had a dream. He saw Maria in a field of flowers, holding out some white lilies to him. Within a few days after this dream, the local bishop requested and obtained an interview with Alessandro. On November 10, 1910, Alessandro wrote a letter to the bishop begging God's pardon for the great sin he had committed.

Assunta took her children and returned to Corinaldo, in accordance with Luigi's last wishes. There she raised her family. She was able to obtain work as the housekeeper of the local priest, and worked there for many years.

Maria's heroic life and death were not forgotten. The Passionist priests asked Assunta's permission to move Maria's body to the sanctuary of Our Lady of Grace. This was accomplished in 1929. Pope Pius X had already held Maria up as an example of true devotion and an inspiration to youth. In this same year, Alessandro was asked to give testimony in Maria's process for beatification. By this time, he had been released from prison and was living a quiet life as a laborer. Alessandro willingly gave his testimony, taking total blame, repeating that Maria's thoughts had been for his soul even at the moment of the attack, and relating the dream which had led to his conversion.

On Christmas eve, 1937, Alessandro went to visit Assunta at the rectory to hear from her own lips the assurance of forgiveness. As he tearfully begged her pardon, she replied that she could hardly refuse when Maria had been so willing to extend this forgiveness. Assunta and Alessandro attended Midnight Mass together at Maria's shrine.

In 1947, Pope Pius XII beatified Maria. Because her death had been that of a martyr, no miracles were required for beatification. But thereafter, those in need began to cry to her for help, and such a shower of favors was received through her intercession that the two miracles necessary for canonization were speedily and unquestionably certified. Maria Goretti's canonization occurred on June 25, 1950, less than three years after her beatification.

Maria's own mother, by that time an old woman, was present, and the crowd was so huge that the ceremony had to be held outside, in front of St. Peter's basilica. The interval between Maria's beatification and canonization was one of the shortest of any cause recorded at the Vatican.

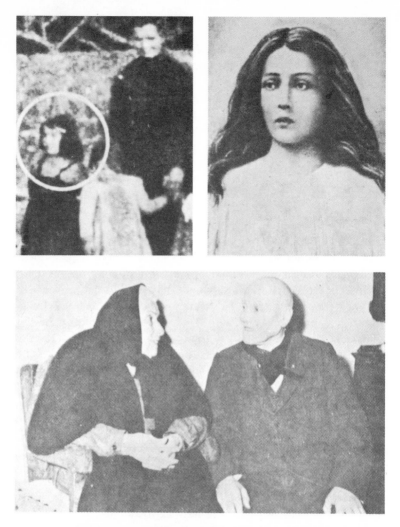

Upper left: Is this the face of St. Maria Goretti as a small child? There is some evidence that the child on the left of this photograph is Maria. It is presumed that she is standing with her mother, Assunta, and her younger sister. This would be the only photograph of Maria Goretti in existence.

Upper right: St. Maria Goretti died from 14 stab wounds at the age of 11 rather than commit a sin; she died after forgiving and praying for the 19-year-old murderer and would-be rapist. This representative painting of Maria Goretti was made in 1929.

Lower: Alessandro Serenelli, Maria's murderer (at age 71), along with Maria's mother. Alessandro repented eight years after Maria's death after having a dream in which he saw Maria in a field of flowers, holding out some white lilies to him.

This is the official portrait of St. Maria Goretti. Painted in 1938, it was approved by her mother and the postulator of her cause as a close likeness.

26

SAINT GEMMA GALGANI

Gemma Galgani
1878 - 1903
Italy
Died Age 25

From time to time, God calls a generous soul to live in reparation for the sins committed by men against their Creator and Savior. Such a lover of the cross was the young Italian mystic, Gemma Galgani, who dedicated herself as a victim of atonement. Gemma could have said "No" to God, in answer to many of His requests for sacrifice. Instead, she modeled herself on Our Lady's answer, "Behold the handmaid of the Lord."

Gemma Galgani was born on March 12, 1878, in a small Italian town near Lucca. Gemma is the Italian word for gem. The child's mother was worried that this name was not a saint's name, but a priest friend comforted her with the remark that perhaps the child would one day be a "gem of Paradise."

At a very young age, Gemma developed a love for prayer. She credited her mother, who died when Gemma was very young, with inspiring in her the desire for Heaven, and with teaching her about God.

Gemma made her First Communion on June 17, 1887. Later, she wrote, "It is impossible for me to describe what passed between Jesus and myself in that moment. He made himself felt so strongly in my soul. I realized in that moment how the delights of Heaven are not like those of the earth, and I was seized by a desire to make that union with my God everlasting."

As a day pupil at the school run by the Sisters of St. Zita, Gemma was loved by her teachers and her fellow pupils. Although quiet and reserved, she always had a friendly smile for everyone. Though by nature a bright and lively child, she exercised great self discipline even as a schoolgirl, keeping her feelings under control.

The superior of the sisters at the school once asked Gemma's teacher and her class to pray for a dying man who refused the Sacraments. After the prayer, Gemma arose from her seat, and going up to her teacher, whispered in her ear, "The grace is granted." That evening the news was brought that the man had indeed converted and received the consolations of the Faith before his death.

Throughout her life, Gemma was to be favored with many mystical experiences and special graces. Often these were misunderstood by others, bringing ridicule. A sensitive person, Gemma suffered these heartaches, too, in reparation, remembering that Our Lord Himself had been misunderstood and ridiculed.

Although she was a good student, Gemma had to quit school due to chronic ill health before completing the course of study. Throughout her life, her frail constitution did not stand up well to several illnesses.

Gemma's father had been a moderately successful pharmacist. But because of his generosity and his willingness to extend credit to those in need, he began to get into financial trouble. His early death in 1897 left Gemma and his other children penniless orphans. Gemma felt the loss of her father keenly, but did not appear to be bothered by the poverty of her circumstances. She must have felt desolate when the creditors came and took away the few possessions left to the family on the very day of her father's funeral, but she maintained her cheerful, patient attitude.

Gemma had an immense love for the poor, and when she went out, many poor people came to her for help. When she could, she gave them things from home. Later, when she too was a "povera," or poor girl, she gave them the gift of friendship. She would weep over their misfortunes, completely ignoring her own.

After her father's death, the nineteen-year-old Gemma became the mother of her seven brothers and sisters. When some were old enough to share this responsibility, she lived briefly with a married aunt. Although she returned the love given by this aunt and uncle, Gemma was unhappy with the busy social life of the couple. They were well off, and wanted Gemma to join in the fun which they could afford to provide. At this time, two young men proposed marriage to her. Gemma, however, wanted silence and retirement, and more than ever she desired to pray and speak only to God.

Gemma returned home, and almost immediately became very ill with meningitis. Gradually she lost her hearing and some of her hair. In addition, she suffered a complete paralysis of her limbs. All earthly remedies proved vain, and Gemma was confined to bed for more than a year. Throughout this illness, her one regret was the trouble she caused her relatives in taking care of her.

News of the heroic patience of the gentle girl spread about the town, and many visitors came to cheer her up. For each visitor, Gemma had a smile and a welcoming comment.

Feeling herself tempted by the devil, she prayed for help to the Venerable Passionist, Gabriel Possenti. (Gabriel was later canonized.) He appeared to her in dreams several times, promising her help and calling her "sister." Through his intercession, Gemma was miraculously cured.

In one of her visions of Gabriel, he placed the badge of the Passionists on Gemma. When she spoke of her desire to enter a convent, he told her to make her vow to be a religious, but not to add anything to this vow. Gabriel was telling her that although she might live the life of a nun, she would never enter any particular convent. Later, Gemma was rejected as a candidate for the religious life on the grounds that her health was too delicate. She offered this disappointment to God as a sacrifice.

Gifted with an ability for prophecy, Gemma predicted that the Passionists would establish a monastery at Lucca; this came to pass two years after her death. When she understood that she would not be able to enter a Passionist monastery, Gemma said, "The Passionists did not wish to receive me; nevertheless, because I wish to stay with them, I shall when I am dead." Today, Gemma's mortal remains are still treasured at the Passionist monastery in Lucca.

On the 8th of June, 1899, Gemma had an interior warning that some unusual grace was to be granted to her. She spoke of this to her confessor and received absolution. She later gave the following account to her spiritual director: "It was Thursday evening, and suddenly I felt an inward sorrow for my sins; but so intense that I have never felt the like again; my sorrow made me feel as if I should die then and there. After that I felt all the powers of my soul in recollection. My intellect seemed to know nothing but my sins and how they offended God . . . Then thoughts crowded thickly within me and they were thoughts of sorrow, love, fear, hope and comfort."

In rapture, she saw her heavenly Mother, who wrapped Gemma in her mantle. At that moment, according to her own account, "Jesus appeared with His wounds all open; blood was not flowing from them, but flames of fire which in one moment came and touched my hands, feet and heart. I felt I was dying, and should have fallen down but for my Mother who supported me and kept me under her cloak. Thus I remained for several hours. Then my Mother kissed my forehead, the vision disappeared, and I found myself on my knees; but I had still a keen pain in my hands, feet and heart. I got up to get into bed and I saw that blood was coming from the places where I had the pain. I covered them as well as I could and then, helped by my Guardian Angel, got into bed."

The next day, covering her hands with gloves, Gemma attended Mass as usual. Later, she showed the marks of the stigmata to one of her aunts, saying, "Just look at what Jesus has done to me!"

Each Thursday evening, Gemma would fall into rapture and the marks would appear. The stigmata remained until Friday afternoon or Saturday morning when the bleeding would stop, the wounds would close, and only white marks would remain in place of the deep gashes. Later, one of Gemma's directors turned to science and had a doctor examine the stigmata. As Gemma had foreseen, the doctor considered them a manifestation of some form of disease, or the delusions of an overly pious soul.

Gemma's stigmata continued to appear until the last three years before her death. At this time, her director forbad her to accept this phenomenon, and through her prayers it ceased, although whitish marks remained on her skin until her death.

Through the help of her confessor, Gemma went to live with a family named Giannini, where she was allowed more freedom than at home for her spiritual life. She was very grateful to this adoptive family, and was more than once overheard in ecstasy praying for its members. In this home, Gemma cheerfully did housework and helped in the training and education of the children.

There is a good record of Gemma's words during ecstasy. In this state of rapture, the soul is so absorbed in God that the normal activity of the senses is suspended. Both her confessor and a relative of the head of her adoptive family, Aunt Cecilia, often overheard Gemma and recorded her conversations.

Father Germano once overheard her arguing with Divine Justice for the salvation of a soul. Some of her words were: "I do not seek Your justice, but for Your mercy. I know, he made You shed tears; but . . . You must not think of his sins; You must think of the Blood You shed. And now answer, Jesus, and tell me You have saved my sinner." Gemma actually named the man she was praying for. Soon afterwards, she broke out joyfully, "He is saved! You have won, Jesus; triumph always thus." Then she came out of ecstasy.

Father Germano had just left the room when he heard a knock and was told that a stranger wished to speak to him. As soon as the man was before the priest, he fell to his knees weeping and said, "Father, I want to make my confession." The priest was stunned to realize that it was Gemma's sinner.

Gemma often saw her guardian angel, with whom she was on familiar terms. Sometimes the angel protected and consoled her, sometimes he counseled her, and occasionally he scolded her very severely for her faults. He would say, "I am ashamed of you." At times Gemma was heard arguing with her guardian angel, so that her spiritual director, Father Germano, had to remind her that she was speaking with a blessed spirit of Heaven and should be very respectful. The angel is mentioned on almost every single page of Gemma's diary. In one entry, Gemma wrote that the devil had been raining down blows on her shoulder for nearly half an hour. "Then my guardian angel came and asked me what was the matter; I begged him to stay with me all night, and he said: 'But I must sleep.' 'No,' I replied, 'the Angels of Jesus do not sleep!' 'Nevertheless,' he rejoined, smiling, 'I ought to rest. Where shall you put me?' I begged him to remain near me. I went to bed; after that he seemed to spread his wings and come over my head. In the morning he was still there."

One of the most extraordinary things is the fact that Gemma often sent her guardian angel on errands, usually to deliver a letter or oral message to Father Germano in Rome. Often the reply was delivered by the priest's guardian angel. Realizing how unusual this was, Father Germano asked Heaven for a sign that it was in accord with God's Will. After Gemma's death, he wrote: "To how many tests didn't I submit this singular phenomenon in order to convince myself that it took place through a supernatural intervention! And yet none of my tests ever failed; and thus I was convinced again and again that in this, like in many other extraordinary things in her life, Heaven was delighted in amusing itself, as it were, with this innocent and dear maiden."

During the apostolic investigations into her life, all witnesses testified that there was no artfulness in Gemma's manner. At the end of each of her ecstasies, she returned to normal and went quietly and serenely about the family life. Most of her severe penances and sacrifices were hidden from most who knew her. Only a few around her were privileged to realize that she was exceptionally favored.

In spite of everything which had happened to her, Gemma understood the true joy of her way of life. She said, "There is neither cross nor sorrow, when we are tightly united to Jesus."

In January of 1903, Gemma was diagnosed as having tuberculosis. To avoid danger to her adoptive family, she was isolated in a small apartment close to the Giannini house. For four months Gemma suffered uncomplainingly from the disease. She died quietly, in the company of the parish priest, on April 11. In his testimony he said, "I have been present at many deathbeds, but never have I seen anyone die like Gemma, without even a precursor sign, nor a tear, nor a panting breath. She died with a smile which remained upon her lips, so that I could not convince myself that she was really dead."

The Church authorities began to study Gemma's life in 1917, and she was beatified in 1933. The decree approving the miracles for canonization was read March 26, 1939—Passion Sunday. Gemma was canonized on May 2, 1940, only thirty-seven years after her death.

A beautiful girl, St. Gemma was untouched by vanity. For most of her life she dressed simply in a black dress, with a cape as protection outside.

St. Gemma Galgani bore the stigmata, had visions of Jesus and Mary, and saw and conversed with her guardian angel. She died at age 25.

27

LAURA VICUNA

Servant of God Laura Vicuna
Laura Vicuna
1891 - 1904
Chile - Argentina
Died Age 13

Laura lived in a society where, as today, many couples lived together in sin. Only thirteen years old at her death, from an early age she knew and understood the type of existence her mother was living. Realizing the near impossibility of drawing her mother away from these bonds, she willingly offered her life to God for this intention. When her mother's lover made repeated advances to Laura, this courageous child defended her own purity with the fortitude of the early Christian martyrs.

Laura was born in Santiago, Chile, on April 5 of 1891. Her father was a soldier who belonged to a noble Chilean family. A revolution and civil war had broken out the previous January, and Senor Vicuna carried his wife Mercedes and his infant daughter into political exile in the Andes mountains.

Shortly before Laura's third birthday and after the birth of her baby sister Julia, Senor Vicuna died, leaving his widow to care for the children. Mercedes took the girls to the frontier town of Las Lajas, where she hoped to find work as a cook and laundry woman. Here she met Manuel Mora, owner of a large hacienda, or ranch. Senor Mora offered to be her protector, and his financial support would pay tuition for the girls at the newly formed missionary school run by the Salesian sisters (Daughters of Mary Help of Christians). In return for his help and protection, Mercedes became his mistress.

When Laura was eight, Mercedes, on the advice of one of the Salesian missionary priests, took both girls to board at the school in Junin. Life at the school was very pleasant. Here Laura learned about God and His love, and learned to repay this love with love for

182

her fellow students and the sisters. Laura was a leader in sports, and a friend to all. She helped the younger children with their daily tasks, such as making their beds, and with their personal chores, such as combing their hair or mending their clothes. She acted as peacemaker for the children's quarrels. When her little sister Julia was naughty, Laura gently corrected her. Laura was looked up to by all. She was serious and wise beyond her age. She had a mature understanding of prayer, and because she was a natural leader, she seemed to build up a joyful spirit of piety in all her fellow students.

On her first summer vacation, Laura began to realize the type of life her mother was leading. In addition, Senor Mora was often drunk. At these times he would attempt to embrace and kiss Laura, who was repelled by his advances and his whiskey-laden breath. Laura's mother demanded that he leave the child alone, which he did except when he was drunk. At these times Laura made every effort to keep out of his way.

Laura made her First Communion when she was ten. Mercedes came to Junin for the festive occasion, but Laura noticed that her mother did not receive the Sacrament. She seemed to realize that her mother was not happy. One of her constant prayers before the tabernacle became, "Jesus, I wish that Mama would know You better and be happy."

Laura was fascinated by the devotion of the sisters. They had courageously left their home countries to dedicate their lives to the service of God in the missions. Laura secretly hoped one day to follow their example and become a sister herself. She said, "I want to do all I can to make God known and loved." She prayed, "My God, I want to love and serve You all my life." When Laura was eleven, Bishop John Cagliero made a visit to the school. Laura asked him if she could become a Salesian sister. Laughingly, he replied, "Just wait a little longer, child." But Laura did not want to wait. Repeatedly she asked her confessor to pray and ask God if it was His Will for her to become a Salesian. This understanding priest agreed that she did, in truth, have a religious vocation, but it remained their secret.

In the summer of 1901, Laura again returned to the ranch for summer vacation. Senor Mora seemed more than ever to be becoming quite interested in her, fawning and fussing over her. Through prayer and vigilance she determined to protect her purity. "Lord, do not let me offend You," she prayed.

One day, the moment she had feared finally arrived; she was caught alone with Senor Mora. He began to make improper advances, and she struggled ferociously, finally breaking away and running outdoors. She knew, however, that he would not give up, and at a fiesta a few days later, he approached her and asked her for a dance. Laura flatly refused in spite of Senor Mora's threats and her mother's entreaties. Laura spent that night hiding outside in the dark, while Senor Mora vented his anger on her hapless mother. For revenge, he refused to continue paying Laura's tuition at school, but the sisters heard of the matter and offered to accept the girls free. Embarrassed at this charitable offer, Mercedes sent only Laura back to school, keeping Julia at home with herself.

At Easter, 1902, Laura was confirmed by Bishop Cagliero. She realized that she had not offered the supreme sacrifice for her mother, and begged her confessor to be allowed to offer her life to God for her mother's conversion. Realizing that he was dealing with a person who had been given great spiritual gifts, the priest granted her request.

During the winter of 1903, Laura became ill. Her mother begged her to come home with her, and the superior told Laura, "Your mother needs you more than you need her. You must go."

At the ranch, Laura's health steadily worsened, instead of improving with the better climate and good care. She felt that her offering had been accepted, and did not believe she would ever get well.

At first, Senor Mora stayed out on the range most of the time. But when he returned, Laura noticed that he had cooled towards her mother, and especially when drunk, he looked at Laura with a strange desire. Mercedes also noticed his attitude, and in spite of his threats, she packed up with the girls and rented a small place in Junin.

On the night of January 14 in 1904, Senor Mora, drunk with whiskey, anger, and lust, rode into town and announced his intention of spending the night at the cottage where Mercedes and the girls were staying. Whip in hand, he demanded that Mercedes accede to his wishes and that his "family" return the following day to the ranch with him.

Though weak and pale, Laura resolutely announced, "If he stays, I will go." She did not wait for an answer, but walked out the door.

Senor Mora was furious. He followed her outside, and Mercedes screamed for Laura to run. Laura attempted to run for safety to the sisters' residence, but Senor Mora caught her in the street. He whipped her and kicked her as she lay in the street crying for help. When some men ran out of nearby houses, Mora picked the girl up and tried to put her across his horse. Then realizing the danger, he tossed her back into the street and rode away.

Laura had been beaten unconscious. She lingered for a week, as her mother and the sisters kept watch over her. She finally revealed her secret. "Mama, I'm dying, but I'm happy to offer my life for you. I asked Our Lord for this."

Mercedes fell to her knees sobbing. She realized what her daughter meant, and begged Laura's forgiveness as well as the forgiveness of God. She promised to begin her life again. After Laura's death at about six o'clock on the evening of January 22, 1904, Mercedes went to the chapel to make her confession. Through the witness of her courageous daughter, she returned to the practice of the Faith.

The diocesan process for the cause of beatification of Laura Vicuna was opened on September 19, 1955.

Laura Vicuna offered her life to God to convert her mother from a life of concubinage. Laura was murdered at age 13 by her mother's paramour; on the day of Laura's death, her mother returned to the practice of the Faith.

28

VEN. ZEPHERIN NAMUNCURA

Zepherin Namuncura
1886 - 1905
Argentina - Italy
Died Age 18

Zepherin Namuncura was destined by birth to be a "cacique" or leader of his people, the Araucano Indians of the Argentine Pampas. The eighth of twelve children of the chief, Manuel Namuncura, Zepherin was slated—by virtue of his intelligence and ability—to be the successor of his father as leader of this fierce, warlike tribe. (The succession was hereditary by family, but did not necessarily fall to the oldest son.) However, Zepherin spent his short life training for a different kind of leadership. His ambition was to lead his people to the religion of the one true God.

Shortly before Zepherin's birth, the Araucano, under the leadership of Manuel Namuncura, had engaged in a last fierce war against the encroaching European colonists. Many atrocities were committed by both sides. At last, the Argentine Minister of War, General Julio Roca, determined to raise a strong army and wipe out the Araucano. In a swift campaign, the army captured two thousand of the Indians, including Manuel Namuncura's wife and four of his children. Surrender was the Indians' only alternative to complete destruction.

Through the arbitration of the one European the cacique would trust, a Salesian priest, a treaty was made, giving the tribe lands and making their chief a colonel in the Argentine army. This treaty was modified in 1894, pushing the Indians further west to worse territory near Alumine, a high valley among the snowy peaks of the Andes mountains.

When Zepherin was two, his father gave him to the Salesian priest, Father Dominic Milanesio, telling him that he was giving this son, the future leader of his people, to be brought up in the white man's religion. The baby was given the baptismal name of Zepherin in honor of a third century pope - martyr. The name means "wind," and perhaps the priest hoped that this new leader of the Araucano would be a cooling wind to put out the flame of war in his people.

In 1897, Manuel Namuncura decided to exercise his rights as a colonel in the army and took the eleven-year-old Zepherin to demand his enrollment at the army academy, El Tigre. It was the chief's wish that there the boy could learn the white man's military tactics. Unfortunately, as Zepherin was the only Indian child at the school, the other students were cruel in their treatment of him. He was so unhappy there that he began to lose weight and actually became ill. At the suggestion of Father Dominic, he was moved to the Salesian mission school in Buenos Aires.

At the mission school, Zepherin studied hard, and his grades remained in the top half of the class. Though not particularly bright when it came to books, he was, in the words of his teacher, a "plugger." Although the schedules and the discipline were hard on a boy used to the freedom of the Indian tribal existence, he felt at home among the students. Asked what he liked best about the school, he replied, "The church and the food"—although he complained that he couldn't eat the "bread" at the altar. At the age of twelve, the "Little Chief" was allowed this Food too.

One day during class, his teacher noticed that Zepherin often appeared to be daydreaming and staring out into the corridor. But despite the fact that the teacher called on him suddenly several times, he could not catch the boy without a ready reply. Later, the teacher moved Zepherin to a new seat where he could not stare off into the corridor. After class, Zepherin asked to be returned to his former place. When asked why, he replied that from his old seat he was able to see the sanctuary lamp burning near Jesus in the chapel. Of course the youth's request was honored.

A child of the outdoors, Zepherin loved sports. He was a good horseman and an expert archer. His clever hands were often occupied in making bows and arrows for himself and his classmates, and sometimes the boys would have archery competitions with "Zeph" as the judge.

One time, when Zepherin's father, Manuel, came for a visit to his son, he was treated as an honored guest, and the two spent several happy days together. When Manuel left, he gave Zepherin the sum of ten pesos with instructions to use it for a special treat for himself.

Like most of the boys at the mission school, Zepherin was poor. His clothes were usually hand-me-downs, and ten pesos would buy something quite nice. The priest was surprised when as soon as his father had left, Zepherin brought him the money, telling him to use it to decorate Our Lady's altar. The priest protested that the money was intended for Zepherin. In turn, the Little Chief replied that, used for Our Lady, it would indeed be a treat for him. He stated that he wanted Our Lady to become the Queen of his people.

Although his outgoing personality and basic honesty made him a favorite at the school, sometimes the boys would unintentionally say things that would hurt Zepherin's feelings. Once, when a fellow student in a discussion about the Indians asked Zeph what human flesh tasted like, the boy bowed his head and a large tear slipped down his high cheeks. He did not remonstrate with the thoughtless student, however, but simply continued the conversation and ignored the question.

As the time for Zepherin to leave the mission school grew closer, he was asked what he wanted to do. He said that he wanted to become a priest in order to take the true religion to his people, and to open a school for the children of the Araucano. Bishop Cagliero, the Salesian superior, liked this sturdy seventeen-year-old, and after warning him that studies for the priesthood would not be easy, arranged for his entrance into the minor seminary at Viedma.

At the seminary, too, Zepherin was well liked. He engaged in sports and small hunting expeditions for recreation, as well as studying hard enough to become second in his class. He enjoyed doing card tricks for his classmates. Zepherin remembered the words of the priest who had come to convert his people: "Serve God with joy."

In addition to the fun and the learning, Zepherin was growing in virtue. He could often be found in front of the Blessed Sacrament, praying for his people. Little Chief did not forget his Indian origins; he wanted to remain an Indian. A favorite devotion was the Rosary—also prayed for the benefit of his people. One of his classmates later said, "During the six months I lived with Namuncura, I saw him relive all the virtues I had read about in the life of Dominic Savio."

On September 24, 1903, with the permission of his superiors, Zepherin organized a procession in honor of Our Lady of Mercy. That night he fell into bed tired from his day's labor. He awoke coughing and spitting up blood. The disease that was slowly wiping out his entire tribe had caught up with him; Zepherin had tuberculosis.

On being informed of Namuncura's condition, the bishop immediately had him sent to the hospital at Viedma. Of his time there, the hospital chaplain said, "Little Chief rarely talked. We often thought he lived in continual prayer. He never gave signs of impatience or disgust. Grateful for any service, he smiled his thanks to all and obeyed every order given him."

In April of 1904, Pope Pius X appointed Bishop Cagliero archbishop, and summoned him to Rome. The bishop asked Zepherin if he would like to accompany him to Rome and remain there to continue his studies for the priesthood. It was thought that he would thus experience warm dry air which might be good for his health.

After a month at sea, the bishop and the young seminarian set foot on European soil. Zepherin was impressed with the strangeness of everything, but the biggest attraction was the large picture of Mary Help of Christians in the basilica at Turin. The picture seemed like a magnet, drawing the young Indian to pray before it for help for his people.

The priest who took care of Zepherin while he was in Turin said, "Every time I looked for him, I found him praying before the picture of Mary Help of Christians." Asked what he was praying for, the constant reply was, "For my people."

At Turin, and later in Rome, Zepherin was privileged to have several fortunate experiences. He was present for the translation of the remains of St. John Bosco, and in company with Archbishop Cagliero, had a private audience with Pope Pius X. During a large mission exhibit in Turin, a well-dressed lady stopped by Zepherin's booth. He had dressed in his native costume for the exhibit, and his manners and refinement were impressive to all. The lady asked that he guide her through the rest of the exhibit. Who was she? The Queen of Italy.

At first, Zepherin attended a seminary in Turin. The director said of him, "He has a heart warm with God's love. It's a heart of gold, and sees no evil in anyone. It's a treat to hear him talk about God and Our Lady. He loves God like we love our mothers . . . warmly, intensely, as though he were always in God's presence." Unfortunately, the Turin climate was not beneficial to his health, so he was transferred to a seminary just a few miles from Rome.

In March of 1905, Zepherin took a sudden turn for the worse. He lost weight alarmingly, and seemed to be often in pain. Nevertheless, his gentleness and the smile in his eyes never left. His director wrote, "He got worse day by day, yet he was never impatient. He suffered, but he held onto his cross generously."

In April, Zepherin was transferred to the hospital run by the Brothers of God in Rome. Here he bore his cross of suffering heroically, constantly praying the Rosary for his people. He died on the morning of May 11, surrounded by several of the brothers who were praying for him. He was buried in Rome, but at the insistence of his people, his body was taken back to Patagonia in 1924 and buried at the Salesian school of Fortin Mercedes. Zepherin was declared Venerable by Pope Paul VI in 1972.

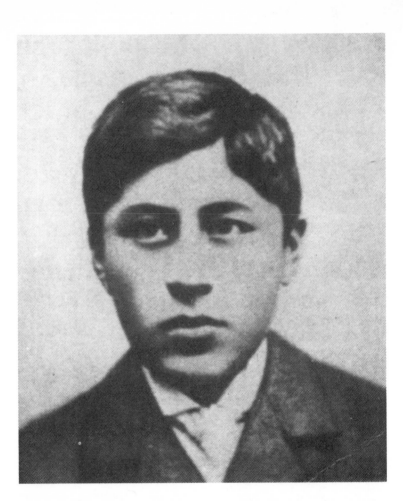

Venerable Zepherin Namuncura, son of the last chief of the Araucano Indians of Argentina, constantly prayed for his people. One of his classmates said of him, "During the six months I lived with Namuncura, I saw him relive all the virtues I had read about in the life of Dominic Savio." Zepherin died as a seminarian at age 18.

29

VEN. MOTHER MARY MAGDALEN BENTIVOGLIO

Venerable Mother Mary Magdalen Bentivoglio, O.S.C.
(Countess) Annetta Bentivoglio
1834 - 1905
Italy - United States
Died Age 71

Annetta Bentivoglio's mother visited the catacombs shortly before Annetta was born. As she knelt before the relics of one of the martyrs, she prayed that the child would grow up to have the virtue of a saint. The baby was so high-spirited and mischievous, however, that more than once her mother was driven to remark, "You are something very different from a saint!"

Annetta was born July 29, 1834, in the Castle of San Angelo in Rome. She was the twelfth of sixteen children of Count Dominic and Angela Sandri Bentivoglio. Her father was a general in the papal army. Her mother was a gentle and religious woman, but not of the same noble lineage as Annetta's father. Five of the daughters of this deeply religious family later entered convents.

As a child, Annetta had many mature characteristics—she was pious, charitable, and deeply thoughtful. She was also strong-willed and full of mischief. On one occasion, she was discovered hanging from a second story window while attempting to escape from a locked room where she had been confined as punishment by one of her teachers.

Like the other children of her family, Annetta attended boarding school. There she was remembered as a child who loved prayer, was thoughtful of others, and who willed to be good. One youthful New Year's resolution in 1840 stated simply, "I will be good." Annetta was also remembered at school, and for the rest of her life, as being high-spirited and full of fun.

During a trip to transfer from one school to another, she was privileged to travel with St. Madeleine Sophie Barat. Madeleine was a friend of the family, and the foundress of the Religious of the Sacred Heart. During the trip, the young Annetta teased, entertained, and tried the patience of the saintly foundress. Later in life Annetta recalled one night when there was only a single bed available for the pair at an inn; she said, "And so I slept with a saint, and I kicked the saint."

By the age of fourteen, Annetta had conquered much of her own self-will, and began to direct her thoughts and activities toward God. After the death of her parents, she lived for a time, in company with two of her sisters, with the Sisters of St. Catherine of Siena, Dominicans. Here she spent many hours in the presence of the Blessed Sacrament, attempting to decide whether she had a vocation to the cloister or to a more active order. The contemplative vocation won, and in July of 1864 Annetta was received as a postulant of the Poor Clares in San Lorenzo. Her sister Costanza entered the same convent. Their sister Matilda also entered there, but was unable to continue because of a serious illness.

On October 4 of 1865, the Countess Annetta Bentivoglio became Sister Mary Magdalen of the Sacred Heart of Jesus. Her sister chose to retain her baptismal name, but Annetta wished to take the name of the penitent who had impressed Our Dear Lord Himself. For nearly ten years, the Bentivoglio sisters remained in the monastery at San Lorenzo. During this time, Sister Mary Magdalen made a constant and concerted effort to overcome her own self-will by following, as perfectly as possible, the rule of St. Clare. Although as a child she had dreamed of being a Christian martyr, her martyrdom as an adult took the form not of a heroic and glorious death, but rather of a constant daily marytrdom of her own will. In her old age, Mother Mary Magdalen confessed that in the early days she had often been tempted to fling the Office book away. In addition, the coarse, plain food was particularly unattractive.

After ten years in the monastery, and largely because of an appeal by an American member of the Third Order Regular of St. Francis, the Bentivoglio sisters offered to go to America in order to found a contemplative monastery. In addition, because of the troubled political situation in Italy, Pope Pius IX was pleased at the thought of having a foundation in America where he could send Poor Clares if it became necessary for them to leave Europe. In his farewell to them, he warned them of the hardships they could expect, and asked them to be an example, a "silent sermon accompanied by prayer and union with God, to make known to many that true happiness is not to be found in things temporal and material."

On October 12, 1875, the Bentivoglio sisters arrived in New York city. They were placed at the house of another order of nuns, forced to accept their charity, since they had practically no money. In addition, the sisters had great difficulty communicating as they spoke only Italian and French. Originally they had planned to travel to Minnesota to make their first foundation. They had been given a priest as a director and told to be obedient to his direction for them. But upon their arrival in New York, the sisters who had requested that they come to Minnesota and the priest who was their legitimate authority had a difference of opinion, which left the two nuns in the uncomfortable position of not having a place to go. They wrote to Rome for instructions, but the reply was not received for nine months! When it finally came, the reply instructed the sisters to travel about and request help from any bishop in the United States, but definitely to make their foundation in that country. Unfortunately, there was no practical advice as to how these two penniless nuns were to get around in such a huge country where they did not even speak the language!

Through the help of friends, the sisters did make application to more than one American bishop. At first, they were not well received. The Americans needed teachers and workers in the vast mission field, and few could recognize the need for a contemplative group. One bishop actually told them he did not want them in his diocese as their vocation was against the American character and the spirit of the country.

The sisters attempted foundations in Philadelphia and New Orleans, but the first good beginning was made in Cleveland, in August of 1877. Here they were joined by a group of German Colettine Poor Clares. Because of the difficulties in trying to adjust the two rules, the Italian sisters gave the German group the house, and with many assurances of good will on both sides, they left for Omaha. There a generous friend gave them a monastery, and the bishop welcomed them.

Even in Omaha, with the help of generous friends, difficulties often arose because of the language barrier. During one particularly upsetting trial, which Mother Magdalen accepted without bitterness, her sister said, "They must think we are fools. We are under the most fearful accusations and here you are laughing."

"I cannot help it, "Mother Magdalen answered. "All my life I have asked God for crosses, and now that He has sent them, why should I not be glad?"

Their friend and benefactor, Mr. Creighton, contributed generous financial support. This, in combination with the money which Mother Magdalen had gained from begging, enabled them to make a firm foundation in Omaha. Several Americans had joined the Italian sisters, and although conditions were poor and primitive, a convent of the Poor Clares of the Strict Observance was finally founded. Mr. Creighton was among the first to recognize the efficacy of the nuns' prayers, and he delighted in telling of a childless couple for whom he had asked the sisters to pray. In due time, he received a telegram from the couple which announced, "Twins born! Call off the Poor Clares."

Mother Mary Magdalen had a particular devotion to St. Joseph. She often confided the young community's material as well as spiritual needs to him. At times, she would place a note or other petition in the folds of the arms of the convent's statue of the saint. Mr. Creighton was once both amused and edified when he noticed that she had placed a potato in the statue's arms.

Strict canonical enclosure of the Omaha community was established in July of 1882, after seven years in America. To help with the building of the monastery, the nuns themselves joined in the work. Enclosure itself brought neither total peace nor freedom from calumny. At one point, Mother Mary Magdalen was forced to undergo four canonical visitations. Through all difficulties, however, she showed herself heroic in accepting what God chose to send, without speaking ill of her accusers or making attempts at self-justification. Her spirit of penitence was exemplary.

Life in the cloister was often difficult, but Mother Magdalen managed to retain her sense of humor. In one letter to her sister, she wrote, "We are without shoes and stockings; we shall see if we can stand it. It is certain that on the one hand we do not want to pamper anyone, but on the other hand we do not want to kill anyone."

Mother Magdalen persevered and the years brought postulants from far and near. Eventually a foundation was made in New Orleans, and then in Evansville, Indiana. Today there are sixteen houses of this branch of the Poor Clares in America.

In 1897, Mother Mary Magdalen traveled to Evansville to join the new foundation. At sixty-three and in poor health, she shared again in the hunger, cold, and poverty of a new beginning. She believed that her calling was not simply to establish a community of Poor Clares in America, but to propagate the order. For this reason she told one of the sisters that she would be willing to begin a new foundation at any time, no matter what her health or age.

The following anecdote illustrates how Mother Mary Magdalen constantly invoked the saints to aid in drawing new vocations to the order. One day, one of the sisters who entered her office noticed five paper dolls cut from a Sears catalog and placed around the statue of St. Anthony. When the sister asked what they were doing there, Mother Mary Magdalen explained that she was asking St. Anthony to send some girls "just like those" to the monastery. According to the account, five young postulants did enter that year, and all persevered and became devout nuns.

Because the Evansville community was not at first cloistered, the nuns were able to meet the townspeople in an informal way. Friendships begun at that time were continued later after the community was enclosed. In addition to her prayer life and the direction of the monastery, Mother Mary Magdalen maintained a large correspondence and was noted for her good advice and spiritual guidance to the steady flow of visitors.

Mother Magdalen was always receptive to what she felt to be God's Will for her. In Evansville, she was nearly blinded in one eye and in danger of losing the sight of the other. In a letter to a friend she wrote, "Thank you for the prayer you offered for my eyes. If it is God's Holy Will to save one, I will be glad; however, I must be satisfied if Our Dear Lord takes away the other one. Then I will have more time to be united with Him in prayer as I will be delivered of all earthly affairs. May His Holy Will be done."

In 1905, Mother Mary Magdalen's health began to fail. Several phenomena which defy natural explanation took place around the time of her death.

Wishing to die as had St. Francis of Assisi, on a bare floor, Mother asked the sisters to remove the furniture from her cell. Dressed in her habit, she was laid on a mat filled with corn shucks, facing the crucifix on the wall. On August 18 of 1905, about a dozen of the sisters were in Mother Magdalen's cell reciting the prayers for the dying. The other sisters were in the hall. Although the shutters were closed, there was a very bright light around Mother Magdalen at the time of her death. This light was observed by all the sisters in the room. After death, the body was only partially embalmed, due to the collapsed condition of the veins. The body was laid out on a plain board awaiting burial, and although it was exposed to the summer temperature for twenty-six days, there was no sign of decomposition. Many people testified that the odor surrounding the body was similar to that of perfume or flowers.

On September 12, 1905, the body in its coffin was sealed in the vault with bricks and mortar. Almost immediately, cures and favors attributed to Mother Mary Magdalen's intercession were reported. In January of 1907, an exhumation took place in the presence of the sisters and a notary public. The body was found to be intact, and although the features had darkened, they assumed a natural color after being exposed. Again the sweet fragrance was noticed by those present.

The coffin was again resealed. The sisters then petitioned the Bishop of Indianapolis to appoint a tribunal to investigate Mother Magdalen's life. After four such appeals in May of 1928, Bishop Chartrand opened the investigation. The investigation took four years, and the report was made to Rome in May of 1932. At this time another exhumation was held and the body was found to be still entirely intact. After this official exhumation, the body was buried again and has remained at rest to the present day.

Mother Mary Magdalen was declared Venerable in 1932. On April 1, 1969, the Sacred Congregation in Rome issued the decree allowing the introduction of the beatification cause of Mother Mary Magdalen Bentivoglio.

Upper: Countess Annetta Bentivoglio at age 26. She was later to become Mother Mary Magdalen Bentivoglio.
Lower: Mother Mary Magdalen Bentivoglio brought the Poor Clares to America from Italy. She founded her first convent in Omaha, Nebraska.

Venerable Mother Mary Magdalen Bentivoglio, foundress of the Poor Clares in America. At the last exhumation of her body around 1930, her body was still entirely intact.

30

TERESA VALSE PANTELLINI

Servant of God Teresa Valse Pantellini, F.M.A.
Teresa Valse Pantellini
1878 - 1907
Italy
Died Age 29

The saints often adopt a motto which becomes their program for life. Shortly before her death, Sister Teresa was asked what her motto was. She replied, "I resolved to pass unnoticed." Although she came from a wealthy family, and had been raised in a home where the walls were decorated with paintings by Michelangelo and Fra Lippi, Teresa chose to enter the Institute of the Daughters of Mary Help of Christians, where she would share a common ward instead of having a room of her own. A talented pianist, she preferred to work in a laundry with poor and forsaken girls. Educated in excellent schools, Teresa could speak French and German as well as her native Italian, but she chose to speak the language of love to girls of the street. Three months before her death of tuberculosis, St. John Bosco appeared to her and offered her the gift of health. Instead, Sister Teresa reminded him of the sick sister in the next room of the infirmary. She understood and lived the beatitude, "Blessed are the poor in spirit: for theirs is the kingdom of heaven."

Teresa was born in Milan on October 10, 1878. While she was still an infant, her family lived for a time in Egypt. Later, they traveled over much of Europe, staying at beautiful hotels in the most luxurious resorts. Teresa's father had won innumerable honorary titles from the rulers of Italy, Portugal, Spain, Tunis, and Egypt. After her husband's death, Teresa's mother and her three children settled permanently in Rome, with a summer home in Poggio Reale. In 1899, Teresa's mother died also, leaving her twenty-one-year-old daughter wealthy and independent.

As a child, Teresa had a strong character. She was impetuous, energetic, and resolute, and was inclined to domineer. The favorite of her father and her grandmother, this intelligent little girl was quite self-willed. Fortunately her mother was strict and helped to keep these tendencies checked. A servant of the family, who herself later became a sister, has given testimony about Teresa's detachment and devotion while she was still living at home. She often led the Rosary with the servants at night, and performed numerous works of charity for the poor.

Teresa retained her impetuous nature all her life. Her even temper, her detachment from worldly things, her serenity—all witness to her heroic self-control. In her little notebook, which was found after her death, she wrote, "God asks us to mortify ourselves in small things rather than in big ones because the big occasions are rare, whereas the small ones are continuous." From the testimony of one of her sisters in religion, one learns that "She practiced virtue so spontaneously that one would imagine it all came naturally to her, whereas it was the fruit of constant sacrifice."

In 1900, Teresa applied to the general director of the Daughters of Mary Help of Christians, Father Marenco, to be admitted to the order. Although impressed with her attitude, the director was afraid that this wealthy young noblewoman would be unable to make the great sacrifice necessary to enter such a poor order. First he mentioned that there was a great need for Christian mothers, and suggested that perhaps that was Teresa's true vocation. Having already turned down an attractive proposal of marriage, Teresa simply said, "No, God does not want that from me." After the first interview, Father Marenco sent Teresa away to think about the type of sacrifice she would be making. In a second interview, he suggested that because of her wealth and cultural background, she should perhaps join the Ladies of the Sacred Heart, with whom she had studied. Teresa calmly but firmly refused to consider this option. The director explained that the Daughters of Mary Help of Christians (co-founded by St. John Bosco and St. Mary Mazzarello) worked mainly among the poor. He told her that the pupils were ignorant and often ill-mannered. As a member of the institute, Teresa would not even have her own room, as do the members of most religious orders. The sisters slept in a common dormitory, and if they were assistants they slept in the children's dormitory. In spite of the fact that Teresa calmly assured the priest that she would be able to adapt to these conditions, he again sent her away unsatisfied. He instructed her to visit the sisters, question them, and observe their life. "If you are still of the same mind, come back."

On the third visit, Father Marenco again tried to argue against Teresa's entrance—but she passed the test and he yielded. Later, he stated that he felt her vocation was no ordinary one.

Why did Teresa insist? Her cousin, a solicitor, had once asked her to take one of his daughters and enroll her at the convent school run by the Daughters of Mary Help of Christians. By mistake she went to the house of another order, and while talking with the superior, she heard a voice within her clearly saying, "This is not where I want you." When she had apologized for her mistake and found the correct house, she heard the same voice saying, "Here is where I want you." From about the age of fifteen, Teresa had felt that she had a vocation to become a sister. The voice simply clarified the choice of order.

Although at first her brother and her uncle opposed Teresa's decision, they became convinced that she had a true vocation, and in 1901 she became a postulant.

At first, the sisters tended to try to grant special favors to Teresa, both because of her status in the world and because of her delicate health. Teresa would have nothing to do with such exceptions, preferring to accept the common state of poverty. The sisters with whom she made her postulancy and her novitiate say that the chief disposition of her soul was humility, and that she displayed no trace of affectation.

Teresa was clothed in 1901 and began her novitiate at Bosco Parrasio, a poor, small house which had one great advantage—it was possible to have an Oratory there for the children of Trastevere. Sister Teresa's novice mistress tells us, "Sister Teresa knew how to deal with those girls. She could keep discipline and overlook much impoliteness and even downright rudeness. Her work was to teach catechism to the older girls because she was one of the best instructed."

Another of her sisters said, "The children, attracted by her kind and gentle manners, ran to her joyfully, showed her great affection, and listened to her stories with rapt attention."

Although many of the children were good, many others were the offspring of anti-religious parents who did not care about their education. Often these children were rowdy or rude, but Sister Teresa's calm response to their antics often won them over. In the words of one of the former pupils, "Sister Teresa was always even-tempered. I felt myself more and more drawn to her. I gave her all my confidence and turned to her in all the difficult circumstances of my life. I always found help and consolation. For this reason I can truly say she protected me and saved me from the many dangers of the world."

Sister Teresa was professed in 1902. In Via Cappelle, a Father Bonanni had opened a laundry to help keep girls off the streets, teach them a trade, and help them earn an honest living. The sisters took over the direction of this laundry, and some of the Oratory girls joined the workers. In 1905, there were thirty young girls employed in the needlework and laundry rooms. Gradually these girls had yielded to the compelling charity of Sister Teresa. They quit loitering on the streets and reading unwholesome literature. Many Trastevere girls who became mothers of families have given testimony on Sister Teresa. One said, "Her beautiful smile, her kindness and gentleness never left her for a moment. She really loved us and her anxiety for us and for our future, her ardent desire to see us good and the sacrifices she made for all of us were such as to baffle description."

The superior of that house tells us that Sister Teresa seemed ready for any sacrifice. If a girl spat in her face, she did not rest until she was able to win her over. In spite of her heavy workload, she was a good listener, hearing tales of family quarrels, drunkenness, impiety, poverty. She would pray with the girls and offer calm and good advice. When a girl was ill, she would visit her in her home. When a girl married, Sister Teresa helped her to get a suitable trousseau.

Even among these good sisters, jealousy would occasionally rear its head. Sister Teresa was young, and because she was extremely capable she was given many responsibilities. One Oratorian recalled, "She not only received just corrections with joy, but received unjust ones in the same manner." Another of the girls remembered, "Whenever any sister corrected Sister Teresa, whether deservedly or undeservedly, she immediately asked pardon without any attempt to excuse herself or justify herself." This was how she taught humility.

One Sunday, five or six rough girls came to the Oratory. They surrounded one of the sisters and pulled her veil off. The Oratorians rushed to the sister's aid, and a fight began. Sister Teresa, who was in bed ill, saw the fight and ran downstairs to intervene. In the meantime the police had arrived and were taking away the troublemakers. Sister Teresa said, "No, no we cannot allow that." She attempted to catch up to the policemen, but she fainted. Later the sisters found out that the girls had been bribed by an anti-Christian sect to go and insult the sisters. Sister Teresa took an interest in them and found work for them, taking one into her own workroom.

At the age of twenty-seven, Sister Teresa was diagnosed as having tuberculosis. She accepted her illness as the Will of God, and wrote, "Do not allow me, O my dear Lord, to be tempted to descend from this cross, for I have already sacrificed my life to You." Even in her illness, the characteristic Salesian sense of humor came to the fore and Sister was able to joke and smile in spite of the pain. When asked how she felt, she replied, "I am now prepared for any of three things: to die, to bear with a long illness, or to be cured." Then, smilingly she continued, "One of the three will certainly happen."

She was to be replaced in the laundry by another sister whom the girls had not yet become close to. The girls did not want to sort and count the soiled linen. In order to avoid a conflict between the girls and the sister replacing her, Sister Teresa secretly went and sorted the linen herself, although the constant bending must have caused a great deal of pain. We might have no record of this act of charity except that one day a benefactress of the house was on a visit and went into the wrong door. Here she saw Sister Teresa sorting the dirty laundry.

In 1907, after a brief visit to her family, Sister Teresa was sent to the infirmary at Turin. In the infirmary, Sister Teresa was given a room next door to a sister who had been ill for ten years. This sister, Sister Lenci, had been making a novena to Don Bosco, who was to be proclaimed Venerable that same month. On the night of July 22, Sister Teresa noticed a bright light in her room. Suddenly, in the center of the light she saw Don Bosco, as if he were alive and real. He drew near her and smiled. She understood in a flash that he had come to her with a gift, but she hastily said to him, "Don Bosco, it is not I who am asking for a cure—it is Sister Giovanna Lenci, in the next room." Don Bosco smiled and made his way toward Sister Lenci's room. She, too, was awake, and on seeing the saint felt herself completely cured. The next day she asked for her clothes and returned to work, continuing to work for another thirty years. Two days later, Don Bosco was proclaimed Venerable.

When the sisters asked her why she did not also ask to be cured, Sister Teresa said, "Oh, I shall be cured in Heaven." For another month and a few days, Sister Teresa continued her uncomplaining acceptance of pain, smiling good-humoredly until the last. On September 2, Sister Genta, her former novice mistress, asked Sister Teresa to dictate a reply to a telegram from her brother asking about her condition. "What shall I say? That you have improved?" Sister Teresa's answer was: "Wait until tomorrow."

The next day, after a repeated request, Sister Teresa said, "Tell my brother that one thing is necessary: to save one's soul." She repeated this message when asked what reply should be sent to other family members' notes, letters, and telegrams.

At midnight on September 2, Sister Teresa asked the infirmarian for her watch and set it for seven o'clock. Thinking she might be confused, the sister said, "Why at seven o'clock? It is midnight."

Sister Teresa quietly replied, "Yes, you are right, it is midnight, but it is all right like this."

At two-thirty in the morning, the infirmarian realized that Sister Teresa was dying, and several of the superiors were sent for. At dawn, the priest arrived and she received her final Communion. The priest then left to say Mass, and a few of the sisters remained in the room praying beside the bed of the almost lifeless sister. Suddenly, they saw her face light up, and three times she softly spoke the word "Paradise." As the sisters watched, Sister Teresa raised her head from the pillow and stretched her arms out toward a corner of her room. Sister Genta asked, "What is happening?"

Smilingly and in a strong voice, Sister Teresa said, "All is finished, Jesus is calling me. Jesus, Mary, Mary Help of Christians. Don Bosco. Oh how beautiful, how lovely Don Bosco is. How beautiful. I am coming." She added, "I am coming quickly."

When Sister Genta asked where the three were, Sister Teresa replied, "They are standing still over there." Asked if they were coming to take her at that moment, Sister replied, "No, they are there and are calling me."

Although all of those present later stated that they felt electrified, Sister Genta took courage and said, "If they are calling you, then go."

Sister Teresa answered, "But must I go like this? Light your candles quickly and accompany me." The sisters lighted a candle, and Sister Teresa continued, "Father Roca told me to wait for him and I cannot disobey him. He has not yet arrived. What shall I do?" She was referring to the fact that when he had left to offer Mass, the priest had said, "Don't go until I come."

After the priest returned, Sister Teresa sank serenely back onto the bed. When one of the sisters attempted to wipe the sweat from her brow, she calmly whispered, "Don't be upset, it doesn't matter, let it alone."

Sister Teresa lay quietly holding her crucifix tightly with her left hand, and for about fifteen minutes her right hand moved as though it were on the keyboard of a piano, playing one of the pieces of music she loved so well. Suddenly her right hand became rigid, and her face relaxed into a peaceful expression of sleep. Seven o'clock chimed from the belfry of the basilica.

After her death, members of Sister Teresa's family requested that her body be interred in a family plot in Rome. However, in accordance with her written request, she was buried with her sisters in religion. The fame of her sanctity began to spread, and many graces obtained through her intercession were reported. The general council of her order introduced her cause for beatification; her cause was initiated in the Curia of Turin on November 29, 1926. The apostolic process was begun on December 3, 1944. The virtues of this Servant of God are now being considered by the Sacred Congregation for the Causes of Saints.

Sister Teresa Valse Pantellini, a wealthy young Italian noblewoman of impetuous and domineering temperament, gave up everything to serve God and the poor. When asked about her life's motto shortly before her death, she replied, "I resolved to pass unnoticed."

31

BLESSED BROTHER MIGUEL

Blessed Miguel, F.S.C.
Francisco Febres Cordero Munoz
1854 - 1910
Ecuador - Spain
Died Age 56

The little son of Professor Cordero was sitting at home with his aunt. Little Francisco—known as "Pancho"—was a delicate child; he had a deformity of both feet, and at the age of five had not yet begun to walk. Gazing out the window toward some rosebushes in the garden, his eyes lit up. "Oh look," he cried to his aunt, "there is a lovely lady near the rosebushes."

Startled, his aunt replied, "Ask her to come in, Pancho."

"How beautiful she is in her white dress and mantle! Can't you see her? She is calling me; she wants me to go to her."

Before the amazed eyes of his aunt, Pancho stood up and went to the window, walking unaided for the first time in his life. The health of the boy improved after this strange incident, although the deformity in his feet remained, making walking difficult for the rest of his life.

Francisco Febres Cordero Munoz was born November 7, 1854, to a well-to-do and prominent family of Cuenca, Ecuador. The little boy was exceptionally bright, and for the first few years he was educated at home by his devout mother. Several unusual incidents during his childhood pointed to the fact that he was specially favored by God.

At the age of eight he was playing with some friends when he was attacked by a wild bull. Bystanders feared he would be killed, but he emerged from the incident completely unhurt.

The de la Salle Christian Brothers came to Ecuador at the invitation of the president of Ecuador, Garcia Moreno. In 1863, Francisco enrolled at the brothers' school. The brilliant nine-year-old immediately fell in love with the brothers and their way of life.

He made the school his second home and often stayed after school to help with any projects he could. Soon he had made up his mind that he wanted to become a brother, and nothing seemed able to dissuade him from this view. The brothers, for their part, quickly realized in Francisco a student of rare intellectual ability and religious fervor.

When Francisco informed his family of his hopes to become a brother, they were appalled. His mother had in mind a great career for him. His father and his grandmother flatly rejected the idea. In an attempt to change Francisco's mind, the boy was removed from the school and sent as a boarder to the seminary at Cuenca.

Years later, Brother Miguel wrote, "I stayed there three months only, but it felt like three years. I suffered intensely even though the teachers and students were very kind and friendly. It just wasn't the place God intended for me and I was like a fish out of water. One of my uncles who was very fond of me used to visit me and give me money to entertain myself, but I used it to buy candles for Our Lady's altar, to beg her to rescue me from this Purgatory and help me to follow my real vocation."

At last the boy's unhappiness began to tell on his health, and he was afflicted with violent headaches. Repeatedly he begged the rector to intercede with his family and point out that his situation was a false one. At last his family relented, and Francisco was allowed to go back to the brothers' school. The family remained adamant about the matter of his vocation until by sheer dogged persistence he finally won their grudging permission to try.

Francisco received the religious habit in 1868 at the age of fourteen. He was the first native Ecuadorian brother. In honor of St. Michael the Archangel, he was given the name Miguel. Because of his delicate health, the brothers allowed him to make his novitiate with the community in Cuenca rather than sending him to a novitiate in France.

At the early age of seventeen, Brother Miguel wrote and published the first of many textbooks! Later, many of his texts were adopted by the government for use throughout the republic. Because of the high quality of his books on grammar and philology, Miguel was elected to the national Academy of Languages in 1892. As a scholar, a writer, and a poet, Brother Miguel was brilliant and outstanding.

The supremely intelligent scholar, at ease in the company of the literary giants of his day, Brother Miguel was also a natural teacher.

At all times he tried to make his lessons interesting to his pupils. He once wrote this resolution in his private notebook: "I must look for every possible way of making the lessons and work agreeable and pleasant to my pupils." He was understanding and patient, and although he set high standards, he never lost his temper even with the slowest of his students.

A young brother once saw Brother Miguel—who had been teaching for many years—poring over a lesson in a rather elementary text. He remarked to Brother Miguel that surely after teaching for twenty years, Brother did not need to "prepare" that lesson.

Brother Miguel replied, "Yes, I know it, at least I think I know it. Even so, I find a better way of explaining it every year, and I think that if I teach it for another twenty years I shall still find new and better ways of putting it over."

An excellent scholar and a good and dedicated teacher—would these attributes serve as the basis for the beatification of Brother Miguel? Indeed not. The basis of the holiness of Brother Miguel was the fact that everything he did was done for God and to promote the kingdom of Christ. He once wrote, "The heart is rich when it is content, and it is always content when its desires are fixed on God. *Nothing* can bring greater happiness than doing God's Will *for the Love of God.*" In his spiritual diary he wrote, "I give myself completely to Jesus so that He can use me just as He wishes. I want every word I write, everything I read, everything I do at my desk and all my work in school to be done for the glory of God."

After his death, Brother Miguel's actions during his life were measured against this stated resolve, and the decision of Church authorities was that he had, indeed, kept to this high purpose.

Brother Miguel considered Our Lady a special helper in his work as a teacher. He wrote several hymns and poems in her honor, and his constant prayer was: "Please inspire me with what I should say to them."

Throughout his life, Brother Miguel was faithful to the ideals and aims of his order. In spite of the fact that he endured a great deal of physical suffering from headaches and the deformity of his feet, as well as from other ailments, he did not speak of them. He simply and quietly offered his suffering in union with Our Lord's passion, and refused to ask for dispensations from any of the religious practices required by the rule. All of his biographers return to the fact that he was a truly happy and cheerful person, never melancholy and sad.

One brother later confessed that whenever he felt depressed he would make an excuse to go and see Brother Miguel, who would willingly lay aside whatever he was doing at the moment in order to listen to him. Invariably he came away cheered. Brother Miguel said that he himself could never be unhappy or bored because "I have such a marvelous friend. I make myself content with God when I am not content with myself."

In 1888, Brother Miguel was delegated to represent the brothers from Ecuador at the beatification of the founder of the order, John Baptist de la Salle. He was charmed to have this opportunity, and said that his trip to Rome was like "being transported to Paradise." At the impressive ceremony, he had many intentions to pray for, but later confessed that he was so overcome that all he could do was repeat over and over, "Thank you, God, for all You have done for me. You know my petitions. Thank you."

In 1905, Brother Miguel was asked to go to Europe to translate some texts from French into Spanish. Although he felt sad at leaving his native land, he wrote, "I am quite calm and serene because I am doing God's Will."

As a translator, he worked first in France, then in Belgium, and finally in Spain. In January of 1910, he caught a severe chill which turned into pneumonia. On the 7th of January he asked to receive the Last Sacraments. When someone told him that he shouldn't die before he finished his work, he smilingly replied, "If the work I am doing is useful for God, He will send someone else to finish it and it will be done better than I could do it." Asked if he was unhappy to be dying so far from home, he answered, "No, I am happy to die in Spain since it is God's wish." He died quietly and peacefully on February 9, and was buried the next day in the cemetery attached to the brothers' residence in Premia.

Although he died far from Ecuador, his saintly life was remembered, and people began to petition for a cause for his canonization. The required documents were forwarded to Rome in 1925. In the meantime, his coffin was transferred to a special place in the novitiate chapel.

On July 21, 1936, the Spanish Communist insurgents sacked the property at Premia and set fire to the chapel. Two months later, a young man came to the Ecuadorian consulate in Barcelona to tell of an unusual occurrence. On the occasion of the attack at Premia, the coffin of Brother Miguel had been opened and the body was found to be intact. The young man felt it his duty to notify the consulate in hopes that this precious relic would not be desecrated or lost. Through the efforts of the Ecuadorian consul, Brother Miguel's remains were identified, claimed, and sent back to Ecuador.

Upon reaching Ecuador, the casket was carried in a procession to a resting place at the novitiate in a suburb of Quito. As it moved slowly through the throng, a young boy on crutches managed to reach out and touch the casket, and to the surprise and delight of the people present, he simply left his crutches there on the pavement and moved off with the crowd. This boy never resorted to crutches again, having been completely cured. Immediately, other favors and miraculous cures began to be reported. On October 30, 1977, with another of his brothers (Brother Mucian of Malonne, Belgium), Brother Miguel was beatified.

Blessed Brother Miguel of the Christian Schools. Brother Miguel wrote
and published his first textbook at age 17. As a child, he had been unable
to walk until the age of five, at which time he saw a vision of a "lovely
lady" and immediately began to walk for the first time.

Brother Miguel is at the left rear in this photograph of the Academy of Languages taken when he was 38 years old. Brother Miguel's body was found incorrupt many years after his death.

32

BLESSED MICHAEL RUA

Blessed Michael Rua, S.D.B.
Michael Rua
1837 - 1910
Italy
Died Age 73

Thirty-one-year-old Father Rua lay at the point of death. While the other Salesians searched frantically for Don Bosco, the head of their order, Don Bosco's trusted lieutenant writhed in agony. The first of Don Bosco's students to join the fledgling order, Rua was the disciplinarian, financial administrator, and general flunky, doing every duty assigned to him with competence and joy. But now, the doctor had diagnosed his illness as acute peritonitis and stated that nothing further could be done. Father Angelo Savio brought the holy oils to the sickroom, where they waited in readiness for the founder to administer the Last Rites.

At last Don Bosco returned, but refusing the entreaties of the others, he carried on with his normal schedule until after supper. When he at last entered the sickroom, the sick priest painfully gasped, "If this is my last hour, tell me—I am ready for anything!"

The gentle reply was, "My dear Michael, I don't want you to die. There are so many things you must help me with." The founder calmed the young priest, and bade him sleep well.

The next morning, as the doctor tried to explain the seriousness of Father Rua's illness, Don Bosco replied, "Let his sickness become as critical as it can be, my Father Rua must recover because he has lots of work to do." Noticing the holy oils for the first time, he asked who had brought them. When Father Savio spoke up, the saint said, "Men of little faith." Then he bent and whispered to his beloved "Michelino": "Don't worry. Even if I threw you out the window this minute, you would not die!" He smiled, and the sick young priest returned the smile as if they shared a secret joke.

Indeed, Father Michael *was* too busy to die. As Don Bosco's "right hand man," there were many responsibilities he felt obliged to carry out. Of a normally frail constitution, this priest continued to carry out his many duties, and after the death of Don Bosco, he led the Salesians until his own death in 1910 at the age of seventy-three. During his beatification homily, the pope hailed Father Michael Rua as a "frail, worn figure of a priest, all meekness and goodness, all duty and sacrifice."

Michael was born in Turin in 1837, the son of a mill worker. At the age of seven, he met the thirty-year-old priest, Don Bosco, and became a member of Don Bosco's Festive Oratory. Michael's father had recently died, and the attraction he felt for the saintly priest helped to fill the void left by the death of his father. To him, Don Bosco became a second father.

Don Bosco had made some enemies through his work, and one day someone warned Michael to keep away from him. "He's sick, you know—up here"—and the man tapped his head meaningfully. Michael burst into tears at the thought that his friend was ill. But upon seeing the priest his usual jovial self the following Sunday, Michael felt much relieved. This lesson in slander would stick with him all his life. Later, Michael always attempted to learn the truth behind any rumors, although slander was still a cross that hurt him deeply.

After finishing his schooling from the Christian Brothers at age ten, Michael attempted to find work in the local arsenal. Hearing of his intentions, Don Bosco offered to pay his tuition for further schooling, and so Michael was able to continue his education. Scholastically, he was at the head of his class in the two private schools he attended.

In 1853, Michael enrolled at the seminary, and he became Don Bosco's right hand man. To him fell the responsibility for all the Oratory's discipline; like its founder, Michael Rua was patient and understanding. Don Bosco entrusted him with the responsibility for paying the Oratory's bills, while he himself went to beg for funds. In addition to these duties, Don Bosco asked Michael to recopy the text of his *History of Italy*. For nearly two months, this task occupied all his spare time.

At the same time the busy young seminarian was performing all these duties, he was also continuing his studies for the priesthood. He made excellent grades by getting up at four in the morning to study, and retiring after midnight. It is in itself a minor miracle that this frail man, whose health was never robust, and whose family counted seven dead by the time he was sixteen, was able to survive such a difficult schedule.

On March 25, 1855, Michael became the first of Don Bosco's followers to take religious vows in the infant society, the Salesians. He was ordained July 28, 1860. On the night of his ordination, he found a prophetic note from Don Bosco on his desk. It read, in part, "You will see, better than I, how the Salesian society will go beyond the confines of Italy and establish itself in many parts of the world." Through the work of Michael Rua, the society did expand to the far corners of the earth. One of his biographers tells us, "His thirst for missionary work was insatiable."

For a year after his ordination, Michael took over the Salesians' first school at Mirabello. Though it was in financial difficulties at his arrival, Father Rua straightened out the situation. Recalled to Rome, by 1884 Michael became the duly appointed vicar of the congregation.

In 1888, he saw that his founder and "second father" was drawing close to the end of his life. Michael was present at Don Bosco's death; he closed the saint's eyes and softly murmured, "We have lost a father on earth, but have gained a protector in Heaven."

Father Michael consolidated the young society, which at that time numbered about seven hundred members. He enjoined them to "faithfully follow the system he [Don Bosco] used and taught us."

Seeming to have inherited Don Bosco's energy and love for the missions, Father Rua opened new houses in eight countries. He sent the missionaries forward with excellent advice, and insisted on respect for the native cultures they found. He advised these Salesians to take up the way of life of their adopted countries. "As regards certain customs of these savages, try not to belittle them, but rather, after the example of the Church in ancient times amidst pagan peoples, try to sanctify such customs, provided they are not harmful to soul or body." Brave enough to accept even somewhat unconventional ideas if he thought they were part of God's plan, Father Rua supported a plan to found a religious order of leprous women. He told the priest who had conceived the idea, "Your institution is a fine thing; it ought to go on and develop."

Father Michael's thoughtfulness and consideration for each member of the order was a mark of his fatherliness. No problem seemed too small to deserve his attention.

Crosses were not lacking in the life of Don Bosco's successor. Floods, earthquakes, and other natural disasters plagued the missions. Suppression of religious orders in some countries and political harassment in others caused him much sorrow. Perhaps the cruelest cut of all was the slander that was spread about the Salesian school near Genoa. On hearing these reports, Father Rua wept openly. Eventually the rumors proved false, but the trial caused him much pain.

On February 15, 1910, Father Rua sat at his desk attempting to open the morning mail. His strength seemed sapped, and he asked his secretary to call Father Rinaldi to take over. After a lingering illness of two months, Father Rua passed away quietly on April 6.

A complete dedication to Christian education was a special characteristic of the life of Father Michael Rua. He reflected a boundless love for children, especially the poor, the orphaned, and the neglected boys of the streets.

The diocesan process for the cause of Michael Rua was completed by 1934. The honor of conducting a beatification ceremony is usually delegated to one of the cardinals, but Pope Paul VI personally conducted the beatification of Michael Rua. This was Pope Paul's second beatification ceremony; it took place on October 29, 1973. During his prepared homily, the pope broke off and asked, "We have declared Father Rua blessed. Are you happy?" The great basilica resounded with cheers and cries of assent. Continuing his homily, he said, "The marvelous fruitfulness of the Salesian family . . . had Don Bosco as its origin, Father Rua its continuation. He was the most faithful, therefore the most humble, and at the same time the most valiant of the sons of Don Bosco."

Blessed Michael Rua was the first follower of Don Bosco to take vows in the infant society, the Salesians. Even in his teens, he was Don Bosco's right-hand man, responsible for the Oratory's discipline and for paying the bills. He became Don Bosco's first successor as head of the Salesians.

Father Rua solicitously bends over the aged Don Bosco in this photo taken in Barcelona in 1886.

33

BLESSED LOUIS GUANELLA

Blessed Louis Guanella, S.C.
Louis Guanella
1842 - 1915
Italy
Died Age 73

To assist the "favorites" of Providence—the incurable, the abandoned aged, the physically and mentally handicapped, orphaned and needy children—Father Louis Guanella lived a life dedicated to charity. From the seed of a moment of special grace in childhood when he felt a call to care for the poor and the disabled, Father Guanella's work has grown to a healthy, blossoming tree comprised of his religious followers who today still shelter these rejects of society. At his death in 1915, many doubted that his work could continue. He replied that the work was God's work, and that "He who brought into existence people and works will also be able to continue them."

Father Guanella believed, spoke, and acted on the premise that "The heart of a Christian, who believes and feels, cannot pass by the hardships and deprivations of the poor without helping them." His entire life proclaimed the Gospel message, "As long as you did it to one of these my least brethren, you did it to me."

Louis was the ninth of the thirteen children of Lawrence and Maria Guanella. The family maintained a simple but comfortable home high in the Italian Alps. Lawrence served as first deputy under Austrian rule, and under Italian rule he was the respected mayor of the little town of Campodolcino. The land was used for pasture, and young Louis worked tending the family sheep and carrying wood and other items long before he had had any schooling. These mountain people were hard workers. They had no animals to help with the work, and horses and wagons were almost unknown.

From his family, Louis learned many lessons he would later put into practical use in his apostolate. He learned how to use his hands to build things, rather than depend on having money to purchase ready-made items. He learned the value and some of the skills of agriculture. Best of all, he learned that a loving spirit of sacrifice can work miracles.

Annually on the Feast of St. Rocco, Lawrence gave away food to all who came. Louis and his sister Catherine played at making "pretend" soup from mud to give to the poor. Perhaps their childish game was an indication of their later work. At one time, Catherine came to help Louis in one of his Houses of Divine Providence, where the soup was still free to the poor—but not made of mud!

Louis' childhood was similar to that of many other little Italian boys of his age and state of life. He learned some reading and arithmetic from a local curate and later attended an elementary school in a village where the priest was a relative of his family. He was entranced at his first sight of horses attached to a wagon. Accidents were no stranger to such an active child, and he had several narrow escapes from serious injury.

At the age of twelve, Louis wanted to enter the seminary. With thirteen children to provide for, his father was uncertain about whether he would be able to afford this. Luckily, through the offices of an uncle, Louis was able to obtain a scholarship. His record at school was excellent and he completed high school in 1859. After this, further studies at the seminary in Como were possible only by sacrifice on the part of his family.

At the seminary, a fellow student came down with a contagious disease and became critically ill. While others used every precaution and avoided the student when possible, Louis disregarded all warnings and cared for the patient until all danger was past.

Louis was ordained in 1866. His first priestly duties were those of an assistant to an elderly pastor. Here his zeal for souls and his sense of responsibility toward them became so strong that he began trying to do penance for those who would not do penance on their own. He prayed for them, fasted for them, and wore a heavy spiked chain. However, the wise old pastor noticed that Louis' health was beginning to be affected, and forbad him such severe penances before his health completely failed.

From 1875 - 1878, Don Guanella went to stay with Don Bosco at the Oratory in Turin. Here, too, he was able to observe the great works of charity carried out by Joseph Cottolengo. He wrote of his time there, "The Lord saw to it that I should meet Father Bosco and Father Cottolengo whom I admired and grew to love the more I learned of them."

The spirit of these two saints of Turin (both have been accorded the honors of the altar) became the greatest example for Louis' priestly life. He followed the example by combining John Bosco's work for the education of youth with Joseph Cottolengo's great works of charity with the poor and the sick. His first houses, indeed, were called Houses of Providence in imitation of Father Cottolengo's home in Turin.

Louis Guanella's vision extended beyond his time to the movements which even today are of concern to Catholics—social action, education, youth movements, and the lay apostolate. In particular, he encouraged the laity to pray the Mass silently along with the priest, and he anticipated St. Pius X's decree by encouraging frequent and even daily Communion. The Italian census of 1861 showed that 74% of the population was illiterate. Father Guanella went so far as to obtain a teaching certificate so that he might not only teach, but also train teachers.

The dignity of the human person was a priority in all of Father Guanella's works. In particular, he wanted to maintain this dignity for those who were classed as society's outcasts. Often the old, the incurable, and the retarded were left in pitiable condition by relatives who had no desire or no knowledge of how to give them this human dignity. In the early days, Father Guanella took these outcasts to be cared for by the followers of Father Cottolengo. Later, he established homes for their care and founded the Servants of Charity and the Daughters of St. Mary of Providence to staff his homes.

Father Louis refused to call his mentally deficient men and boys "retarded." Instead, he wished them to be called his "good boys" or "good children." He believed that a human life has value because it is a gift from God, and that it cannot be measured by its achievements. When he died, he left these "good children" to his priests and sisters as most precious gifts; he called them his "treasures."

During most of Father Guanella's lifetime, Italy was in a state of political unrest. The infamous law of July 7, 1866 suppressed all religious communities. Several later laws, including the Suspect Law of 1866, were enacted by the anticlericals and the socialists. Because of his popularity with the people, Father Guanella was seen as a threat by these groups as well as by the Freemasons. He was a gifted writer, and published a small book and several stirring pamphlets against the liberalization then prevalent. In 1873 the book was banned by the civil authorities, and Father Guanella was forbidden to teach. He was placed under surveillance, and several times had to offer Mass under the watchful eyes of the police. Time and again, political ploys were devised against him.

Father Louis spent the last of his inheritance from his father in an attempt to open a small free school for boys. He had made most of the furniture himself. After only two years, the secular authorities closed the school and threatened him with fines and severe punishment. Through all this political oppression and suppression, Father Guanella put complete trust in Divine Providence. Rather than fight against these trials, he saw them as the fire that would temper and strengthen his works.

The first House of Providence was begun at Como in April of 1866. By 1890, there were two hundred poor and afflicted persons of all ages living there. In 1895, a mob of anticlericals set fire to the House of Providence. As Father Guanella comforted the people, he advised them to tell God, "Lord, in Your designs You have permitted that our house be burned down! We will stay here in Yours." They slept that night in the church, and immediately, plans for rebuilding were begun.

"The Lord ordinarily wants everything here on earth to follow a natural course," said Father Guanella. He believed that the help of Providence was merited by faith, prayer, and work. Sometimes, however, the ordinary course of events gave way to the extraordinary. At one time, Father Guanella decided to rebuild the chapel. Patients, workers, and Father Guanella himself were working happily one day when he suddenly gave the order to halt and directed all the workers to leave the area. Within minutes, the scaffolding crashed to the ground without a single injury. On another occasion, the superior at one of the schools discovered that there was no food for dinner. When she told Father Guanella, he replied, "It is only 11:30; Providence still has half an hour to provide." The sister asked the students to pray, and at noon a cart delivered a sack of rice. No one knew where the cart had come from.

Father Guanella did not believe that his priests and sisters should simply sit back to watch God work, although he often said, when asked how he accomplished so much, "It is God who does the work." He advised his priests that "the Servant of Charity must go to bed each night so tired from work that he will think he has been beaten."

As he saw it, practicality went hand in hand with trust in God's Providence. Although Father Louis relied on Providence to care for his dependents, he also worked to improve their lot. When a fellow priest asked how Father Louis could hope to care for all who came to him for help, he simply advised the priest that God would provide for His own.

Noticing a large parcel of swampy, mosquito-infested land at the end of Lake Como, Father Guanella decided to attempt to reclaim the land. His detractors thought that he was crazy, and laughed that he had at last found a swampy grave for himself and his work. Using the labor of his "good children" who were physically strong, and the directive and administrative ability of some of the old men from his homes, he began slowly to reclaim the swamp. Within a few years, the work of leveling, filling, plowing, and planting had changed it into fruitful land. People began to move into the area to make new homes. Father Louis designed a statue of Mary for his faithful workers and called it "Our Lady of the Worker." Soon a church was dedicated in this "swampy grave." For his work in reclaiming unusable land, Father Louis was awarded a medal of honor by the minister of agriculture.

Humorous incidents often arose from what some considered Father Guanella's foolish charity. Once when some of the sisters tried to prevent his giving away some money, he literally threw money out the window to a poor man standing outside. Another time, not having any money to give, he tossed out a pair of new shoes.

In other facets of his apostolate, Father Guanella began the return of Catholicism to Switzerland, promoted the Lourdes devotions, led a pilgrimage to the Eucharistic Congress in London, and himself traveled to the United States to investigate the plight of Italian immigrants. Later he sent his sisters and priests to assist these immigrants.

A friend and contemporary of Pope Pius X, Father Guanella often appealed to him for help in his work. After the construction of one home for the retarded, he asked Pope Pius if he might name the new home in honor of His Holiness. Laughingly the pope replied, "Yes, yes, put me at the head of your retarded patients. Immortalize me through them; call it the Pius X Home." These two great men of their age often joked in this manner while carrying out numerous works of charity. When the pope asked Don Guanella if all his responsibilities did not worry him a great deal, the priest replied, "I worry until midnight and from then on I let God worry. I even sleep too much. Sometimes when I am in the streetcar and should get off at [one place], I sleep and it takes me to [another place]. And then quietly, and well rested, I return without telling anyone so they will not make fun of me."

Father Guanella did much to rescue the victims of the Italian earthquakes of 1905 and 1915. He assisted on the disaster sites and sheltered refugees in his homes all over Italy. During World War I, he was active in relief and aid and was presented with a gold medal by the board of deputies for his outstanding work.

Louis Guanella died on October 24, 1915. He was beatified by Pope Paul VI on October 25, 1964, only forty-nine years later.

Above: Blessed Louis Guanella founded the Servants of Charity to care for society's rejects. He said, "The Servant of Charity must go to bed each night so tired from work that he will think he has been beaten." At his first parish assignment, Father Guanella's great zeal for souls led him to fast, pray, and wear a heavy spiked chain in penance for those who would not do penance on their own.

Opposite: These photographs of Blessed Louis Guanella show him as a youth, carrying burdens and tending cattle. In the lower picture, the boy on the left is Louis Guanella.

34

BROTHER ISIDORE OF SAINT JOSEPH

Servant of God Isidore of Saint Joseph, C.P.
Isidore De Loor
1881 - 1916
Belgium
Died Age 35

The priests and brothers of the Congregation of the Passion enter the monastery for a threefold purpose—to sanctify their own souls, to save other souls, and to spread devotion to the Sacred Passion. In the instructions to the novices, it is plainly stated that they should not think that to reach these high goals they must perform extraordinary works or submit themselves to rigorous austerities. Their path to sanctity is to follow the Will of God by obeying their rule and their superiors. By and large, the life of these dedicated religious is a quiet one.

Brother Isidore of St. Joseph lived this rule in uncomplaining submission to his superiors. At his death in 1916, no legacy of scholarly writings or miraculous events in the monastery during his lifetime was discovered. However, within thirteen years, the memory of his sanctity had so survived the descent of his mortal remains into the grave that a cause for him was begun. In 1952, at the ritual exhumation of the relics, more than thirty thousand people came to pay their respects in a period of only six hours.

What was there in the personality of this humble lay brother which could attract such a multitude? The key to Brother Isidore's sanctity lay in his knowledge that all, religious and lay, are called upon to do God's Will humbly and devotedly. Brother Isidore found his strength to know and do God's Will in prayer.

Isidore De Loor was the oldest child of hard working Belgian peasants. His parents had married rather late in life, and with their three children, they formed a close-knit, loving family. Work on the family farm was never easy, and chores kept the parents from attending daily Mass. Isidore went as the faithful family representative to daily Masses, and the whole family attended on Sunday. Love of God and each other formed Isidore's family background, and at the end of the day's work the entire family knelt to pray the Rosary. To omit this daily prayer was unthinkable.

Isidore helped his father with the farm work to the extent of his age and capabilities. He also had other chores such as running errands for his mother and babysitting his younger brother and sister. Because young rural farmers in Belgium in the late 1800's did not need much formal education, he attended school for only six years. By the time he was twelve, he had quit school to help on the farm.

As Isidore grew, so did his wish to dedicate himself entirely to God's Will. Prayer and work were the rule of his life at this time.

On Sundays, Isidore served early Mass, and after a hasty breakfast at home, walked back to the parish church to teach catechism to the younger parishioners. On Sunday afternoons he often walked the hour's distance to the next closest church to assist with the catechism lessons there. All who knew him at this time spoke well of him, and always with respect. Although Isidore had a pleasant manner and a ready laugh, he greatly disliked coarse or vulgar talk and refused to sacrifice his principles in this matter. "Men don't speak of such things," he admonished. "Stop and think of God who hears and sees you at every moment."

During slack times on the farm, Isidore could have rested or pursued some hobby or interest of his own. Instead, he first finished any repairs or extra work he could find at home and then volunteered his help to neighboring farmers.

Although Isidore dreamed of a vocation of total dedication to God, at first he spoke only to God about this matter. He knew that his ageing parents needed him at home. Finally, at the age of twenty-six, he attended a mission given by a Redemptorist priest. To this priest, Isidore confessed his wish. The wise priest counseled him to follow his vocation by entering the Passionist congregation as a lay brother.

Isidore's parents had normal human reservations about what they at first saw as the loss of their son. In their desire to follow God's will, however, they allowed him to leave to try his vocation. His father could not bear to be present at the parting from his beloved son.

As Isidore left for the station in a small donkey cart, his mother bade him farewell. Tearfully she called after him, "Isidore, if it doesn't suit you at the monastery, hurry back home."

Turning and pointing to himself, Isidore called back, "Mother, this one is never coming back."

Though resolved not to return home, Isidore almost did not find the monastery. Belgium is a bilingual country and Isidore, who spoke only Flemish, was traveling to a monastery in the French-speaking section of the country. On arrival in the town, he could not locate the monastery. He tried with signs and a drawing of the Passionist emblem to elicit directions, but to his embarrassment he had attracted quite a crowd before he was able to get directions from a Flemish-speaking carriage driver.

At the monastery, the shy farm boy was overwhelmed by the presence of so many priests and knowledgeable brothers. The kindness of all soon overcame this barrier and soon he was able to write home a letter of praise for the equality he found in the monastery. "Here we are all the same from superior to the most lowly: same food, same bed, same rest, same recreation." Isidore's name there was Brother Isidore of St. Joseph.

From his first days at the monastery, Brother Isidore decided to do his best to follow the rule perfectly and obey all the orders of his superiors without question or grumbling. His novice master apparently recognized that Brother Isidore had a special character, and was exceedingly hard on him. Isidore never complained.

Knowing that the rule forbad the brothers to attempt extraordinary penances and austerities, Isidore performed his penances in small, largely unnoticed ways. As cook for the monastery, he waited until all had eaten before serving himself from the leftovers. Rather than cook a simple, easy to fix menu, he went out of his way to prepare the items which the various individuals liked. One brother noticed that when making himself a sandwich, Isidore would pass the butter knife over the bread as if he were spreading the customary allotment of butter on his slice. No butter, however, actually got on the bread. Small penances of this type became, for him, presents for God.

On one occasion when Brother Isidore was mowing hay, the weather became unbearably hot. A brother was sent to take a cool drink out to him. Isidore thanked him most kindly, but was later observed slipping the full bottle back into the kitchen. Although he preferred the outdoor work that he had grown up loving, such as gardening and working in the fields, he did not complain about tasks assigned him in the kitchen or laundry.

If Isidore could help another he was quick to offer his assistance. If he, on the other hand, needed help, he did not ask for it. Once, two kitchen helpers who were very lazy were assigned to him. They failed to peel enough potatoes or complete their other kitchen chores. Rather than complain about their conduct, Brother Isidore simply did their work in addition to his own, until another of the brothers noticed their actions and reported them to the superior.

Isidore regarded his superior's wishes as direct commands from God Himself. At one time during World War I, the brothers were advised to leave their monastery, since it was in a dangerous location. The superiors withdrew most of the brothers to safety in Holland, leaving only a few to guard the monastery. When asked if he would stay, Brother Isidore willingly acceded to the request, though he knew it was a dangerous job. Another act of submission took place on Isidore's deathbed. There, he confessed to his brother that he was more than ready to die. "But," he said, "my superiors do not will it, and therefore I remain alive."

In the summer of 1911, Isidore contracted an extremely painful disease of the eye. Although the doctors said that the pain must have been terrific, Isidore never mentioned it until it became unbearable. The disease was diagnosed as cancer of the right eye, and the eye was removed. Furthermore, Brother Isidore was told that he had intestinal cancer, and that he would probably have only a few more years to live. He accepted this diagnosis with calm resignation. He wrote to his parents, "Resigned to God's Will, we will make the best progress. May Our Blessed Lord grant me a resignation without murmur or complaint."

In 1914, Brother Isidore was given the duty of porter at the monastery at Kortrijk. This duty is the most disruptive and often the most disagreeable duty for a monk. When the doorbell rings, the porter must stop his work or prayers to go and admit the visitors. Brother Isidore made this chore a joyful task, leaving immediately when he heard the summons and gladly welcoming all comers.

By the end of summer, 1916, Brother Isidore was exhausted. An attack of pleurisy sent him to bed and the doctor said that the cancer was spreading rapidly. As the end drew near, the attacks became increasingly painful. Finally, he could not even remain in bed. Instead, he sat in a chair and rested his head in the infirmarian's arms when the pain was at its worst. This nurse states that he never once heard Brother Isidore complain. "When I asked him about his condition, he answered only that he regretted that he could not make a better thanksgiving after Holy Communion and asked me to help him." Brother Isidore felt very keenly that his pain disturbed his prayers at this time, causing him to be unable to concentrate well. Although his brother was able to come for a last visit, Brother Isidore did not have the consolation of a final visit with his much-loved parents. Again, he did not complain about this.

About one o'clock in the morning of October 6, Brother Isidore suddenly said, "Father Superior, call the members of the community—I am dying." Another priest in the room said that he felt the end was not at hand, but at Brother Isidore's insistence the whole community was called. Brother Isidore humbly asked forgiveness for any wrong he might have done them and promised to pray for each one when he reached Heaven. With his head in his superior's hands, he sighed quietly and passed to his reward.

He was buried quietly within two days. The number of persons visiting his grave and asking for his intercession slowly began to grow. Soon many were claiming spiritual and temporal favors received. Eventually, Belgium could not contain his fame, and people began to come from other parts of Europe. The diocesan investigation was begun in October of 1950, and within two years a favorable report was sent to Rome.

Brother Isidore of Saint Joseph, a humble Passionist lay brother who died of cancer at age 35. Though he was almost unknown during life, after his death many favors were granted through his intercession. 30,000 people came to pay their respects in a period of six hours at the ritual exhumation of his relics.

35

VEN. CHARLES DE FOUCAULD

Little Brother Charles of Jesus
Charles Eugene, (Vicomte de) Foucauld
1858 - 1916
France - Algeria
Died Age 58

In his mid-twenties, Viscount Charles de Foucauld thought that the best part of life consisted in shocking the little French town where he was stationed as a second lieutenant in the French army. He tried in every way to shock the people, both with his extravagant spending and his wild behavior. Having inherited a fortune from his maternal grandfather, Charles was able to indulge any whim of self-gratification. Greatly attracted to women, he told each of his new mistresses, "I rent by the day, not by the month." No one who knew him at this time suspected that the playboy would one day give up all worldly pleasures for the love of God. The thought that he, like the desert fathers of early Christian times, might eventually be attracted to a life of serving God as a hermit in the desert would have amazed his contemporaries.

Charles was left an orphan by the age of six, and he and his sister were brought up by their grandfather. By the time he was fifteen, less than a year after his First Communion, Charles had ceased to be a Christian and was an agnostic. At school he did so little work that he was expelled. For a few months he studied hard in order to be admitted to Saint-Cyr, a military school. But he became so lazy that he grew fat, and by the entrance date, no uniform could be found to fit him; he had to have one specially tailored. At age seventeen, he was, in his own words, "all egoism, vanity, impiety, and evildoing."

In 1878, his grandfather died. Love for the old man had prevented Charles from indulging in the worst excesses, but at his death, Charles began to "live." On receiving his inheritance, he set about spending it in riotous living. In 1880, his regiment was sent to Algeria. Charles took with him one of his numerous mistresses, and lived in such blatant dissipation that he was suspended from the army. Soon, though, an insurrection broke out in Algeria; he re-volunteered and was reinstated.

After eight months of active service, in which the young soldier fought bravely and well, he resigned his commission. For the next year he traveled through Morocco, exploring and taking such excellent notes that on his return he wrote two books which won for him a gold medal from the French Geographical Society in 1885.

Back in France, however, Charles returned to his old life of self-indulgence. For a time he lived in Paris, where he took an apartment near a cousin, Marie de Bondy. Marie, who had first entered his life when he was about eleven, was a deeply spiritual young woman. Gradually, through her example, the gay and reckless young man began to change.

Realizing the devoutness of his cousin, and knowing her intelligence, Charles began to question whether religion was truly the fairy tale he had thought it. He began to go to church, praying that God would make Himself known to him. Finally came his dramatic return to the Sacraments.

His religion, when he rediscovered God, was a highly personal discipleship and love of the Person of Jesus Christ. Regarding his conversion, Charles said, "The moment I realized that God existed, I knew I could not do otherwise than to live for Him alone."

Marie had felt that the best means of converting a person was to show him that one loved him, a concept that Charles was to remember later and make a large part of his life. Between Charles and this cousin, who was eight years older, grew a spiritual friendship that was to last until his death. The fact that Marie never scolded him, attempting to win him only by her example, led Charles to the idea of an apostolate for a new order in the Church—an apostolate of presence, not preaching.

Before his return to France, Charles had become engaged to the daughter of a prominent French geographer in Algeria. This fiance later testified and gave evidence to the postulator of his cause. The young woman was a Catholic convert, but after the engagement was broken, she was broken-hearted and left her religion. In 1913, Charles and his ex-fiance met by chance on a street of Algiers. She was a married woman and he was a priest. At this meeting, she informed him that she had left the Church. Feeling that her leaving was his fault, Charles prayed for her, and in time she did return to the practice of her Catholic Faith. At the age of sixty-five, ten years after the death of Charles de Foucauld, this woman told the postulator of his cause: "I have pined for him all my life, and I loved him and will love him until my dying day."

For a time after his return to the Sacraments, Charles lived as a Trappist monk. Although he is remembered as an exemplary religious, the conviction grew that this was not his vocation. Charles felt that God's Will for him lay elsewhere, although his advisor felt that he should remain a Trappist. The decision, however, was in the hands of the superiors of the order. At the end of January, the Father General of the order told Charles to leave the order, the better to follow Christ in abjection and poverty. In February of that same year, 1897, he was to have taken his final vows as a Trappist. After being released from his temporary vows, Charles went to the Holy Land where he became a servant for the Poor Clare nuns. Living in a small room near their monastery, he spoke to no one except in the line of duty, often slept outside on the ground, and ate frugally. He worked as a gardener and handyman for the sisters, only one of whom, the superior, knew who he was.

Rumors about the handyman with the cultured voice and manners began to fly. When at last a gossipy man from town inquired if it were true that in France he held the title of Count, Charles smilingly replied, "I am an old soldier," avoiding the actual question.

Mother Elizabeth, the superior of these Clarist sisters, was a woman of uncommon wisdom. She helped Charles to the realization that he should become a priest in order to serve God better. Charles wished to remain hidden, living a poor, unknown life, but his confessor and Mother Elizabeth won out, and Charles finished his studies for the priesthood and was ordained in 1901. Later that year he left for Algeria to take up the life of a hermit in the desert.

In the desert, one thing became increasingly clear to Father de Foucauld. Neither the Mohammedans nor the pagans of Africa were yet ready to be converted. Ignorance and prejudice were too great for that. He must live in such a way as to make himself a personal example to these people. He would make the first personal contacts that later, much later, would lead to conversions.

Little Brother Charles of Jesus, as he called himself, thought up and wrote down a plan for two religious orders. The members of these orders would live a life patterned on the life of Jesus at Nazareth. They would go and live among the world's poor, sharing all they had, working each day for a living. They would teach only by the example of living a good Christian life in small groups of three to five.

At the time of Brother Charles' death, neither his missionary contacts nor his designs for new religious orders had borne visible fruit. In ten years in the desert, he had not made a single convert, although many of the natives who knew him were devoted to him and thought of him as a holy man. His plans for new orders had not been carried out—the only recruit who came to join him left after only a short while.

In 1916, living among the fierce Tuaregs of Tamanrasset, Charles de Foucauld was murdered in an attempt to warn two Arab soldiers of danger from a group of Senussi rebels. On the evening of December 1, Charles was called out of his house by a familiar voice. Outside, he realized that he had been betrayed, and he was seized by a group of rebels. Leaving a fifteen-year-old boy to guard him, they began to ransack the building. Suddenly, two Arab horsemen were sighted. The captive priest made a gesture to warn them off, and the boy panicked and shot. Little Brother Charles was dead instantly, with a bullet in his brain. Three weeks later, the monstrance with the Host before which Brother Charles had been praying when the marauders appeared was found in the sand, where they had tossed it as a useless object.

The life of Charles de Foucauld was like the biblical seed which had to die before it sprouted into a healthy plant. Within twenty years after his death, there appeared three congregations which derived their inspiration, purpose, and rules from Charles de Foucauld. These Little Brothers of Jesus, Little Sisters of the Sacred Heart, and Little Sisters of Jesus live in small groups all over the world, preaching by the lives they lead. Two other orders, founded later, trace their heritage to Little Brother Charles of Jesus. Each of these groups bases its apostolate on the ideas of the orders which the martyr of the desert had planned, but did not live to see.

A brief resume of the ideals of the Little Brothers of Jesus— founded in 1933—will give an idea of the basis for all five orders. The brothers have an apostolate of presence, rather than of preaching. They live among men and witness to Christ by their actions rather than their words. For the brothers, nothing takes precedence over prayer. They do not take over the leadership of social or civic works, but band together for a life of shared Christian prayer. When a fraternity comes to an area, the Little Brothers do not bring jobs, skills, teachers, or other benefits provided by other orders of the Church. They have an apostolate of personal friendship; their mission is to be friends and make friends, to share the friendship of Jesus Christ. The brothers' homes and their clothes, except for a badge, are the type common to the people among whom they live. Their work does not separate them from the environment they have chosen. Finally, the brothers live a life of poverty rather than security. The need for their type of Christian witness is especially great among the poor and the least favored. They could not share the work and social conditions of their neighbors without being committed to the poverty and uncertainty of such a life. As a part of their family responsibility, each fraternity contributes out of its earnings to the education of the congregation's candidates.

The Little Sisters of Jesus are also based on the above ideals. They consider themselves contemplatives in the world.

Knowledge of the life of Charles de Foucauld has spread throughout the Church. After preliminary investigations, all proved positive, and he was declared Venerable on April 13, 1978.

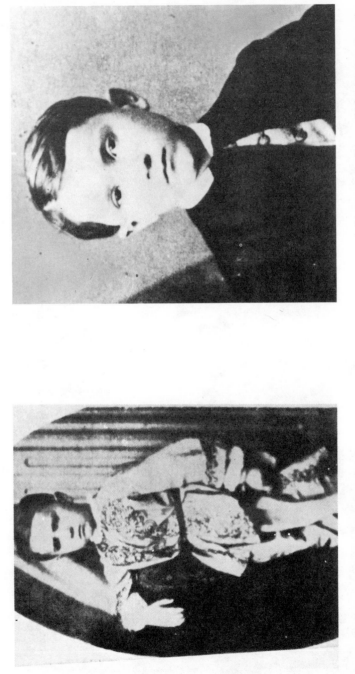

This photograph of the young Viscount Charles de Foucauld shows the willfulness he displayed for most of his early life.

Charles de Foucauld at age six. By age 15 he was an agnostic.

Charles de Foucauld was expelled from school for not doing his work, and later was suspended from the French army in Algeria because of his dissipated life.

The rich young libertine told each of his new mistresses, "I rent by the day, not by the month."

Regarding his conversion, Charles de Foucauld said, "The moment I realized that God existed, I knew I could not do otherwise than live for Him alone."

Gradually, through the example of his cousin Marie, an intelligent and deeply spiritual young woman, the reckless Charles began to regain his faith.

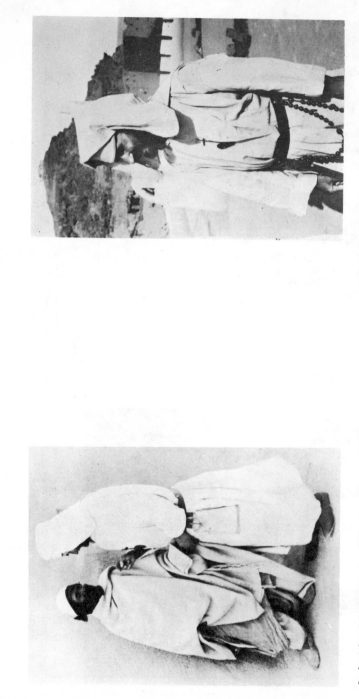

Left: After his conversion, Charles (on the right) took up the life of a hermit. He made himself a simple habit patterned after the common dress of his neighbors in the desert, adding a badge showing the cross and a heart.
Right: Venerable Charles de Foucauld, the hermit of the desert, in his homemade habit.

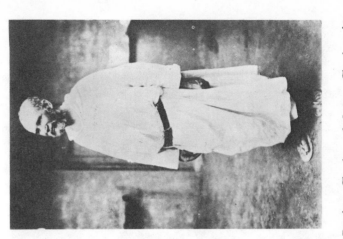

Known as Little Brother Charles of Jesus, Charles de Foucauld was killed at the age of 58. At that time he was living in Tamanrasset, Algeria.

Charles de Foucauld with Paul Bonifa and little Abd-Jesus (Servant of Jesus).

The face of Venerable Charles de Foucauld bears witness to his great transformation of soul.

36

SAINT FRANCES CABRINI

Saint Frances Xavier Cabrini, M.S.C.
Maria Francesca Cabrini
1850 - 1917
Italy - United States
Died Age 67

Though born prematurely and afflicted with chronic poor health, little Maria Francesca Cabrini grew up to be one of the most active missionaries the Church has ever known. She opened sixty-seven charitable institutions and houses of her religious order. In carrying out this prodigious activity, she practiced such heroic virtue that in 1946 she became the first American citizen to be canonized a saint. Her canonization took place within only twenty-eight years of her death.

Francesca was born July 15, 1850, at San Angelo in Lombardy, Italy. Her devout parents, Agostino and Stella, had the frail baby baptized the same day for fear she would not live. They maintained an ideal Catholic family life. Francesca was the youngest of thirteen children; her older sister, Rosa, took particular interest in Cecchina, as the new baby was called. Rosa's discipline greatly influenced Francesca.

When Francesca was about thirteen, a visiting missionary preached about the Chinese missions, and the young girl began to dream of being a missionary herself. In spite of the teasing of her older sister, she held to her dream. Geography became her favorite school subject.

Francesca attended the boarding school of the Daughters of the Sacred Heart at Arluno, and studied for the teaching profession. She passed her finals with distinction.

For several years, she taught in a village school, spending her spare time nursing the sick poor. She felt she had a vocation to become a sister, but two communities turned her down because of her poor health. When she was twenty-four, her bishop and her parish priest asked that she go to the House of Providence at Codogno to work with the young girls there. Although she believed she would be there only a short while, Francesca actually stayed for six years, until the Bishop of Lodi closed the institution and sent for her. At Codogno, Francesca had been considered an intruder, and several of the women had treated her with insults and disrespect. Here, under impossible circumstances, Francesca made great strides in the practice of humility and the formation of her religious spirit.

In an audience, the bishop told Francesca, "You always wanted to be a missionary. I know of no such order for women. Why not begin one yourself?"

The suggestion that this quiet and retiring young woman begin a new religious order—at a time when the anticlericals were shutting down many religious works and suppressing entire orders—was a daring and apparently foolhardy one. But after a moment of silence, with no argument about the difficulty of such a task, Francesca quietly answered, "I will look for a house."

The beginnings of the Institute of the Missionary Sisters of the Sacred Heart were modest and poor. Francesca added the name Xavier to her own, in honor of the great apostle of the Indies.

The first convent of Mother Cabrini's order was an abandoned Franciscan monastery. She and seven other young women spent the first night in their new home with no light, and said their prayers in the dark. For beds, they dragged in clean piles of hay from the fields. On November 14, 1880, the first Mass was offered in a room hastily fitted as a chapel.

Soon, young girls from the neighboring towns began to flock to the new order. Mother Cabrini's wise and gentle direction and her obvious love for her sisters and zeal for the missionary apostolate drew recruits.

Although funds were often scarce, Mother Cabrini's great trust in the Providence of God helped the sisters maintain their own unlimited confidence. Soon, expansion to three other houses was necessary in order to take care of the many postulants. In Milan, the sisters ran a home for girls attending the university and teacher training schools there.

Mother Cabrini's next target was Rome. When a good friend and advisor heard of her projected trip there, he cautioned her that she might make a laughingstock of her institute. "Are you mad? You should leave this sort of thing to the saints!" he exclaimed.

In spite of the opposition and the fact that the young institute had no funds with which to open a house in Rome, Mother Cabrini and another sister went to Rome to request an audience with the pope. In Rome, the sisters were unable to obtain a personal interview with the pope, but they spoke with his vicar, Cardinal Parocchi. After Mother Cabrini expressed her wish to establish her sisters in Rome, the vicar questioned her closely. When asked whether she had the necessary funds, or patrons who would provide the money, Mother Cabrini calmly told him that she did not. In addition, the institute was young. The cardinal was puzzled, but the large blue eyes of the nun were full of trust. He advised her to return home and come again in a few years. Mother Cabrini left the audience and hurried to a nearby church where she poured out her grief to Our Lord in prayer.

A few days later, the cardinal received her again. He asked if she was ready to obey. "Of course," she answered.

"Well then," he smiled, "you will not open one house in Rome, but two."

Early in 1889, Pope Leo XIII called Mother Cabrini to him. Her missionary dreams were to be fulfilled—but not to the East. Pope Leo told her to go to America, where there were many poor Italian immigrants who needed help in many forms. With no hesitation, Mother Cabrini and six of the sisters prepared to go.

In spite of her own great fear of water, Mother Cabrini and the sisters sailed for America, landing in New York in March of 1889. She had been promised that a house would be waiting for her.

Mother and the sisters spent their first night off the ship in a dingy boardinghouse near Chinatown. Still exhausted from seasickness, they sat up in hard chairs, for the beds were filthy and crawling with bugs.

After Mass the next morning, the sisters called on the archbishop, who was greatly embarrassed. The plans for the Italian orphanage had fallen through, and he had mailed a letter telling the sisters to remain in Italy—but they had already left. He regretfully advised them to return on the same ship which had brought them over.

Mother Cabrini solemnly told him, "No, Your Excellency, this I cannot do. I came here by order of the Holy See, and here I must stay."

Three months later when she returned to Italy, Mother Cabrini had already managed to open an orphanage and a school. In all,

Mother Cabrini crossed the ocean twenty-five times, and on succeeding trips she made foundations in more than eight American cities as well as in Central and South America. Everywhere she went, schools, orphanages, hospitals, and other charitable institutions sprang up. In the sick and poor of the slums, Mother Cabrini saw Christ. She did all in her power to help them through spiritual and corporal works of mercy.

Mother Cabrini was naturalized as a citizen of the United States in 1909, in Seattle.

Throughout all her bustling activity and her great missionary accomplishments, Mother Cabrini kept a peaceful inner life, never forgetting that she was made for God alone, to do His Will. Her maxim was, "I can do all things, *in HIM*." Some lines from her retreat notes show her total submission to the Will of God for her own life: "O Jesus, I love You very much. . . Give me a heart as big as the universe. . . Tell me what You wish that I do, and do with me as You will."

There are several recorded instances indicating that Mother Cabrini's prayer life was rewarded with a number of special favors. She made light of these few instances, and attempted to keep her own interior life hidden. A minor case in point is that of a sister who had suffered for several years from varicose veins. Her doctor advised her to wear elastic stockings at all times. Instead, she somehow obtained a pair of Mother Cabrini's cotton stockings, put them on, and felt instantly cured. The next day, seeing the sister walking briskly, Mother Cabrini asked what had happened. When the sister confessed about wearing her stockings, Mother Cabrini became serious and told her, "I hope you are not so foolish as to say my stockings cured you. I am wearing them all the time and they do me no good. It was your faith that did it. Say nothing about it."

In 1917, Mother Cabrini died peacefully in her room in Columbus Hospital in Chicago. In spite of the fact that she had discounted any talk of "miracles" in her life, soon after her death God began to answer prayers through the intercession of this fervent missionary.

More than 150,000 petitions and reports of favors were addressed to the Holy Father by people of every walk of life and from all parts of the world. Pius XI appointed a postulator, and at his request the Archbishop of Chicago, Cardinal Mundelein, opened the informative process in 1928. This was eleven years after Mother Cabrini's death. Her beatification in 1938, within twenty-one years of her death, was one of the fastest in modern times. Mother Cabrini was canonized on June 7, 1946.

St. Frances Xavier Cabrini at age 55. This photograph, taken in 1905 at the opening of Columbus Hospital in Chicago, has become her official portrait. It has been retouched to show a halo.

This picture was taken when Mother Cabrini first came to America at age 39. The sisters caught her by surprise when she was praying.

This photograph is from a group shot made July 4, 1914, at the dedication ceremony the mission at Dobbs Ferry, New York, three years before St. Frances Cabrini's death. Many years earlier, her missionary zeal had led a friend and advisor to exclaim, "Are you mad? You should leave this sort of thing to the saints!"

37

BLESSED MARY FORTUNATA VITI

Blessed Mary Fortunata Viti, O.S.B.
Anna Felice Viti
1827 - 1922
Italy
Died Age 95

The gift of free will means that man must spend his entire life on earth making choices. At times, the choice between good and evil is clear, and decision is easy. At other times, the situation is unclear, and decision is difficult. The measure of heroic virtue lies in the choices made between good and better than good. The life of Blessed Fortunata Viti was a continuing series of choices made for that which was better, in humility and devotion to the love and power of God.

Blessed Fortunata's life provides an example of the goodness which can grow despite a background of family problems. Anna Viti was the third of nine children born into a pleasant and somewhat prosperous home. Her mother remained true to her religious beliefs until her early death at the age of thirty-six. Her weak father, however, provided a bad example for the family. He became an alcoholic gambler, and soon squandered the family resources by his intemperate mode of life. Anna's mother, worn with the care of her children, died of a heart attack when Anna was only fourteen.

The care and running of the entire household fell onto the young but capable shoulders of Anna, as her older sister had left home to enter a convent. Anna's attitude toward her father, whose behavior embarrassed and distressed her, was the result of a first great decision. This father who had brought about the ruin of his family and the early death of their well-loved mother was always treated with love and respect by his daughter. When her younger sister declared that she hated her father, Anna gently instructed her and the other brothers and sisters by telling them, "It is the command of God that we honor and love our father and mother; who disregards this commandment offends Almighty God and does not share in the blessings of the fourth commandment." Anna knew that God's law still held, even when the parent in question was a weak man and apparently a great sinner. This father was a burden to his children for thirty-four years, but Anna never failed in her respect. On his death she recorded this simple message in her prayerbook: "March 22, 1875. Today our very dear father, Luigi, died."

Because they had so many mouths to feed, for a time the family lived on the charity of the Benedictine nuns of the town. In gratitude, Anna gave her only earthly treasure, her mother's pearls, to the shrine of Our Lady at the monastery. For three years she worked as a servant for a wealthy family in a nearby town.

Anna began to think of entering the cloister in a convent a few miles away. By this time her brothers and sisters had grown enough to be able to survive without her financial help. Here, too, she faced a difficult choice. Anna was an attractive young woman, physically graceful with lovely blond hair. In addition, she had a cheerful and pleasing disposition. A wealthy young man fell in love with her and proposed marriage. In spite of the fact that she was poor and nearly illiterate, he wanted to marry her. As he said, "She is good, and kind, and beautiful."

Anna realized that marriage to the young man would assure her family of comfort and education. However, she felt that God was calling her to dedicate herself to Him in the convent, and she kindly declined the young man's proposal.

Anna decided to enter the cloister in her home town of Veroli, rather than the one a few miles away, the one to which she had first felt attracted. The choice was fortunate, for later this first convent was confiscated by the government. In the end, the few sisters left there were sent away from the religious life entirely, to live on the charity of friends and relatives.

At the age of twenty-four, Anna entered the cloistered Benedictine convent. Here another choice awaited her. Although she had had little schooling, and could not read and write well, her superiors noticed her native intelligence which they thought would fit her for the life of a choir religious. They offered to continue her education in preparation for this vocation. Anna, however, declined, preferring the simple life of a lay sister. In this order, lay sisters carry on the domestic work of the community.

The reason for her decision came to light a few years later. A fellow lay sister complained that in her work she was no better than a servant. Sister Fortunata replied, "Don't let that bother you. I was offered the choice of becoming a choir nun, and I would have loved to sing the praise of God. To me, these sisters are like God's angels. But I chose rather to be a lay sister, in order to have greater opportunity to practice humility."

The following note was found jotted in her diary: "I am fortunate to be given this opportunity to become a saint. I want to become a saint. If I bungle in this life, I will spoil things forever. If things turn out well, and I am equal to the task, I will achieve happiness and become a saint."

Many people living in the world today consider cloistered nuns to be useless, impractical, or escapists. The active orders are admired for their work, but those who "shut themselves off from the world" are somehow suspect in our active age; they seem to be only a carry-over from the Middle Ages. But how fortunate are those who have seen the happiness and total dedication to God in the cloister, or felt the effects of the great unceasing work of prayer there. The vocation to the cloister is understandable if we realize that loving God is the most important work there is. And, rather than shutting the world out, these sisters love God's creatures all the more deeply; they spend their lives interceding for mankind.

Sister Fortunata received the special grace needed for the cloistered religious life. Her physical work as a lay sister consisted of all manner of domestic service to the other sisters. In particular, she mended clothes and altar vestments, served for a time as infirmarian, and spun thread. She spent seventy-two years in a routine that, for anyone who did not make her entire existence a prayer in honor of God, would have quickly become boring or stifling.

During this great length of time, Sister Fortunata did not go back into the world, but the world nevertheless came to her. If a visitor to the convent, or any of the school children were missing, it was taken for granted that they would be found with Sister Fortunata, listening to her warm and loving advice. She attempted to remain in the background, but visitors sought her out. She was apparently gifted with an uncanny ability to see into the hearts of people and give them the words of encouragement and advice they needed. When one of her sisters asked how she knew just the right words of understanding to say to her, Sister Fortunata simply replied that God had told her what to say. By this she did not mean that she heard a voice from

Heaven. She simply meant that God gave her the ability to speak the appropriate words of comfort and love.

Following the advice of St. Benedict, the founder of her order, Sister Fortunata practiced no excessive penances. Indeed, she counseled against them. Her penances consisted in small things which would not damage her health, but which were equally fine gifts for God. She would deny herself seasoning for her food, or stretch herself out on the bare floor to pray.

God bestowed several extraordinary supernatural gifts on His faithful servant, Fortunata, but they were not made much of during her lifetime. By and large, these were stored and treasured in the hearts of her fellow religious, confessors, and friends until after her death.

One such gift was the gift of prophecy. Occasionally Sister would predict an unexpected event, and in time it would happen. For example, two aspirants once entered the monastery; one was healthy, apparently with a strong vocation. The other was weak, and entered with doubts. Sister Fortunata comforted the weaker of the two, telling her to persevere as she would stay and the other would not. In spite of the belief of the sisters to the contrary, this is exactly what happened. Another time, Sister Fortunata quietly began to cry during Mass. She had seen that this priest would leave the priesthood, and she was filled with sadness for and with him. She predicted that yet another priest would abandon his vocation but would repent and return.

At times, mystical phenomena caused her trials and sometimes physical suffering. She attempted to keep these to herself, but they came to the notice of her superiors. At first they thought Sister Fortunata might be afflicted with a nervous disorder, so they investigated very thoroughly. Their investigations showed her to have a very well-balanced personality. She calmly resisted the attacks with prayer and the Sign of the Cross.

When Sister Fortunata was eighty-eight years old, her confessor apparently recognized that hers was a uniquely favored soul, and he told her to write a spiritual diary. This was an extreme act of humility for Fortunata, as she knew she could not spell or write well. Obedient to the wish of the confessor, she trusted him to see through her mistakes in grammar and spelling in order to read her meaning.

After more than twenty-five thousand days in the cloister, Sister Fortunata became too ill with old age to carry on any longer. Until three days before her quiet and peaceful death, she struggled to make herself useful to her sisters, even at the advanced age of ninety-five. She was buried simply and quietly in the local cemetery. Few, if any, of her sisters suspected that a saint had been living so long with them.

The people of Veroli who had visited her in the convent now began to visit her grave, still seeking Sister Fortunata's wise counsel and help. For the next thirteen years, devotion to this humble lay sister spread over Europe and across the ocean.

The decree proclaiming her heroic virtue was published in 1964, and by 1967 the two miracles necessary for beatification were certified. Two women, who as children had been cured of tubercular meningitis through the intercession of Fortunata, were happy to stand with the crowd at the beatification ceremony on October 8, 1967.

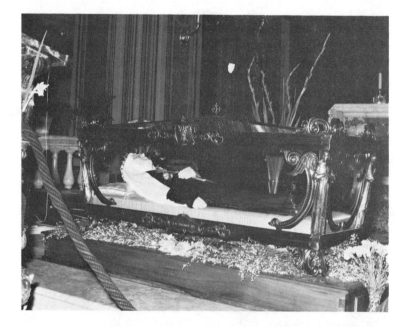

Blessed Mary Fortunata Viti spent 72 years in prayer and domestic work in the cloister and died at age 95. The wax figure in this glass casket covers her skeleton; it is located at her shrine in Veroli, Italy.

Before leaving home to become a nun at age 24, Sister Mary Fortunata insisted that her brothers and sisters respect their father, although he was an alcoholic and a gambler, and had brought about the early death of their beloved mother. Regarding her religious vocation, she wrote, "I am fortunate to be given this opportunity to become a saint. I want to become a saint. If I bungle in this life, I will spoil things forever. If things turn out well, and I am equal to the task, I will achieve happiness and become a saint."

38

MOTHER MARY WALSH

Mother Mary Walsh, O.P.
Mary Walsh
1850 - 1922
England - United States
Died Age 72

On Friday morning, November 10, 1922, the solemn Requiem Mass for Mother Mary Walsh was offered at the Church of St. Vincent Ferrer in New York city. Into the large, cathedral-like church filed hundreds of men and women from all walks of life and of all races and creeds. Numerous members of the clergy—from the Archbishop of New York to simple parish priests—women religious from many orders, representatives of lay organizations, and individual mourners came to pay their last respects to this remarkable woman who had dedicated her life to God in the service of His sick poor. Perhaps most impressive of all were the hundreds of poor people in shabby clothes who came with a final tribute of love and gratitude to the humble Irish immigrant who had begun a great work, a work carried on today by the religious order she founded, the Dominican Congregation of the Immaculate Conception.

On her way to work as a laundress one sweltering summer day in 1876, Mary Walsh noticed a small girl of about seven sitting in a doorway crying. She stopped to ask what was the matter, and the child led her to a dingy tenement room in the Hell's Kitchen section of New York city.

In this small room on the fourth floor, incredibly hot, dirty, and gloomy, Mary found a critically ill woman with a newborn child dead at her side. Three other children under five huddled in a corner. No food or medicine were to be found among the filth. Mary washed the woman's face and wrapped the dead infant in a blanket, removing it from its mother's sight. After talking to the sick woman, Mary learned that her husband was in jail for drunkenness and fighting. Telling the woman that she would be back shortly, Mary returned to her own room and got out her small savings. Meeting several friends on the way, she told them of the Dunne family's situation, and begged them in the name of Christ to help in any way they could. Within a few days, she had begged aid and substantially helped the family in several ways. Fresh bedding and clothes were brought. The dead child was buried, food and medicine were purchased, and the gas bill was paid. Mary talked to the father upon his release from jail, and persuaded him to promise to try to stop drinking so much. A good man, he had simply been overwhelmed by steadily decreasing fortunes. Mary talked to his employer and persuaded him to give Mr. Dunne another chance. Her dedicated care for this family brought more than simply material improvement—it also brought hope.

For Mary, these efforts brought the loss of her job as a laundress for a well-to-do family. In dismissing her, the employer told Mary that her actions were foolish and impractical. However, she acknowledged Mary's courage; faced with the choice of keeping her job or helping the Dunne family, she had unhesitatingly chosen the latter. From this incident, Mary turned her steps to a path of service to the poor that never wavered for the next forty-six years.

Mary Walsh was born in an Irish section of London, probably in 1850. Her parents had moved to England because of the economic pressures in Ireland after the potato famine. Mary's parents died of black diphtheria while she was an infant, and her paternal grandmother came over to take her back to Ireland. Mary lived with her grandmother and her aunt in Knockaderry, County Limerick, until she was eighteen. As a young child she first attended a Catholic school taught by the Sisters of Mercy, and later a National School. She would get up early and finish her chores, then travel to school by walking or riding a donkey. It was not far to the school, but the roads were rough, and travel difficult.

Mary's grandmother, who was like a mother to her, gave Mary a good, well balanced religious upbringing. In addition, she saw to it that Mary learned several practical skills such as embroidery and fine needlework. When her grandmother died, the eighteen-year-old girl was faced with the task of making her own living. Her maternal uncle urged her to go with him when he returned to the United States, and offered to pay her fare. He had a large family, and Mary's help would be welcome. She traveled with him to Pennsylvania, but lived with the family for less than a year. Her aunt was a difficult woman, and as soon as Mary had repaid the price of her ticket through service, she left for New York to seek domestic employment. Her specialty was laundry work, and for ten years she served as a laundress in the homes of several wealthy families.

During this time Mary attended the parish of St. Vincent Ferrer, where the pastor, Father Dominic Lilly, was a Dominican priest. Under his direction, she became a Dominican tertiary, a member of a secular order or "third order" whose members lived their lives with special striving toward perfection. Her days were filled with work to earn her living, attending the meetings of the tertiaries, and giving help to the poor whom she began to seek out. Feeling drawn to the religious life, she asked Father Lilly about the possibility of becoming a nun. She wished to enter a cloistered order, but he dissuaded her from this idea, and counseled her to wait.

As Mary went daily to help those in need, she became more and more aware of their problems. This awareness translated itself into immediate action. Father Lilly said of her, "It is amazing . . . what Mary Walsh can accomplish for the poor and sick with no funds or resources. Sometimes it is hard for me to believe the evidence."

The sympathetic interest shown by this plain young woman seemed to draw forth confidences from all who came in contact with her. She was shocked by the marriages being broken because of the discouragement of extreme poverty. Men and women lived in constant fear of eviction from even the filthy overcrowded tenements they called home. New York at this time had few relief agencies and no visiting nurse service. The poor were frightened of the impersonal hospitals. Mary realized that if these people could be aided temporally, they might then also be reached spiritually. She recognized the souls that hid inside the broken bodies and crushed spirits she saw.

Mary realized that her life's work was to be among the poor. At the time of her reception into the Third Order of St. Dominic in the fall of 1879, she had chosen the name of Sister Mary Magdalene. Shortly after this date, she and a co-worker, another tertiary, moved into rented rooms in the parish of St. Paul the Apostle, and began to support themselves and their work by taking in washing.

To this first helper, Mary said, "Our road will be rocky and the human side of us will get discouraged sometimes, but we cannot fail, for God is our ally. When you think of it like that, it is truly wonderful, isn't it?"

Mary's road was indeed rocky, and personal hurts and insults often came her way. But through every trial and personal injury, she trusted implicitly in the Providence and direction of God.

The two women began a plan of prayer, manual labor, and works of charity. As far as possible, they worked the first three days of the week and spent the rest of their time working among the poor. On Thursdays, they solicited money and begged food and clothing. The large wicker baskets they carried soon became known to all in the neighborhood. On Saturdays they distributed the food and goods they had earned or begged earlier in the week. Then, too, they gave nursing care to those who needed it, cleaning house and bathing the children when this was necessary. During their first two years, they cared for about twenty families on a regular basis.

The two women worked hard, often ironing late into the night. They spent little on their own accomodations, preferring to give what they had to those who were in greater need. In the spring of 1881, Sister Mary's co-worker became ill, and as they had no money for coal, the rented room was uncomfortably cold. One morning, after her helper had complained bitterly about their circumstances, Sister Mary found a quarter on the street as she was starting out to collect the laundry. With this coin, she went to Murphey's Coal and Wood and ordered a quarter's worth of coal. She realized that the amount of coal would be small, but the store owner promised to deliver it that morning. At least it would provide heat for a short while, and enable her to have hot water for the laundry. When she reached home, a smiling co-worker and a warm room greeted her. An oversized container of coal leaned against the wall, with a note from the vender. It read, "Miss Mary, a man standing near you overheard your order for a quarter's worth of coal. He questioned me after you left and then paid for a five dollar order to be delivered to your flat. He didn't tell me his name. I had never seen him in my store till this morning. So I am returning your money. You'll be using it now on someone else, I know." This incident and the anonymous benefactor were never forgotten. This was only one of the many gifts that supported and encouraged Sister Mary in her work throughout the years.

A friendly and sympathetic pastor of the Paulist church, Father Nevins, sent for Sister Mary and told her of his appreciation of her work. He was convinced that her vocation was to nurse the sick poor in their homes, and expressed his willingness to help the work expand. He hoped to enlist other young women. In 1885, two new recruits came to join the original tertiaries in their life of service. Through the years, some of the recruits left; the extreme hardship and poverty were too difficult for some who were attracted to the good they saw being accomplished.

In the early days, the sisters were often no better off financially than the poor they served, but Sister Mary's keen sense of humor got them through many a depressing time, once with quite surprising results. On this occasion, the sisters were entirely without food. Sister Mary began telling her companion, Sister Dominic, stories of her childhood in Ireland, and she perfectly imitated an old rooster that had lived on the family farm. Sister Mary was a good mimic, and the two sisters began laughing. Sister Mary had just repeated her imitation when a knock on the door signaled the presence of the next door neighbor, whose apartment was separated from theirs by a thin wall. The irate man exclaimed, "For Heaven's sake, get rid of that rooster and let a man get some sleep!" With that, he pushed a five dollar bill into the surprised sister's hand and went back home to bed.

In 1887, Sister Mary was called to a basement apartment where she found an old man in his final illness. With him lived a little five-year-old child, Mary Cepheda Napp, his cousin's orphaned daughter. The old man asked Sister Mary to care for her after his death, which she promised to do. Although she probably intended only to care for the child until a suitable home could be found, somehow Mary Cepheda stayed on. After consulting her spiritual director, Father Nevins, Sister Mary opened her home to the little girl until she was grown. At eighteen, she became a tertiary and one of the helpers until her early death from spinal meningitis.

At this time, a change became apparent in the attitude of the first co-worker who had come to assist Sister Mary in her work. Shortly after Mary Cepheda's arrival, this woman severed her association and left. Twenty-four years later, this same woman wanted to rejoin the group of sisters who had just been given official recognition as affiliates of the Dominican order. The novice mistress who interviewed her refused to admit her, and she left angrily, swearing to "get even." One of Sister Mary's greatest sorrows came through this woman.

Although Sister Mary had had nothing to do with refusing her admittance, the woman determined on a cruel revenge for her rejection. In 1913, this former co-worker wrote a letter to Sister Mary Walsh. Sister Mary shared the letter only with her sub-prioress, and that only to ask help in planning how to defend her sisters. This former friend and companion had written a slanderous accusation that Sister Mary was the mother of Mary Cepheda. Further, she stated that the accusation had been sent to the Archbishop of New York and the Dominican provincial. She also promised to spread the slander to everyone. In the presence of the sub-prioress, Sister Mary wept unrestrainedly, but her concern was for the damage such slander might do to the infant community. After a few moments, she told Sister Reginald, "I'll put this in the hands of God. He will protect our community. With all my heart and soul I believe that." Then she cautioned Sister Reginald, "The sisters must not know. God will take care of us. I am not afraid now."

But what were Sister Mary's feelings toward the one who had become, in effect, a Judas? Her words to Sister Reginald were, "There is only one thing I wish for [the name of the first associate], and that is if she ever needs us, I hope that we will learn of it in time to take care of her." This wish came true after Sister Mary's own death. Nearly fifteen years later, someone reported a woman badly in need of care. One of the sisters went to help, and soon learned that this was the foundress' first helper. At first unresponsive, she gradually warmed to the sister's love. One day, the repentant woman told the sister, "I hurt Mother Mary [Walsh] terribly when I wrote that lie and I did her a great harm. Many times, I have been sorry that I ever left her." Within a few months, the woman died. The sisters who cared for her knew that they had carried out the express wish of their foundress.

Mother Mary Walsh is remembered for the wise and practical advice she gave to her sisters. She often told stories on herself as illustrations. Humility was a virtue she prized highly and strived constantly to attain. Though practicing humility was not always easy for her, many people will testify that this was one of her most outstanding character traits. She herself said, "Humility can be given a dignity of its own."

She recalled an incident that occurred when one other sister and three children were living with her. "When I delivered a big basket of freshly laundered clothes to a certain woman, she was indignant at my price, but I knew my rate was fair and that she was able to pay what I asked. She mumbled and grumbled and then she paid me, but in a most ungracious manner. She threw the money on the floor at my feet. My Irish blood boiled for a moment! I was really furious and I was tempted to let the money lie there, turn my back and go. But I realized that if I did not take it up the children would not have any supper that night and they should not be put to bed hungry because my pride had been hurt. So I got down on my knees and picked up the money, piece by piece. When I arose, the woman seemed ashamed of what she had done and she said hesitatingly, 'Sister, I'd like to give you some apples to take to the children.' I accepted them, of course, for the children loved apples which I could not often buy for them, and I knew the gift was an attempt to make amends for the rudeness."

Sister Mary's humility led her, in the early days of the community, to request that a seemingly more able superior be appointed in her place. This young woman was educated and capable. Indeed, she accomplished much good for the group. However, like many others who have easy access to drugs, she began to misuse them to help in coping with the strain of her life. When Sister Mary noticed this, she quietly went to her spiritual director to present the problem to him. Misunderstanding her motives, and unwilling to believe what she was telling him, he sent Sister Mary herself away for a "rest for her health," strictly cautioning her not to speak of the matter to anyone. Sister Mary spent almost three years in this exile from her community. No one who was associated with her at this time recalls a single uncharitable word about the reason she had been sent away from the other sisters. At last, someone—possibly a member of the superior's own family—spoke to the proper ecclesiastical authorities who investigated and quietly had the woman placed in a private psychiatric hospital, where she eventually recovered.

Vindicated, and reassured that both her spiritual director and the sisters were eager to have her back, Sister Mary returned—not in a spirit of triumph, but rather with humility, holding no grudge and refusing to talk of the past. She simply began quietly to look to the future and rebuild the young community.

On August 4, 1910, Sister Mary received word that a dream she had cherished for many years was finally a reality. The little group which over the years had come together to serve the sick poor was officially affiliated with the Dominican order. Up to that time, Sister Mary had spent thirty-four years working for God in the slums of New York city. To many, she had become known as the "holy washerwoman." Now, at the age of sixty, this humble tertiary became a Dominican religious. What did Sister Mary Walsh think of her own role in founding this little congregation? She said, "Who am I, to think that I am somebody? Poor and uneducated, I could never have done anything on my own. No one knows my unworthiness more than I do. I am God's instrument, but why He chose me I will never venture to guess."

Sister Mary humbly refused to be dispensed from making a novitiate with the others when they were formally affiliated with the Dominican order. A sister from another order was brought in as novice mistress and temporary superior; in company with her sisters, most of them years younger than she, Sister Mary followed the prescribed training. The novice mistress said, "Sister Mary accepted correction better than any religious I ever knew. I gave her many penances and humiliations, but never once did she show any sign of disobedience or pride."

The first group of sisters was professed in 1911. Sister Mary was elected Superior General, an office she was to hold for life. Her efforts to guide the sisters in living their vocations were outstanding. The group expanded and accepted an invitation to work in another city. Mother Mary Walsh believed she should communicate with the new group, and when her fingers stiffened with arthritis to the point where she could barely hold a pen, she learned to type.

The sisters took no pay from those they served. Mother Mary taught them to trust completely in God to provide generous benefactors, which He always did. She called God her "Banker."

Mother Mary Walsh recognized the need for annual renewal and refreshment both for her sisters and the sick poor. For the sisters, she insisted on an annual vacation away from their stressful daily environment, and through the generosity of several people, was able to provide a summer home and transportation to it. Also through the generosity of benefactors, she arranged a summer rest for the sick poor. For some, these trips were the first vacations they had ever had. For some of the children, the trips marked their first time out of the city.

Fear was never a part of Mother Mary's life. Once asked if she wasn't afraid of meeting bad characters in the places her work took her, she replied, "When you try to live in the presence of God and do all your work for love of Him, then your fears disappear completely and with them much of what you call 'danger.' "

During her lifetime, Mother Mary's work took her into all sorts of situations, but she never considered a single soul beneath her or undeserving of her help. Once in 1901, a neighbor had reported to the Paulist Fathers that an old woman living alone was dying. One of the priests, believing that the woman might need personal attention before his arrival, asked Sister Mary to hurry to help her prepare for the Last Sacraments. Sister had not known the woman before, but hurried off to see what she could do. On her arrival, the room was so dark that she had to light a candle to see. The smell in the room was terrible, and as Sister Mary entered, a large rat pulled at her skirt. Hearing a pitiful moan from what she took to be a bundle of rags in the corner, she investigated and discovered an elderly woman, distorted with pain. One of her feet was mutilated from the attack of rats. The woman expressed her fear of rats and her gratitude that Sister Mary had come to help. When told that the priest was on his way, she wept to think of the state in which he would find her, but Sister Mary calmly assured her that she would handle everything. Sister made the woman comfortable in a small area of cleanliness she managed to make in the center of the room. She assisted the priest upon his arrival, and stayed with the woman until the city ambulance came to take her to the Almshouse Hospital.

Another time, a rookie policeman was startled in the early hours of a winter morning to see Sister Mary emerge from a house known as the home of a prostitute. In amazement, he asked if she realized the sort of place it was, and how long she had been there. She replied that of course she knew what the house was, and that she had been there most of the night. "But I couldn't let that stand in my way when one of those poor unfortunate women sent for me, could I?" When he learned that the girl had sent for Sister Mary, he began to expostulate about the matter, but Sister Mary scolded him. The young policeman later remembered her parting words, "Never forget, Mr. Clancy, that those people have souls too."

During the last few years of her life, Mother Mary Walsh was often occupied with the business of governing the young religious order she had founded. Under her direction, several new foundations were made, but she never ceased being actively involved in the work her sisters were carrying on. When she was seventy-two, she went to Hampton Bays to see some of the sisters who were convalescing there and to talk with the sister who would be the superior of the new mission soon to be opened in Denver. While there,

Mother Mary suffered an attack of angina pectoris, and died two days later, after receiving the Last Sacraments.

Today Mother Mary Walsh's sisters continue her work in five dioceses in the United States. They are known as the Dominican Sisters of the Sick Poor.

Mary Walsh, a young Irish immigrant living in New York, was dismissed from her job for helping a family in distress. She and a helper began an apostolate to the sick poor; they supported themselves and their work by taking in laundry. Mary Walsh became known as "the holy washer-woman." This photograph shows her as a Dominican tertiary.

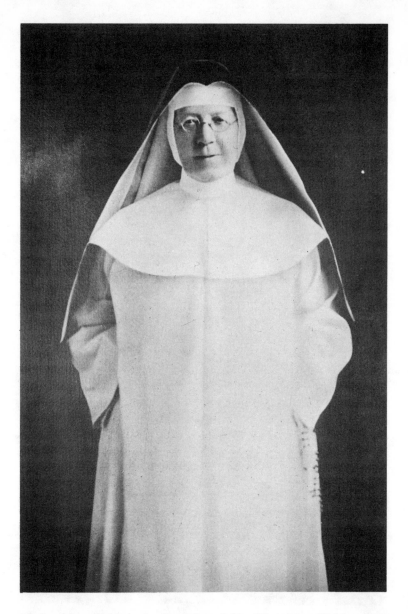

Mother Mary Walsh in the Dominican habit. When Mary Walsh was 60 years old, her community was officially recognized by the Church; she and her followers became the Dominican Congregation of the Immaculate Conception (also called the Dominican Sisters of the Sick Poor).

Mary Cepheda Napp came to live with Mother Mary Walsh when she was a five-year-old orphan. She later became a Dominican tertiary and helped with the charitable work until her early death of spinal meningitis.

39

SAINT RAPHAELA

Saint Raphaela Mary of the Sacred Heart, A.C.J.
Raphaela Francisca del Rosario Rudesinda de Porras
1850 - 1925
Spain - Italy
Died Age 74

In the early years of the 1920's, an elderly nun could be seen dusting and sweeping in the convent of the Handmaids of the Sacred
Heart in Rome. She was known as Mother Raphaela Mary of the
Sacred Heart, but few people know the true story of her life.
Although Mother Raphaela Mary had founded the order and been
its first superior, dissension led her to resign her office for the good
of the community. The leaders of the order, including her own
sister, then declared her mentally deficient and sent her to this
Roman convent of the order to keep her away from their community. They even went so far as to claim all the credit for the
beginning of the order. In her obituary, Mother Raphaela Mary is
listed simply as "one of the first members of the institute."

For almost thirty-three years, Raphaela's only concern was to
fulfill God's Will by leading a humble and obedient life. This she did
with silent serenity and great charity. In 1977, this saint of silence
was given to the Universal Church as an example of heroic charity
and humility.

Raphaela was born March 1, 1850, to a Spanish family of well-
to-do landowners with extensive olive groves. When she was five,
her father died nursing the victims of the cholera plague then raging
in the district. Raphaela, her only sister Dolores and her brother
Henry were taught at home by a priest tutor. Many years later,
Raphaela recalled the most important lesson she learned from him.

One day, she was vainly admiring herself in the mirror, rearrang-
ing her curls and smiling at how attractive she was. Suddenly, her
tutor came up behind her and asked, "Raphaelita, how do you think
you will look a quarter hour after your death?" Even at an early age,

she had had the opportunity to observe death closely; her father and four of her brothers and sisters had died. Years later, as she told the story, Raphaela said, "That was my conversion."

When Raphaela was nineteen, her mother died. She asked herself a question—and answered it. "For what was I born? To save my soul." For the rest of her life, she held firm to her decision to save her soul. Later, she willingly endured a life of silence and exile as reparation to save the souls of others.

Raphaela and her only sister, Dolores, loved each other very much, but throughout their lives a personality conflict led to many difficulties. Dolores had a very forceful personality and felt that as the elder she was automatically the wiser and more capable.

Raphaela, on the other hand, was a peaceful person. Although she had her own opinions, she learned at an early age that for the sake of peace it was often better to voice them but rarely. Her refusal to enter into arguments was misinterpreted by her friends as a sign that she was mentally slower than they. Although humble, Raphaela was also sensitive, and these attitudes hurt her.

After the death of their mother and a younger brother shortly thereafter, Raphaela and Dolores went into mourning. In the late 1800's, persons in mourning wore plain dark clothes and did not attend parties or other social entertainments for about a year. The sisters met these conditions, and began doing several charitable works. Their friends and relatives thought they were simply being scrupulous about their period of mourning, but in reality, Raphaela and Dolores were living a deeply spiritual life. At the end of the customary mourning period, when the girls failed to resume fancy clothes and begin attending social events, their relatives began to mutter about lost opportunities for marriage and excessive piety.

Both girls felt that they had vocations to the religious life. Knowing that their relatives would object strenuously, Raphaela decided on a daring plan. She and Dolores wished to live for a while as guests of the Franciscan sisters while deciding which order to apply to for admission. With two cousins and a friend, they left for a visit to the convent.

At the convent, a sister appeared and Dolores and Raphaela entered the enclosure, leaving the other three in the waiting room. Finally, one of the sisters came to inform the bewildered trio that the girls were not planning to return. These three were left to spread the news to the other relatives.

The two sisters decided to promise obedience to the clerical superiors and allow them to make the decision of the proper order. These superiors first decided that the girls should become Visitation nuns, and later that they should join a French order which had been recently invited to establish a house in the diocese. Although the girls began their novitiate with this order, difficulties arose between the superiors and the local clergy which resulted in the French sisters' return to France. The sixteen Spanish novices stayed to begin a new community, and the bishop appointed Raphaela as the superior. Again, difficulties arose; the bishop re-wrote the rule, and the sisters felt that the new version was not a true reflection of their vocation. Late one night, they left the convent for Madrid.

From its small beginning in Madrid, the community began to grow rapidly. The sisters' life was both contemplative and active. One reason for the community's rapid growth was the fact that Raphaela combined love with a great deal of common sense in her advice to the sisters.

To a sister who was "languishing," Raphaela wrote, "Take good care of yourself . . . have a good appetite. God does not want His spouses to look as though He fed them on lizards."

To another sister, in danger of losing her serenity, she wrote, "When you are in a panic, mosquitoes look like elephants." A vigorous plea for cheerful service was made with the words, "For God's sake, don't let me hear that you have sour faces!"

Formal approval of the Handmaids of the Sacred Heart was given in 1887. The constitution of the new order required the election of a superior general and four advisors. Raphaela was unanimously elected superior and her sister Dolores, Mother Purisima, and two others were elected advisors. Of these four nuns, Raphaela later wrote in some retreat notes: "I . . . am nailed to my cross with four painful nails. There is no offence on their part, for like Our Lord's nails, they are put there by the Will of the Eternal Father.[I must] live willingly nailed by them."

The advisors were supposed to help the superior govern. Instead, they were a great hindrance to effective government. There were a number of reasons for their actions—a scanty knowledge of canon law, their belief that they were better administrators than Raphaela, and a misunderstanding of their role. The disunion was especially painful for Raphaela because of her own sister's part in it. But she believed that the assistants were doing what they considered best, and never blamed them. Once out of office, she accepted them as legitimate authority to whom she gave unfailing obedience. It is a tribute to Raphaela that no one outside the government of the congregation suspected the strife.

Raphaela resigned her post in March of 1893. At the age of forty-three, at the prime of her physical and mental powers, she ceased to have any part in the government of the order which she had founded. "My duty is to be silent, to pray and to suffer."

Raphaela was well-loved in the community. The new superiors wanted to remove her from the rest of the sisters for fear she would tell the true story of her resignation. She was sent to the Roman house of the order where she was refused any status except that of a former leader. For the next thirty years she did sewing and domestic chores which she found needed to be done, but she was not given any official job to do. Before her resignation, the assistants had spread false rumors about Raphaela, one of which was that she was mentally incompetent. This may partially explain why she was never assigned any official duties.

After Raphaela's resignation, Dolores was elected to the top position. She found the job no easier than her sister had. When the same pattern was repeated in her own life, she began to realize how much she had hurt her sister, and asked how she could make amends. Raphaela simply told her to work for the good of the congregation. Dolores tried, but was not successful. In 1903, she too resigned, and went to Valladolid where she lived the remaining thirteen years of her life. During this time, Raphaela continually wrote to encourage her not to be bitter about her treatment.

Mother Purisima became superior general, and in 1911 was elected to the post for life. Later, however, she was removed from office because she was failing both in mind and in body. In spite of her cruel treatment of Raphaela, Mother Purisima had many qualities for which she was justly admired. During the beatification process, she gave evidence in Raphaela's favor.

In 1906, Raphaela was allowed to tour some of the Spanish houses of the order, but because the nuns received her so joyously, Mother Purisima recalled her to Rome and canceled the remaining scheduled visits. Raphaela was not allowed to visit Dolores before her death.

When Raphaela died at the age of seventy-four, only a few of the sisters remembered her as a superior. The rest, if they even knew she existed, had no idea she was the foundress. At the general council of the order in 1911, Mother Purisima had stated that both the de Porras sisters were mentally deranged. She had gone so far as to accept, in Raphaela's presence, tributes to herself as being mainly responsible for the foundation of the order. To have told the truth when Raphaela died would have gravely damaged her own reputation. Therefore, neither Mother Purisima nor any of the assistants even attended her funeral. No inscription on her tomb even hinted at the part Raphaela had played in the formation of the order. As mentioned earlier, in her obituary she is described only as "one of the first members of the institute."

Within the last ten years of her life, Raphaela developed a serious condition which even after several operations left her with a stiff knee and caused a great deal of pain. Later, a sore which was constantly infected added to the problem. Still she managed to drag herself about with the help of a stick, and she did mending and other small tasks for the sisters. In 1922, she became ill and received the Last Sacraments. She and all the sisters at the Roman house thought her death was imminent. Her prayers at that time for the community so impressed the other sisters that they began to realize that Raphaela was far more than simply a feeble-minded elderly sister.

Raphaela rallied, and for the next three years her sickroom was a magnet, drawing the sisters to the presence of this holy nun. Still, no words of condemnation or attempt at self-vindication came from her. Her days were spent in praying, mending, and suffering. Following the pattern of her life, her last days were days of suffering borne silently and serenely. On her final day, Raphaela knew she was dying, and she said to the infirmarian, "When you think I am dead, keep on saying [prayers] into my ear for I shall hear." Later, she said, ". . . only a little while now. I will await you all in Heaven."

One of Raphaela's confessors had once advised her, "Have a little patience and one day you shall shine as bright as the sun." He did not know how prophetic his words were to be.

"How do you think you will look a quarter hour after your death?" she had been asked. Neither she nor her tutor imagined the wondrous expression of peace and happiness which her face would show after she died.

Thirty years after Raphaela's death, her body was still incorrupt, and thousands came to see one who had loved and been loved by God. Her body has since decomposed. The skeleton lies in a beautiful wax figurine in the chapel dedicated to her in Rome.

In 1938, the superior general elected after the forced resignation of Mother Purisima courageously began an examination of Raphaela's life. After the required investigation by the Church, she was beatified in 1952 and canonized in 1977.

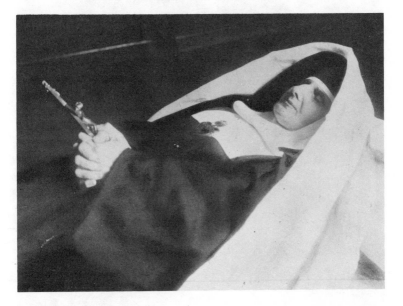

This picture was taken right after St. Raphaela's death. Her body remained incorrupt for 30 years.

St. Raphaela Mary de Porras before she became a nun. Her "conversion" took place when, as a young girl, she was vainly admiring her curls in a mirror; a priest came up behind her and asked, "Raphaelita, how do you think you will look a quarter hour after your death?" This picture has been retouched.

St. Raphaela Mary de Porras, foundress of the Handmaids of the Sacred Heart of Jesus. She was falsely declared mentally incompetent and sent away from the order she had founded. She practiced constant obedience and resignation in this trial, which lasted the rest of her life.

40

ROSE HAWTHORNE LATHROP

Mother M. Alphonsa Lathrop, O.P.
Rose Hawthorne
1851 - 1926
United States
Died Age 75

When the young society matron, Rose Hawthorne Lathrop, heard that her friend Emma Lazarus was stricken with the dread disease, cancer, she hurried to visit her. Emma, a wealthy woman, died soon afterward, surrounded by the best care money could buy.

Rose wondered what happened to the *poor* who were afflicted with this terrible disease. She discovered that they were often shunned like lepers. Once they were diagnosed as incurable, no hospital would continue to care for them, and often their own families rejected them for fear of catching the disease themselves. The only other recourse for the cancerous poor was Blackwell's Island, New York city's last resort for the impoverished. Rose's question, "Why doesn't someone do something for them?" soon changed to "What can I do for them?"

Rose Hawthorne was born on May 3, 1851, the third child of Nathaniel and Sophia Hawthorne. As a young child she lived first in Massachusetts, and then for seven years in England, where her father served as the American consul.

Brought up as a Unitarian, Rose learned many lessons in compassion and kindness from her parents. In one of his writings, her famous father stated, "If a single one of these helpless little ones is lost, the whole world is lost." Rose's later work was in the service of some of God's most abandoned "little ones."

On a trip to Rome after her family's return from England, Rose was walking one day in the gardens of the Vatican. Bumping into a stately priest, she realized to her surprise and horror that it was Pope Pius IX. As her stricken mother rushed forward to apologize, the Holy Father smilingly patted the little girl's red curls and gave her his blessing. Rose never forgot this incident, and one of her childhood treasures was a tiny medal bearing the pope's image.

The family returned to the United States and settled in Concord, Massachusetts. Here Rose's father died when she was thirteen. At fourteen, she entered a school for the first time. Previously, she and her sister had studied at home, concentrating on painting, music and the study of classic literature.

In 1868, the family moved to Germany. Here Rose met a handsome young man who aspired to be a writer. George Lathrop was the son of a New York physician, and he and Rose soon fell in love.

Both families moved to England, and there Rose's mother died.

On September 11, 1871, Rose and George Lathrop married. The young couple soon returned to the United States.

Although Rose and George were both immature and financially unstable, their life was relatively happy until George began to exhibit the intemperance that later would cause the couple much sorrow.

George's literary talent was soon recognized, and he obtained a position as staff critic of the *Atlantic Monthly*. In 1876, a son, Francis Hawthorne, was born and the little boy became the light of both his parents' lives. Unfortunately, he was stricken with diphtheria when he was four and a half, and in spite of excellent medical care, he died.

The heartbroken parents moved to New York, where George's drinking problem worsened. The couple attempted several times and with several moves to make a fresh start to their marriage. In New London, Connecticut, they began to study the Catholic religion, and both were received into the Church in 1891, almost twenty years after their marriage.

The Lathrops soon became associated with many Catholic activities in more than one city. Rose's deep spirituality found an outlet in religious services and practices, and in small attempts at aiding those in need of charity. Her spiritual director cautioned her not to let her religious duties interfere with her duties as a Christian wife; her diary of the time reveals that George held a very high place in her concern and affections.

Unfortunately, George's drinking grew worse, and even dangerous. Life with him became so unbearable that in 1893 Rose applied to the diocesan authorities for permission to leave him, and the request for the separation was granted. Although she never resumed her life with George, notations in her diary show that her love and her prayers stayed with him long after his death.

George's constant drinking led to his death in 1898 at the age of forty-six. Rose had been called to his side at Roosevelt Hospital in New York, but he died before she arrived. She knelt beside his body and offered her prayers that Our Lord would continue to care for him.

When Rose left George, she had no definite plans for her future, but she did feel called to devote herself to God in some charitable work. After hearing the description given by a priest-friend of the death of a poor young woman on Blackwell's Island, she determined to search out and care for cancer patients who were destitute. After the death of her friend Emma Lazarus, Rose had come to a vivid realization of their plight. She later acknowledged, "A fire was then lighted in my heart where it still burns. I set my whole being to endeavor to bring consolation to the cancerous poor."

To prepare for her work, she took a three-month course in nursing at the New York Cancer Hospital. Thinking that the attractive society matron would not last through the first morning, much less the entire course, her instructor began by having Rose watch her change the bandages on the tumorous face of one of the worst-afflicted patients. Although the effort to watch the terrible sight was great, Rose stood the test. Later, one of her primary rules for her helpers was that they must never show their aversion to the terrible wounds and tumors with which they came in contact.

At the age of forty-four, Rose rented a small flat on the lower East side of New York city and began the work she would continue for the rest of her life. She instinctively knew that if she were to work effectively among the poor, she would have to live among them. She began to seek out and nurse the cancerous poor in their own homes, and soon she took in the first of those who had no other place to go. Soon her tiny rented home was too small and she was forced to move to larger quarters. Seeing the abundance of the misery caused by cancer in this area of the city alone, she prayed earnestly for help in her work. In 1897, a young art student from an excellent family, Alice Huber, came to join her. Together the two women continued their charity, constantly besieging Heaven for more help. In time, more help came.

To enlist the aid of the public, Rose began writing articles for newspapers, telling of the problem of the cancerous poor and soliciting bedding, bandages, and financial aid. From the beginning, she determined that she and her followers would accept no pay from, or through contacts of, their patients. She expressed a fear that if they did so, they would wind up caring for those who could afford aid, and neglecting the poor they originally intended to serve. To this day, her sisters maintain this policy, depending on the aid and assistance of their benefactors to provide them with the means to carry on their work.

After George Lathrop's death, Rose and Alice decided to adopt some form of religious life. They even came up with a name—The Daughters of the Puritans—and in spite of Rose's initial reluctance, made a distinctive costume patterned after the early pilgrims' dress. In this somewhat strange attire, they called on the Archbishop of New York to ask permission to wear this mode of dress and to consider themselves a religious work. At this first visit the archbishop spoke sharply to the women, finally advising them to join with a widow who was planning to open a charitable establishment nearby. Although Rose and Alice followed this advice, nothing came of it, for they found that the widow's aims were not at all like their own. In a subsequent interview, the archbishop allowed them to wear their semi-religious habit, and advised them to affiliate themselves with an established religious order. The "Servants of Relief" emerged as a more suitable name, and the archbishop recognized in the two "servants" a true dedication. He later publicly acknowledged and approved their work, and in the years to come was to provide much aid and encouragement to them. During the following year, when the widow he had advised them to join requested that he stop the work of Rose and Alice, the archbishop said, "If it is not God's work, it will fail. If it is His work, no one can destroy it."

In the first years, many hardships befell these two women whose early lives had been so sheltered. Rose found prayer to be a powerful support, and one which never failed. In spite of the hardships, she and Alice persevered in their daily work in the tenement world.

In 1899, after using the newspapers to bombard the public with pleas for help, Rose was able to make a substantial payment on a house on Cherry Street. She and Alice became The Servants of Relief for Incurable Cancer. Following the advice of Father Clement Thuente, O.P., Rose and Alice became Dominican tertiaries. Rose became Sister Mary Alphonsa, while Alice took the name Sister Mary Rose. In 1900, they called on Archbishop Corrigan again, and to their joy he gave them permission to wear the Dominican habit. As more patients came to be cared for, more workers came to join the two sisters in their work.

The Cherry Street home and a small flat across the street for male patients were soon outgrown. One morning on her way to a sick patient, Sister Alphonsa was stopped by a little girl who asked that she come and see her father. The child expressed the belief that he was dying. When Sister Alphonsa reached his room she realized that indeed he did not have much time left, for a sudden hemorrhage had occurred. He died before the doctor could reach him. This incident made her realize that a home was needed where patients could receive constant care. It would have to be large enough for men as well as women. As usual, Sister Alphonsa had recourse to prayer. Her prayers were answered when a group of French Dominican priests who were returning to their homeland offered to sell her a large house, a former hotel, which they had been using for their monastery. The property, located at Sherman Park (now called Hawthorne), stood on top of a hill which the Fathers had named Rosary Hill. The house had sixty rooms, and there were nine acres of land.

Easy terms were arranged, and Sister Alphonsa and four postulants moved in during the summer of 1901. Sister Alphonsa became the superior of this group. They began with five women patients that same month, and soon others came to fill the empty rooms. Sister Rose remained in New York as superior of the group there.

Mother Alphonsa always tried to let the patients do as they liked, as far as this was possible. She maintained a happy, cheerful atmosphere, and believed in spending money on luxury items for the patients as well as on necessities. One time when Sister Rose was out of town, Mother Alphonsa found the key to her cashbox and went on a shopping spree, buying presents for everyone except herself. She spent $150 on a radio, and bought a dog for one of the patients. On another occasion, a parrot was acquired for a patient who had always been glum; he finally cheered up. Many residents perked up remarkably after experiencing the love and tender care given by Mother Alphonsa and the sisters. They no longer felt abandoned. It is no wonder that often a patient would exclaim: "This is Heaven!"

Fire, which had been a constant worry of Mother Alphonsa, finally came to Rosary Hill in 1922. Fortunately the fire was contained, but Mother Alphonsa determined to build a new building which would be fireproof. This was the last of her great dreams, and the work was begun under her direction, although not completed before her death.

Mother Alphonsa died quietly in her sleep in July of 1926. The eulogy at her funeral was given by Bishop Walsh of Maryknoll. Several pages of jottings found after her death give testimony of Mother Alphonsa's constant thought of God in all her work. One of the pages contained these lines: "I will see all things only through the presence of God, thus freeing myself of personality and forgetting my existence. I will regard creatures in the spirit of Jesus Christ."

After Mother Alphonsa's death, *Century Magazine* published a letter from Matilda Chenault Nash, a Protestant lady who had visited the Cherry Street home during Mother Alphonsa's life. She described the experience thus: "How she gained the strength to do what she did, I learned when she led me into a tiny Oratory she had fashioned out in a dark, otherwise unusable corner of the upper hall. The hinges of my heretic knees bent easily enough to prayer when our journey of inspection ended at the foot of the little cross. She strove to comfort me, weakly overcome as I was by what I had seen, and whispered, 'If they bear patiently their suffering here below, they will not be left long in Purgatory.' "

Mother Alphonsa's daughters, the Dominican Servants of Relief, continue her work among poor cancer patients in six dioceses in the United States.

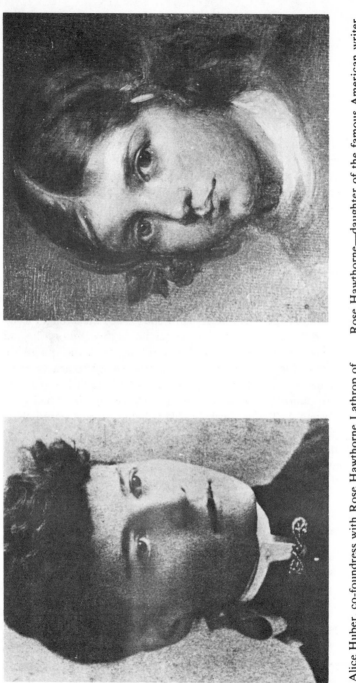

Alice Huber, co-foundress with Rose Hawthorne Lathrop of the Dominican Servants of Relief for Incurable Cancer.

Rose Hawthorne—daughter of the famous American writer, Nathaniel Hawthorne—at age nine.

Rose Hawthorne Lathrop. Rose and her husband George became Catholics almost 20 years after their marriage. Tragically, George's drinking problem became so bad that Rose was granted permission for a separation 22 years after their marriage. The couple's only child died of diphtheria at age four.

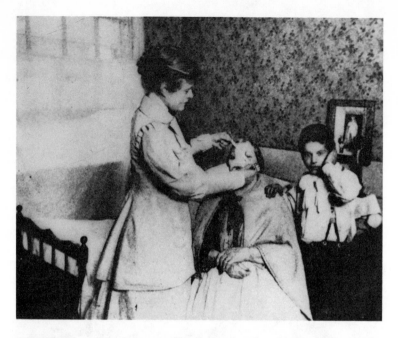

Rose Hawthorne Lathrop nursing a cancer patient in the relief room on
Cherry Street. Later, one of her primary rules for her helpers was that they
must never show their aversion to the terrible wounds and tumors they
saw.

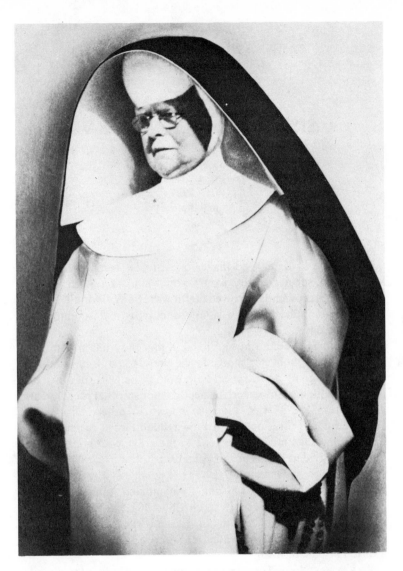

When her community was officially recognized by the Church as a religious order, Rose became Mother Alphonsa. Mother Alphonsa did not like to have her picture taken; here she poses reluctantly. She always tried to let her cancer patients do as they liked, as far as this was possible. Although cancer victims were treated as outcasts by society, Mother Alphonsa and her sisters took them in and were so good to them that often a patient would exclaim, "This is Heaven!"

41

SISTER MIRIAM TERESA

Sister Miriam Teresa Demjanovich, S.C.
Miriam Teresa Demjanovich
1901 - 1927
United States
Died Age 26

From time to time, God makes a particular truth of our Faith known with special clarity to a favored soul. To Sister Miriam Teresa Demjanovich He showed that it was His Will for all, no matter what their state in life, to attain sanctity by a close union with Him every day.

Sister Miriam Teresa herself lived in this close union with God, although throughout her short life she presented a somewhat ordinary, if very good, appearance. Few, even those who knew her well and lived with her, suspected the depth of her spiritual life. God also gave Teresa the mission to make known to others His Will of sanctity for all. Still, outside her own small circle, Sister Miriam Teresa's message might have gone to the grave with her, had God not also provided the means of spreading it.

Miriam Teresa Demjanovich was the youngest of seven children born to Alexander and Johanna Demjanovich, immigrants from Slovakia. Teresa was born March 26, 1901, in Bayonne, New Jersey. She was baptized in an Eastern rite Catholic church, although her family later attended a Latin rite parish after moving to a different part of town.

As a young child, Teresa was the much-loved baby of the family. She preferred boys' games, particularly baseball, and from an early age one of her favorite pastimes was reading. Her brother Charles was her favorite playmate. Teresa remained close to Charles as she grew older; his ordination to the priesthood was an event of great joy for her.

Teresa was exceptionally bright, and began school at the age of four. She entered high school at twelve, and graduated before she was sixteen. She was valedictorian of her elementary class, and graduated with honors from the public high school she attended. Although she was somewhat quiet and retiring, she enjoyed activities with the glee club and other youth-related programs at her parish church. Throughout these years, she was considered a "good," intelligent girl with a gift for writing and a good sense of humor. None who knew her realized the depth of her interior life.

For almost two years after she finished high school, Teresa stayed home to help with the housework and in nursing her mother who was ill. After the death of her mother, and following the wishes her mother had expressed, Teresa entered the College of St. Elizabeth. In June 1923, she received a bachelor's degree in literature with highest honors.

Her college professors recalled that her ability was not confined to a single subject; she excelled in all. She was especially noted for the fact that in scholastic discussions her remarks showed much good, common sense. She made posters, played musical accompaniments, was a graceful dancer, and wrote witty verses. One of her "junior jingles" begins:

> "One night we felt that life was dull, we formed into parade;
> The hour was late, the hall was dim, but we were not afraid.
> We marched, we ran, we slid, we hid . . ."

Teresa put her utmost effort into everything she did.

When her friends needed help, Teresa was always glad to provide it. She was witty, and from time to time she even indulged in a practical joke, although she always stopped such jokes before any unpleasant consequences could arise. In many ways, she seemed to be an ordinary American college student of the twenties, enjoying to the fullest the happy things of life. It was noticed, however, that she liked to spend long periods of time in the chapel.

After her graduation, Teresa taught for a year at St. Aloysius Academy in Jersey City. For many years she had thought of entering a Carmelite convent, but in making a novena asking God to tell her where she should go, she became convinced that He wished her to become a Sister of Charity. She entered the novitiate of the Sisters of Charity of St. Elizabeth at Convent Station, New Jersey, on February 11, 1925. Her new name was Sister Miriam Teresa.

In the novitiate, Sister Miriam Teresa tried to follow the rule of her order as perfectly as possible. She was kind and helpful to the sisters, wrote and directed a play at Christmas, and lived the routine life of the novice. Novices generally did not teach, but since Sister Miriam Teresa had finished college and already had a year's experience, she was sent to teach at the academy run by the sisters. She did not enjoy teaching; in fact, she felt a great aversion to it, but did her best faithfully, as this was God's Will for her.

Most of her fellow novices liked Sister Miriam Teresa and enjoyed her company. One, Sister Maureen Maroney, remembers several acts of special kindness which Sister Miriam Teresa performed for her. The Mistress of Novices had assigned Sister Maureen to read out loud at dinner. She suggested that Sister Maureen go to Sister Miriam Teresa if she needed help in preparation for the readings. In addition to this help, Sister Maureen had trouble in getting used to the proper way to fix the headpiece of her habit, and Sister Miriam Teresa went several times to her dormitory to help her fix it properly.

Another time, one of the novices was scrubbing the floor. She had begun late and would be late finishing, thereby missing part of her afternoon rest—a special allowance permitted only during retreat. Soon, all the other novices passed by on the way to their rooms. In a few moments, one returned. It was Sister Miriam Teresa, ready to help. Small acts of charity such as these were an everyday part of her life. She wrote, "If all would only make use of the ordinary duties and trials of their state in the way God intended, they would all become saints." Sister Miriam Teresa firmly believed that God yearns for the sanctification of men.

The spiritual director of the novices, Father Benedict, O.S.B., realized that he had been given charge of a specially favored soul. Indeed, he was later to recall, "Though Sister Miriam Teresa had enjoyed from childhood the extraordinary privileges of many of the great mystics, such as ecstasies, raptures, visions, locutions, she carefully concealed from all the secrets of the King. It was not until she entered the novitiate that she revealed to her spiritual director the hidden privileges of her spiritual life . . ."

But despite the many such gifts she had received from God, Sister Miriam Teresa realized that sanctity consists not in visions and revelations, but rather in doing God's Will at every moment. Sister's own life of obedience and humility appeared very ordinary; to some, her fidelity in all details of the rule was annoying. Yet her constant submission to God's Will for her—which included great physical and mental suffering—brought her to the heights of holiness. Her longing for Heaven grew deeper. To her spiritual director, she wrote, "Oh, Father, I'm madly in love and getting madder every minute. And what a little price has been the paying—purgatory and a taste of perdition and the boot of the world. But it's nothing, nothing, nothing, though it has been awful and is getting worse. God, my wonderful God, if people only knew You, they'd die on the spot . . . God, my very own God, slay me breath by breath, torture me body and soul as You please, but let me bring the world to Your feet . . ." After Sister Miriam Teresa's death, her spiritual director wrote, "For her own sanctification He [Our Lord] permitted her to be terribly misunderstood, and this proved the heaviest cross of her life, I think. This form of suffering hurts most . . ."

Father Benedict thought of a plan to spread Sister Miriam Teresa's message, and at the same time to shed more light on the workings of her soul. Part of his job was to give a conference to the sisters each week, on the way they could better attain perfection. He directed Sister Miriam Teresa to write these conferences.

Father Benedict would preach what Sister Miriam Teresa had written. He told her not to mention the fact that she was writing the conferences. The superior gave her permission for this arrangement, and in addition, she found time for Sister to do the actual work of writing the conferences. Later, Sister Miriam Teresa wrote to Father Benedict, "I never knew what I was going to write or say, but when obedience imposed the task, He took care of everything."

As the priest preached the conferences, Sister Miriam Teresa seemed to listen to them in the same way as all the other novices. No one suspected that the words of Father Benedict had been written by Sister Miriam Teresa. Some of the sisters did speculate that perhaps the words were not Father's own, and that possibly they were from the writings of the saints, but none suspected that they had come from one of their own companions.

These conferences became very popular for the down-to-earth yet deeply spiritual advice they contained. They were copied and sent to other houses of the order, and later to houses of other orders. After Sister Miriam Teresa's death, the conferences were published in book form under the title *Greater Perfection*. This book has gone through several editions in several languages, and the path of spirituality outlined in it is becoming known worldwide.

Two brief quotes from the conferences show the simple style of writing which Sister Miriam Teresa used in presenting religious truths and guidelines for the everyday life of the Christian who desires a closer union with God.

On seeking a life of fullest perfection, she wrote, "To find this perfect life, you have only to keep the ways of the Lord. His way is the way of the cross which you must shoulder daily, cheerfully and courageously, if you wish to have realized in you the name of disciples. The way of the cross is the path of sacrifice and self-denial. Only a humble soul can walk this path securely."

In writing of cooperation with grace, Sister tells us, "Union with God, then, is the spiritual height God calls everyone to achieve— 'any one,' not only religious, but 'any one' who chooses, who wills to seek this pearl of great price, who specializes in the traffic of eternal goods, who says 'yes' constantly to God the Holy Ghost." She goes on to point out that even the greatest of saints have often lived their lives in the world: Catherine of Siena, Joan of Arc, and Queen Elizabeth of Hungary who managed a contemplative life among the bustle of a royal court.

Sister Miriam Teresa first became ill in 1926—at first with tonsillitis and later with appendicitis. Although most thought that the minor operations were successful, her brother requested and received permission for her to make her final vows, which she did. Her death came as a shock to most of the community. There is some evidence that she willingly offered her death as a sacrifice for the success of her mission, which was to help sanctify her community and all sisters living a life of active apostolate.

When her body was being arranged for burial, it was found that her head had assumed a somewhat strange shape. Sister Miriam Teresa's spiritual director affirmed that she had suffered the pain of the crown of thorns.

Sister Miriam Teresa was buried in the community graveyard with a simple white marble cross to mark her grave. A few days later, the following notice was posted on the community bulletin board: "The conferences which I have been giving to the sisters were written by Sister Miriam Teresa." It was signed by the spiritual director. The sisters were astonished.

On Friday afternoon after Sister Miriam Teresa's death, her spiritual director came to give his weekly talk to the novices. He spoke about Sister Miriam Teresa, and stated that she had truly been a saint, and might one day be canonized. He continued, "I know the secrets of her life, and I know that she lived entirely for God from the time she had arrived at the age of reason. She never offended God by a deliberate venial sin."

After Sister Miriam Teresa's death, many of her sisters began to realize that they had been living with someone specially chosen. Prayers for Sister Miriam Teresa's intercession began to be answered. In the latter part of 1945, Rome authorized Bishop McLaughlin of the Paterson, New Jersey diocese to institute an ordinary informative process concerning Sister Miriam Teresa's life and virtues. The official investigation began early in 1946. Sister Miriam Teresa has made many friends all over the world, and her cause is progressing. The ritual exhumation of relics required in the process was carried out on May 8, 1979, exactly fifty-two years after her death.

This photograph of "Treat," as her friends called her, shows Miriam Teresa Demjanovich shortly before she joined the Sisters of Charity in New Jersey at age 24.

Above: After her death at age 26, Sister Miriam Teresa's spiritual director stated, "I know the secrets of her life, and I know that she lived entirely for God from the time she had arrived at the age of reason. She never offended God by a deliberate venial sin." This painting is considered a good likeness of her.

Opposite left: Miriam Teresa Demjanovich was born in Bayonne, New Jersey, the youngest of seven children. Though she seemed like an ordinary good person, her spiritual director later declared that she had received extraordinary mystical gifts from God since her childhood.

Opposite right: Sister Miriam Teresa shortly after she entered the convent. Almost no one suspected the depth of her spiritual life. She wrote, "If all would only make use of the ordinary duties and trials of their state in the way God intended, they would all become saints."

297

42

FATHER MIGUEL PRO

Servant of God Miguel Pro, S.J.
Miguel Augustin Pro Juarez
1891 - 1927
Mexico
Died Age 36

There is more adventure, excitement, and danger in the life of the Mexican priest, Father Miguel Pro, than in many modern spy thrillers. His life of danger began when, still only a toddler, he managed to escape the watchful eye of his nursemaid and crawl out onto a window ledge three stories above a busy street. Here his horrified mother found and rescued him. A final dangerous episode led to his death by firing squad at the age of thirty-six.

Miguel was born January 13, 1891 at Guadalupe. His father, Miguel, was the senior engineer at the Concepcion del Oro mine. His mother, Josefa, was a good and gentle influence on Miguel as he observed her charity to the mine workers.

From childhood, laughter and high spirits were hallmarks of Miguel's personality. He enjoyed practical jokes which he often played at the expense of his sisters. Once, while taking a stroll with his favorite sister, Concepcion, he darted over and knocked at the door of a house they were passing. When the man of the house came to the door, Miguel explained that his sister—and he indicated the horrified Concepcion—had noticed a beautiful statue of the Virgin in the man's window and wished to purchase it. Concepcion later told her parents that it was the gaudiest, most hideous statue she had ever seen. Luckily, it was a family treasure and the man refused to part with it.

Another time, Miguel attended a mission in a nearby town with some visiting Jesuits, friends of his family. Secretly, he dressed himself in the soutane belonging to one of the missionaries and went out on his own little preaching expedition to the neighboring ranchos. He was accepted as a genuine priest by the simple country folk who loaded the appealing young Padre with eggs, cigarettes, and fresh cheeses. Soon the real priests caught up with him but as he had apparently done a good job of preaching, they did not expose him as a fake. Instead, they dragged him back to their room where they relieved him of his hard earned contributions.

Miguel had his embarrassing moments. On one occasion, he was on the roof trying to catch his sister's escaped canary. As he leaned over the side to request help, a shower of cigarettes fell from his pocket into the startled face of his father. The excuse he managed to manufacture on his way down from the roof sounded weak to all who heard it.

On another occasion, he mistakenly mailed to his mother a letter intended for his non-Catholic girlfriend; the letter intended for his mother was mailed to the senorita in question. Providentially, this error led to a break-up with the girl.

The Pro family shared a warm and close-knit life. On many nights they gathered for musical entertainment, and Miguel added to the festivities by playing his mandolin or guitar. Although the family was devoutly Catholic, for a time Miguel remained away from the Sacraments and became lukewarm toward his religion. Finally, after two of his sisters became nuns, he began to think about his vocation. More and more, he felt drawn to the priesthood.

At the age of twenty, he decided to apply for admission to the Jesuits. His reputation as a jokester had preceded him, and the superiors wished to make certain that the young man could take a joke as well as play one.

The first appointment he had with the rector found the man reading a newspaper. Miguel stood for a full half hour before the rector put down his paper long enough to suggest that Miguel return the next day as he was quite busy at the time. The next day, the rector was busy writing. Again Miguel stood for a long time before being noticed. At the final interview, there was a whole group of young Jesuits in the courtyard loudly complaining about all the things wrong with the Society of Jesus. It dawned on Miguel that this was a test—a test he sucessfully passed. He entered the Jesuit novitiate on August 10, 1911.

In 1910 a revolution had begun in Mexico. By 1914, the fighting was too close for comfort, and the rector of the seminary prepared for the worst. He packed and hid or buried the best possessions of the novitiate, and bought street clothes for the members of the community. On August 15, they began leaving in small groups. Miguel was dressed as a peasant, and he attended his friends so well that no one suspected he was not their servant. By foot and train they made their way to Laredo, Texas. From Texas to California, through Nicaragua and Spain, to Belgium the young seminarian traveled. At each place he stopped and worked as teacher and assistant, as well as continuing his studies. In Belgium he trained as a priest for the workers. Miguel had worked with his father as a manager at the mines, and was deeply interested in the labor issues.

Miguel's sense of humor remained unchanged by the Jesuit training, but he did learn to accept rebukes with humility. He began to control his impetuousness, and his love of prayer made him stand out even in a Jesuit community.

Miguel suffered from a severe stomach ailment which he successfully concealed for some time by making a joke whenever the pain came. The joke gave him an excuse to hold his stomach. Finally, this was noticed, and he underwent a series of operations to correct the condition.

Miguel was ordained in Belgium on August 31, 1925. His only sadness about the day was that none of his family members could be there with him.

When Father Miguel's health did not improve, his Belgian superiors decided to send him back home to Mexico. It is probable that they did not realize how severe the persecution had become. For his part, Father Miguel believed that it was his mission to spend the rest of his life in bringing Christ to his countrymen, without counting the cost or worrying about the danger. He arrived back in Mexico in 1926, and went to Mexico City. Within twenty-three days of his arrival, an order suppressing all public worship was issued. Any priest the police came across was thus subject to arrest and prosecution.

Because he was unknown as a priest, Father Miguel was kept busy ministering secretly to the Catholics in several parishes. He wrote to a friend, "I have what I call 'Eucharistic stations' where, fooling the police, I go each day to give Communion."

Two of Father Miguel Pro's brothers were active supporters of the Religious Defense League. On one occasion, Father Miguel and his brothers and some friends were picked up and thrown into jail. The jailer laughingly suggested the group have Mass, as one of them was a "presbitero" (priest). Father Miguel wrote a friend regarding the incident, "We all looked one another over from head to toe wondering who might be the unfortunate priest among us." The jailer said, "He's a Miguel Augustin."

Father Pro continued his account: " 'Hold on!' I cried loudly. 'This Miguel Augustin is I, but I'm going to say Mass just like I'm going to sleep on a mattress tonight! [The prisoners slept on the floor.] And this "presbitero" before the name—that's my family name, "Pro," which someone has confused with "Pbro." [the abbreviation for "priest"].' "

This escape was close, but no closer than many other escapes which Father Pro made. As in the jail incident, he sometimes used his wits to escape from tight situations. Often, though, it was the sturdy faith of the Mexican Catholics who kept his secret. At last an order was issued for his arrest, and he went into strict hiding.

To continue his secret ministry, Father Pro adopted a number of disguises. He dressed as a mechanic to give a talk to a group of chauffeurs. Or, wearing secular clothes, he would calmly walk past a policeman to give a message about Mass to someone less than a block from the official. During one narrow escape, he was barely fifty yards ahead of his pursuers. Spying a passing girl, he linked arms with her and whispered, "Help me—I'm a priest." Speedily the girl reacted perfectly, and the police search group passed by the "lovers" without a backward glance.

To bring Christ to his countrymen, Father Pro raced back and forth across the capital on a bicycle to give Communion, baptize, perform marriages, hear confessions, and administer the Last Rites. In addition to these spiritual tasks, he also took many risks to help the poor of the city, collecting and distributing food and other supplies.

On November 13, 1927, a bomb was thrown from an old Essex at another car, that of Calles, the newly elected president. The Essex had at one time belonged to Miguel's brother, Humberto. Although all the Pro brothers had solid alibis, they were considered marked men. They were forced into strict hiding, but within four days were betrayed unwittingly to the police by a young boy who feared for his mother's life.

The order for the execution of the three Pro brothers was given. They were to be shot, along with two other prisoners.

On the day of the execution, the sweater-clad Father Miguel was the first to be led out of the prison. No due process had been accorded him; he had not received a trial. For the attempt on the life of the president, Miguel had a solid alibi; he was, however, guilty in the eyes of Calles of a worse crime—being a Catholic priest.

The prisoners had not been told of their death sentence, although they seem to have sensed it. A few days before the arrest, while serving Mass at a convent, Miguel had told the Mother Superior: "I offered my life for the saving of Mexico some time ago, Sister, and this morning at Mass I felt that He had accepted it." During his time in jail, Father Pro prepared his brothers and the other prisoners, and counseled his jailer.

As one of the policemen who had helped to hunt him down was leading him out to his execution, the man turned, and with tears in his eyes, begged Father Pro to forgive him for leading him to his death. Miguel put his arm about the shoulders of the shaking man and told him, "You have not only my forgiveness but my thanks." He also softly told the members of the firing squad, "May God forgive you all."

Asked if he had a last request, Miguel asked to be allowed to pray. He knelt in front of the bullet-pocked walls and fervently prayed for two minutes. After his prayer, he stood with his arms outstretched in the form of a cross, rejecting the offered blindfold. In a firm clear voice, he said, "Viva Cristo Rey!" (Long live Christ the King!).

A lawyer and Miguel's sister Anna arrived with an *amparo*, that is, a stay of execution, but shots from the other side of the locked gate announced that they were too late. Although they had been there several minutes, and several people had taken up the cry, the guards refused to open the gates. A phone call from the Argentine ambassador did save the life of Roberto, Miguel's youngest brother, who was later exiled to the United States.

Contrary to Calles' expectations, Father Pro met his martyrdom calmly and heroically. The firing squad did not kill the courageous priest; though mortally wounded, he still breathed. General Cruz walked over to him, placed a revolver to his head, and fired into his brain.

The fanatic General Calles had seen the executions as an occasion for celebration of the cowardice of the Mexican Catholics. He had invited the press, photographers, and many others to attend, and for this reason we have a good photographic record of the martyrdom. But the deaths were so heroic that the photos produced the opposite effect; possession of them quickly became a crime.

That night the bodies of Miguel and Humberto lay in their father's house. One of their sisters, overcome with emotion, was weeping bitterly. Her father asked, "Is this how you behave in the presence of a saint?" All night, people streamed past the caskets. The next day, over five hundred cars were in the funeral procession, and thousands thronged the streets to throw flowers on the caskets. Although Calles had forbidden any public demonstration, the people acted in open defiance, knowing that there were not enough jails in Mexico to hold all who wished to pay homage to the saintly priest and his martyred brother.

Before his death, Father Pro had told a friend, "If I am ever caught, be prepared to ask me for things when I am in Heaven." He also jokingly promised to cheer up any long-faced saints he found in Heaven by performing a gay Mexican hat dance! Not only this friend, but many of his countrymen believed that Father Miguel would answer their prayers. An old blind woman in the crowd who came to touch his body at the funeral left with her sight restored. Three others testified to his aid within a week of his death. Early in the 1930's, the cause for Father Pro's beatification was introduced in Rome.

Above: Father Miguel Augustin Pro, S.J., who offered his life to God to save Mexico.

Opposite upper: The young Jesuit, Miguel Pro, in his study.

Opposite lower: The Pro family. Standing (left to right) are Edmundo, Miguel, and Ana Maria (Anita). Seated (left to right) are Maria de la Concepcion (later to become a nun), Roberto, Senora Pro, Humberto, Senor Pro, and Maria de la Luz (later to become a nun).

305

The last year of Father Pro's life was spent carrying out his priestly duties in great danger amid religious persecution, as he dodged the Mexican police during the Revolution.

Father Pro in one of his many disguises.

Upper: Flashlight photo of Father Pro, taken in prison at 1:00 a.m. on the day of his execution. His crime: being a Catholic priest.
Lower: Father Pro is led to his execution.

Refusing the blindfold, and stretching out his arms in the shape of a cross, Father Pro speaks his last words: "Viva Cristo Rey!" (Long live Christ the King!)

Father Pro's last request is honored—a moment of prayer before the execution.

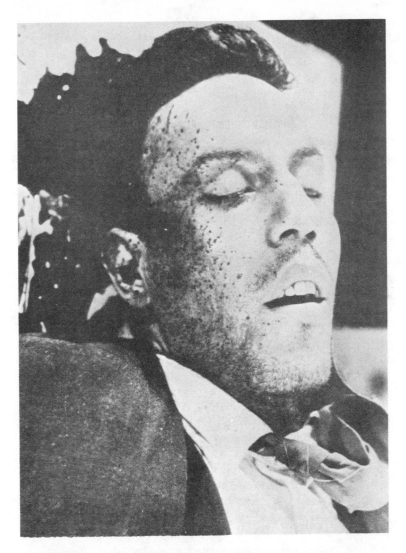

Opposite: To make sure of his death, a soldier fired a bullet at close range into the priest's head.

Above: Father Miguel Pro in death. Thousands thronged to the funeral of the saintly priest and his brother Humberto, who was executed with him. Upon seeing the bodies of his two dead sons, their father tenderly kissed their faces. To his daughter, Ana Maria, he said, "There is nothing to weep over, my child." He blessed God that he was the father of two martyrs.

311

43

FATHER LUKAS ETLIN

Servant of God Lukas Etlin, O.S.B.
Augustine Alfred Etlin
1864 - 1927
Switzerland - United States
Died Age 63

The ancient axiom, "Mighty is the power of the pen," holds true still today. Father Lukas Etlin used this power to spread devotion to the Blessed Sacrament, the Sacred Heart of Jesus, and the saints. In addition, he used it to move hearts to charity through the Caritas program, and to provide for the education of many seminarians.

Augustine Alfred Etlin was born in Sarnen, Switzerland on February 28, 1864. He was the son of a minor government official. There are few records of his early life other than his school reports. He was consistently listed as an excellent student except in the field of foreign language study. In 1880, Alfred entered Engelberg College on a scholarship provided by the board of education of Sarnen. Here he took a healthy interest in all the activities of the college, especially in those of the dramatic club. Artistically talented, he painted much of the scenery used in various plays. He also enjoyed acting in some of the productions, usually in a comedy role. His favorite recreational activity from youth until his death was fishing. At Sarnen, Alfred joined the Sodality of the Blessed Virgin, and renewed his membership each year of his life.

While Alfred was still a student of the university, a Benedictine monk from America came to make an appeal for young men to join the monks in the United States. After the monk's return to America, the abbot received the applications of Caspar Lussi and Alfred Etlin for admission to the novitiate at Conception Abbey.

Alfred's parents would have preferred that he enter a monastery in Switzerland. His decision to enter a monastery which was still newly formed, in a land across the ocean, caused these devoted parents much heartache. But when they realized that this was their son's vocation, they gave their permission. Alfred and Caspar left for America on September 9, 1886. The Benedictine sisters had also made a new foundation near the monastery, so some candidates for this convent traveled to America with the two young men. The ocean voyage and cross-country trip took nineteen days.

After he completed his novitiate in 1887, Alfred's name became Brother Lukas. He was ordained a priest in 1891.

At the request of the sisters, who wished to have one of the newly ordained priests celebrate his first Mass in their chapel, Father Lukas offered the Holy Sacrifice there on August 20, 1891. Earlier that morning, a storm had torn several holes in the roof and walls of the chapel; the sisters had hurriedly repaired the damage as best they could. Father Lukas was so absorbed in the joys of the day that he did not even notice the damage until it was pointed out to him after Mass by the sisters.

Some of Father Lukas' greatest talents were in the fields of art and architecture. For a while after his ordination, he continued to help with the decoration of the monastic church which was nearly completed. There were about seven painters who worked on the church, including Father Lukas and Father Solanus, O.S.F., of Quincy, Illinois. Some of the beautiful frescoes on the walls of the basilica at Conception Abbey and a picture of the Immaculate Conception in the apse of the abbey church were painted by Father Lukas.

In 1892, Father Lukas was appointed chaplain to the Benedictine Sisters at Clyde, Missouri. For a while he walked the two miles to the convent each morning for Mass. The winter of 1893 - 94 was so severe that on one trip Father Lukas became lost in the snow. Luckily a neighboring farmer found him and took him to the convent, nearly frozen. After this incident, his abbot and the superior of the sisters insisted that he make his residence at the convent.

Father Lukas believed that devotion to the Blessed Sacrament, the Sacred Heart of Jesus, and the saints should not be only for the clergy and religious. In order to spread these devotions among the laity, he advised the sisters to begin an apostolate of printing, and he brought skilled printers from his abbey to train them. The apostolate proved to be a popular one, and Father Lukas and the sisters began printing a magazine as well as pamphlets. From its beginning, the magazine particularly emphasized the importance of the Mass and Communion in the lives of the faithful.

Along with adoration of the Blessed Sacrament, the love of the

Sacred Heart of Jesus took first place in the life of Father Lukas. He worked closely with Father Mateo Crawley-Boevey, SS.CC. to promote this devotion, and especially emphasized the enthronement of the Sacred Heart in Christian homes in the United States.

After World War I, Father Lukas launched one of the most amazing one-man relief programs the world has ever seen—the Caritas program. Father Lukas knew about the starvation and pitiful circumstances of many of the people in Europe. In particular, many monasteries and convents which had previously been supported by endowments were in dire straits, and in more than a few cases, the religious were actually dying from hunger. Father Lukas published an editorial on this topic in June, and by the end of August, $24,907.50 had already been collected and distributed to various institutions in Europe—including monasteries, convents, orphanages, and seminaries. Most of this money came in as small donations. From June of 1920 to December of 1927, the Caritas program collected and distributed funds exceeding two million dollars to thirty-two countries, including Russia and China.

Father Lukas had always spent considerable time in thanksgiving after Mass. On the Feast of St. Joseph, 1921, he retired abruptly to his room immediately after Mass, startling the sisters, who became worried that he was ill. Father Lukas was not ill; instead, he had had an idea. The war had left many countries in Europe with a severe shortage of priests. Because of lack of money, many young men who would have become priests could not afford the necessary education.

Father Lukas' next editorial began, "You, too, can have a priest in your family. You can adopt a youth who studies for the priesthood." Scholarships raised through this program helped 2,800 young men to finish their studies for the priesthood. The list of these young men includes the names of three cardinals, five archbishops, eleven bishops, nine auxiliary bishops, and fourteen abbots of religious orders.

Even though Father Lukas carried on a remarkable amount of activity—in addition to his duties with the convent, his writing, and the Caritas program, he taught religion and carried on many additional activities—he maintained his prayer life and a great spirit of self-denial. While working in the fields, he kept the Benedictine custom of abstaining from water between meals, although field work carried an automatic dispensation. Though he encouraged the sisters to look on their daily work as a mortification and refused to allow them to undertake unusual penances, he was undoubtedly severe with his own personal mortifications. He did not, of course, practice them in public or speak of them, but after his death several instruments of penance were found in his room. In spite of the fact that he was frequently in poor health, especially in his last years, he always insisted on saying Mass daily if he was physically able to do so. If he was unable to go to the chapel, he requested permission to say Mass in a room adjoining his own.

Father Lukas anticipated the liturgical apostolate by many years in the United States by urging the sisters to "pray the Mass" rather than to pray at Mass. He arose at night for adoration of the Blessed Sacrament, and when not actively engaged elsewhere, was usually to be found in the chapel.

Father Lukas had a deep devotion to Our Lady. His secretary recalls that whenever she went to his room to take dictation or do other forms of work, they usually began by kneeling before a picture of Our Lady for a short prayer. One day they began their work as usual, but then Father Lukas appeared to have forgotten the secretary's presence. After about half an hour, she quietly withdrew and left him absorbed in his prayer.

On December 16 of 1927, Father Lukas arose, offered Mass, and went to teach religion to the girls of St. Joseph Academy. Among other things, he told them: "We must at all times be ready to die. We should not wish to live even a single day longer than God wills. Should death overtake us in an automobile, also then we should accept it with resignation to the Will of God."

Less than eight hours after this remark, Father Lukas lay dead at the side of the highway, the victim of an automobile accident. A piece of his rosary was clutched tightly in his hand.

The diocesan process for his beatification was opened on August 13, 1960. Currently the process has been given an inactive status, and prayers are sought in order to discern the Will of God with regard to a cause for Father Lukas Etlin.

Alfred Etlin (on the left)—later to become Father Lukas Etlin—enjoyed playing in theatrical productions while a student in Switzerland. He usually played a comedy role.

Alfred Etlin is shown here before leaving Switzerland to join the Benedictines in the United States, where he was to begin an Adopt-a-Seminarian program to help war-devastated Europe with its severe shortage of priests. Scholarships raised in this way helped 2,800 young men to finish their studies for the priesthood; 42 of these became bishops or abbots.

Hours before he was found dead in an automobile accident, a piece of his rosary clutched tightly in his hand, Father Lukas Etlin had told a class of school girls, "We must at all times be ready to die. We should not wish to live even a single day longer than God wills. Should death overtake us in an automobile, also then we should accept it with resignation to the Will of God."

44

BISHOP LUIGI VERSIGLIA
and
FATHER CALLISTO CARAVARIO

Servant of God Bishop Luigi Versiglia, S.D.B.
Aloysius Versiglia
1873 - 1930
Italy - China
Died Age 56

Servant of God Father Callisto Caravario, S.D.B.
Callisto Caravario
1903 - 1930
Italy - China
Died Age 26

The first Salesians were greatly fascinated by China, the "Celestial Empire." According to an oral tradition, Don Bosco had once had one of his vivid, prophetic dreams about future missionary work in that country. He had seen two large chalices raised up in the sky—one filled with sweat and the other filled with the blood of Salesians.

In 1917, a mission in Kwantung Province was offered to the Salesians, and Father Versiglia sent to this province a group of newly arrived confreres, as well as some from the mission of Macau. The leader of this new expedition, Father Garelli, brought Father Versiglia a present from the superiors in Italy; it was a new chalice. To Father Garelli and the superiors, this was simply a fitting gift for the mission. For Father Versiglia, however, it awakened the memory of Don Bosco's "dream." When he was presented with the gift at a dinner in Macau on the night of the arrival of the new confreres, Father Versiglia said, "You brought me a chalice, and I accept it. Don Bosco saw the Chinese missions flourish when a chalice would be filled with the blood of his sons. This chalice was sent to me, and"—his voice trailed away to a whisper—"I will have to fill it."

Luigi Versiglia was born on June 5, 1873, at Oliva Gessi, Italy. Luigi and his two sisters came from a good, religious family. They attended Mass often, and Luigi was an altar boy who served Mass with a great deal of pleasure. Noticing his attitude, family friends sometimes teased that he would probably grow up to be a priest, but he had no such intention. In fact, when one of his teachers, a priest, offered to help him through his studies as far as the university level, Luigi turned the offer down as he felt that the teacher was trying to induce him to become a priest.

Luigi had a very lively nature and was a good student, particularly in arithmetic. He loved animals, especially horses, and in 1885 he agreed to join Don Bosco's Oratory in Turin in order to study and eventually enroll in a well known veterinary school in the city.

Luigi spent the next three years at the Oratory, although at first his adjustment was difficult. Soon after arriving there, the homesick boy wrote to his father asking him to come and take him home. Happily, the atmosphere had captured Luigi by the time his father arrived, and he decided to stay.

At first, his grades at school were poor, but with hard work he eventually attained marks near the top of his class. On Don Bosco's feast day in 1887, Luigi was chosen to read a composition of good wishes from the boys to the ageing saint. Don Bosco was very pleased with the young student, and invited Luigi to come and see him as he had something to tell him. Unfortunately, however, Don Bosco was ill at the time of Luigi's visit and so could not receive him.

During his last year at the Oratory, the young Luigi became attracted to the missionary life of the Salesians. He determined to become a priest and a missionary.

In 1886, Luigi began his novitiate. His clothing ceremony was the first one conducted by Father Michael Rua, the first successor of Don Bosco. Because of his intelligence, in 1890 Luigi was sent to the Gregorian University of Rome, where he earned his doctorate in 1893. His first assignment upon graduation was to Foglizzo, where he taught philosophy and was supervisor of novices. By a special dispensation he was ordained at the age of twenty-two, eighteen months short of the required age. He spent nine years training the novices at Foglizzo and at the novitiate at Genzano where he was appointed rector. But dreaming impatiently of life in the missions, he often said, "My trunk can be packed at a minute's notice."

At last, in 1905, arrangements were made for the first group of missionaries to go to China. They were to open a mission and orphanage in Portuguese Macau, an old Portuguese colony opposite Hong Kong. The most logical choice for leader of the group was in poor health at the time. Asked to nominate someone else for leader, this man chose Father Versiglia.

At this first Chinese mission, the six young Salesians—three priests and three lay brothers—began to study the difficult Chinese language. In cooperation with some Jesuits, they opened a school and orphanage for poor and orphan Chinese boys. In addition to their regular studies and religious instruction, the students were taught Gregorian chant, were trained in tailoring and shoe making, and were able to form a brass band. There were fifty-one pupils, the most that could be accommodated at the tiny school.

In 1910, another house was given to the missionaries so that they could enlarge their work. Unfortunately, their joy was short-lived. The Portuguese Revolution of 1910 led to a suppression of religious orders, both in the homeland and in the missions. The little band of missionaries had to leave their work and find shelter in Hong Kong where they were welcomed by the bishop and the Fathers of the Pontifical Institute for Foreign Missions. The students were sent home, if they had homes to go to. The orphans were entrusted to the care of the local bishop.

After the superiors learned of the forced departure, a decision was sent back to Father Versiglia that the missionaries were to remain in the Far East. Joyfully, they accepted work in the district of Heung Shan, adjacent to Macau. This district, previously taken care of by the diocesan clergy of Macau, presented many challenges to the missionaries. It was overrun by pirates, subject to frequent civil wars, and because of the superstitions of the people, conversions to the Faith had been few. Four other missionaries came from Europe to join the group in their work, which included visiting a small colony of Christians and two leper colonies on nearby islands. In 1912, plague broke out in the district; Father Versiglia and his companions were unstinting in their efforts to aid the people.

That same year, 1912, saw the fall of the Manchu dynasty. When the revolutionary troops arrived in the district capital, many of the frightened people surrounded Father Versiglia for their own protection. The imperialist troops surrendered easily, however, and the revolutionaries did no harm, contenting themselves with cutting off the long pigtails worn as a sign of submission to the dynasty. Also in 1912, the Salesians were allowed to reopen their mission in Macau; Father Versiglia became the superior there.

In 1917, Father Versiglia returned to Italy to request new mission territory in China for the Salesians. By request of the Sacred Congregation for the Propagation of the Faith, and in accord with his own wishes, the Bishop of Canton turned over the northernmost portion of Kwantung Province for the new mission. Shiu Chow was the town designated as the center of the mission.

In 1920, the mission was raised to the rank of vicariate, and Father Versiglia was consecrated a bishop on January 9, 1921. Realizing that plans to make the mission a Vicariate Apostolic were underway, Father Versiglia had written to his superiors, humbly requesting that he not be made bishop. He asked them to look for a better man, and to allow him to stay with his work. His wish was overruled.

What type of man was this new bishop whose consecration was greeted enthusiastically by the Chinese Christians of his diocese with a torchlight procession and plenty of firecrackers? Who was this bishop who gave his first pontifical blessing in a pro-cathedral which was only a tiny, dark, unadorned chapel, and whose original episcopal clothes had belonged to a deceased bishop in Turin? The new bishop fully exemplified the Salesian spirit, especially the joy which had been enjoined by John Bosco.

Bishop Versiglia was a builder, always building for others—never for himself. When an episcopal residence was eventually built, he deemed it too large and luxurious for his own use. Refusing to call it the Bishop's House, he termed it the Missionary's House, and brought the seminarians to live there, too. He was a traveler; he refused to stay in his episcopal city, and traveled continually throughout his diocese. He chose the cheapest, least comfortable modes of transportation, going on horseback, by boat, and on foot.

Like all Christians, Bishop Versiglia had crosses to bear. In particular, he suffered from misunderstandings with some members of his own order, from the poverty of his diocese, and from the political unrest of his adopted country. He weathered all storms without complaint or self-justification, bearing his trials with joy and resignation to the Will of God.

A deeply Eucharistic priest, Bishop Versiglia began and ended his days in front of the Blessed Sacrament. Devoted to Our Lady

Help of Christians, he had his mission consecrated to her. Believing that authority was meant only for service, he made himself constantly available to others—his religious, the orphans, the aged, the catechumens.

Inspired with a true spirit of penance, he offered himself as a victim for the sake of his mission. Although his mortifications were secret during his lifetime, after his death several instruments of penance were found among his effects. It was at this time that people realized why he had always troubled to rinse his personal linen before sending it to be washed.

*   *   *

Callisto Caravario was born in a small town in northern Italy on June 8, 1903. When Callisto was five, his family moved to Turin where he attended a public primary school for three years. His teachers there remembered him for his intelligence and goodness, and the sisters who taught him religion were impressed by his devotion at a young age. On Sundays, he attended the Oratory of St. Joseph, and he finished two final years of primary education at the Salesian School of St. John the Evangelist.

Callisto felt drawn to the priesthood, but his family was too poor to afford the necessary education. Father Garelli, his future superior in Shanghai, located benefactors to bear the expense, and he completed his secondary education at the Oratory in Valdocco. In 1918 he applied for admission to the Salesians. He was accepted and began his novitiate, making his profession in 1919.

After completing his education, Callisto received approval on his application for the Chinese missions; he left for the Far East in 1924. He first worked in Shanghai, then later in Macau and on the Portuguese portion of the Island of Timor in the East Indies. He learned to speak Chinese, Portuguese, and the local dialect of the island. The young Salesian loved working with the boys in his charge, and inspired a number of vocations to the priesthood. However, he was afflicted with chronic poor health, and suffered from time to time with bouts of malaria.

Political unrest caused several moves, and Callisto's ordination was postponed due to the absence of the local bishops. Finally in 1929, Callisto was sent to the mission of Shiu Chow where he was ordained by Bishop Versiglia. At an entertainment held in his honor after his ordination, Father Caravario thanked his friends, speaking partly in English and partly in Chinese dialect. His linguistic ability was a pleasant surprise to all present.

The exceptional ability and maturity of the young priest led to his assignment to a solitary post at Linchow, where he was visited monthly by another of the missionary Fathers. Father Caravario's love for souls helped him to accept the penance of such a lonely way of life, without close contacts with other members of his order or race.

After six months there, he returned to the episcopal center of the diocese to report on the growth of his community. Bishop Versiglia decided to accompany the priest back for a visit to the mission, and they set out on February 24, 1930. In addition to these two, the traveling party was composed of two young male teachers (one was a Christian) recently graduated from Don Bosco School and three young women. Two of these were sisters of the teachers. Tong Su-lien Mary, who was twenty-one years of age, was herself a newly trained teacher who was returning home to tell her family that she had decided to become a nun. Sixteen-year-old Ng Yu-che Pauline was giving up her studies and returning home. Tzen Tz-yung Clare was a young catechist returning to work in Linchow. All five of the Chinese were originally from the Linchow district.

The little group traveled by train to Lin Kong How. While aboard, they were questioned by three soldiers as to their destination. Recognizing one of them as an opponent of the mission, Mary managed to wink at Bishop Versiglia to warn him to be careful. The soldier treated them with courtesy. After spending the night at Lin Kong How, the group embarked by boat for the second leg of their journey. They were joined by a ten-year-old student and an elderly Christian lady who planned to live with the young catechist, Clare. In addition, there were the boatmistress, her twenty-year-old son, and two young people to help propel the boat with oars or long poles. A flag proclaimed the boat as property of the Catholic mission. Such a flag had served in the past as a guarantee of safety and protection for those on board.

In the districts through which the group was traveling to reach the Linchow mission, there was a dearth of troops, and local pirates ran a "protection" racket, exacting tolls and often robbing the boats of cargo. Familiar with their ways, the boatmen simply paid the "tolls" in order to escape with their lives. The local people never betrayed the pirates, as these pirates were frequently local people who simply led a double life. The Catholic missionaries were not frightened of the pirates because up until this time they had been largely left alone by them. Whether because the pirates realized the missionaries were friends of the people, and were poor, or whether they feared reprisals by authority, it was a fact that on the few occasions when missionaries had been ambushed, they were released unharmed to go on their way. Both Bishop Versiglia and Father Caravario had been ambushed by pirates in the past.

The pirates who perpetrated the tragic encounter of February 25, however, were not simply the "locals." In addition to these, there were some ex-soldiers, some Communists—who hated and feared foreigners, especially religious—and possibly a rejected suitor of Mary Tong, determined to take her for himself by force. It is also possible that the attack was planned by the soldiers who encountered the missionary group on the train.

About nine o'clock, Bishop Versiglia, Father Caravario, and the two male teachers disembarked and followed the boat on foot along the bank for a time. Passing through a small village, they noticed a number of people in town for market, among whom were some armed with rifles and revolvers. The people looked mildly surprised at seeing foreigners, but the bishop's polite greetings were returned politely. At eleven, the men boarded the boat again and everyone took a lunch break.

After lunch, while the bishop was taking a nap and the priest was praying his office, a sharp command rang out from the bamboo lining the river bank: "Stop the boat! Who is on board?"

A group of ten to twelve armed pirates demanded that the boat land, and in spite of being assured that the group was made up of missionaries, they asked for $500 protection money. Father Caravario showed the pirates his visiting card, which in normal times would have ended the incident. One of the boatmen later declared that these were no ordinary pirates, but "evil people" he had never seen before. The outlaws cursed and increased their demands that the enormous toll be paid, although both sides realized that no missionary would be carrying such a sum. Losing their tempers, the pirates began shouting invectives against the "foreign devils." They boarded the boat, and then caught sight of the women who were crouching fearfully in the bottom of the vessel. The pirates shouted their intention to steal the "wives."

Father Caravario intervened and told them the women were not wives, but pupils. "Do not touch them!"

The pirates then informed the missionaries that as they had no money, they would take the women instead, and they threatened to beat the men if they interfered. The pirates tried to grab the women, but the two missionaries stood bravely in their way, attempting politely to argue the pirates out of their plans. The pirates tried to set fire to the boat, but since the wood was wet, the bishop easily put it out. A scuffle ensued, with the pirates attempting to capture the women and the missionaries fighting to protect them. The bishop and priest were repeatedly hit with heavy sticks and rifle butts, but were determined not to give up. Two shots were fired and hit the side of the boat; eventually the bishop and then the young priest collapsed.

The women clung desperately to the fallen bishop who begged faintly that the pirates leave them alone. The women were captured, but before the pirates could tie her up, Mary Tong leaped into the river, determined to die rather than be captured. The water was so shallow that the pirates had no difficulty in grabbing her by the hair and arms and dragging her to shore.

Instructed to come on land immediately, Father Caravario walked off the boat. The fallen bishop was too weak to move, so the outlaws demanded that the young Christian teacher help him off. The valiant priest went on begging for mercy on behalf of the women, but was ignored while he and Bishop Versiglia were searched and relieved of their watches and a small amount of cash. The bandits, probably through superstition, did not touch the bishop's ring and cross. The missionaries' arms were tied behind their backs, leaving their hands and forearms free, and they were lashed together with bamboo strips to prevent their attempting to escape.

Before being taken into the nearby bamboo thicket, the priests were asked if they were not afraid of dying. The bishop replied, "We are priests; why should we fear death?"

The boatmen and the two teachers were told to unload the baggage. Everything was opened and the religious articles and books were thrown into the river while the other items were taken. During the looting, the pirates made constant insulting references to religion and foreigners, and eventually demanded that the two teachers carry the booty. The boat was sent on its way. The teachers were soon dismissed, and they ran to catch up to the boat. They traveled to Lin

Kong How and reported to the priest there what had happened.

In the meantime, the pirates took the women into the woods, trying to calm them by assuring them that they would be set free. The women were seated a short distance away from the captive missionaries, and realized that the missionaries, speaking quietly, were making final confessions. The bishop winked at the three and raised his eyes to Heaven to give them courage. The young women began to say the Rosary, but this annoyed the pirates who snatched away their beads and threw them away.

The missionaries began to pray aloud, and some of the outlaws believed they were placing charms or spells on them. The pirates announced their intention of killing the missionaries because they were members of the hated foreign religion. Father Caravario again attempted to negotiate, going so far as to promise ransom. In reply, the bandits stated that this alternative was unacceptable because of possible revenge from the foreigners. At this point, Father Caravario and Bishop Versiglia apparently realized that their death was imminent, and decided to accept the martyrdom calmly. Two former Communist soldiers carried them further into the woods. The young women were stopped in their attempt to follow and were taken to a small white temple on the river bank. Later testimony of people from nearby houses revealed that the bishop's last request was this: "I am an old man, kill me; but he is still young, spare him!" The request was refused, and the two missionaries knelt in prayer to await death.

Five shots rang out through the silence of the woods. Upon returning to the group in the temple, the executioners were told to go back and make certain the missionaries were dead and to pay someone in the village to bury the corpses. The pirates then fled to the mountains, taking along the terrorized women.

The corpses were originally buried where they fell, but the landowner later took them by boat across the river and re-buried them on a sandy part of the river bank. The rude graves were covered with bamboo branches to conceal them. The following day, the bishop's secretary and another priest traveled to the site in an attempt to learn the fate of the mission party. The local people were terrified, and it was with difficulty that the two finally learned that Bishop Versiglia and Father Caravario had been murdered. Later, they returned to the site with a local police chief who, although he knew what had happened, kept silent through fear for the safety of the people. He arranged matters so that the clerics would discover the bodies.

Five days after the murder, the regular army was in the area. After a skirmish with the pirates, the three young women were rescued. Seeing the bodies of the saintly priest and bishop, they fell to their knees in prayer.

The bodies were taken to Lin Kong How and placed in wooden coffins. On March 4, 1930, official identification of the bodies was made. They were transferred to zinc coffins and taken to Shiu Chow. Father Caravario was buried to the left of the door of the Church of St. Joseph, and Bishop Versiglia was buried in his pro-cathedral, after a solemn funeral.

At the funeral, for the first time since Christians entered China in 1589, the cross was carried in solemn procession through the city. Christians and non-Christians alike attended, and many of the civil authorities formed an honor guard for the casket. One of these authorities said, "The Catholic Church is marvelous which gives to society such men whose duty compels them to sacrifice their lives for their spiritual children."

In Mary Tong's sworn deposition for the process, she stated that she had always had great respect and affection for the bishop. She said, "He died for me."

The Chinese "cultural revolution" wrought havoc to the tomb of Bishop Versiglia. Red guards opened his tomb and that of another bishop, attempting to find valuables. Finding none, they burnt the remains and threw the ashes on the rubbish heap. We have no information about the fate of the tomb of Father Caravario.

The process for beatification of the two missionaries was begun in late December of 1934. They became known as Servants of God in 1963, and Pope Paul VI issued the decree declaring them martyrs on November 13, 1976. Bishop Versiglia and Father Caravario are the Protomartyrs of the Salesian order.

Mary Tong, a young Chinese teacher, was traveling with the missionaries to inform her parents of her decision to become a nun. It is believed that the attack on Bishop Versiglia and Father Caravario may have been instigated by one of her rejected suitors.

Bishop Luigi Versiglia, missionary Bishop to China. Bishop Versiglia knew that St. John Bosco's prophecy of martyrdom was meant for him. After the Bishop's death, Chinese Communists entered the cathedral where he was buried and opened his tomb looking for valuables. Finding none, they burnt his remains and threw his ashes on the trash pile.

330

Father Callisto Caravario, who, along with Bishop Versiglia, was martyred by a group of Chinese pirates, ex-soldiers, and Communists.

45

SISTER CARMEN MORENO
and
SISTER AMPARO CARBONELL

Servant of God Sister Carmen Moreno, F.M.A.
Carmen Moreno
1885 - 1936
Spain
Died Age 51

Servant of God Sister Amparo Carbonell, F.M.A.
Amparo Carbonell
1893 - 1936
Spain
Died Age 43

No. 4676. A woman. Brought from the Hippodrome. Tall and healthy. About 50 years of age. Dressed in black. Undergarments marked with S. Moreno C. Gunshot wound. Entrance hole in left temple, exit right temple. Traumatic cerebral hemorrhage.

No. 4677. A woman. Taken from the Hippodrome. Medium height. Healthy. About 40 years. Dressed in a white habit. Gunshot wound in right shoulder and in neck. Traumatic cerebral hemorrhage.

Thus the police records identified two martyrs to charity, victims of persecution by the Red army during the Spanish Civil War.

Carmen Moreno was born at Villamartin on August 24, 1885. She was educated at the college of the Daughters of Mary Help of Christians. Overcoming her mother's opposition, she followed her sister's example in dedicating her life to God through the order of her teachers. After completing her teacher training, she began teaching young girls. She made her final vows in 1914.

Sister Carmen is remembered by her fellow religious and former students for her extreme devotion to duty and an exceptional charity to the sisters and the pupils. After teaching in several schools of the institute, she was sent to a house near Barcelona. Here, because of her piety and her prudence, she was named superior. She was serving as vicar at the house in Sarria when the revolution caught up with her in 1936.

Amparo Carbonell was born November 9, 1893. As a child, she was noted for her humility, her constancy, and her generosity. Her family placed many obstacles in the way of her vocation, but she confidently went daily to pray before the Blessed Sacrament. Although she was often in poor health, the desire to make the total gift of herself was finally recognized, and she made her vows in 1923. Shortly thereafter, she suffered from high fevers, but in a spirit of sacrifice she continued her work without considering herself. Although she had made her final vows, the revolutionary movement of 1931 caused a brief return to her home. Eventually Sister Amparo rejoined her sisters in Sarria, where her favorite occupation was working in the garden.

In July of 1936, the Red army began severe persecutions of religious orders. The sisters left their beloved house in Sarria and fled to a nearby village in preparation for leaving the country. The passports for all the sisters were in order, awaiting only the necessary permissions. To stay would mean disaster. On August 6, the permission came. The sisters prepared to leave to seek asylum with the members of their order in Italy.

One of the sisters, Sister Carmella, was in a nearby hospital recovering from surgery. The surgery had not been successful, and the disease was fatal. She had only a few more months to live. Refusing to abandon her, the valiant superior, Sister Carmen, determined to stay with the sick sister. Sister Amparo also decided to stay. Both were aware that although their invalid sister might recover from the operation, she would probably not survive much longer. Both sisters were well aware of the danger they faced in refusing to leave. In spite of these two grave arguments against their decision, they bravely told the other sisters good-bye and took a small apartment near the hospital. Sister Carmella was released from the hospital on August 12, and moved into the apartment with Sisters Carmen and Amparo. Between them, they shared the duties of nursing her back to health, and all three waited for an opportunity to leave the country.

On August 29th, an elderly fruit and vegetable vendor knocked on the door of their apartment. Furtively he slipped inside and shut the door. Actually he was a Jesuit priest, and had come to give the sisters Communion and to console them. He spoke of possible martyrdom, and when he left, he left the Blessed Sacrament with them, promising to return in a few days.

On the evening of September 1, there was another and far more authoritative knock on the door. This time, it was a group of soldiers, who took the sisters before a people's tribunal. The tribunal freed Sister Carmella, as her disease was incurable. Sisters Carmen and Amparo were identified as religious and condemned. No details of the next five days are known. On September 6, the sisters were taken to the Hippodrome, a stadium in Barcelona. There, it is probable they were beaten before being executed. After the execution, the bodies were taken to the civil hospital, where they were tagged for identification.

Sister Carmella escaped to the motherhouse in Italy and died shortly afterward without ever knowing of her sisters' martyrdom.

Together Sister Carmen Moreno and Sister Amparo Carbonell won the twin palms—virginity and martyrdom. They are currently awaiting Rome's official declaration of their martyrdom.

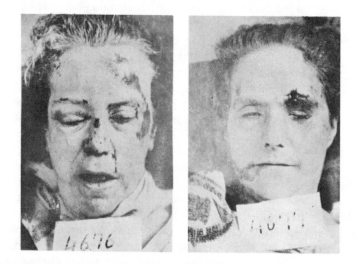

The two nuns were killed in the religious persecution by the Red army during the Spanish Civil War in 1936. These are official police photographs made for later identification.

Sister Amparo Carbonell. She and Sister Carmen were taken before a "people's tribunal" and condemned for being Catholic nuns.

Sister Carmen Moreno, who chose to remain in Spain during the dangerous days of the Spanish Civil War with a sister recuperating from surgery.

46

BLESSED BROTHER ANDRE

Blessed Brother Andre, C.S.C.
Alfred Bessette
1845 - 1937
Canada
Died Age 91

Long before his death at the advanced age of ninety-one, people were talking of "miracles" worked through the intercession of the humble lay brother of the Holy Cross, Brother Andre. In press reports he was known as the "Miracle Worker of Montreal" or the "Saint of Mount Royale."

Brother Andre deplored such publicity, and assured everyone that he had not worked any miracles. Time after time he insisted that the person's own faith or the intercession of St. Joseph had moved the good God to action to effect a cure. He said, "I am only a man, just like you." To many who came for cures, he replied, "Thank the good God for having visited you through suffering; if we knew the value of suffering, we would ask for it." Yet time after time he quietly said, "I will pray for you." And time after time, miraculous cures took place.

Often, Brother Andre suggested a novena to St. Joseph, a rubbing with oil from the lamps burning in front of his patron's statue, or wearing a medal of the saint. When asked about this, he replied, "Such things are acts of love and faith, of confidence and humility." He also said, "Can one bargain with the good God? The best way to be cured is to submit to His Will."

No one who knew Alfred Bessette as a child would have believed he would live to reach the age of ninety-one. He was so weak and frail at birth that the midwife baptized him immediately. His health remained poor his entire life. The Holy Cross superiors hesitated to admit him to final vows until his novice master assured them that "if this young man becomes unable to work he will at least be able to pray for us." In old age, when asked how he had managed to live so long, Brother Andre laughingly replied, "By eating as little as possible and by working as much as possible."

Alfred was born August 9, 1845, in a small town thirty-two miles southeast of Montreal. He was the sixth of ten children. His father worked as a carpenter and a woodcutter, and when Alfred was nine, his father was killed in a lumbering accident. His mother died a few years later of tuberculosis. At twelve, Alfred went to live with an aunt and uncle, and his brothers and sisters were also parceled out to live with their relatives. An orphan and almost illiterate, Alfred was faced with the necessity of beginning some type of work to help pay for his keep.

As a young child, because of his poor health and low family finances, Alfred had not had much formal schooling. His mother had tried to teach him the little she herself knew, but by the time of her death he was barely able to write his name and to read a very little. His letter requesting admission to the Congregation of the Holy Cross was actually written by his parish priest. Later, the brothers taught him to read, but he always read with difficulty. He had a copy of the Gospels, and this was his favorite book. This book and the sermons to which he listened intently helped him learn about the word of God. But the *love* of God he had known about from childhood. His brothers and sisters had noted his absorption in and devotion to prayer, and his aunt was horrified to discover some of the severe penances he performed. Regarding education, Brother Andre said, "It is not necessary to have been well educated, to have spent many years in college, to love the good God. It is sufficient to want to do so generously."

For the next thirteen years, Alfred worked at a number of unskilled jobs in Canada. For a time, he lived in the United States. Like many Canadian boys of his time he had heard of the better job opportunities there. Living with his aunt and uncle he had been apprenticed at a number of skills, but always his health failed him.

In 1870, Alfred joined the Congregation of the Holy Cross. For the next forty years he joyfully and uncomplainingly washed floors and windows, cleaned lamps, carried firewood, and worked as a porter and messenger. Afterwards, he served as the doorkeeper for the college.

Throughout his life, Brother Andre had a great devotion to St. Joseph. In a dream while he was still a young man, he had seen a church in an unfamiliar setting. He believed that a large church in honor of the saint should be built at the top of beautiful Mount Royale. Through his initiative and efforts, such a church was begun, enlarged and rebuilt; the oratory which stands in its place today is the largest church in the world dedicated to St. Joseph. Brother Andre never spoke of "my project." Instead he said, "Personally, I am nothing. God chose the most ignorant one. If there was anyone more ignorant than I am, the good God would have chosen him."

Though he had a deep devotion to St. Joseph, Brother Andre's main devotion was to the Passion of Our Lord, on which he often meditated. He loved the Passion as the supreme act of God's love for man.

Brother Andre knew how to speak of the love of God with such intensity that he inspired hope in all those who met him. His portrayal of God as a loving Father, his common-sense advice, and his empathy with those he counseled—along with a warm sense of humor—were outstanding. Though almost painfully shy, Brother enjoyed a good laugh with his friends. He was, in addition, a bit of a storyteller. He said, "You mustn't be sad; it is good to laugh a little."

Especially with the poor and the unfortunate, Brother Andre was merry, and his own inner happiness communicated itself to others. After his work for the day was finished, he spent many hours visiting the sick and the elderly in their homes or in the hospital. And thousands of the poor, the hurt, the unhappy, visited Brother Andre. In his little office he counseled them, cried with them, and prayed for them.

Brother Andre had high principles, and could be quick or sharp at times. In addition, fatigue made him nervous or cross. One Protestant woman was so offended that she left in tears and it was some minutes before she realized that her lameness had been cured. When Brother knew he had spoken sharply, he was sorry and consoled himself with the thought, "Well at least they see that I am nothing but a poor sinner."

Brother Andre had a particular love for the Eucharist, and wished to see people go to Communion more often. With sadness, he would say to a visitor, "If you ate only one meal a week would you survive? It is the same for your soul. Nourish it with the Blessed Sacrament. A nice table is set there for us, with something good on it—we don't pay any attention to it."

Brother Andre made no distinction among those who asked for his help. He prayed for all, no matter what their race or religion, their wealth or education. In his words, "Our Lord is our big Brother, and we are the little brothers. Consequently, we should love one another as members of the same family."

Brother Andre died peacefully in his hospital room in Montreal. A few days before his death, he said, "The great Almighty is coming . . ." Two days before he died he lapsed into a coma. A few instants before his death he cried out, and bending close they heard him whisper, "Here is the grain."

When he died on January 6, 1937, an estimated one million people climbed the slope of Mount Royale to St. Joseph's Oratory. In the rain, sleet, and snow on the seven days following his death, they filed past the small wooden coffin to pay their final respects to the little brother. And today, many still come to ask his help.

Brother Andre was beatified by Pope John Paul II on May 23, 1982.

This photograph of Alfred Bessette—later to be called Brother Andre— was taken at his First Holy Communion when he was 12. The picture was damaged and has been airbrushed in an attempt at restoration.

Brother Andre at age 30, at the time of his profession as a lay brother in the Congregation of the Holy Cross in Montreal. For the next 40 years he joyfully and uncomplainingly washed floors and windows, cleaned lamps, carried firewood, and worked as a porter, messenger and doorkeeper.

Blessed Brother Andre around age 80. Many miraculous cures took place through Brother Andre's prayers. He always insisted that the person's own faith or the intercession of St. Joseph had moved the good God to effect the cure.

Through Brother Andre's efforts, the magnificent Oratory of St. Joseph was built. The huge shrine, which took 50 years to complete and furnish, is the highest point in the city of Montreal—over 500 feet above street level and 850 feet above sea level.

Above: Brother Andre around age 80. When Brother Andre died at age 92 in 1937, newspapers reported that over a million people climbed the slope of Mount Royale to attend his wake and burial. Many of the mourners came from Maine, Massachusetts, Connecticut, Rhode Island, New Hampshire, New York and Vermont.

343

47

BLESSED LOUIS ORIONE

Louis Orione
1872 - 1940
Italy
Died Age 68

The fiery-tempered little Italian priest seemed to do everything with great speed. By the age of twenty, Louis Orione had established a boarding school for poor boys; while still a seminarian he began the foundation of a religious order; within three years of his ordination one of his orders had been canonically formed; his cause for beatification was underway a bare seventeen years after his death.

The benefactor of outcasts and the abandoned—the old, the sick, the insane, the retarded, maimed, orphaned, poor—Don Orione (Father Orione) had such complete trust in Divine Providence that time and again he was able to get whatever he needed for his work. Call it what you will—miracle or coincidence—there are a multitude of well-documented instances that bear out this fact. If Don Orione needed half a million lira by three p.m., a generous benefactor would show up with the money just in the nick of time. If one orphanage was filled, another house would be offered. His works of charity are best described in the words of St. Joseph of Cottolengo: "They are like pyramids upside-down, starting very small and growing rapidly." Today, in over two hundred institutions all across the globe, the spiritual sons and daughters of Don Orione carry on some of the most diversified charitable works of any religious order.

The son of a stone cutter and a strict but loving mother, Luigi—or Louis—Orione began life in poverty. As a young man he was good-looking and intelligent. Practically everyone who has recorded testimony about his appearance has been struck by his large, penetrating eyes. They seem to have served as a focal point for his forceful personality. Although noted for good manners, he was equally known for a short temper and impatience. He fought to correct these flaws in his personality all his life, and even in old

344

age was able to joke about his lack of success. When his doctor expressed astonishment that such a sick man should have lost more weight, Don Orione laughingly replied that he still had his sins and that they were very heavy.

Louis seems to have felt a vocation to the priesthood from an early age. By thirteen, he was eager to begin his training but had no money or contacts. As he was to do throughout his life, he turned to his Heavenly Mother for help. Shortly thereafter he was accepted into a Franciscan minor seminary. The life there was rugged and harsh, and Louis contracted a severe case of pneumonia. His parents were sent for in haste, and for one of the few times he could remember, the feverish fourteen year old heard his mother crying. He assumed he was going to die, and later said he was not nearly so disturbed by the thought of dying as he was by his mother's weeping.

While still critically ill, Louis dreamed he was surrounded by priests dressed in white habits, not the brown of the Franciscans. A few days later, the doctor advised the superiors that Louis' health would never be able to stand the Franciscan life, so he was sent home.

Later, Louis went to the newly formed Salesians in Turin at the Oratory where the saintly Don Bosco still presided over the work among the poor boys of the city. Louis was well liked for his good disposition and his sense of humor. He became the friend of Don Bosco, who told him to remember, "We are always going to be friends."

After two years, when he was just on the point of entering the Salesian novitiate, Louis left. This action surprised many, for he seemed particularly fitted for the Salesian life. However, as one of those who knew him there said, "Although we were surprised, we knew that it must be all right, since what he was doing was approved by his superiors." Within a year, he was accepted at the diocesan seminary in Tortona, where he was eventually ordained a diocesan priest.

On casual examination, it might seem that his actions merely indicated indecision over his vocation. However, since the ideas Louis gained while he was with the Salesians contributed greatly to the work he was to initiate, it seems that God wanted Louis to spend some time with them and then to move on. While with the Salesians, Louis not only observed their work of rehabilitation and technical schooling, but also the multiplicity of corporal works of mercy carried on at the great institute of the Cottolengo nearby. In addition, Don Orione never seems to have lost the Franciscan spirit of poverty which magnified his complete trust in God's willingness to provide for his works.

At the diocesan seminary, the other students at first teased Louis cruelly about his shabby clothes and his frugality, even going so far as to throw bread under the table in order to watch him solemnly pick it up and eat it with the words, "Bread comes from God and must not be wasted." He seemed "different" to them, and they teased him with the idea that they might be able to run him off. He worked as assistant sacristan to help pay his way, and spent much of his spare time helping the other seminarians. He made their beds, cleaned their rooms, and tended them when they were ill. Different and poor though he was, gradually the others began to accept him and eventually came to admire him greatly. Instead of them influencing him to leave, he influenced them to improve. One priest who was a seminarian at the time claims that he actually owes his vocation to Louis Orione. Throughout his life, Don Orione used the same principle; without trying to argue or explain, he used the best weapon he knew of—love.

When an orphan boy in trouble appealed to him for help, Louis remembered the work the Salesians were doing in Turin, and began his own oratory, or boys' club. After obtaining permission from the rector, the group began meeting in his room, and soon the boys were coming in droves. Their noise disturbed the canons, so Louis asked and received permission to move to the bishop's own garden. Soon even this grew too small.

Italy was in the throes of an economic depression at this time, and many boys spent much of their time in bad company on the streets. In addition, there was a severe shortage of priests. Louis, still a twenty-year-old seminarian, again approached the bishop and told him of a plan to start a boarding school for these boys. It would help keep the boys off the street, train them in technical skills as well as regular studies, and possibly foster much-needed vocations to the priesthood. This seemed logical to the bishop, so he told Louis he might have permission if he could make suitable arrangements.

Louis set off to see what he could do about getting a place and pupils. In the meantime, some people persuaded the bishop that he had acted hastily in granting permission for such a major work to a young, impetuous seminarian. At the end of the day, Louis was summoned and sent to the bishop, who withdrew his permission for the school. The young man expressed his disappointment and explained that he had already been given a donation which paid for the entire first year's rent on a suitable house and had accepted his first pupil—in only a few hours! The bishop recognized this as God's Will and said, "Kneel down. I'll give you my blessing again and I'll never take it away."

This incident marked the beginning of a relationship that for many years found the bishop in support of and generous to Louis Orione's projects. In spite of occasional differences, he time and again gave permissions that few others would have dared to grant.

Louis was ordained in 1895. He celebrated his first Mass served by boys from his school who were dressed by special permission in what later became the habit of the men's congregation he founded.

Soon a second and third school were established, the third being for the purpose of agricultural education, an intensely practical idea for the time. By now, Don Orione had gathered a group of priests and lay teachers to work with him. When, under pressure, the bishop attempted to remove the young priest as head of this group and replace him with an older man, a group of these teachers threatened to resign. The angry bishop realized that if this happened, the whole project was doomed, so he deferred his decision. Don Orione himself then went to talk with the bishop. His followers were afraid that with his fiery temper there would be a head-on clash that would result in a fiasco. Don Orione, however, exhibited such tact and diplomacy, and so successfully controlled his temper, that he got his way, as usual.

The work was growing and Don Orione, a man of prayer as well as of action, began to worry about the fate of the little group of workers. He decided they needed a powerhouse of prayer to support them, so he established a group of men which he named the Hermits of Divine Providence. He submitted this plan to Pope Leo XIII and the group was canonically formed only three years after his own ordination.

By 1906, his Work of Divine Providence had been given formal approval by the bishop. Don Orione wrote a rule for the Work, and traveled to Rome to present it to the new pope. On the way, he worried about an incident that had happened when he was a seminarian. He hoped the pope had a short memory, or would not bear a grudge over it.

While still in the seminary, Louis had asked about a friend of his, a fellow seminarian, who was a talented musician and was attending a music school run by the cardinal who later became the pope to whom Don Orione was to submit his rule. The boy's father was worried that the cardinal had made the boy a particular friend. The father felt that the cardinal was spoiling his son by showering him with favors.

Louis, too, was upset, and he went home and wrote an angry, impetuous letter to the cardinal, sharply expressing his disapproval. He mailed the letter and then cooled off. Crushed, he realized the brashness he had displayed. The thought of himself, a young seminarian, scolding one of the cardinals, shocked him greatly. For weeks he waited for repercussions, but they never came. He finally concluded, hopefully, that the letter had gone astray. No word came from Venice until right before his ordination when he received an anonymous gift of cloth for a new cassock. He assumed his young musician friend had sent it.

The audience with the pope went well. He approved the rule and gave Don Orione a gift of money and a promise of help. As the interview drew to a close, the pope rose and brought his breviary to Don Orione. He told the priest to look at what was inside it. Don Orione immediately recognized his own sprawling handwriting.

"Even the pope, you know, needs frequently to be reminded of the need for humility. For this reason I have kept your letter and have it with me all the time. By the way, did you get the material all right for your first cassock as a priest?" This pope, Pius X, did manage to keep his humility. He was canonized in 1954.

In 1908, a tremendous earthquake hit Sicily and part of Italy, killing nearly 100,000 people. Thinking of those who had been orphaned, Don Orione immediately set out for the disaster area. His exceptional qualities as an organizer were soon seen. He was rewarded by the government with a medal and by the pope with a fine new house near Rome for use as an orphanage.

For various reasons, the earthquake left, among its other dreadful legacies, a wave of problems with the clergy of the area. The pope appointed Don Orione as vicar general, a position he filled loyally and capably in spite of the fact that it was a most uncomfortable job. Recognizing its difficulties, the pope sent a message expressing his support. "Tell Don Orione to have patience, patience, patience, for it is with patience that miracles are worked." From that day, one of the special works of this saintly priest and his followers has been the help and support of priests in trouble. They do not preach to them, or attempt any rational arguments. They simply try to win them back by showing them Christian charity.

In 1915, another appalling earthquake struck and the civil authorities requested Don Orione's help. With 30,000 dead, conditions were pitiful, and everything was shrouded with a blanket of snow. At one village Don Orione gathered six hungry, poorly clothed and wounded children to take them back to a reception center in Rome. Large hungry wolves roamed the hillside, joining in the grisly search for bodies. Five of them, probably attracted by the smell of blood, were soon snarling about the coach carrying Don Orione and the children. Don Orione comforted the terrified children by saying, "Look how fond of us those big dogs are."

One young woman assisting with the disaster relief later told her father that the destruction had raised drastic questions for her until she noticed a small secular priest calmly moving about the area carrying two infants, one on each arm. Wherever he moved he brought order, hope, and faith into the midst of the destruction and despair. She says it was at that point that she felt the great love that could make itself felt through the completely self-oblivious tenderness of the priest.

One boy, later to become a priest, was twelve years old at the time of the earthquake. Both his parents and most of his family had been killed. Traveling by train to a relief center, he and another boy were sitting on either side of Don Orione. The three talked until the children began to fall asleep. Nodding off, this boy felt a large hand creep around his shoulder and draw him close. Sleepily, he noticed that the hand inconspicuously held a rosary. He says, "I kept that same picture [of Don Orione]—always combining prayer with action, inspired with love, with no affectation, no smarminess, no bunk."

Don Orione felt that the type of work his priests were doing would clearly benefit by support from an order of women, so in 1915 he founded the Little Missionary Sisters of Charity. Soon both orders were growing. To back them up spiritually, he began another order of contemplatives, the Blind Sacramentine Sisters. These sisters live a simple life of prayer and work which they can do in spite of their handicap. At the time of its foundation, it was the only order of this kind in the world. Each community Don Orione began stemmed from his vision of it as a practical and necessary part of his work. In his own words, "The Little Work exists to serve and to serve with love. With God's help it intends to live on in order to practice the works of mercy for the moral and material well-being of the most abandoned . . . its program is Dante's 'Our love has no closed doors.' " Don Orione's charity was extended to all, without question, and no matter what their beliefs.

A diabetic for years and in poor health, Don Orione suffered two strokes in 1939 and 1940. He retained his humor and his humility until his death. Sent to an infirmary a short time before suffering a third and fatal stroke, he found in the room set aside for him no light other than a small votive candle before a picture of Our Lady. Laughingly he inquired of the infirmarian, "Don't you think that this place is exactly like a mortuary chapel?" Later, the same infirmarian found him sitting up in bed trying to pare corns, gained from much time spent in prayer, off his knees. He said, "I don't know what is going to happen to this old body, but I want to get rid of these things before I die. We don't want a lot of people to see them and start making something of it." Scolded for working too hard when his nurse discovered he had just written twenty-two letters, he joked, "It's all right. We'll have a long rest in Paradise."

He died quietly a few days later, murmuring the name of Jesus.

In March of 1965, on the twenty-fifth anniversary of his death, Don Orione's body was exhumed in the presence of a medical examiner. In the words of Sister M. Bertilla Disegna: "To find and see the intact body of a person who died twenty-five years before is something which happens very rarely. When they took the top away from the tomb, they found the body, incorrupt, floating in water because the casket and even the clothes had all fallen apart. The same day . . . I went to see it. It was lying on a table still wearing its worn out cassock and covered by a sheet. Usually when I go to see and pray for a dead person, I take a very quick look at the body, and from far away, too, because it gives me an uncomfortable feeling. That time not only did I stand close to Don Orione's body, but I put my hands on his hands, praying him to intercede for me with God." This is only one more example of the drawing power this priest was able to exercise over those with whom he came in contact.

Don Louis Orione was declared Blessed by Pope John Paul II on October 26, 1980, only forty years after his death.

Everyone is struck by Blessed Louis Orione's large, penetrating eyes. All his life he strove to control his fiery temper. Though he was dismissed from the Franciscans because of poor health, Don (Father) Orione founded four religious orders to care for the old, the sick, the insane, the retarded, the maimed, orphaned and poor.

351

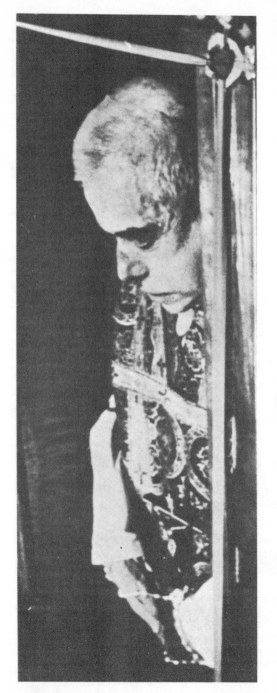

Actual photograph of Blessed Louis Orione's unembalmed body, found marvelously incorrupt exactly 25 years after his holy death. Cardinal Cushing stated, "Don Orione was one of the greatest apostles of charity and benefactors of the poor in modern times."

48

SAINT MAXIMILIAN KOLBE

Saint Maximilian Maria Kolbe, O.F.M. Conv.
Raymond Kolbe
1894 - 1941
Poland
Died Age 47

Raymond Kolbe was born January 7, 1894, in the small Polish village of Zdunska-Wola. His parents were poor; they were hard workers, as well as dedicated Catholics and patriotic Poles. As a child, Raymond was so mischievous that one day his mother, in exasperation, asked him, "Raymond, what is to become of you?" The boy asked himself the same question, then went to church to pray and repeat his question to the Blessed Mother. Later, he confided to his mother that at this visit he had had a mystical experience in which he saw Our Lady. In her hands she held two crowns: a white one for purity and a red one for martyrdom. "Which do you choose?" the apparition seemed to say. Raymond's heart leaped as he answered, "I choose both." Silently Our Lady smiled approval of the choice and faded from view.

Though money at the Kolbe household was always in short supply, the devout parents promised to make every sacrifice to aid their oldest son, Francis, in his plans to study for the priesthood. One of the sacrifices would be to keep Raymond at home to help his father and follow him in a trade. A local pharmacist noted the brightness of the young man and tutored him. Eventually he was able to attend a local technical school, and finally, in 1907, he joined his brother at the secondary school in Leopoli.

Raymond had a special talent for mathematics and physics, and was fascinated by astronomy and the prospects for space flight. He sketched many plans for rocket ships, and while a student in Rome, actually designed a spacecraft and applied for a patent on it. Although few took the idea of space travel seriously in the early days of this century, today the seminarian's plans do not seem foolish at all—only far-sighted.

The Conventual Franciscans opened a minor seminary, and Raymond and his brother both asked for admission. Raymond was invested in the Franciscan habit on September 4, 1910, and took the name of Maximilian.

During his novitiate, the young friar was beset by many interior trials, and for a time he thought of leaving. More and more, the fascinating world of science seemed to draw him away from the ideal of the priesthood. But on the verge of leaving, he again became firm in his resolve, and made his first vows on September 5, 1911. Friar Maximilian's superiors sent him to Rome to study, and by the early age of twenty-one, he had already earned a doctorate in philosophy. Later he also earned a doctorate in theology.

He was ordained a priest in 1918. Although supremely intelligent, Father Kolbe had no trouble recognizing the supremacy of faith over reason. Time and again, he practiced the virtue of obedience by following the instructions of his superiors in spite of his first inclinations.

Shortly after his ordination, he wrote to his younger brother, also a Franciscan: "The most deadly poison of our times is indifference. Its victims are found not only among worldly people, but in our own ranks as well. And this happens, although the praise of God should know no limits . . . Let us strive, therefore, to praise Him to the greatest extent of our powers." He had already recognized his mission—to combat religious indifference. For this purpose, he founded the Knights of the Immaculata. Father Maximilian had heard the story of the conversion of the Jewish agnostic, Alphonse Ratisbonne. He reasoned that if Mary could use the Miraculous Medal to conquer Ratisbonne, this medal would be an ideal means to gain other souls.

The program for the Knights was simple. The purpose was to conquer all souls for Christ through Mary. Each member was to dedicate himself to Mary Immaculate and become a tool for her use. Each Knight of the Immaculata was charged to work for the salvation of all souls, particularly the enemies of the Church. Each member wears the Miraculous Medal and daily prays the simple prayer inscribed on it—O Mary conceived without sin, pray for us who have recourse to thee—adding the words, "especially for the enemies of the Church and those recommended to you." The group was given the status of a Primary Union by Pope Pius XI in 1926, and has spread throughout the world.

In 1920, chronic tuberculosis flared up, and Father Kolbe was confined to a sanatorium for two years. All activity ceased, and even the work with the Knights hung in limbo. Although beset by interior trials, Father Kolbe was still able to say, "The Immaculate Virgin will maintain her victory over the devil, and to make this victory even more imposing, she will take us to her service, us weak ones with our not especially qualified talents." Father Kolbe expressed the seriousness and purpose of his mission thus: "Modern times are dominated by Satan and will be more so in the future. The conflict with hell cannot be engaged by men, even the most clever. The Immaculata alone has from God the promise of victory over Satan."

At the end of his confinement, Father Kolbe returned to work in Krakow and the movement began to grow. Soon, auditoriums grew too small, and the need for a printed form of communication became obvious. The first issue of *The Knight of the Immaculata*, sixteen pages long, carried this note from the publisher: "As capital is lacking, we cannot guarantee readers that *The Knight* will appear regularly." But through donations which often came just in the nick of time to avoid bankruptcy, *The Knight* continued its apostolate. Soon, the brothers were given land, they bought presses, and the first City of the Immaculata came into being for a publishing apostolate dedicated to spreading the glory of God and His Immaculate Mother. Of this, Father Kolbe said, "The best inventions are meant to serve her most of all . . ." Growth was rapid. By 1938, there were seven hundred sixty-two friars, most of whom were specialists in some phase of printing. By 1939, the circulation of *The Knight* had grown to nearly a million readers, and several other periodical publications had been added.

During the early 1930's, Father Maximilian himself traveled extensively to promote the publishing apostolate. He began in Japan, and worked there for some time. Always his own personality attracted volunteer translators to aid him in translating the material into as many languages as possible. Always, too, he counseled and warned his brothers not to look at the enterprise in terms of success and profit. He said, "The wrath of St. Francis would come upon the kind of city that strives for security in this world. It would be a blessing of Heaven if it were exploded in the air." He saw in this work a means to gain the salvation of men, and he insisted on personal poverty and dedication for all his workers.

In 1939, Father Kolbe was recalled from Japan to attend a provincial chapter in Poland. He was appointed superior at the City of the Immaculata, and intended to continue with his work there. But World War II broke out, and almost immediately after the German occupation, this Catholic publishing apostolate became the target of bitter and increasing reprisals. Calmly, Father Kolbe assured his brothers, "The true City of the Immaculata is in your hearts."

He was arrested by the Gestapo, then released in December of 1939. In February of 1941, in the company of four other priests, he was arrested again and imprisoned in Warsaw, where an inflammation of the lungs confined him to the infirmary. On May 28, 1941, Father Kolbe and three hundred twenty other prisoners were transferred to Auschwitz.

Though Father Kolbe was at first assigned to domestic work, within three days the commandant came and announced, "The parsons come with me." Handing several priests over to a subordinate named Krott, he said, "Take these useless creatures and parasites of society and show them what work means." Their work became the hauling of gravel for the walls of the crematorium. The priests were singled out for exceptionally cruel treatment, and at one point Father Kolbe was severely beaten and left for dead under a pile of brush. His companions carried him back to camp where he gradually recovered.

A fellow prisoner, an artist named Koscielniak, has given us an idea of Father Kolbe's attitude at the time. In June, Father Kolbe spoke to some of the prisoners, exhorting them to manly forbearance and speaking of the suffering by which God would prepare them for a better life. Father Kolbe said, "No, they will not kill our souls . . . They will not be able to deprive us of the dignity of a Catholic. We will not give up. And when we die, then we die pure and peaceful, resigned to God in our hearts."

Because Father Kolbe publicly acknowledged that he was a Catholic priest, many extra sufferings were heaped upon him, including beatings, attacks by dogs, the dirtiest and heaviest work, and the carrying of corpses. Totally exhausted, he at last succumbed to the lung inflammation and was placed in the infirmary. Though he was in wretched condition, a fellow priest who knew him there says that often Father Kolbe whispered, "For Jesus Christ I am prepared to suffer still more." He gave conditional absolution to each dead person, heard confessions, and prayed and spoke with all who asked for help.

Another prisoner in the infirmary recalled that he and several others often crawled across the floor at night to be near the bed of Father Kolbe, to make their confessions and ask for consolation. Father Kolbe whispered, "Hate is not creative. Our sorrow is necessary that those who live after us may be happy." He pleaded with his fellow prisoners to forgive their persecutors and to overcome evil with good.

A Protestant doctor who treated the patients in Block Twelve testified that Father Kolbe waited until all the others had been treated before asking for help. He constantly sacrificed himself for others. The doctor testified, "From my observations . . . the virtues in the Servant of God were no momentary impulse such as are often found in men; they sprang from a habitual practice, deeply woven into his personality. In Auschwitz, I knew of no other similar case of such heroic love of neighbor."

Father Kolbe recovered enough to be transferred to Block Fourteen and assigned to farm labor. At roll call one sultry night in July, one of the prisoners was missing. According to the rules of the camp, if a prisoner was not caught, ten would die in reprisal. The next morning the members of the cell block were stood in the broiling sun all day. By roll call that evening, the escapee had not been caught, and the commandant, Fritsch, imperiously went through the ranks pointing out ten victims who were then separated out, screaming, by armed guards. One Polish soldier, Sergeant Francis Gajowniczek, cried out, "What will happen to my family?" For the extraordinary events which followed, we have the word of several witnesses.

Father Maximilian silently slipped out of line, took off his cap, and stood before the commandant. Astounded, Fritsch asked, "What does this Polish pig want?"

Father Maximilian pointed with his hand to the condemned Polish sergeant. "I am a Catholic priest from Poland; I would like to take his place, because he has a wife and children."

Observers believed in horror that the commandant would be angered and would refuse the request, or would order the death of both men. The commandant remained silent for a moment. What his thoughts were on being confronted by this brave priest we have no idea. Amazingly, however, he acceded to the request. The sergeant was returned to the ranks, and the priest took his place.

With nine companions, Father Maximilian entered the starvation bunker. Before entering, the men were made to strip completely in the face of the guard's cruel gibe: "You will come out like dried-up tulip bulbs." From this time on, the unfortunate victims received neither food nor water. The secretary and interpreter for this underground bunker was so impressed by the heroism of Father Kolbe that he kept an exact record of the last days, more detailed than his job required.

Daily the guards removed the bodies of those who had died. Instead of continuous weeping and wailing, the sounds that arose from the bunker were the sounds of murmured prayers, the Rosary led by Father Kolbe, and hymns to Mary Immaculate. While the guards were away the secretary would sneak in to converse with and console the prisoners. At times the prisoners were so engrossed in prayer that they failed to notice the return of the guards until rude shouts interrupted them.

Reduced to the state of animals, some of the prisoners begged the guards for food or drink, or attempted to get close to the door of the cell. Some were kicked away rudely, and died from the blows. At all times, Father Kolbe remained constant, and neither whimpered nor whined. He encouraged and comforted the others. Constantly the guards found him praying, whispering his prayers when he could no longer speak them aloud. They were amazed.

At the end of two weeks, only four of the ten were left alive. The cell was needed for more victims, and the camp executioner came in and injected a lethal dose of carbolic acid into the left arm of each of the four. With a prayer on his lips, the last prisoner, Father Kolbe, raised his arm for the executioner. It was August 14, the eve of the feast of the Assumption of Our Lady into Heaven. The next day, Father Kolbe's remains were cremated.

Some time previously, at the death of one of his workers at the City of the Immaculata, Father Kolbe had composed an epitaph which applies equally well to himself: "He has left nothing of himself, for he gave everything to Mary Immaculate."

Maximilian Kolbe was beatified by Pope Paul VI on October 17, 1971, as a confessor. On October 10, 1982, Pope John Paul II canonized Father Kolbe—as a martyr! Thus did the apostolic authority of the pope fulfill in a marvelous, totally unexpected way the choice of the ten-year-old boy: a white crown for purity and a red crown for martyrdom.

The work of St. Maximilian Kolbe is carried on in the United

States by the Franciscans at Franciscan Marytown in Libertyville, Illinois. This is the American headquarters of the Knights of the Immaculata and Youth Mission for the Immaculata.

Raymond Kolbe as a youth. (He was later to be called Maximilian Maria Kolbe as a Franciscan priest.) At age ten he saw a vision of the Blessed Virgin Mary holding two crowns: a white one for purity and a red one for martyrdom. "Which one do you choose?" Our Lady seemed to say. Raymond's heart leapt as he answered, "I choose both." *(Picture courtesy of Ave Maria Institute, from I Knew Blessed Maximilian Kolbe, by J. Mlodozeniec.)*

In Poland and Japan the Knights of the Immaculata carried on an extensive publishing apostolate for the glory of God and His Immaculate Mother. Father Kolbe said, "The best inventions are meant to serve her most of all."

Upper: Father Kolbe in 1931 in Nagasaki, Japan.
Lower: Father Kolbe with Japanese students.

St. Maximilian Maria Kolbe founded the Knights of the Immaculata. Their purpose was simple: to conquer all souls for Christ through Mary Immaculate. Father Kolbe wrote, "Modern times are dominated by Satan and will be more so in the future. The conflict with Hell cannot be engaged by men, even the most clever. The Immaculata alone has from God the promise of victory over Satan." *(Picture courtesy of Ave Maria Institute, from I Knew Blessed Maximilian Kolbe, by J. Mlodozeniec.)*

361

Father Kolbe at Niepokalanow, the City of the Immaculata, in Krakow, Poland. During the German occupation in World War II, when this Catholic publishing apostolate became the target of bitter reprisals, Father Kolbe assured his brothers, "The true City of the Immaculata is in your hearts."

This picture of Father Maximilian Kolbe was taken at the time of his internment by the Gestapo, Warsaw, 1939.

Above: At Auschwitz, Father Kolbe told fellow prisoners, "No, they will not kill our souls . . . They will not be able to deprive us of the dignity of a Catholic. We will not give up. And when we die, then we die pure and peaceful, resigned to God in our hearts." This picture was taken in 1940, the year before Father Kolbe was sent to Auschwitz.

Opposite: St. Maximilian Maria Kolbe at Auschwitz concentration camp (painting by M. Koscielniak). Because Father Kolbe publicly acknowledged that he was a Catholic priest, many extra sufferings were heaped upon him, including beatings, attacks by dogs, the dirtiest and heaviest work, and the carrying of corpses. Though exhausted and in wretched condition, he whispered, "For Jesus Christ I am prepared to suffer still more."

Upper: St. Maximilian Kolbe offered to die in the starvation bunker at Auschwitz in place of another man. This is the artist's conception of the heroic offering. (Painting by M. Koscielniak.)
Lower: Sergeant Gajowniczek, the man for whom Father Kolbe gave up his life, and Sergeant Gajowniczek's family.

366

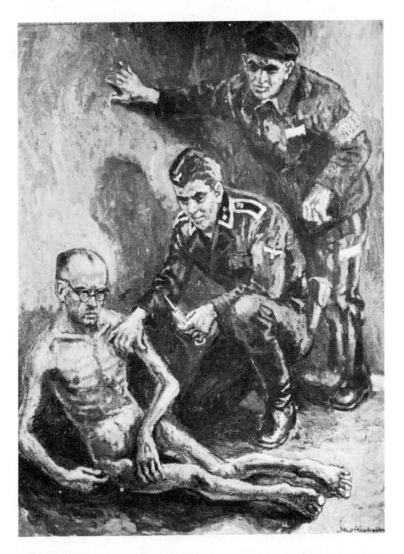

In the starvation bunker, Father Kolbe prayed aloud and comforted the other prisoners. At the end of two weeks, when the cell was needed for more victims, he and the three other inmates still alive were given an injection of carbolic acid. With a prayer on his lips, Father Kolbe raised his arm for the executioner. It was August 14, the eve of the Feast of the Assumption of the Immaculate Virgin Mary into Heaven. (Artistic representation by M. Koscielniak.)

49

TITUS BRANDSMA

Servant of God Titus Brandsma, O. Carm.
Anno Sjoerd Brandsma
1881 - 1942
The Netherlands - Germany
Died Age 61

When Titus Brandsma made up his mind that a certain course of action was the correct one, no amount of persuasion would change it. This determination eventually cost him his life. As spiritual advisor to the Dutch Catholic journalists, Titus declared that it would be morally wrong to accept Nazi propaganda ads. His stand was so firm that he was sent to the German concentration camp at Dachau, where he died in 1942.

Anno Sjoerd Brandsma was born February 23, 1881, in a Frisian area of The Netherlands. His birth took place at the family farm near Oegeklooster. As a boy, he was small for his age, having a slight build. He had blue eyes and dark blond hair. Typical of the farmers of the area, Anno's family had a rather stern attitude, although Anno was a lively, happy little boy. A good student, he enjoyed his studies, especially philosophy and language. He earned his doctorate when he was twenty-eight.

Anno's family members were staunch Catholics, in an area populated mainly by Calvinists. At home he acquired a deep devotion and strong prayer life. When he announced his intention of becoming a Carmelite priest, the only objection his family members put forward was that they had expected him to choose the Franciscan order. That the family was a deeply religious one is shown by the fact that three of Anno's four sisters became nuns, and his only brother became a Franciscan priest.

As a Carmelite priest, Anno chose the name Titus. He was involved in many activities. He was a professor of philosophy at the Catholic University of Nijmegen for nineteen years; in addition to his duties as a teacher, he traveled all over The Netherlands and part of Europe in the interest of many different causes, often doing his paper work on the train. Father Brandsma did a great deal of research in the field of mysticism, and was sent to lecture on the subject to his order in the United States. He managed to gain acceptance for the work of two modern religious artists, worked to promote Christian unity, and attempted to gain recognition for the Frisian language.

If Titus was a hard worker for groups, he was a harder worker for individuals. Once he phoned the superior of a convent to ask if he might pay her a visit. Upon his arrival, she was much astonished to learn that he had made the forty-five minute journey to ask her to help him find work for an unemployed man. The visit was more personal and more likely to succeed than a mere telephone call.

Until the time of his arrest, Titus offered Mass every Sunday at an old folks' home. He had heard that they wanted a priest but could not afford the expense involved.

Titus was himself a journalist and an author. He was therefore the logical choice for the position of National Spiritual Advisor to the Dutch Catholic journalists.

In 1935, marriage laws against the Jews were announced at Nuremberg. Father Titus wrote a protest to the press, and traveled up and down the country to make it known that the Church makes no such distinctions between races or peoples. Many children of Jewish origin were in The Netherlands receiving a Catholic education. Still extant is one of the priest's papers which explores the possibility of taking Jews to Brazil where the Carmelite Fathers had a mission.

Finally, Titus took the step that started him on the road that was to end at Dachau. He delivered a mandate to the Catholic press, stating that it was not possible for a publication to print Nazi propaganda and still claim to be Catholic. After this mandate, he knew that he would probably be arrested. Already the Nazis called him "that dangerous little friar."

For himself, Titus ruled out the option of hiding. He reasoned that if he himself did not stand firm, he could hardly expect the Catholic journalists to do so. When people reminded him of the danger he was in, he replied, "Well, now I am going to get what has so seldom been my lot, and what I have always wanted—a cell of my own. At last I shall be a real Carmelite."

Titus was arrested and held in several prisons before Dachau. In one of his letters home, he wrote, "I don't need to weep or sigh. I even sing now and then, but of course not too loud." His fellow Carmelites had to smile at this last remark, for at home Titus sometimes forgot himself in choir and practically roared out the songs in enjoyment. In prison at Amersfoort, the guards were less than kind, and Titus urged the other prisoners to pray for them. When they replied that this was a difficult request, Titus remarked matter-of-factly, "Well, you don't need to pray for them all day long. God is quite pleased with a single prayer."

There is no firm evidence to show whether Titus was actually given the opportunity to recant after he was sent to Dachau. However, more than once Nazi guards told other prisoners what a fool that priest Brandsma was, since by making a retraction he could have walked out a free man.

Titus Brandsma had only a short stay in Dachau—five weeks. However, the impression he left was a lasting one for many people.

Titus was not very good at making his bed in the approved fashion, and he received a severe beating each day on this account. He was also poor at marching; the instructor took great pleasure in stepping on the back of his heels so that the blood ran down his feet. The prisoners worked from 5:30 a.m. to 7:00 p.m., with only a thirty minute break at noon for some weak vegetable soup. Back in camp, the much-hated "ministers of God" were often made to do an extra thirty minutes of exercise. In spite of this extreme punishment, Titus never condemned his guards; rather, he calmly urged the others to pray for them. To one of his friends there, he mentioned, "Now I will have to practice what I have previously taught others."

For some reason, the barracks where the German priests were housed had a chapel where they were allowed to celebrate Mass. Frequently, one of the German priests slipped a consecrated Host to a man who passed it to Titus who then hid it in his eyeglass case until he could distribute it to others.

On one occasion when Titus had the sacred Host on his person, he was stopped by a guard. The guard searched him. He did not find the Host, but was not convinced that the little priest was not up to something, so he beat Titus severely anyway. Titus crawled back to the barracks where he was helped inside by a friend. The frail sixty-one-year-old priest smiled through his pain and said, "I knew Whom I had with me." Then he removed the eyeglass case from under his arm where it had been pressed the whole time.

Finally Titus became so weak that the supervisor of his unit insisted that he go to the camp "hospital." We have the word of the nurse who attended him regarding his last days there.

When Titus entered the hospital, he was already ill. He lay on a straw mattress; he had no crucifix to gaze at, no friendly religious to give him comfort. The doctors carried out some inhumane "experiments" on his body, while he merely repeated aloud, "Not my will, but Thy Will be done."

Titus spoke seriously to the nurse, and by questioning her discovered that she, too, was from a Catholic background in The Netherlands. When he asked her why she was there, she muttered something about "bad priests," and tried to excuse herself. He told her to observe closely the priests in the camp, and said he was glad to undergo his own sufferings for God's sake.

Titus gave this nurse the last thing he had to give, his rosary. She protested and said she had forgotten the prayers. "Well," he said, "if you can't say the first part, surely you can still say 'Pray for us sinners.'"

This nurse administered the final poisonous injection to the priest on July 26, 1942. Titus Brandsma was dead within ten minutes. His body was cremated three days later in the camp crematorium.

The Carmelite was not forgotten by the nurse who witnessed his last days. After the war, she returned to the Catholic Faith and eventually came forward of her own accord to testify for him.

The decree approving the writings of Titus Brandsma was issued on April 2, 1964. The decree officially introducing his cause was issued December 10, 1973.

Left: Anno Brandsma (later to be called Titus Brandsma) as a student.
Right: When Father Brandsma was in prison, another priest would sometimes slip a consecrated Host to a man who passed it to Father Brandsma who would hide it in his eyeglass case until he could distribute it to others. This drawing of Father Titus Brandsma was made by John Dons, a fellow prisoner in the Amersfoort concentration camp, who was later executed.

Father Titus Brandsma, a Dutch Carmelite priest who died in the Dachau concentration camp during World War II for refusing to allow Catholic periodicals to print Nazi propaganda ads.

50

EDITH STEIN

Sister Teresa Benedicta of the Cross, O.C.D.
Edith Stein
1891 - 1942
Germany - Poland
Died Age 51

Some girls from even very devout Catholic homes meet family opposition to a religious vocation. Edith Stein met family opposition to her call to Carmel on two counts. First, although she was from a devout home, it was a Jewish, not a Catholic family; and second, she was the beloved youngest of seven children of her widowed mother. In later life, Edith recalled that the first time she saw her mother break down and cry bitterly was the day Edith told her she had become a Catholic.

After her father's death when Edith was just a young child, her mother faithfully followed all the precepts of the Jewish religion. Although Edith attended services with the rest of her family, she had become an atheist by the time she was thirteen.

Throughout her life, Edith was considered a brilliant scholar. She was sent to kindergarten at the age of four, but this exceptionally bright little girl soon wore out the teacher. Kindergarten was no place for a budding genius, so she was sent back home to wait until she was six and could enter a regular school. Throughout her education, Edith scored high marks in all subjects except arithmetic, and by the time she was twenty-five she had earned a doctorate in philosophy.

Edith did not study simply to beat her classmates and take top honors. She was a girl who loved learning for its own sake. The headmaster of her high school made a German pun on her name: "Strike the stone [Stein] and wisdom will spring forth."

During her college days, Edith was able to study philosophy under the phenomenologist Edmund Husserl. She became friends with his assistant, Adolph Reinach, and with Reinach's new wife. When this friend was killed in 1917, Edith went to pay a visit to his young widow, whom she expected to find crushed in spirit. Instead, Anna Reinach was completely calm because her Christian faith had given her the strength to bear her loss. Of this visit, Edith later wrote, "It was then that I first came face to face with the cross and the divine strength which it gives to those who bear it."

On another occasion, Edith noticed the autobiography of St. Teresa of Avila at the home of friends. She could not put the book down; she finished it in a single night, and the next day she went into town and bought a Catholic catechism. After attending her first Mass, she followed the priest out of the church and asked to be baptized. When he asked where she had received instruction, she simply smiled and asked him to question her.

Shortly after Edith became a Catholic, she felt that she must also become a Carmelite. However, for fear of upsetting her mother too greatly, she decided to wait. In the end, she had almost twelve long years to wait.

For a while, Edith taught school at the Dominican school in Speyer. There the students remembered her as being a teacher with very high standards, one who could be stern if necessary. They also remember, however, that she always had time to help anyone who needed her in both scholastic and personal matters. They remember the little kindnesses she showed to homesick and lonesome girls.

Edith Stein had studied and was trained as a philosopher. With this background, it seemed only natural that she should turn to Catholic philosophy. She translated several important works and then wrote commentaries on them. This work led to her giving small talks to those at the convent. Her lectures became so popular that she was increasingly in demand as a lecturer to large public audiences. When she spoke to her spiritual advisors about her vocation to Carmel, they advised her to wait. They felt that her outstanding gifts were more needed in the world. So Edith taught, lectured, wrote, and waited. During this time she began to develop an increasingly deeper interior life of prayer. She was also often seen slipping quietly into town with small presents for some poor family, or for someone who was temporarily in hard straits.

In 1933, Hitler took power in Germany, and Edith's lecture schedule began to slow down. At last, largely because her public influence was at an end, her spiritual advisors allowed her to request entrance into Carmel. She was accepted as a postulant in the Carmel at Cologne, Germany.

Edith took a short vacation to Breslau to tell her mother of her decision. Again her mother was grief-stricken. Later, writing of her feelings at the time, Edith said, "There could be no rapturous joy. What lay behind had been too terrible for that. But I was perfectly at peace in the harbor of the Divine Will."

In 1934, at the age of forty-three, Edith was clothed as a Carmelite. She immediately put behind her the years as an intellectual and scholar in order to become a simple nun, seeking only a closer union with God. Her name was changed to Sister Teresa Benedicta of the Cross.

In the convent, Sister Benedicta was expected to attend to the domestic chores, as were all the sisters. Although she was never proficient, the sisters remember that she honestly put her best efforts into sweeping, mopping and dusting. She followed her patron, Teresa of Avila, in her regard for laughter. Sister Benedicta is remembered as being a very warm and cheerful person.

In the cloister, Edith was allowed to continue her writing. She wrote several pamphlets and booklets on Catholic subjects. She also continued a large correspondence with friends and former pupils, and through her influence several of these became converts. There were also some others who entered religious life. Her sister Rosa became a Catholic convert.

In 1938, the persecution of the Jews was in full force in Germany. There was danger not only for the Jews, but also for all who sheltered them. Sadly, the sisters realized that their much-loved Sister Benedicta must leave them.

Late one night, a doctor friend drove Sister Benedicta over the border into Holland, where she joined the sisters at the Carmel of Echt. Sister Benedicta had left the Carmel of Cologne out of love for her sisters, not for her own safety. This is shown by a note she gave to her new prioress, formally requesting permission to offer her own life as a sacrifice of atonement. "Dear Mother, I beg you, give me permission to offer myself to the Heart of Jesus as a [sacrifice] of atonement for the sake of true peace, that the Antichrist's sway may be broken." Edith prayed and suffered that God would comfort the Jewish people in their sufferings and lead them to the Catholic Church.

In 1940, Sister Benedicta's sister, Rosa, came to Echt and lived in one of the rooms of the convent outside the enclosure. Holland was occupied by the Germans.

In 1942, the Archbishop of Utrecht had voiced the Catholic protest against the horrible treatment of the Jewish people. Because of this and other Catholic protests, all Jewish members of the Dutch religious orders were arrested and taken to concentration camps.

Two German S.S. men appeared at the Carmel of Echt and gave Sister Benedicta and her sister Rosa ten minutes to pack. They escorted them to a police van while the local people stood and watched helplessly. Sister Benedicta and Rosa were first taken to a transit camp at Amersfoort, then to Westerbork. Some who escaped from this camp have testified regarding Sister Benedicta. Many of the mothers at the camp were so crazed with fear that they forgot to care for their children. Witnesses state that Sister Benedicta moved calmly and composedly about the camp giving assistance wherever she could, and taking care of the young children. This intelligent woman surely knew that she herself was on her way to die.

On August 7, 1942, one of her former students happened to be in the railroad station at Schifferstadt. Hearing her name called, she noticed Sister Benedicta standing at the window of a train.

"Give my love to the sisters," she called. "I am traveling eastward." She was traveling into Poland toward the German concentration camp of Auschwitz. Two days later, Edith Stein and her sister Rosa died in a crowded gas chamber at Auschwitz.

The decree approving the writings of Sister Teresa Benedicta of the Cross was issued in 1978.

Edith Stein (on the right) at age nine with her favorite older sister, Erna. Edith was the youngest of the seven children of a devout Jewish family.

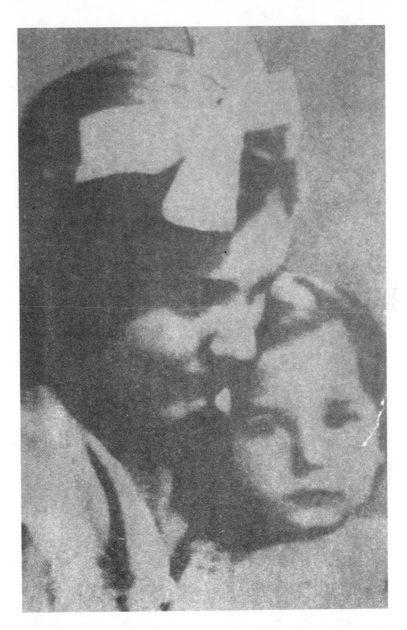

Edith Stein with her niece. This picture was taken when Edith was 14; although Edith attended Jewish services with the rest of her family, she had become an atheist by age 13.

Edith Stein (at left) at age 15 with her sister Erna and niece. From early childhood, Edith was considered a brilliant scholar.

Edith earned a doctorate in philosophy by age 25. She studied under Edmund Husserl and Adolph Reinach, searching for truth. One evening in 1921, Edith came across the *Autobiography of St. Teresa of Avila*. She stayed up all night and finished the book, and was immediately convinced that she had finally found the True Faith. This picture was taken around 1921.

Edith Stein as a Red Cross nurse in World War I. When Edith became a Catholic at age 30 (in 1922), her devout Jewish mother broke down and wept bitterly.

Shortly after she became a Catholic, Edith felt called to become a Carmelite nun. However, her spiritual advisors counseled her to wait. Thus
she spent many years writing, teaching, lecturing, and praying. This photograph was taken in 1931, when Edith was 40 years old.

The doctor of philosophy, Edith Stein. This photograph was taken in 1931. When Edith finally told her beloved mother of her decision to enter Carmel, the 84-year-old woman was heartbroken.

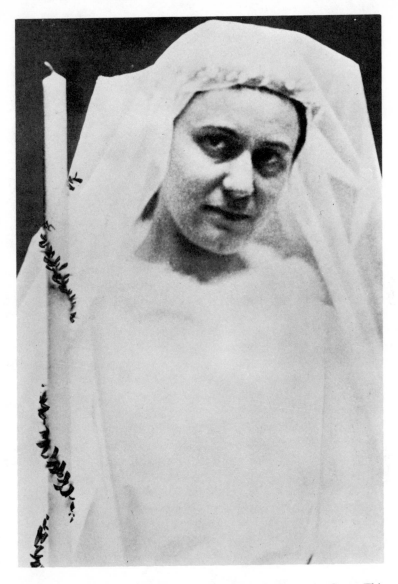

Edith Stein as a bride of Christ, Sister Teresa Benedicta of the Cross. This picture was taken on her Clothing Day as a Carmelite nun when she was 42 years old.

As a Carmelite nun, Edith gave herself completely to God. She prayed and suffered that God would comfort the Jewish people in their suffering and lead them to the Catholic Church.

This is the last picture of Edith Stein; it was taken in the summer of 1942, shortly before she died in a gas chamber at Auschwitz. Concentration camp witnesses later told of Edith Stein's great charity and unshakable peace of soul. A Carmelite announcement of her death stated, "She has been called to God who accepted her sacrifice, which will bear much fruit in the people for whom she prayed, suffered and died."

51

SISTER ALPHONSA

Servant of God Sister Alphonsa
Anna Muttathupandatu
1910 - 1946
India
Died Age 35

On July 28, 1946, an Indian Poor Clare lay serenely on her death-bed. Smiling, the sister reassured her superior, "Mother, I am in perfect peace." A few moments later, her life in this world quietly ended. Two days later, there was a simple funeral for this nun who had been confined to her sickbed for most of her few years in religion. Her sisters from the convent carried the coffin; the funeral was also attended by a few priests and relatives and a good many children from the convent school. Though she was virtually unknown outside her own small sphere, within six years thousands of visitors from all parts of India had flocked to her tomb. There they forgot caste and class distinctions; there an orthodox Hindu, a strict Muslim, and a zealous Christian knelt together. Ladies bedecked with jewels prayed beside pariah (untouchable—lowest Indian caste) women. Some were pleading for Sister Alphonsa's help; most were kneeling in thanks for favors received. Many of the thanksgivings were for miracles of healing. In addition to miracles of restoration of sight to the blind and of hearing to the deaf, more than forty cures of clubfeet have been attributed to Sister Alphonsa's intercession.

Sister Alphonsa was born on August 19, 1910. Baptized Anna Muttathupandatu, she was given the nickname Annakutti. Her father was a doctor, and in addition worked at cultivating a small plot of land belonging to the family. Her mother died within a few weeks of Annakutti's birth, and her aunt, Annamma, became her "second mother." As a young child, Annakutti lived in a small three-room cottage with a thatched roof and mud floor. The family were devout Syrian Catholics, and even as a child, Annakutti was known for her joyous observance of all the religious exercises common to this rite.

Anna attended the state primary school of Tonnankuzhi, where she was noted for her good scholastic record. In addition to her love for her Creator, she loved His creatures, and showed this love by her disposition and small acts of kindness. On one occasion when her elders were out, some beggers came to the door. Without the least hesitation, Anna gave them the supper which had been prepared for the family's evening meal. On the family's arrival back home, it is to be feared that she received a severe scolding.

Another time, at the age of eight, Anna was walking to school together with a Hindu friend. The friend later recounted the following incident in a deposition to the diocesan tribunal:

"A mischievous boy pushed us down a fence when crossing it. I was wild with anger and was determined that the boy should not go unpunished. I told Annakutti that I would report the matter to his father and also to our teacher. 'Look here, Lashmikutti,' she said in very persuasive tones, 'our pain is momentary; on the other hand, a report may produce more lasting consequences. He will be punished and may continue to be in the bad books of the teacher. If we forgive those who offend us, God will forgive our offenses.' This argument had its desired effect, and my anger gradually cooled down."

After completing primary school, Annakutti went to live with her aunt in Muttuchira in order to attend the state school there. There she had a dream in which a young Carmelite nun told her that her vocation was to become a sister. But Anna's aunt, who had no daughters of her own, loved Anna and wished to arrange a good marriage for her. Although she was quite strict in her supervision of the young girl, she dressed her in the finest clothes and jewels. As Annakutti was an attractive girl, her friends used to tease her and call her "little bride."

There were proposals of marriage even before Anna was in her teens. Canon law had not yet been made applicable to the Syro-Malabar rite, and it was not uncommon for young girls to be given in marriage at a very early age. After reviewing a number of proposals, the delighted aunt chose a young man from a well-to-do family. No one even consulted Annakutti. When she learned of the plans, she prayed and appealed to her uncle to forbid the marriage, but the plans proceeded.

Having read some early lives of the saints who had marred their beauty to prevent unwelcome attention from earthly lovers, Annakutti decided to cause some physical injury to herself so that she would not be able to go to church for the betrothal. The thirteen-year-old who had been promised in marriage but who wished to enter a convent went to a pit near her house where chaff and husks left after the harvest were burned. Sitting on the edge of the pit, she intended to put one of her feet into the fire and cause a burn which would make her unable to walk to church. However, she slipped and fell into the pit, burning her feet and legs, as well as her skirt and the ends of her hair. Somehow she managed to climb out of the pit, and went back to the house to change her clothes so that her aunt would not see what she had done. However, she fainted, and a goldsmith had to be called to remove the bangles from her ankles. The burns were serious indeed, and it was more than three months before they were healed and Anna was able to walk about. The scars remained for the rest of her life.

None of her relatives knew until after Anna's death that she had deliberately burned herself in order to escape marriage. When she confessed this action to her spiritual director in the convent, he scolded her. Her simple and childlike defence was, "I didn't know there was so much fire!"

But even this drastic action did not dissuade her aunt from planning a good marriage, so in desperation Annakutti appealed for mercy to her uncle, telling him that she preferred death to marriage. At last, her uncle gave in, and Anna was allowed to join the Poor Clares. (The Clarist Sisters of Malabar are Franciscan tertiaries who have adopted a community life and the usual religious vows. Though called Poor Clares, they are not the same as the Poor Clares elsewhere.)

In 1927, at the age of seventeen, Annakutti went to live at the convent of the Poor Clares to continue her education. In 1928, she became a postulant, and was given the name Alphonsa in honor of St. Alphonsus Liguori. As a postulant, she continued her schooling, working toward teacher certification. Postulants were allowed to go home for visits, and on one visit Anna's aunt showed that she still had not given up her dreams of a marriage for her niece.

As Annakutti arrived home, she noticed a goldsmith sitting at one end of the porch, hastily making ornaments. Her aunt approached and told her, "We have given our word for the marriage. We can't possibly retract. It would be kinder to kill us."

The postulant was sad to cause her aunt grief, but told her, "I, too, have pledged my word—to my Divine Lover. I cannot possibly retract it. I would rather die than break my word with Him."

In spite of all her aunt's recriminations and entreaties, Annakutti remained firm. Her uncle refused to allow any further marriage plans.

From the time of her clothing in the Poor Clare habit, Sister Alphonsa was rarely free from suffering caused by a number of diseases and ailments. Her vocation seems to have been to keep Our Lord company in His troubles. Willingly she submitted to the Will of God. She said, "Let the Lord do with me what He wills . . . for the benefit of a world which is marching to its ruin." An account of her physical sufferings reads like a study in pathology, and spiritually, like many saints, she had to pass through what is commonly called a "dark night of the soul." What were her feelings about this life? In one of her notes is this statement: "I made my perpetual vows on August 12, 1936. From that time it seemed as if a part of the Cross of Christ was entrusted to me . . . I have a great desire to suffer *gladly* . . . I wish to suffer without betraying even the least sign of suffering."

After a vision of St. Therese the Little Flower, Sister Alphonsa confided to her superior that the saint had promised her she would never again suffer from any contagious disease, but would still have various ailments until the time of her death. In her humility, she told Mother Ursula, "This was probably no vision, but a mere fancy of mine. Anyway, I would that you don't tell anyone about this."

Toward the end of her life, Sister Alphonsa's agonies had become so intense that the mother superior once asked her if she would not be glad to die. Sister Alphonsa humbly replied, "When I consider what a burden I am to others, I desire to die. But when I think of the many indignities Our Lord suffers at the hands of His own chosen people, I wish to suffer not only this, but far more until the end of the world. I am glad to suffer. A day without suffering is a day lost." In her wisdom, she realized that her sufferings for the intentions of others were a pleasing gift to Our Lord. Not content with the crosses given to her, she offered to take the crosses of others. Hearing that the local bishop and one of the teaching sisters were ill with malaria, Sister Alphonsa worried that they would be unable to do their work. She prayed that God would allow her to suffer the fever instead of them—a prayer that was answered almost immediately.

In 1932, during a period of comparative health, Sister Alphonsa had taught at the convent school while making her novitiate. The children sensed her great love for them, and loved her in return. When she became bedridden, the children considered it a great privilege to be able to assist her in any way, and often visited her with requests for advice and prayers.

A number of miraculous occurrences are related of the days when this humble sister was still alive. Her reputation for extraordinary sanctity began to be spoken of by those who had visited her sickroom. She was noted for giving good advice, and her prayers on behalf of people were answered speedily. She made a number of predictions which later were fulfilled. Most remarkable of all were the serenity and the loving smile on the face of this nun who suffered so intensely. A visiting bishop remarked, "Is this the face of a person who has been ill and sleepless for so long? There is no sign of illness." Later, he told the mother superior, "This is no illness. There is some divine mystery in it."

Sister Alphonsa had willingly accepted all the crosses God was pleased to send her, asking only that she be allowed to suffer gladly. All who knew her say that even when her agony was obviously causing her much suffering, she attempted to smile and spoke only cheerful words.

A few examples will illustrate the extraordinary events that were commonplace in the life of Sister Alphonsa. The local bishop had issued a pastoral letter defending the Church's right to run schools in opposition to the directives of the educational minister. The bishop was told that if he did not retract the letter he would be jailed. He visited Sister Alphonsa to ask her advice. She assured him that it was the minister, not the bishop, who would go. For some reason, the minister failed to order the arrest, and shortly afterwards was forced to relinquish his office under very tragic circumstances.

One evening Sister Alphonsa surprised a thief in her room while the community was at prayers. The man was frightened off by her screams, and left his "loot" beneath the window. Unfortunately, however, the shock caused Sister to lose her memory temporarily—including, for a period of about eleven months, her ability to read. On the day she regained her ability to read, she asked for a book. By mistake, someone handed her a book written in a dialect and an alphabet with which she was unfamiliar. As she began reading the book aloud, one of the sisters realized that she was translating from

Tamil, and asked how she could understand it. She could give no good explanation for this phenomenon.

On another occasion, the brother of one of the nuns, a man who lived several miles away, was suffering from tuberculosis. The doctors had still given him some time before they felt the disease would reach the critical stage. At eleven o'clock one night, Sister Alphonsa woke up and roused several of the sleeping sisters, asking them to pray for the sick man, as he had just died. The next morning, word was sent to the convent that he had died at eleven o'clock the night before.

In July of 1946, Sister Alphonsa requested permission from her spiritual director to pray for death, as she felt that she had become a burden to the community. He gave her permission with the requirement that she add the words, "if it be Thy Will." Sister Alphonsa then predicted she would die after her next agony, a prophecy that was fulfilled on Sunday, July 28. She died quietly after telling her superior that she was at peace, and asking the sisters to dress her in a clean habit for burial.

That afternoon and evening, her body lay in state, adorned with flowers in the convent chapel. Many friends came to pay their last respects. The homily at Sister Alphonsa's quiet funeral was given by her spiritual director, who said, "I assure you that as far as human judgement can be relied upon, this young nun was almost as saintly as the Little Flower of Lisieux."

How did such an obscure life attract the attention of thousands? After Sister Alphonsa's death, the children of the convent school missed the company of this nun who had been their good friend. During her life, they used to visit her sickroom with their requests for prayers to aid them in all the small trials of childhood—successful marks on exams, matters of friendship with their peers, happiness in their lives at home. After her death, they went to her tomb to continue their requests. When their prayers were answered, they were vocal in their gratitude. They told their elders, and soon the elders too began asking for Sister Alphonsa's intercession. In affectionate devotion, they began to light candles at the tomb. No one thought to consult the ecclesiastical authorities. Though the authorities frowned on this unauthorized devotion, soon the people's fervor could no longer be ignored. The fame of the humble sister began to spread, and people from all over the country began traveling to her tomb.

The echo of the extraordinary events taking place at Sister Alphonsa's tomb reached Rome, and the Cardinal Secretary of the Sacred Oriental Congregation, which attends to matters regarding the Malabar rite in Syria, sent a personal letter to the Bishop of Palai to start the preliminary diocesan investigation for Sister Alphonsa's beatification and canonization. The tribunal began its work in the extraordinarily short time of less than seven years after her death. Sister Alphonsa's writings were approved on January 8, 1970.

The body of Sister Alphonsa, decked in flowers, lay in state while people paid their last respects. At her funeral, her spiritual director said, "I assure you that as far as human judgement can be relied upon, this young nun was almost as saintly as the Little Flower of Lisieux."

Sister Alphonsa, an Indian Clarist nun. At an early age she decided to give herself to Our Lord by becoming a nun, although her family planned marriage for her. At age 13, she deliberately burned herself in order to escape the betrothal ceremony.

— 52 —

VEN. MARIA TERESA QUEVEDO

Venerable Maria Teresa of Jesus Quevedo, Ca. Ch.
Maria Teresa Quevedo
1930 - 1950
Spain
Died Age 19

The third child of the prominent Doctor Calixto Quevedo and his wife was born April 14, 1930, only a year before the fall of the Spanish monarchy. The infant girl was baptized Maria Teresa Josephina Justina Gonzalez Quevedo y Cadarso, after Ss. Teresa, Joseph, Justina, and Our Lady. She was often called Teresita or Tere, but she lived the "Maria" of her name.

At age thirteen, Teresita consecrated herself to Our Lady in the formula composed by St. Louis De Montfort. Her beautiful motto was, "Mother, may all who look at me see you." Explaining her Marian devotion to her cousin, Teresita said, "I love Our Lord with all my heart. But He wants me to love Our Lady in a special way and to go to Him with my hand in Mary's."

Teresita's mother described her children in a letter to her sister-in-law when her youngest was three: "Louis has the manner of an army general, Conchita is quiet and thoughtful . . . Teresita is a bundle of happiness. Everyone loves her . . . pretty as a picture, but terribly self-willed. Perhaps we have indulged her more than we should because she is the youngest. Whatever the reason, she cannot be crossed. We shall have to do something about it."

"No me gusta!" (I don't like it!) was Teresita's frequent comment at table. Her finicky appetite often led to such outbursts of rudeness. Later, she said, "After such disagreeable outbursts—there were a number of them before I received my First Holy Communion—Tia [Teresita's aunt] would watch for the first sign of sorrow on my face. I never apologized, I am ashamed to say. What patience and kindness she possessed! Not a word about my bad behavior to me, nor to Mama and Papa. She taught me many lessons in that way—

patience and repentance. Without a word, she forced me to grow truly ashamed of myself."

The happy but headstrong little girl apparently took the matter of her self-control upon herself. After her First Communion, her father noticed quite a change in Teresita. He wrote to his brother, "The extraordinary power she had acquired over her quick, impulsive nature touched me deeply."

Later, as we learn from her confessor and her notes, she found another aid to self-control; this was her love for Mary. Every time Teresita triumphed over her revulsion for certain foods, or managed to put away her own will, she silently counted the incident as a little gift for Mary.

During much of the time of the Civil War in Spain, the Quevedo family lived away from their apartment in Madrid. During one of their stays in a fishing town, the cook noticed cakes and breads disappearing from the larder. Teresita's sister later confessed that Teresita had "snitched" them to take to the children of the fishermen. Even the plainest of fare from the wealthy Quevedo household was a rare treat for these children.

After the war, the family moved back to Madrid, where the girls attended Our Lady of Mount Carmel Academy. Teresita worked hard and made relatively good grades, but she also got into her share of schoolgirl mischief. At a designated period each day, the students were all supposed to be working in absolute silence on handwork. On one occasion, Teresita was embroidering a large tablecloth and enjoying a forbidden conversation with her cousin Angelines. Suddenly the two magpies heard the measured tread of a sister coming down the hall. Angelines had no book or embroidery—what was she to do? Quickly, her cousin threw the large tablecloth over Angelines, and with a smile and a nod Sister passed by the industriously sewing Teresita.

Teresita was not fond of books, and often said school would be fine if there were no books to study. In study hall, she often spent time sketching on her paper or jotting notes rather than working on one of her assignments. Nevertheless, she got along well with her teachers, and her happy nature made her a favorite with the other students. She was elected best dressed of her class, president of the sodality, and captain of the basketball team which won the school championship in 1947. A good dancer, she enjoyed most things a normal Spanish girl her age enjoyed—including the bullfights, although she clapped for the bull as often as for the matador.

Each year the academy girls of a certain age made a retreat. In 1941, at the age of eleven, Teresita would normally have been too young to attend. However, she asked for and received special permission to go along with the other girls. During the retreat, each girl kept a little notebook of points to remember from the lectures and discussions. It is probable that Teresita did not understand all the items in the discussions, but one thought which the priest presented and which Teresita quickly grasped was the necessity of making a resolution for life. Teresita's resolution, later found in this notebook, was: "I have decided to become a saint."

The road Teresita decided to travel to fulfill this resolution was paved with numerous small conquests of her own will. Always, her companion and guide on this road was Our Lady. Like St. Therese of Lisieux, she realized that even the smallest personal sacrifices were pleasing gifts for God.

Tennis was Teresita's favorite game, but no matter how hard she tried she usually came in second. By her senior year, she had improved her game so much that everyone felt certain she would win the championship. After the big game, Teresita returned home with such a happy expression that her mother asked if a new champ had been added to the family. Teresita said, "If you consider one who has won a spiritual victory a champion, then you have your champ, but not a tennis champion."

Teresita then told her mother that before the match one of her friends had jokingly said that she was going to order a larger crown for the champion, as Teresita's head would be swelled by her victory. Although the remark was made only in jest, Teresita began to wonder if her desire for the championship might be only vanity. In regard to the match, Teresita asked Our Lady for whatever would please Jesus. Then at the match she played her best, but she lost. On the way home, Teresita stopped at the church to tell Our Lady that she understood the decision. An old woman was begging at the church door and Teresita gave her some money. In turn the beggar handed Teresita a card; she carried this with her to Our Lady's altar without glancing at it. As she knelt, the card fluttered to the floor, and she noticed that it had no picture, only a slogan—"Love makes all things easy."

One of Teresita's friends remembers her party days. "Everyone flocked around Tere at a party, especially the boys, because her [conversation] was sparkling. Tere loved people, and she loved parties . . . I never knew her to miss one."

In 1947, with the consent of her confessor, Teresita petitioned the Mother General to be admitted to the Carmelites of Charity. In the same interview, Teresita asked, "Then may I go to the missions in China?"

Laughing, the superior replied that she would have to go to the novitiate first. It seemed that Teresita had always wanted to speed up everything. Several times her father had to restrict her use of the car, for she drove too fast to suit him. And many times she asked her aunt how she could become holy more quickly.

Throughout her postulancy and novitiate, Teresita tried hard to overcome even the slightest fault. She was known for her recollection in prayer and her charity to the other sisters. Even during her school days this recollection had been noticed by one of her teachers, Sister Ramona. Sister Ramona tells us that one day, wishing to see exactly how recollected Teresita was, she knelt beside her for ten minutes while she said the Rosary. Later that afternoon she asked Teresita, "Who was the sister kneeling on the prie-dieu with you after lunch today?" Teresita replied, "No one knelt on the prie-dieu while I was saying the Rosary, Sister. At least, I don't remember anyone." Teresita, or Sister Maria Teresa, liked nothing better than to keep Mary in all phases of her life.

In May of 1949, Teresita became ill with a bronchial disorder, and her father came to the convent to persuade her superiors to send her home with him for treatment. They decided to wait a few days. Teresita seemed to recover after a dose of streptomycin, so she was allowed to stay to continue her novitiate.

During advent of that year, a group of novices were discussing the coming holy year (1950) and the pope's intention of proclaiming the dogma of the Assumption. Teresita mentioned that she felt she would be allowed a special favor that year. After much questioning, she admitted that she believed she would be allowed to celebrate the proclamation in Heaven.

Some laughed, some protested, none took her very seriously. She replied, "Go on, little sisters, laugh at me. But remember what they say about the one who laughs last! Every one of you will probably sing my requiem before the close of 1950. I know I shall be with my Mother on her glorious day. Can you imagine, sisters, what Heaven will be like when the dogma of the Assumption is declared?"

During the last part of January, 1950, Dr. Quevedo was called in to examine Teresita to see what was causing her such severe head and back aches. With a heavy heart, he admitted to the superior that he suspected tubercular meningitis. At the most, she had only a few months to live. Although his natural inclination was to bring his child home, Dr. Quevedo realized that Teresita would be happier to die in God's house. He decided to ask the superior to allow her to stay in the convent. As he was bringing up the subject, Reverend Mother interrupted to ask him if he would please not take Teresita home.

Although she had not completed her novitiate, Teresita was allowed to take her vows to become a fully professed sister. She was also given Extreme Unction, as her father feared she might lose her mental faculties. Although her mind did wander at periods toward the end, she never totally lost the use of her reason.

Teresita's whole community began to pray for a miraculous recovery. Asked why she was in such a hurry to get to Heaven, she replied, "In Heaven, nothing will separate me from Jesus and Mary. Besides, I am of very little use here, but from Heaven you will see how busy I shall be."

The next three months were filled with pain for Teresita. The only way to relieve the intense agony of the headaches was to draw off some of the spinal fluid by a spinal tap. In all, the doctors punctured her spine a total of sixty-four times. At all times, Teresita attempted to accept the pain without complaint.

Finally, Holy Week of 1950 arrived. On Monday, Teresita was in great pain, and she was in a coma part of Tuesday and Wednesday. Thursday she seemed better, and asked for a snack in mid-afternoon. A severe spasm of pain hit Thursday evening and left her with a stiff neck and a headache. She was barely conscious, but fought having another spinal tap, although it would have provided some relief. On Holy Saturday, the community began to chant the prayers for the dying. "Pray for her," the community intoned. "Pray for me," came the weak response.

Around eleven p.m., Teresita suddenly smiled and looked up. "How beautiful, O Mary, how beautiful you are." The sisters looked wonderingly at each other. Did Teresita see the Blessed Mother? Or was she merely thinking of things soon to be? Teresita gave a final soft sigh, and then quietly passed away.

Before her death, Dr. Quevedo had asked Teresita to pray for her mother, as she was taking her daughter's illness very hard. Teresita promised that the first thing she would do when she got to Heaven would be to ask God to send complete resignation to her mother. From the time she was told of Teresita's death, Senora Quevedo was completely resigned to God's Will.

The preliminary investigations into Teresita's life and virtue were opened in the Marian Year 1954. In 1959, her cause for beatification was presented to the Sacred Congregation in Rome, and a decree confirming the validity of the cause was issued in 1971. Teresita has been declared Venerable, and the cause for her beatification is nearing completion.

Venerable Maria Teresa Quevedo, or "Teresita," at age six. She was born in Spain in 1930. Teresita was a happy but terribly self-willed child, given to outbursts of rudeness. But after her First Communion, she acquired extraordinary control over her quick, impulsive nature.

Teresita at 17, in a pensive mood. She wanted to do everything in a hurry—including becoming a saint. At a retreat at age 11, Teresita had written down this resolution: "I have decided to become a saint."

Teresita around age 18, shortly before she joined the Carmelites of Charity. She consecrated herself to Mary at age 13, and lived this consecration the rest of her life.

Teresita as a novice (age 19) in the Carmelites of Charity, where she was called Sister Maria Teresa. She predicted that she would be in Heaven to celebrate the proclamation of the dogma of the Assumption of Our Lady into Heaven.

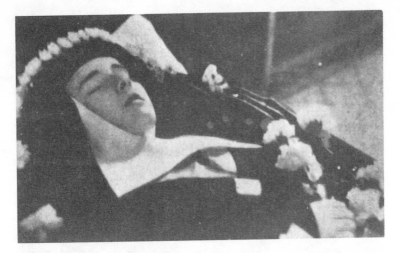

This photograph of Teresita in her coffin shows her dressed as a fully professed Carmelite of Charity (note the black veil). She was allowed to take her vows shortly before her death at age 19, although she had not yet completed her novitiate. Teresita's last words were, "How beautiful, O Mary, how beautiful you are."

53

MARY ANN LONG

Sister M. Loretta Dorothy
Mary Ann Long
1946 - 1959
United States
Died Age 12

A fatal disease is usually sad, no matter who its victim is. When this disease includes the problems of disfigurement, it becomes a tragedy—and when it strikes a child the sadness is almost unbearable. Today as never before, many suffer martyrdom by the dread disease of cancer. Disfiguring, painful, often causing loss of wealth, family and friends, this killer is on the rampage. In spite of significant advances in prevention and control, many battles are still lost daily to cancer.

Mary Ann Long suffered from all the tragic consequences of cancer, and in 1959 she lost her battle with the disease. How, then, is her life remembered not with grief but with joy, love, and thanksgiving? The answer to this question lies in the life of the child herself. Even at so young an age, she had a definite mission in life, and she fulfilled this mission to the best of her abilities. No cause for canonization has been begun; however, those who knew Mary Ann and came under her influence feel that her beautiful soul now resides in Heaven.

Mary Ann was one of four children of a family from Kentucky. Misfortune had followed the family, leaving it in poor circumstances. Mary Ann's mother was ill and could not care for a sick child. At the age of three and a half, in spite of X-rays, radium, and the removal of her eye, Mary Ann was diagnosed as incurable at the Tumor Clinic in Louisville. The hospital could no longer keep her. The family doctor advised her parents to send her to the home run by Dominican sisters in Atlanta. The thought of sending their dying child so far from home and to strangers was terrible to her loving parents. However, no other option was financially possible, so they reluctantly agreed to let her go there until her mother could regain her health.

Sister Veronica, at that time superior of the home, saw Mrs. Long arrive in a taxi with the new patient. She was eager to meet this child about whom a social worker in Louisville had written to her, "This patient is a very loveable little girl and one who touches the hearts of all who come in contact with her."

As Sister walked out to greet the new arrivals, Mrs. Long felt apprehensive about Mary Ann's reaction to a woman who was dressed so strangely. Mary Ann had never seen a nun before. But before her mother's astonished eyes, she ran to the welcoming arms. Once inside, she was lovingly passed from one set of arms to another. Laughingly she greeted each, sister and patient alike, with no shyness or hesitation.

One of the sisters described her first view of Mary Ann in this way: "She does look awfully tiny and kind of thin, but her face is round and happy-looking. One cheek is swelled badly, and the eye is closed. You should see her hair—it's so soft and curly." Mary Ann's one good eye was brown, and sparkled with the joy of life.

Mary Ann was distracted by the sisters while her mother sadly left. The sister on duty that night was afraid that Mary Ann would cry for homesickness. Instead, she slept quietly and in the morning investigated the entire ward. At the bed of one of the patients Mary Ann stopped, climbed up on the bed, sympathetically looked at the patient and stroked her hand. For the rest of her short life, Mary Ann was to continue to console all the residents of the home in her own cheerful and sympathetic way.

Tales of pious and religiously oriented children are often exaggerated, and sometimes the teller mistakes the innocence of childhood for something out of the ordinary. Mary Ann exhibited all the ordinary goodness of childhood, but there was also something special about her life and her ability to console those who came to console her.

Our Lady of Perpetual Help Home in Atlanta, Georgia, is a pleasant place of refuge and love for the poor who are suffering from incurable cancer. Although most of the residents are adults, child patients are not unknown there. The sisters who staff the home, Servants of Relief, see more human misery and physical corruption in a single day than many others meet in a lifetime. These sisters truly understand what Christ meant when He said that those who serve the least of His brothers actually serve Him. They are able to see beyond the tragic outer shell of a patient to the presence of God in the soul within. Mary Ann's special gift was the ability to display her interior beauty despite her disfigured outer self. She strove completely to forget her own self in favor of the needs of others.

Mrs. Long had explained to the sisters that the family had no religious affiliations, and when asked if she wished Mary Ann to be baptized, she promised to consult with her husband and write her decision. The parents decided to ask the sisters to have Mary Ann baptized, and the patients joyfully prepared for the ceremony. A Methodist contributed a white satin nightgown she had received as a gift, and a Baptist patient made it into a white dress for the beginning of Mary Ann's Christian life.

The sisters tried to provide all the things possible to make a comfortable and happy home for their youngest patient. The other patients and friends of the home derived much pleasure from her childish joy in their small gifts. In addition to caring for her temporal needs, the sisters provided for Mary Ann's spiritual needs as well. She was intelligent and a quick learner, and the sisters taught her much about the love of God. When one of the sisters tried to explain the Stations of the Cross, she ended by lifting Mary Ann up close to the stations so she might see better. Sadly, Mary Ann said, "Oh, poor Jesus." This is perhaps a normal childish reaction to such a sad depiction. But Mary Ann seemed to take her lessons in religion and absorb them in a mature way for so young a child. Her prayer, "Jesus I love You with all my got," was as close as she could get to "with all my heart." She did not stop with the formal, rote prayers taught to her, but soon began adding her own intentions.

Once, Mary Ann wistfully questioned Sister Loretta about Heaven, suggesting that it would be light and she would be able to see with both her eyes. Sister Loretta told her, "Heaven is everything that is perfect and is our true home, but this must not make us forget our work here, the things God put us here to do."

The tiny four year old shocked Sister by her immediate grasp of this definition. Mary Ann said, "You mean we make it so bright and cheerful here that everyone will know what it'll be like in Heaven?"

Mary Ann rarely cried, but when she did she usually had a good reason. Good reason or not, she would struggle against this display. One day when she was leaving the chapel with one of the sisters, the tears began to fall. When questioned as to the reason, she told the sister that she wanted to have Jesus come to her, as He came to everyone else. The sisters began to prepare her for First Communion, and promised to pray that she be allowed to make it within that year. Trying to explain to her what was meant by an examination of conscience, Sister Loretta doubted if she could grasp this concept fully. However, Mary Ann seems to have understood the "zamination," for after telling Sister of a particular piece of self-willed naughtiness she had performed that day, Mary Ann contritely said, "I'm sorry, Baby Jesus."

She was allowed to make her First Communion at the age of five, and was confirmed at six. She chose the name Joseph for her confirmation name, explaining that since he had taken care of Baby Jesus and Blessed Mother, he would also take care of her.

Mary Ann's parents loved her dearly. Financially they were unable to visit her often, but they came when they could. In spite of her cheerful behavior, her father was troubled at the thought of having sent his child to an "institution." When Mary Ann was six, her parents took her home with them, but after a short time her mother called the sisters and asked them to take her back. She said, "We just don't seem to be able to make her happy here." Although Mary Ann loved her family, she was more comfortable at the home, away from the unkind stares of those outside her family who saw, at first, only her deformity. A few years later another attempt was made to take Mary Ann back to Kentucky. This, too, failed, and she spent the rest of her life with the sisters and patients she loved so dearly.

The retreat master of the nearby Trappist monastery paid a visit to Mary Ann soon after this incident. She told him about her family, her trip to Kentucky, and the bad children who had mocked her there. He asked her, "Mary Ann, do you want to help those children become good? They haven't been taught to be good and they need help." After Mary Ann indicated how willing she was to help, the priest explained to her how she could accept her disappointments, hide them, and offer them as a gift to the Baby Jesus to help these children. She never forgot the lesson, and if she ever shed tears after that, it was not over little things.

Mary Ann made many friends through her lively and charming personality. Sometimes visitors asked her why she did not pray that God would cure her. She would simply smile and say, "This is the way God wants me." By this time, Mary Ann had seen herself in a mirror, and she knew what she looked like. Her calm obedience to God's Will for her impressed and inspired all who knew her.

Some of Mary Ann's greatest joys came from the times her sister Sue was allowed to come and spend the summers with her. The two girls were very loving, and Sue was the first of Mary Ann's family to follow her into the Catholic religion. Mary Ann had once asked a visiting priest if she might become a nun; one of the sisters sewed little habits for Mary Ann and Sue to play in.

After seeing a cloistered Visitation monastery, Sue began to slip off to the chapel when the two girls played at being nuns. Mary Ann continued to help the patients in the ward. When she could not locate Sue, she exclaimed in exasperation, "All I say is if all Sue wants to do is go to chapel and pray, she just better join another order . . . We work!"

Mary Ann loved to do things for other people. Often, her gentleness and cheerful acceptance of her own state in life made it easier for the other patients to accept their state. One patient was almost helpless. Mary Ann went often to help her brush her hair or do other small things the patient herself could not do. When Mary Ann asked this lady if she would like to say her night prayers with her, the lady admitted that she did not know how to pray. Mary Ann began to teach her and then enlisted the aid of others in the project. She was thrilled to become this patient's Baptismal sponsor.

Another patient came to the home from Kentucky because her husband had deserted her after discovering she had incurable cancer. Mary Ann did not know the background of this case, but she recognized that the woman's spirit was crushed. She informed the lady that she, too, was from Kentucky. She brought the patient a drink of water, and became her special "nurse" in the next couple of days. This woman told one of the sisters, "Now I know why I came all the way from Kentucky. Years ago I was a Catholic. I've wanted to come back for a long time and didn't know how." That night she died. Again it seemed that Mary Ann had helped a soul to find God.

Mary Ann's mission appears to have been to live her own life in such acceptance of her state that she continually drew others to God. Her constant prayer was that her own family would become Catholic, and within a few years after her own First Communion, her three sisters, one by one, began to follow her example. The summer after her death, her mother, too, was baptized.

Mary Ann had often expressed a wish for a baby that she could care for. When Mary Ann was eleven, her wish was fulfilled by Stephanie. This very young cancer victim was the seventh child of warm and loving parents. These parents, particularly the mother, found it very hard to give up their baby. Only the counsel of their priest convinced them they should take Stephanie to the home.

Mary Ann met the parents at the door. Recognizing the parents' inner turmoil, she told them, "I didn't pray for a baby to be sick, but I prayed that if a baby was sick it would come here." Later, Stephanie's mother said that Mary Ann's words helped her to understand God's purpose for the baby. Her doctor and others had told her that the baby was useless, and the kindest thing would be simply to let it die. But Stephanie's mother understood the situation better after Mary Ann's remarks. In the mother's words, "Stephanie was needed; she wasn't useless; this child with a bandaged face and a heart full of love needed her. My whole attitude changed and as the months passed and we came back to see Stephanie the hurt healed and was replaced by a quiet joyful gratitude for her. Not only did she bring happiness to Mary Ann but she brought it to all in the home."

Mary Ann, for her part, was an excellent nurse and a real help with Stephanie. She never complained when the baby kept her awake at night. She comforted Stephanie and helped to feed and care for her. Mary Ann seemed very pleased when Sister assured her that she really was a big help in caring for this child.

In September of 1958, Mary Ann's physical condition began to grow much worse. One of the sisters remembered that Mary Ann had always wanted to be a sister, and she was allowed to become a Dominican tertiary. When the sisters suggested that the ceremony be performed in her own room, Mary Ann insisted on going to the chapel, where she received the name of Sister Loretta Dorothy and the scapular of the Order of St. Dominic.

A large growth appeared in Mary Ann's mouth, and it soon became impossible for her to eat normally. She never complained, and when her parents came for a visit and a sister suggested that they eat in the breakfast room rather than in her room as they had done on past visits, Mary Ann was quick to understand the suggestion. "Oh yes, Sister, because it wouldn't be good for Mama and Daddy to watch me struggling to eat." Even in this small matter, Mary Ann was concerned about her parents rather than about herself.

Shortly before Christmas, another serious hemorrhage occurred.

The sisters lit the candle which now always stood ready at Mary Ann's bedside. Over and over, Mary Ann repeated, "Dear Jesus, I love You."

In January, Mary Ann was visited by a self-styled faith healer. This boy's mother had at one time been a patient in the home. As he entered her room, he greeted her with the words, "The Lord Jesus can heal you, Mary Ann." When she made no reply, he repeated his statement.

Mary Ann looked at him. "I know Jesus can heal me," she said. "I know He can do anything. It doesn't make a bit of difference whether He heals me or not. That's His business."

Mary Ann died quietly in her sleep during the night of January 18, 1959. In her hands she clutched the rosary she was saying when she fell asleep.

At Mary Ann's funeral, Bishop Hyland pointed out two possible attitudes toward her death. "From the viewpoint of the world, the death of Mary Ann was indescribably sad. This viewpoint fails to take into account that the primary purpose of our existence on earth is to know, love and to serve God, and to prove thereby our worthiness of eternal happiness with Him in Heaven."

None who knew her can doubt that Mary Ann, in the space of the twelve years allotted to her, did indeed know, love, and serve her God.

Mary Ann Long was thrilled to meet Santa Claus.

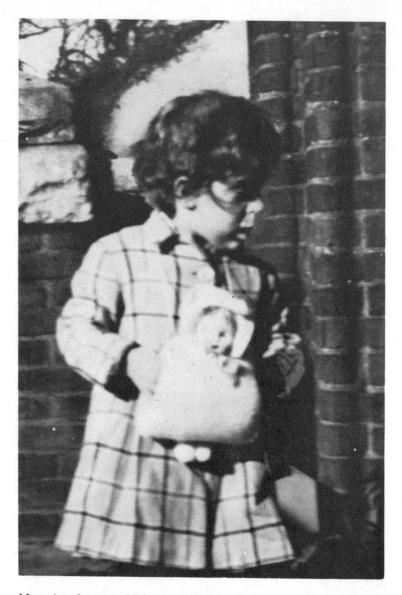

Mary Ann Long, a child cancer victim, grew up at a home run by the Dominican Sisters. There she was baptized and embraced the Catholic Faith, receiving her First Communion at age five and being confirmed at age six. She inspired joy in all who came in contact with her, and died at age 12 in complete acceptance of God's Will.

54

PADRE PIO

Servant of God Padre Pio of Pietrelcina, O.F.M. Cap.
Francesco Forgione
1887 - 1968
Italy
Died Age 81

The little son of Grazio and Maria Forgione was baptized Francesco in honor of St. Francis of Assisi. Later in life, he became more like his holy namesake when he received the stigmata, the wounds of Our Lord.

Francesco was one of eight children of a poor peasant family. On two occasions, his father migrated to America as a laborer in an attempt to make enough money to support his family. Francesco was very devout even as a child, and at an early age felt drawn to the priesthood. He was first taught by private teachers and then enrolled in a school run by the Capuchin friars. During his teens his health was not robust, and he was often subject to mysteriously high fevers. Later in life, under obedience, he disclosed that although he had felt a religious vocation at an early age, the sweetness of the world also appealed to him very much, and a fierce struggle took place in his soul. Twenty years later, he wrote that the memory of that struggle between God and the world still made his blood curdle. Francesco was granted a vision which helped him to make the extremely difficult decision. The parting from his family was particularly painful, but Jesus and Mary consoled him and assured him of their love. Francesco became a Capuchin novice at the age of sixteen; the Capuchins are one of the three independent branches of the Franciscan order. He received the habit in 1902.

Francesco was ordained to the priesthood in 1910 after seven years of study. He became known as Padre Pio.

In 1916, along with many other young priests in Italy, Padre Pio was drafted into the army to be a soldier. Here he became ill. When he was taken to the military hospital, doctors quickly admitted puzzlement as to his exact condition. Ordinary thermometers broke from his high fevers. Special thermometers indicated temperatures from one hundred twenty to one hundred twenty-five degrees. In spite of the fever, Padre Pio did not go into delirium. Finally, the doctors declared him unfit for military service, and diagnosed tuberculosis. His Capuchin superiors, convinced that he was dying, sent him to the monastery in San Giovanni Rotondo. Here he lived much longer than the few months they expected; he lived fifty-one more years.

On September 20, 1918, Padre Pio was kneeling in front of a large crucifix when he received the visible marks of the crucifixion. One of the brothers passing along the hall noticed Padre Pio lying apparently unconscious on the chapel floor. He and the superior of the monastery carried Padre Pio to his cell. They immediately notified the superior of their order of the inexplicable marks; the superior asked that a photograph be made of the unusual phenomenon and that a doctor examine the wounds.

The doctor who examined Padre Pio could not find any natural cause for the wounds. In the normal course of events, wounds of the human body either heal, or fester and become infected. Padre Pio's did neither. These wounds were still bleeding at the time of his death in 1968, fifty years later.

At the time he received the stigmata, Padre Pio's wounds bled profusely. For the next fifty years they oozed blood continually. The wounds in his hands were about two centimeters in diameter, round and near the middle of his palms. The provincial superior of the Capuchins who examined these right after they first appeared said that he was almost able to see through Padre Pio's hands.

When such phenomena as the stigmata of Padre Pio take place, the Church authorities are very cautious. They investigate such matters closely so that people are not led to believe that there is something miraculous about anything which might be the effect of natural causes. Because of this caution on the part of the Church, there were many restrictions placed on Padre Pio from time to time. Always, he willingly and cheerfully complied with the requests of his superiors. At one time, he was forbidden to show his stigmata to anyone, and people were forbidden to come to see him at the monastery.

During this time, it became necessary for him to have an operation on his gall bladder. Arrangements were made for the doctor to come to perform the surgery at the monastery, and a room was fixed up as an operating room. After arising at an early hour and attending to his chores, Padre Pio entered the makeshift hospital room and got into position on the table. Quietly he refused any anesthetic. When the horrified doctor asked why, he explained that he was afraid that the doctor would take the opportunity to make a detailed examination of the stigmata which he had been forbidden to show.

In the spirit of strict obedience, Padre Pio obeyed his superiors even to the point of undergoing a major operation without anesthetic. For two hours he suffered quietly. Tears streamed down his face. He was heard to say, "Jesus, forgive me if I do not know how to suffer as I should." Eventually, he passed into unconsciousness from the pain, and the doctor did, at that time, make some notes on the condition of the stigmata.

The wounds of the stigmata were not the only mystical phenomenon experienced by Padre Pio. The blood from his stigmata had an odor described by many as similar to that of perfume or flowers, and the gift of bilocation was attributed to him. Padre Pio had the ability to read the hearts of the penitents who flocked to him for confession in ever-increasing numbers. He heard confessions for ten or twelve hours per day. Many people stated that he announced things to them before they even said a word in the confessional— things he could not ordinarily have known about them. Sometimes, he would refuse absolution to a penitent he knew was not sincere enough. At other times, he would take upon himself a painful penance for someone else's sins. Sin caused Padre Pio great suffering, as he realized its horror and how it offended God. Often when he absolved a penitent from serious sins, his face would become contorted in great pain; afterwards, a grave sinner who had just been absolved would sometimes feel as though he were literally walking on air, or floating.

Padre Pio used the confessional to bring both sinners and devout souls closer to God; he would know just the right word of counsel or encouragement that was needed. A Russian prince, who later became a brother, has recorded his impression of the individual attention he received from Padre Pio: "Everything he said was for me exclusively. There was no phrase, no advice which was applicable to all, nor was there any trace of over-sweetness, or rhetoric, or pastoral admonition . . ."

Padre Pio had thousands of spiritual children and even today, people become his spiritual sons and daughters. There are many, many stories told of his great love and tenderness toward those who came for his help. There are also numerous stories of conversions and cures through his intercession. Although the great crowds of people who came to him caused him much suffering, and although he was sometimes stern or gruff if the circumstances required this, he had a heart full of compassion. He wrote, "If I know someone who is afflicted in soul or body what would I not do with the Lord to see him delivered from these evils? I would freely take upon myself all his pains to free him, leaving him the reward of his sufferings, if the Lord would allow me to do so. I know that this is a very special favor from God because at other times, even though by the mercy of God I have never failed to help the needy, I naturally had little pity for their miseries." Padre Pio wanted a hospital built near the monastery; the Home for the Relief of Suffering has now been completed.

Padre Pio's prayer was very efficacious. In 1914 he described his prayer experiences in a letter: "I no sooner begin to pray than my heart becomes filled with a fire of love; this fire does not resemble any fire of this lowly earth. It is a sweet and delicate flame which consumes yet causes no pain. It is so sweet and delicate that it satisfies and satiates my spirit to the point of insatiability. Dear God! The most marvelous part for me is the fact that perhaps I will never comprehend it until I get to Heaven . . ."

In the late 1940's and early 1950's, in response to Pope Pius XII's repeated calls for the faithful to band together in groups for prayer, Padre Pio promoted the formation of many "Prayer Groups," both in Italy and beyond. Though he exercised leadership over these groups, he always directed them to be obedient to the local authorities. He wanted Prayer Groups for both adults and children. In 1968 there were seven hundred twenty-six groups in about twenty nations, with a membership of 68,000. On July 31, 1968, the Holy See appointed a first Director General for the Prayer Groups.

The devil was not happy with Padre Pio's love for God, and often attacked him both mentally and physically. He was afflicted with temptations to despair and temptations against faith in God, and many times was thrown to the floor, dragged around his room, or beaten. These things caused him great suffering.

From the time of their reception, the stigmata were a source of pain for Padre Pio. He wore brown half-gloves on his hands to avoid staining everything with blood. His manner of walking showed vividly that the wounds in his feet were painful. Shortly after receiving the stigmata, he wrote to his spiritual director that they caused him embarrassment and humiliation. Yet he wanted to suffer; he wrote, "I wish to be inebriated with pain." He also said, "The cross doesn't overwhelm; if its weight makes one stagger, its power gives relief."

Padre Pio's love for the Eucharist was experienced as a burning fire; Padre Pio wrote that to receive Jesus only increased the hunger and thirst he felt for Him. Of the Mass, he said, "It would be easier for the earth to carry on without the sun than without Holy Mass." Those who attended his Masses—these lasted an hour and a half or more—came away with the feeling that they had been in the presence of a saint.

For a long portion of his priestly life, Padre Pio was forbidden to write letters of spiritual direction. In spite of a storm of controversy which grew up about the mystical phenomena, in his mission as confessor and priest Padre Pio was known to be deeply humble. At times he wrote to his director that he felt like a very unfaithful soul. Like all Capuchins, he lived an austere life. He was always obedient, and in counseling was known to scold people who asked his opinion about certain matters, such as unapproved apparitions, which lay in the province of local church authorities.

Padre Pio had a wonderful sense of humor, and often made witty remarks using puns or funny vernacular expressions. Even in the confessional he would point out the folly of a sinner with a quick and sometimes caustic remark. Often he would speak to someone in a chiding, yet gentle way.

Even before his death, people spoke to Padre Pio about his possible canonization. On one occasion when the subject was brought up, he alluded to the northern Italians' accusation that southern Italians were "macaroni eaters." In defense of the South, he stated, "If they make me a saint, anyone who comes to me seeking a favor will have to bring me first of all a crate of macaroni; for each crate of macaroni I'll grant a favor!"

Padre Pio died on September 23, 1968, at the age of eighty-one. His funeral was attended by about 100,000 people.

Padre Pio's cause for beatification is currently quite active. His process was begun in Rome in 1973.

Padre Pio as a young monk.

On September 20, 1918, Padre Pio received the stigmata, the visible marks of the crucifixion of Our Lord. These five painful wounds neither healed nor became infected, and doctors could find no natural explanation for them. The wounds were still bleeding at the time of Padre Pio's death in 1968, fifty years later.

421

Thousands of people from all over the world traveled to San Giovanni Rotondo to go to confession to Padre Pio and to listen to his spiritual counsel. Padre Pio often spent ten to twelve hours a day in the confessional; many times he was able to read a penitent's heart before the person had said a word. Padre Pio said, "Divine Goodness not only does not reject penitent souls, but goes out in search of obstinate souls."

The center of Padre Pio's life was the daily offering of Holy Mass. He said, "It would be easier for the earth to carry on without the sun than without Holy Mass."

Padre Pio pouring the cleansing waters of Baptism. He lived entirely for God and souls.

Padre Pio offering Holy Mass. On the altar, his face was transformed, and suffering shone through his features. Those who attended his Mass came away with the impression that they had been in the presence of a saint. Note the brown half-gloves worn by Padre Pio to avoid staining everything with blood.

The beautiful smile of Padre Pio. All those who knew Padre Pio heard him tell funny stories; he seemed to have a whole anthology of them in his head.

In addition to the stigmata and the reading of hearts, Padre Pio possessed other unusual qualities, such as bilocation, celestial perfume, miraculous cures, remarkable conversions, and prophetic insight. Padre Pio died in 1968, at the age of 81.

55

BROTHER ELIAS

Brother Elias, o.c.s.o.
Charles William Simpson
1939 - 1970
United States
Died Age 30

In an age in which absolute commitments are often sneered at, the monastic life led by Brother Elias is a firm statement on the value of a life totally dedicated to God. This man strove to live God's Will for him by following as perfectly as possible the ancient Trappist rule. Though no cause for canonization is anticipated, Brother Elias is remembered by his brothers as a holy monk.

Charles William Simpson was born on December 15, 1939, in Cincinnati, Ohio. One of nine children, his early childhood and youth were similar to that of many other American boys of the time. Like most American boys he loved sports—in particular the Cincinnati Reds baseball team. He played baseball and football, although he excelled at neither. A mischievous child, Billy always seemed happy, with a ready smile and a quick laugh. His brother Albert remembers that he rarely saw Billy angry.

As is common with pre-schoolers, young Billy's antics often provided the occasion for a hearty laugh on the part of his family. At Mass with his mother, Billy would wave and call out to his older brother who was serving, or to his sisters in the choir loft, unfortunately causing something of a distraction to the other parishioners. He was given a little shoe-shine kit, and once when he was shining his father's shoes, his father recommended that he use more elbow grease. Noticing Billy looking around, his dad asked what he was hunting for. "I don't see any elbow grease," came the innocent reply.

Billy attended Catholic grade school in Norwood, a suburb of Cincinnati. When the Simpson family went to the regular Friday confessions, his brother remembers having to stifle his laughter when it was Billy's turn. In the confessional, Billy humbly and contritely confessed his sins—in so loud a voice that the entire church could hear. The adults just grinned and bowed their heads in prayer.

Like many youngsters, Billy loved animals. He was always bringing home a stray dog or cat, and was overjoyed when his parents allowed him to keep it. When an animal died, an elaborate play funeral with flowers on the back yard grave was called for. On one occasion, Billy was bitten and had to have the full series of rabies shots as the dog could not be located. This love for animals carried over to his life in the monastery. During the winter when the farms were covered with snow, Billy was the one who remembered to put out food for the wild birds. Stray dogs and cats were certain of a treat if they could find him in the kitchen.

On a visit to the monastery, Billy's brother once teased him that since he had the care of the pigs so much, he was beginning to look like one. "Thank you; they are also God's creatures," came the quiet reply.

"All-American boy" is an apt description of Billy during most of his childhood. On his way home from school each day, he sang happily at the top of his voice. The neighbors always knew what time it was when they heard him come singing or whistling down the street. He never missed an opportunity to kick a can or rock along the road, and a trash can was an open invitation for him to jump over it, instead of walking around it. Once when Billy saw another boy hitting a girl, the youthful Sir Galahad rushed to her rescue, and got a beautiful shiner for his trouble. In the eighth grade, he had a girl friend in his class. Sometimes he and his friends would take their girl friends to a movie or a party.

A few events in Billy's childhood gave a glimpse of his future mission. At the age of eight, he made friends with a boy who was mute. He brought the boy home and shared his comic books and play time with him. In spite of the boy's handicap, the two were able to communicate with each other.

On one occasion when Billy was a young child, he ran home crying after a scuffle with one of his friends. He was not unhappy about the physical pain, but questioned his mother, "Why would Gary hit me? He's my *friend!*"

Once when Billy was in the eighth grade, his teacher had the boys folding and stacking chairs. The other boys were having a fine time, joking and laughing, but Billy remained very quiet as he helped.

When Sister asked him why he wasn't acting like the other boys, he replied that he couldn't joke around just then—he was praying the Rosary as he worked.

At the end of eighth grade, Billy entered Brunnerdale Seminary for high school. Although he gave his parents no full explanation of his reasons, he wanted to become a priest. But a bit of a dreamer, Billy was never an outstanding student, and his superiors felt that he would probably not be able to complete the difficult class work required for the priesthood.

This apparent failure actually led to the biggest adventure of his life—his life as a modern contemplative at the Abbey of Gethsemani, Kentucky. His superior at the Precious Blood seminary in Brunnerdale wrote to the monks, "Billy's fidelity in coming for direction, his spirit of obedience and his over-all earnestness and interest in the things of the spirit, all these make me feel that he deserves the opportunity which a postulancy and novitiate will afford." A former teacher said, "He was not brilliant in his studies, but he was extraordinarily good."

After about two years in the seminary, Billy's application to the monastery was accepted. He became known as Brother Elias. Brother Ferdinand, one of the monks, gives us this description of his assignments there: "Brother Elias held down jobs in the tailor shop, bakery, guest house, kitchen, and finally, electrician from 1967 on. Most of his assignments were distinguished, if that is the word, by the fact that they were a little undesirable, demanding some sacrifice of time and participation in the community life. Brother was never known to complain; on the contrary, he seemed to radiate peace and joy wherever he went. His cheerfulness and ready smile were always a great lift to those with whom he worked. What he did, he did gladly and so lent encouragement to those around him."

At the monastery, his sense of humor endeared him to all the brothers. Once he admonished his spiritual director to slow down: "Look at me, I'm never in a rush—especially when that bell starts ringing for me to get up at three a.m." He was much loved by his brothers; he loved each of them and showed his love daily by doing all he could for them. Ever ready to give of himself, he might often have been imposed upon. If so, he never seemed to be aware of it, or to give any indication that any chore was "beneath" him. In the final months of his life, he certainly suffered. But unless directly asked, he made no mention of any pain or discomfort.

Brother Elias once suffered a rather serious eleven-foot fall while working on one of the buildings. Concerning this accident, his confessor later wrote: "I was called to see some brother who had fallen from the high ceiling to the basement floor, luckily escaping the tools and cement blocks that were scattered about. I looked down from the floor above and saw Brother Elias lying on his back—smiling—and making the sign of offering . . . He told me later that he made an offering of his pain or his life to the good God. And all with a smile! He did not evince any sign of fear. Elias was ever ready to meet his God."

Brother Elias became interested in electricity, and studied the subject during his "free time." Later he was given electrical work to do and became quite an expert. Eventually, Brother Elias became the chief electrician for the monastery. After the diagnosis of his incurable cancer, he took pains to train his successors in the electrical and refrigeration fields, as both are extremely important to the community's cheese industry.

Brother Elias was particularly fond of reading the Bible, and after his death his confessor was given the Bible he used for his readings during "free hours." This priest discovered three hundred ninety-three annotations and underscorings which Brother Elias had made. He chose Scriptural readings for a Mass celebrated in his room the day before his death, which were also used for his funeral Mass. One of the readings, from the eighth chapter of *Romans*, begins: "Brethren, I consider that the sufferings of this present time are not worth comparing with the glory that is to be revealed to us."

In 1969, the mobile health unit visited the monastery. Spots showed on the X-ray of Brother Elias' lungs, and he entered the hospital for further tests and exploratory surgery. The diagnosis was terminal lung cancer.

Even then he kept his sense of humor. In a letter to the brothers he wrote that in the hospital he had several distinct advantages—"plenty of time for prayer, reading, and visiting the sick."

Brother Elias faced something—prior knowledge of his own death—that might shake the faith of any man. His reaction to the news was human, and yet showed his courage and faith. In a letter to the monastery shortly after learning of the diagnosis, he wrote, "I consider this a great grace to be able to know the approximate time of my own death, although I have to admit, my surface reaction to this knowledge is fear. However, Our Lord will continue to guide me through this time and I will continue to believe in what He says about death and the Resurrection. This will be a way for me to draw closer to Him and to seek my true life from Him through the death of this merely earthly body. It definitely will require a complete abandonment of my own thoughts and desires in regard to it, and openness to receive from Him, His life, and His love. My ideas of what is happening are distorted and darkened, but He will instill truth if I remain in an attitude of openness full of faith."

Later, to one of the brothers assigned to stay with him when his disease approached its last stages, he confided, "I have known that I was going to die soon, six months ago. Understandably, all kinds of expectations as to what death would be like crowded in on my mind. But the reality has been so different. I never imagined that it would be so sweet to die."

At the hospital, Brother Elias was not content merely to be a patient. He wanted to be of service, and at suppertime, he helped the nurses deliver the trays. He visited the other patients and took his portable radio to the room of an old mountain woman who enjoyed hearing the music from her part of the state. When this woman died, he went to help console her daughter. His letters to his brothers spoke of prayers for others and detailed the tragedies being suffered around him.

Brother Elias returned to his monastery in February; early in June he developed blood clots in his leg which necessitated his staying in bed. It was obvious that the end would come sooner than originally expected. Brother Elias' comment was, "I didn't expect this, but Jesus wants it. Whatever He wants."

His parents in Cincinnati were notified and drove down immediately. By request of his superiors, papal enclosure was lifted to allow his family to visit him in the infirmary. His mother, three sisters, two brothers, and his father visited with him on Saturday before his death on Sunday.

The majority of the abbey monks gathered in the corridor of the infirmary to recite the prayers for the dying. Three of the priests and two infirmarians were in the room where Brother Elias lay under an oxygen tent. Father James said that Brother repeated twice the words of Our Lord, "Father, into Thy hands I commend my spirit." Seconds later, he whispered, "Lord Jesus Christ, Son of God, have mercy on me a sinner." These were his last words. The next second he drew his last breath and was gone.

No cause for the canonization of Brother Elias is anticipated. Nevertheless, his brothers at Gethsemani remember him as an exemplary brother.

Mischievousness sparkles from the eyes of four-year-old Billy Simpson, later to become a Trappist monk in Gethsemani, Kentucky.

Billy Simpson had a life-long love for all God's creatures. Here he poses his dog, Lady, for the photographer.

Stray dogs and cats were always sure of a treat if they could find Brother Elias in the monastery kitchen. This little chipmunk knows he has nothing to fear.

Turned down as a seminarian because of a lack of scholastic ability, Billy Simpson embraced a humble and hidden life of obedience as a Trappist monk. In the monastery he was known as Brother Elias. Here Brother Elias stands with his mother in front of the Abbey of Gethsemani, Kentucky.

SOURCES BY CHAPTER

The individual bibliographical entries in this book consist of publications and names of correspondents who gave information or leads to information. American archivists' addresses are listed in the *Official Catholic Directory,* a copy of which is on file in the chancery office of each diocese.

1. SAINT JULIE BILLIART

Publications

> Anna of the Sacred Heart, Sister. *Rose of Picardy.* Cincinnati: Provincial House, 1946.
>
> Cushing, Richard Cardinal. *Blessed Julie Billiart.* Boston, 1964.
>
> Sisters of Notre Dame. *Illustrated Life of the Blessed Julie Billiart.* Cincinnati, 1936.
>
> Spagnola, Mary-Eunice. "St. Julie: Pioneer of Religious Education." *Liguorian,* Sept. 1978, pp. 12-15.

Correspondence

> Sister Mary Christine, S.N.D. The Provincial House, Cincinnati.

2. BLESSED PHILIPPINE DUCHESNE

Publications

> Bascom, Sister Marion, R.S.C.J. *Rose Philippine Duchesne.* Purchase, N.Y.: Manhattanville College.
>
> Duffy, T. Gavan. *Heart of Oak.* Pondicherry, India, 1940.

Correspondence

> Sister Marion Bascom, R.S.C.J. St. Louis, Mo.
>
> Sister Marjorie Erskine, R.S.C.J. St. Charles, Mo.

3. SAINT JOAQUINA

Publications

> Lang, M. E. *Rooted in Love.* Castro Valley, Calif.: Carmelite Sisters of Charity, 1954.
>
> *Saint Joaquine de Vedruna: Foundress of the Carmelite Sisters of Charity.* Canonization booklet. Rome.
>
> Various pamphlet materials.

Correspondence

> Sister Maria Rosa, Ca. Ch. Vedruna House of Studies, Washington, D.C.

4. SAINT DOMINIC SAVIO
Publications

> Aronica, Rev. Paul, S.D.B. *The Boy-Saint.* Savio Club pamphlet.
>
> Bosco, St. John. *St. Dominic Savio.* Transl. and notes, Paul Aronica, S.D.B. New Rochelle, N.Y.: Don Bosco Publications, 1979.
>
> Lappin, Rev. Peter. *Dominic Savio: Teenage Saint.* New Rochelle, N.Y.: Salesiana Publishers, 1965.
>
> O'Brien, Terence, S.D.B. *Dominic Savio: Teenage Apostle-Saint* [including Dominic's life as written by St. John Bosco]. New Rochelle, N.Y.: Salesiana Publishers, 1969.
>
> Phelan, Edna Beyer. *Don Bosco: A Spiritual Portrait.* Garden City, N.Y.: Doubleday, 1963.
>
> *Salesian Bulletin,* May 1970.

Correspondence

> Rev. Dominic Britschu, S.D.B., Secretary General of the Salesians. Rome.

5. SAINT JOHN NEUMANN
Publications

> Manton, Joseph A., C.Ss.R. *Venerable John Neumann.* St. Paul: Catechetical Guild, 1960.
>
> Murphy, Gerald, C.Ss.R. *Blessed John Neumann, C.Ss.R.* Techny, Ill.: Divine Word Publications, 1964.
>
> Various beatification brochures and pamphlets.

Correspondence

> Rev. Francis Litz, Vice-Postulator. John Neumann Shrine, Philadelphia.

6. SAINT GABRIEL POSSENTI
Publications

> Ferdinando, P., C.P. *S. Gabriele dell'Addolorata.* Teramo, Italy: Casa Editrice Tip., 1961.
>
> Lovasik, Rev. Lawrence, S.V.D. *Picture Book of Saints.* New York: Catholic Book Publishing Company, 1970.
>
> Poage, Godfrey, C.P. *Son of the Passion.* Milwaukee: Bruce, 1962.

Correspondence

> P. Enzo Annibali, C.P., Archivist General of the Passionist order. Rome.
>
> Passionist Fathers. Holy Name Retreat Center; Houston, Texas.
>
> Passionist Fathers. L'Eco Di S. Gabriele; Teramo, Italy.

7. SAINT BENILDUS
Publications

Battersby, Bro. Clair, F.S.C. "Our New Saint: Brother Benilde." Canonization press release. Memphis, Tenn.: Tennessee Christian Brothers College, 1967.

Christian Brothers. *Tall in the Sight of God.* Canonization pamphlet. Christian Brothers, 1967.

Christian Brothers Today, Vol. II, No. 1; Feb. 1980.

Christian Brothers Today, Vol. II, No. 2; May 1980.

Curriculum Vitae on Brother Benildus, F.S.C. Lockport, Ill.

Gerard, Bro. Hubert, F.S.C. F.S.C. National Public Relations press release. Lockport, Ill.; Oct. 1967.

Gilmartin, Bro. Hilary, F.S.C. Homily at Pontifical Mass in honor of canonization of Brother Benildus. Basilica of St. Mary, Minneapolis; Nov. 19, 1967.

Liddy, A. J., F.S.C. *Chalk Dust Halo.* London: Macmillan, 1956.

Maria, Bro. Leone di, Postulator General. "The Two Miracles of Blessed Benilde Accepted for Canonization." Mimeographed report. Rome, 1967.

Various archive materials.

Correspondence

Bro. Hilary Gilmartin, F.S.C., Director of Public Relations. Christian Brothers Conference; Romeoville, Ill.

Bro. Luigi Morell, F.S.C., Postulator General. Rome.

Bro. John H. Mulhern, F.S.C., Archivist. Rome.

8. HENRIETTE DELILLE
Publications

Detiege, Sister Audrey Marie. *Henriette Delille, Free Woman of Color.* New Orleans: Sisters of the Holy Family, 1976.

Various brochures from the Sisters of the Holy Family.

Correspondence

Sister Audrey Marie Detiege, Archivist. Sisters of the Holy Family; New Orleans.

9. FRANCIS SEELOS
Publications

Artz, Thomas, C.Ss.R. *Father Francis X. Seelos, C.Ss.R.* New Orleans: Father Seelos Center, 1979.

Cicognani, Most Rev. Amleto Giovanni. *Sanctity in America.* Paterson, N.J.: St. Anthony Guild Press, 1945.

Curley, Michael J., C.Ss.R. *Cheerful Ascetic.* New Orleans: Redemptorist Press, 1969.

Father Seelos and Sanctity. Various issues. New Orleans: Vice-Postulator.

Vaughn, John N. *Do You Need an In with God?* New Orleans: Seelos Center, 1962.

Correspondence

Rev. William Grangell, C.Ss.R., Vice-Postulator. New Orleans.

10. SAINT PETER JULIAN EYMARD

Publications

Dempsey, Rev. Martin. *Champion of the Blessed Sacrament.* New York: Sentinel Press, 1962.

The Eucharist, Feb. 1963; Aug. 1963; Nov. 1968; Nov. 1969; July 1970; Sept. 1970; July 1971.

Life Sketch, Saint Peter Julian Eymard. New York: Eymard League, 1962.

Paul VI, Pope. Letter to Roland Huot, Superior General of the Congregation of the Priests of the Most Blessed Sacrament; July 19, 1969.

Tesniere, Rev. Albert, S.S.S. *Saint Peter Julian Eymard.* New York: Eymard League, 1962.

Various pamphlet and mimeographed materials.

Correspondence

Rev. Norman Folardeau, S.S.S. Blessed Sacrament Fathers, Office of the American Provincial; New York.

Rev. Ralph A. Lavigne, S.S.S. Eymard League, New York.

Alice M. Lavin, Assistant Editor, *The Eucharist.*

11. SAINT ANTHONY MARY CLARET

Publications

Blocs Claretians. Archival set of postcards. Barcelona, 1928.

Mahoney, John. *St. Anthony Claret: Restless Apostle.* Chicago: Claretian Fathers, 1964.

Nino, Macrinus, C.M.F. *Saint Anthony Claret.* Chicago: Claretian Fathers, 1950.

Correspondence

Rev. Leo A. Mattacheck, C.M.F., Director, Claretian Center; New York.

Rev. Louis A. Olivares, C.M.F. Claretian Center, Los Angeles.

12. SAINT BERNADETTE SOUBIROUS

Publications

Cruz, Joan Carroll. *The Incorruptibles.* Rockford, Ill.: TAN Books & Publishers, 1977.

de Saint-Pierre, Michel. *Bernadette and Lourdes.* Garden City, N.Y.: Doubleday Image, 1955.

Husslein, Joseph, S.J., ed. *Heroines of Christ.* Bruce: Milwaukee, 1949.

Lovasik, Rev. Lawrence, S.V.D. *Picture Book of Saints.* New York: Catholic Book Publishing Co., 1970.

Pauli, Hertha. *Bernadette and the Lady.* New York: Farrar, Straus and Cudahy, 1956.

Trochu, Francis. *Saint Bernadette Soubirous.* Translated and adapted by John Joyce, S.J. New York: Pantheon, 1957.

Werfel, Franz. *The Song of Bernadette.* Pleasantville, N.Y.: *Reader's Digest,* Summer 1970.

Correspondence

Sister Marie Bernadette. Bureau Bernadette; Nevers, France.

13. SAINT MARY MAZZARELLO

Publications

Bianco, Enzo, S.D.B., & Maraldi, Assunta, F.M.A. *First Centenary of Don Bosco's Missions.* Rome: SDB Publishers, 1977.

Centenary, Daughters of Mary Help of Christians. Asti, Italy: Isag-Colle Don Bosco, 1972.

Daughters of Mary Help of Christians. Rome: Generalate of the Institute, Daughters of Mary Help of Christians, 1972.

Lappin, Peter, S.D.B. *Halfway to Heaven.* New Rochelle, N.Y.: Don Bosco Publications, 1981.

Passero, Sister Louise, F.M.A. *Hands for Others.* Boston: St. Paul Editions, 1971.

Salesian Bulletin, April 1934, Nov. 1976, & Sept. 1979.

von Matt, Leonard, and Henri Bosco. *Don Bosco.* New York: Universe, 1965.

Correspondence

Rev. Dominic Britschu, S.D.B., Secretary General of the Salesians; Rome.

Sister Virginia D'Alessandro, F.M.A., Secretary to the Provincial. Salesian Sisters; Haledon, N.J.

Sister Rosalie Ann Ragusa, F.M.A. Baton Rouge, La.

14. SAINT CHARLES LWANGA AND COMPANIONS

Publications

Faupel, Rev. J. F. *African Holocaust.* New York: P. J. Kenedy, 1962.

Marion, Francis. *New African Saints.* Milan, Italy: Ancora Publishers, 1964.

Mimeographed biographies of the individual martyrs. White
  Fathers.
Various pamphlet materials and publications.
Correspondence
  Miss E. I. Demkovich, Secretary. Provincial Office of the White
    Fathers; Plainfield, N.J.
  Rev. Rene Lamey, Archivist General. The White Fathers, Rome.
  Rev. Jack Jackson. St. Thomas Episcopal School, Houston.

15. SAINT SOLEDAD
Publications
  Javierre, Rev. Jose M. *As a Grain of Mustard Seed.* Trans. by Nan-
    cy Avetta and Jane Courel. Edited by Sister Donna Gunn,
    C.S.J. Kansas City, Kans.: Sisters, Servants of Mary, 1974.
  Peman, Jose Maria. *Saint Maria Soledad Torres Acosta.* Madrid:
    Graficas Horizonte, 1969.
  The World Was Her Cloister. Kansas City, Kans.: Sisters, Servants
    of Mary, 1967.
Correspondence
  Sister Nieves Bierrun, S.M., Provincial Superior; Kansas City,
    Kans.
  Sister Piedad Davila, S.M.; Oxnard, Calif.
  Sister Cristela MacKinnon, S.M.; Kansas City, Kans.
  Sister Conception Pedrido, S.M.; Kansas City, Kans.
  Sister Bernarda Ruiz de la Prada, S.M.; Curia General, Siervas de
    Maria, Rome.

16. SAINT JOHN BOSCO
Publications
  Aronica, Rev. Paul, S.D.B. *A Man Sent by God.* New Rochelle,
    N.Y.: Salesiana Publishers, 1968.
  Bosco, St. John. *St. Dominic Savio.* Transl. and notes, Paul
    Aronica, S.D.B. New Rochelle, N.Y.: Don Bosco Publica-
    tions, 1979.
  "A Canonization Tribute to Our Saint." *The Salesian Bulletin,*
    April 1934.
  Forbes, F. A. *St. John Bosco: The Friend of Youth.* New Rochelle,
    N.Y.: Salesiana Publishers, 1966.
  Lappin, Peter. *Give Me Souls! Life of Don Bosco.* Huntington,
    Ind.: Our Sunday Visitor, 1977.
  Phelan, Edna B. *Don Bosco: A Spiritual Portrait.* Garden City,
    N.Y.: Doubleday, 1963.
  The Salesian Bulletin, various issues.

Sheppard, Lancelot C. *Don Bosco*. Westminster, Md.: Newman Press, 1957.

Von Matt, Leonard, and Henri Bosco. *Don Bosco*. New York: Universe Books, 1965.

Correspondence

Rev. Paul Aronica, S.D.B. New Rochelle, N.Y.

Rev. Dominic Britschu, S.D.B., Secretary General of the Salesians; Rome.

Rev. John Docherty. Thornleigh Salesian College; Bolton, England.

Rev. William Kelley, S.D.B., Secretary to the Provincial; New Rochelle, N.Y.

Rev. Joseph Perozzi, Vice-Provincial; New Rochelle, N.Y.

17. FATHER DAMIEN

Publications

Daniel-Rops, Henri. *The Heroes of God*. Hawthorne, N.Y., 1959.

Hanley, Boniface, O.F.M. *Ten Christians*. Notre Dame, Ind.: Ave Maria Press, 1979.

Jourdain, Vital, SS.CC. *The Heart of Father Damien*. Trans. by Rev. Francis Larkin, SS.CC., and Charles Davenport. Milwaukee: Bruce, 1955.

Various brief materials.

Correspondence

Rev. Francis Larkin, SS.CC. Washington, D.C.

18. AUGUSTUS CZARTORYSKI

Publications

Phelan, Edna. *Don Bosco: A Spiritual Portrait*. New York: Doubleday, 1963.

The Salesian Bulletin, April 1934 and Jan. 1979.

Correspondence

Rev. Paul Aronica, S.D.B., Editor, *The Salesian Bulletin;* New Rochelle, N.Y.

Rev. Dominic Britschu, S.D.B., Secretary General of the Salesians, Rome.

Sister Virginia D'Alessandro, Secretary to the Provincial; Haledon, N.J.

19. AGOSTINA PIETRANTONI

Publications

Duffet, Sister Antoine de Padoue, ed. *Sister Agostina*. Rome: Suore della Carita, 1972.

Archive material.

Correspondence

Sister Mary Pia Panfili. Motherhouse, Rome.

Sister Maria Sophia Tevarotto, Secretary to the Provincial Superior, Milwaukee.

20. ANDREW BELTRAMI

Publications

The Salesian Bulletin, April 1934 and May 1970.

Various Italian language pamphlet materials.

Correspondence

Rev. Dominic Britschu, S.D.B., Secretary General of the Salesians, Rome.

Sister Virginia D'Alessandro, Secretary to the Provincial; Haledon, N.J.

21. SAINT CHARBEL

Publications

Cruz, Joan Carroll. *The Incorruptibles.* Rockford, Ill.: TAN Books and Publishers, 1977.

Mahfouz, Rev. Joseph. *Saint Charbel Makhlouf: Monk and Hermit of the Lebanese Maronite Order.* Rome: Sacred Congregation for the Causes of Saints, 1976.

Correspondence

Rev. Joseph Mahfouz, Postulator General of the Maronite Lebanese Order, Rome.

22. MARIA DROSTE ZU VISCHERING

Publications

Mulen, Dr. F.; Strube, Peter; and Sisters of the Good Shepherd. *Maria Droste zu Vischering.* Osnabruck, Germany: Meinders & Elstermann, 1975.

Correspondence

Sister Annunciata, R.G.S. Motherhouse; Angers, France.

Sister Mary Angela Donohoe, R.G.S., Communications Director. Sisters of the Good Shepherd, Rome.

Betty Holmes, Secretary. Provincial Convent of the Good Shepherd, St. Louis.

23. MOTHER ANGELA TRUSZKOWSKA

Publications

Cegirlks, Gtsnvid S. *The Pierced Heart.* Bruce: Milwaukee, 1955.

Da Voltri, P. Teodosio, O.F.M. *Sofia Truszkowska.* Roma, 1960.

Dmowska, Sister M. Bronislawa, C.S.S.F. *Matka Maria Angela Truszkowska.* Buffalo, N.Y.: Felicjana Pub., 1949.

Doman, Suor Maria Tullia, C.S.S.F. *Madre Maria Angela Truszkowska.* Rome: Felician Sisters, 1955.

Doman, Sister Mary Tullia, C.S.S.F. *Mother Mary Angela Truszkowska.* Livonia, Mich.: Felician Sisters, 1954.

Doman, Sister Mary Tullia, C.S.S.F. *The Spirit of the Foundress of the Felician Sisters.* Livonia, Mich.: Felician Sisters, 1967.

Frankowska, Sister Mary, C.S.S.F. *Excerpts from the Writings of the Foundress.* Warsaw: Wawer, 1967.

Frankowska, Sister Mary, C.S.S.F. *The Spirit of the Felician Congregation.* Buffalo, N.Y.: Felicjana Pub., 1967.

Gorski, Artur. *Angela Truszkowska.* Pozi: Pallottenum, 1967.

Tkacz, Sister Aiarwe Mary Casimir, C.S.S.F. *Mother Angela.* Rome: Pauline Editions, 1967.

Truszkowska, Mary Angela. *Excerpts from Her Letters.* Lodi, N.J.: Felician Sisters, 1967.

Wilson, R. H. *Mother Angela and the Felician Sisters.* Felician Sisters, 1980.

Correspondence

Miss Anna Bobak, translator. Dearborn, Mich.

Sister Mary Celine; Ponca City, Okla.

Mother M. Liliose, Provincial Superior; Ponca City, Okla.

Sister Mary Magdalene, Felician Sisters, Rome.

Sister Mary Raphael, Secretary for the American Provinces; Lodi, N.J.

24. BLESSED GREGORY AND COMPANIONS

Publications

The Twenty-Nine Martyrs of China. Providence, R.I.: Franciscan Missionaries of Mary, 1947.

Individual French language mini-biographies of the Seven Protomartyrs. Quebec.

Correspondence

Sister Anne M. Richards, F.M.M., New York.

Sister Agnes Willmann, F.M.M. Franciscan Missionaries of Mary; N. Providence, R.I.

25. SAINT MARIA GORETTI

Publications

Buehrle, Marie Cecilia. *Saint Maria Goretti.* Bruce: Milwaukee, 1950.

Ciomei, P. Fortunato, and Sconocchia, P. Simone, M.R.P. *S. Maria Goretti, Nelle Paludi Pontine.* Nettuno, Italy: Basilica della Madonna delle Grazie, 1978.

Correspondence

> P. Enzo Annibali, C.P., Archivist General of the Passionist order, Rome.
>
> Marie Cecilia Buehrle, Rome.
>
> Simone Sconocchia, M.R.P. Sanctuary of Maria Goretti; Nettuno, Italy.

26. SAINT GEMMA GALGANI

Publications

> Husslein, Joseph, S.J., ed. *Heroines of Christ.* Milwaukee: Bruce, 1949.
>
> Lovasik, Rev. Lawrence G., S.V.D. *Picture Book of Saints.* New York: Catholic Book Publishing Company, 1970.
>
> *A Lover of the Cross: St. Gemma Galgani.* Lucca, Italy: Monastero-Santuario di S. Gemma, 1940.
>
> Parente, Rev. Pascal P. *Beyond Space: A Book About the Angels.* Rockford, Ill.: TAN Books and Publishers, 1973.

Correspondence

> P. Enzo Annibali, C.P., Archivist General of the Passionists, Rome.
>
> Mother Superior of the Passionist Nuns. Monastero-Santuario di S. Gemma; Lucca, Italy.

27. LAURA VICUNA

Publications

> Aronica, Rev. Paul, S.D.B. "Laura Vicuna, Rose of the Andes." *The Salesian Bulletin,* March - Apr., 1971.
>
> Bianco, Enzo, S.D.B., and Maraldi, Assunta, F.M.A. *First Centenary of Don Bosco's Missions.* Rome: SDB Publishers, 1977.
>
> *Centenary, Daughters of Mary Help of Christians.* Asti, Italy: Isag-Colle Don Bosco, 1972.
>
> *Daughters of Mary Help of Christians.* Rome: Generalate of the Institute, Daughters of Mary Help of Christians, 1972.
>
> *The Salesian Bulletin,* Vol. 33, Sept. 1979.
>
> Various short Italian language publications.

Correspondence

> Rev. Paul Aronica, S.D.B., Editor, *The Salesian Bulletin;* New Rochelle, N.Y.
>
> Rev. Dominic Britschu, S.D.B., Secretary General of the Salesians, Rome.
>
> Sister Lydia Carini, F.M.A. Motherhouse of the Daughters of Mary Help of Christians, Rome.
>
> Sister Virginia D'Alessandro, F.M.A., Secretary to the Provincial. Salesian Sisters; Haledon, N.J.

28. ZEPHERIN NAMUNCURA

Publications

Aronica, Rev. Paul, S.D.B. *Little Chief of the Andes.* Paterson, N.J.: Salesiana Publishers, 1957.

Bianco, Enzo, S.D.B., & Maraldi, Assunta, F.M.A. *First Centenary of Don Bosco's Missions.* Roma: SDB Publishers, 1975.

The Salesian Bulletin, July-Aug., 1972.

von Matt, Leonard, and Henri Bosco. *Don Bosco.* New York: Universe Books, 1965.

Correspondence

Rev. Paul Aronica, S.D.B., Editor, *The Salesian Bulletin;* New Rochelle, N.Y.

Sister Virginia D'Alessandro, F.M.A., Archivist, Daughters of Mary Help of Christians; Haledon, N.J.

Rev. Peter Lappin, S.D.B. West Haverstraw, N.Y.

29. MOTHER MARY MAGDALEN BENTIVOGLIO

Publications

Cicognani, Most Rev. Amleto Giovanni. *Sanctity in America.* Paterson, N.J.: St. Anthony Guild Press, 1945.

A Poor Clare Nun. *A Seraphic Seed: Sketch of the Life of the Servant of God Mother Mary Magdalen Bentivoglio, Poor Clare, 1834 - 1905.* Omaha, Neb.: Monastery of St. Clare.

Zarrella, Mary Alice. *I Will . . . God's Will.* Evansville, Ind.: Poor Clare Monastery Press, 1975.

Various brief printed materials.

Correspondence

Sister M. Bernardine, O.S.C. Monastery of St. Clare; Evansville, Ind.

Sister Mary Clare, O.S.C., former Abbess. Monastery of St. Clare; Omaha, Neb.

30. TERESA VALSE PANTELLINI

Publications

Centenary, Daughters of Mary Help of Christians. Asti, Italy: Isag-Colle Don Bosco, 1972.

Daughters of Mary Help of Christians. Rome: Generalate of the Institute, Daughters of Mary Help of Christians, 1972.

Grassiano, M. Domenica. *My Decision Is Irrevocable.* Bombay: St. Paul's Press, 1971.

The Salesian Bulletin, April 1934 & Sept. 1979.

Correspondence

> Rev. Dominic Britschu, S.D.B., Secretary General of the Salesians, Rome.
>
> Sister Virginia D'Alessandro, F.M.A., Secretary to the Provincial. Salesian Sisters; Haledon, N.J.

31. BROTHER MIGUEL

Publications

> Delehanty, Bro. David, F.S.C. "A Tale of Two Brothers." *The Christian Brothers Today,* Nov. 1977.
>
> *LaSallian Liturgies.* Romeoville, Ill.: Christian Brothers National Office, 1977.
>
> O'Toole, Bro. Lawrence, F.S.C. *Brother Miguel of Ecuador.* De la Salle Christian Brothers, 1977.
>
> Various brief works in Spanish and Italian.

Correspondence

> Bro. Hilary Gilmartin, F.S.C. Christian Brothers National Office; Romeoville, Ill.
>
> Bro. Luigi Morell, F.S.C., Postulator General, Rome.

32. MICHAEL RUA

Publications

> Bianco, Enzo, S.D.B., & Maraldi, Assunta, F.M.A. *First Centenary of Don Bosco's Missions.* Rome: SDB Publishers, 1977.
>
> Forbes, F.A. *St. John Bosco: the Friend of Youth.* New Rochelle, N.Y.: Salesiana Publishers, 1962.
>
> *The Salesian Bulletin,* April 1934, March 1971, July 1972, Sept. 1972, Nov. 1972, and Jan. 1973.
>
> von Matt, Leonard, and Henri Bosco. *Don Bosco.* New York: Universe Books, 1965.
>
> Various pamphlets and mimeographed materials in English and Italian.

Correspondence

> Rev. Dominic Britschu, S.D.B., Secretary General of the Salesians, Rome.
>
> Sister Virginia D'Alessandro, Secretary to the Provincial; Haledon, N.J.

33. LOUIS GUANELLA

Publications

> Buehrle, Marie C. *His Brother's Keeper.* Chicago: Servants of Charity, 1964.
>
> *Father Guanella: The Good Samaritan.* Special Issue. Rome: Guanellian Studies Center, 1978.

Correspondence
> Rev. Peter Di Tullio, S.C. Servants of Charity, Don Guanella Seminary; Springfield, Pa.

34. BROTHER ISIDORE OF SAINT JOSEPH

Publications
> A Passionist. *Isidore of St. Joseph: Brother of the Passionist Congregation.* Antwerp, Belgium: Passionist Fathers, 1960.
>
> *Servo di Dio Fratel Isidoro di S. Giuseppe.* Rome: Passionist Fathers.

Correspondence
> P. Enzo Annibali, C.P., Archivist General of the Passionist Fathers, Rome.
>
> Sebastian MacDonald, C.P., V. Provincial; Passionists, Chicago.
>
> Passionist Fathers; Wezembeek-Oppem, Belgium.

35. CHARLES DE FOUCAULD

Publications
> Bazin, Rene. *Charles de Foucauld: Hermit and Explorer.* London: Burns-Oates, Ltd., 1923.
>
> Daniel-Rops, Henri. *The Heroes of God.* Hawthorne, N.Y., 1959.
>
> Graef, Hilda. *Mystics of Our Times.* Garden City, N.Y.: Hanover House, 1962.
>
> Hovda, Rev. Robert. *Jesus Caritas: The Little Brothers of Jesus.* Detroit: Helicon Press, 1964.
>
> Knowles, Leo. *Candidates for Sainthood.* St. Paul: Carillon Books, 1978.
>
> Six, Jean Francois. *Spiritual Autobiography of Charles de Foucauld.* New York: P. J. Kenedy & Sons, 1964.

Correspondence
> Brother Bernard of Jesus, Detroit.
>
> Little Sister Damicue J. of Jesus; Washington, D.C.
>
> Little Sister Jacqueline of Jesus, Secretary to the Postulator, Rome.
>
> Little Sister Madeleine Augustine of Jesus; Washington, D.C.

36. SAINT FRANCES CABRINI

Publications
> Lovasik, Rev. Lawrence, S.V.D. *Picture Book of Saints.* New York: Catholic Book Publishing Company, 1970.
>
> *Mother Cabrini Messenger,* April 1950 and other issues.
>
> *Saint Frances Xavier Cabrini.* Compiled from approved sources by the Missionary Sisters of the Sacred Heart, Chicago, 1965.
>
> Various pamphlets and other short works.

Correspondence
> Mother Cabrini League, Chicago.
> Sister Phyllis Gerbarowski, M.S.C., New York.

37. BLESSED MARY FORTUNATA VITI, O.S.B.

Publications
> Locher, Rev. Gabriel, O.S.B. *A Brief Biography of Sister Mary Fortunata Viti.* Collegeville, Minn.: St. John's Abbey, 1940.
> *Mount Angel Letter,* various issues. St. Benedict, Ore.
> Sarra, Andrea. *La Beata Suor Maria Fortunata Viti.* Veroli, Italy: Tipografia Dell'abbazia di Casamari, 1967.
> Sarra, Andrea. *The Blessed Mary Fortunata Viti.* St. Benedict, Ore.: Benedictine Press, 1972.
> Various pamphlet materials.

Correspondence
> Rev. Thomas Brockhaus, O.S.B., Vice-Postulator for the Cause of Sister Fortunata. Mount Angel Abbey; St. Benedict, Ore.
> Miss Antoinetta Panico. Benedictine Monastery; Veroli, Italy.
> Sisters. Benedictine Convent of Perpetual Adoration; Clyde, Mo.

38. MOTHER MARY WALSH

Publications
> Boardman, Anne Cawley. *Such Love Is Seldom.* Ossining, N.Y.: Mariandale Publishers, 1950.
> "Dominican Sisters Carry on 100-Year-Old Nursing Tradition." Gannett Westchester Newspapers, Jan. 29, 1979, sponsor notes.
> *The Story.* Newsletter of the Dominican Sisters of the Sick Poor. Vol. IV, No. 1.
> Sister M. Teresa, O.P. Letters to Mother Mary Walsh.

Correspondence
> Sister M. Assumpta, O.P. Dominican Sisters Congregation of the Immaculate Conception; Ossining, N.Y.
> Sister M. Virgine, O.P., Archivist. Dominican Sisters Congregation of the Immaculate Conception; Ossining, N.Y.

39. SAINT RAPHAELA

Publications
> Lawson, W., S.J. *Blessed Rafaela Maria Porras.* Dublin: Clonmore and Reynolds, 1963.
> Purcell, Mary. Life of Blessed Raphaela Mary of the Sacred Heart. Dublin: The Handmaids of the Sacred Heart, 1956.

Thoughts of Blessed Raphaela Mary of the Sacred Heart. Faversham, Kent, England: Carmelite Press, 1963.

"Years of Silence." *Young Catholic Messenger,* Dec. 28, 1962.

Correspondence

Sister Irene, A.C.J. St. Raphaela Mary Retreat House; Haverford, Pa.

Sister Ruth Nuckols, A.C.J. Handmaids of the Sacred Heart of Jesus, Philadelphia.

Sister Rosalia, A.C.J. Ancelle del Sacro Cuore, Rome.

40. ROSE HAWTHORNE LATHROP

Publications

The Anthonian. Special issue, Vol. 46, 1st quarter, 1972.

Dominican Sisters, Congregation of St. Rose of Lima, 1900 - 1975. 75th anniversary brochure.

Joseph, Sister M., O.P. *Artistry Indeed.* Dominican Sisters, 1975.

Joseph, Sister M., O.P. *Out of Many Hearts.* Hawthorne, N.Y.: Servants of Relief for Incurable Cancer, 1965.

Maynard, Theodore. *A Fire Was Lighted: The Life of Rose Hawthorne Lathrop.* Milwaukee: Bruce, 1948.

Correspondence

Mother M. Angela, O.P., Mother General, Rosary Hill Home; Hawthorne, N.Y.

Sister M. Joan, O.P., Vocation Director, Rosary Hill Home; Hawthorne, N.Y.

41. SISTER MIRIAM TERESA

Publications

Demjanovich, Sister Miriam Teresa. *A Blueprint for Holiness.* Convent, N.J.: S.M.T. League of Prayer, 1979.

Demjanovich, Sister Miriam Teresa. *Greater Perfection.* Charles Demjanovich, 1946.

Harris, Elizabeth. *Sister Miriam Teresa.* Ireland, 1965.

The Sister Miriam Teresa League of Prayer Bulletin, various issues including Oct. 1970, Dec. 1970, and Dec. 1979.

A Sister of Charity. *Sister Miriam Teresa.* New York: Benziger Bros., 1957.

The Story of the Exhumation of the Remains of Sister Miriam Teresa Demjanovich, S.C. 1978.

Correspondence

Sister M. Zita. The Sister Miriam Teresa League of Prayer; Convent, N.J.

42. FATHER MIGUEL PRO
Publications

Dragon, Rev. A., S.J. *Le Pere Pro*. Montreal: Les Editions de L'Atelier, 1958.

Forrest, Rev. M.D., M.S.C. *The Life of Father Pro*. St. Paul, Minn.: Radio Replies Press, 1945.

Knowles, Leo. *Candidates for Sainthood*. St. Paul: Carillon Books, 1978.

Marmoiton, Victor. *Le Pere Pro: Apostolat de la Priere*. Toulouse, France, 1953.

Roberto, Bro., C.S.C. *Dawn Brings Glory*. Notre Dame, Ind.: Dujarie Press, 1956.

Correspondence

Rev. Enrique Cardenas, S.J., Vice-Postulator; Chihuahua, Mexico.

Rev. A. Dragon, S.J., Montreal.

Rev. Andrew Smith, S.J., Spring Hill College; Mobile, Ala.

43. FATHER LUKAS ETLIN
Publications

Malone, Very Rev. Edward E. *Father Lukas Etlin, O.S.B.: Apostle of the Eucharist*. Clyde, Mo.: Benedictine Convent of Perpetual Adoration, 1961.

Various pamphlet materials.

Correspondence

Rev. Louis Meyer, O.S.B., Vice-Postulator; Conception, Mo.

44. BISHOP LUIGI VERSIGLIA and
FATHER CALLISTO CARAVARIO
Publications

Bianco, Enzo, S.D.B. *I Buoni Pastori Danno La Vita, Mons. Versiglia E Don Caravario*. Rome: Publicazione a cura dell'Ufficio Stampa Salesiano, 1980.

Bianco, Enzo, S.D.B., & Maraldi, Assunta, F.M.A. *First Centenary of Don Bosco's Missions*. Rome: SDB Publishers, 1977.

Rassiga, Marius. *Blood on the River Bank*. Hong Kong: Salesian Provincialate, 1980.

"Two Martyrs in China." *The Salesian Bulletin*, Vol. 33, Jan./Feb. 1979.

Various extracts from Salesian biographical records, Italian language.

Correspondence

> Rev. Dominic Britschu, S.D.B., Secretary General of the Salesians, Rome.
>
> Sister Virginia D'Alessandro, F.M.A., Secretary to the Provincial. Salesian Sisters; Haledon, N.J.
>
> Rev. James Hurley, S.D.B. Don Bosco College; Newton, N.J.

45. SISTER CARMEN MORENO and SISTER AMPARO CARBONELL

Publications

> *Centenary, Daughters of Mary Help of Christians.* Asti, Italy: Isag-Colle Don Bosco, 1972.
>
> *Daughters of Mary Help of Christians.* Rome: Generalate of the Institute, Daughters of Mary Help of Christians, 1972.
>
> *La Serva di Dio Suor Amparo Carbonell.* Torino, Italy: Superiora Generale delle Figlie di Maria Ausilatrice, 1960.
>
> *La Serva di Dio Suor Carmen Moreno.* Torino, Italy: Superiora Generale delle Figlie di Maria Ausilatrice, 1960.

Correspondence

> Sister Lydia Carini, F.M.A. Generalate, Rome.

46. BROTHER ANDRE

Publications

> Hanley, Boniface, O.F.M. "All He Could Do Was Pray." *The Anthonian,* Vol. 53, 1979.
>
> Knowles, Leo. *Candidates for Sainthood.* St. Paul: Carillon Books, 1978.
>
> Lafreniere, Rev. Bernard, C.S.C. *Brother Andre's Beatification Cause.*
>
> *The Oratory.* Special issue dedicated to Brother Andre. Montreal, May 1971.
>
> Various pamphlet materials.

Correspondence

> Rev. Bernard Lafreniere, C.S.C. The Oratory, Montreal.

47. DON LOUIS ORIONE

Publications

> Aronica, Rev. Paul, S.D.B. "No Closed Doors." *The Salesian Bulletin,* Vol. 34, Dec. 1980.
>
> Disegna, Sister M. Bertilla. "The Exhumation of Don Louis Orione's Body." March 9, 1978.
>
> *Don Orione, l'homo che ha creduto.* Fossano: Sezione Pastorale Editrice Esperienze.

Hyde, Douglas. *God's Bandit.* Ireland: Sons of Divine Providence, 1957.

Knowles, Leo. *Candidates for Sainthood.* St. Paul: Carillon Books, 1978.

Il Servo di Dio Don Luigi Orione. Rome: Instituto Don Orione, 1954.

Various brief mimeographed works.

Correspondence

Rev. Paul Aronica, S.D.B., Editor, *The Salesian Bulletin;* New Rochelle, N.Y.

Sister M. Bertilla Disegna; East Boston, Mass.

Leo Knowles; Manchester, England.

48. SAINT MAXIMILIAN KOLBE

Publications

Elliott, Lawrence. "The Heroism of Father Kolbe." *Reader's Digest,* July 1973.

Francis Mary, Bro., O.F.M. Conv. *The Hero of Auschwitz.* Kenosha, Wis.: Prow Books, 1970.

Hanley, Boniface, O.F.M. *Ten Christians.* Notre Dame, Ind.: Ave Maria Press, 1979.

Treece, Patricia, and Chatton, Ray. *Soldier of God: The Gripping Story of Maximilian Kolbe* (comic book). Libertyville, Ill.: Prow Books/Franciscan Marytown Press, 1982.

"The Two Crowns Fulfilled." *Immaculata Review,* Oct. - Nov., 1982. Libertyville, Ill.: Franciscan Marytown Press.

Correspondence

Regis Barwig, Community of Our Lady; Oshkosh, Wis.

Bro. Francis Mary, O.F.M. Conv. Libertyville, Ill.

49. TITUS BRANDSMA

Publications

Knowles, Leo. *Candidates for Sainthood.* St. Paul: Carillon Books, 1978.

Rees, Joseph. *Titus Brandsma: A Modern Martyr.* London: Sidgwick & Jackson, 1971.

Rhodes, Elinor D. *His Memory Shall Not Pass.* New York: Scapular Press, 1958.

Correspondence

Rev. Roger Bonneau, Librarian. Mt. Carmel High School; Houston, Texas.

Rev. Joseph Rees. Catholic Presbytery; Ware, England.

Rev. Joachim Smet, O. Carm. Whitefriars Hall; Washington, D.C.

Rev. Adrian Staring, O. Carm., Rome.

Rev. Felix Wezenbeek, O. Carm., Vice-Postulator; Nijmegen, The Netherlands.

50. EDITH STEIN

Publications

de Fabregues, Jean. *Edith Stein*. Staten Island, N.Y.: Alba House, 1965.

Graef, Hilda. *The Scholar and the Cross*. London: Longmans Green, 1955.

Grant, Cecily. *Edith Stein*. London: Catholic Truth Society, 1957.

Knowles, Leo. *Candidates for Sainthood*. St. Paul: Carillon Books, 1978.

Correspondence

Sister M. Amata, O.C.D. Edith Stein Archives, Karmel Maria vom Frieden; Cologne, Germany.

Edith Foss, Edith Stein Guild; New York, N.Y.

51. SISTER ALPHONSA

Publications

Chacko, K.C. *Sister Alphonsa*. Trivandrum, India: Alphonsa Publishers, 1949.

Kappen, J.C. *The Passion Flower of India*. Bharananganam, 1964.

Minattur, Dr. J. *Flame and Flower*. Trivandrum, India: Alphonsa Publishers, 1963.

The Passion Flower. Bharananganam, India; Aug. 1969, Nov. 1969, Feb. 1970, May 1970.

Sister Alphonsa and Her Clients. Elthuruth, Trichur, India: St. Joseph's Press, 1950.

Correspondence

Rev. Antonio Cairoli, O.F.M., Postulator General for the Franciscan Order, Rome.

Rev. Thomas Moothedam, Vice-Postulator for the Cause of Sister Alphonsa; Bharananganam, India.

52. MARIA TERESA QUEVEDO

Publications

Pierre, Sister Mary, R.S.M. *Mary Was Her Life*. New York: Benziger Bros., 1960.

Teresita. Newsletter from the beatification cause headquarters. Madrid, No. 91 and No. 92.

Weber, Leonora Mattingly. *She Walked With Mary*. Castro Valley, Calif.: Carmelite Sisters of Charity.

Correspondence

> Sister Rose Amelia. Carmelite Missionary Sisters, Houston.
>
> Sister Maria Rosa, Ca.Ch.; Washington, D.C.
>
> Sister Maria Rosa, Ca.Ch.; Novitiate of the Carmelites of Charity, Madrid.
>
> Sister Maria Luisa Uralde, Ca.Ch.; Carmelites of Charity, Madrid.

53. MARY ANN LONG

Publications

> *Dominican Sisters, Congregation of St. Rose of Lima, 1900 - 1975.* 75th anniversary brochure.
>
> Evangelist, Sister M., O.P. *Mission Fulfilled.* New York: Dell Publishing Co., 1961.

Correspondence

> Mother Mary Angela Bott, O.P., Mother General. Dominican Sisters, Congregation of St. Rose of Lima; Rosary Hill Home, N.Y.
>
> Sister M. Joan, O.P.; Rosary Hill Home, N.Y.
>
> Miss Doris Long, Ky.
>
> Mr. & Mrs. George Long, Ky.

54. PADRE PIO

Publications

> Parente, Pascal P. *A City on a Mountain.* Grail, 1952.
>
> Pio, Padre, O.F.M. Cap. *The Agony of Jesus.* Rockford, Ill.: TAN Books and Publishers, 1974.
>
> Pio, Padre, O.F.M. Cap. *Meditation Prayer on Mary Immaculate, with a Translation and Sketch by Laura Chanler White.* Rockford, Ill.: TAN Books and Publishers, 1974.
>
> *The Voice of Padre Pio: Periodical of the Postulation for the Beatification and Canonization of Padre Pio of Pietrelcina.* San Giovanni Rotondo, Italy: Our Lady of Grace Capuchin Friary, various issues.

Correspondence

> Rev. Antonio Cairoli, O.F.M., Postulator General of the Friars Minor, Rome.
>
> Mrs. Vera M. Calandra, Director of the National Center for Padre Pio, the official Postulation office for the Cause for Padre Pio in the United States and Canada.
>
> Rev. Armand Dasseville, O.F.M. Cap.
>
> Rev. Sigmund Hafemann, O.F.M. Cap. The Capuchins' Public Relations Office; Yonkers, N.Y.

55. BROTHER ELIAS

Publications

Burns, Flavian. *Homily for the Funeral Mass of Brother Elias.*

The Exodus of Our Brother in Christ Elias Simpson. A collection of Letters by the brothers of Gethsemani Abbey, Ky.

James, Rev. M., o.c.s.o. Letter circulated to the other Trappist monasteries.

Merton, Thomas. *Gethsemani, A Life of Praise.* Gethsemani, Ky.: Abbey of Gethsemani, 1966.

Simpson, Albert (brother of Brother Elias). Letter of remembrance. Cincinnati.

Correspondence

Bro. Athanasius Doll, o.c.s.o. Abbey of Gethsemani, Ky.

Frances Simpson, mother of Brother Elias. Cincinnati.

Timothy Kelly, o.c.s.o., Abbot of Gethsemani.

GENERAL SOURCES
AND SELECTED BIBLIOGRAPHY

Publications

Antonelli, Franciscus, O.F.M. *De Inquisitione Medico-Legali Super Miraculis in Causis Beatificationis et Canonizationis.* Roma: Antonianum, 1962.

Attwater, Donald. *A Dictionary of Saints.* New York: P. J. Kenedy & Sons, 1958.

Attwater, Donald. *Martyrs.* New York: Sheed & Ward, 1957.

Blaher, Damian Joseph, O.F.M. *The Ordinary Procceses in Causes of Beatification and Canonization.* Washington, D.C.: Catholic University of America Press, 1949.

Butler, Rev. Alban. *The Lives of the Fathers, Martyrs and Other Principal Saints,* 4 vols. Chicago: The Catholic Press, 1961.

Codex Iuris Canonici, c. 2116.

Delaney, John J., and Tobin, James. *Dictionary of Catholic Biography.* Garden City, N.Y.: Doubleday, 1961.

Farmer, David Hugh. *The Oxford Dictionary of Saints.* Oxford: Clarendon Press, 1978.

Foy, Felician A., O.F.M., ed. *The Catholic Almanac.* Huntington, Ind.: Our Sunday Visitor, 1973 - 1979 editions.

General Catechetical Directory. Warrenton, Va.: Society for the Christian Commonwealth, 1971.

Habig, Rev. Marion, O.F.M. *Saints of the Americas.* Huntington, Ind.: Our Sunday Visitor, 1974.

Holweck, Rt. Rev. F. G. *A Biographical Dictionary of the Saints.* Detroit: Gale Research Co., 1969.

Index ac Status Causarum Beatificationis Servorum Dei et Canonizationis Beatorum. Roma: Sacra Congregatio Pro Causis Sanctorum, 1962 edition & 1975 edition.

"The Long Road to Sainthood." *Time,* July 7, 1980.

Mother Cabrini Messenger. Vol. 12, No. 2, April 1950.

Official Catholic Directory. New York: P. J. Kenedy & Sons, 1978.

Paul VI, Pope. "Sanctitas Clarior." Apostolic Letter of March 19, 1969 on reorganizing procedures in causes for beatification and canonization. Washington, D.C.: U.S. Catholic Conference, 1969.

"Sacra Rituum Congregatio." *Acta Apostolicae Sedis,* 61 (1969).

Schamoni. *The Face of the Saints.* London: Sheed & Ward, 1948.

Correspondence

Rev. F. Beaudoin, Archivist. Sacred Congregation for the Causes of Saints, Vatican City.

OTHER TITLES AVAILABLE

At your bookdealer or direct from the Publisher.

The Glories of Mary. St. Alphonsus.
The Prophets and Our Times. Culleton.
St. Therese, The Little Flower. Beevers.
The Life & Glories of St. Joseph. Thompson.
An Explanation of the Baltimore Catechism. Kinkead.
Humility of Heart. da Bergamo.
Christ's Appeal for Love. Menendez.
The Cure D'Ars. Trochu.
The Divine Mysteries of the Rosary. Ven. M. of Agreda.
Preparation for Death. St. Alphonsus.
St. Joseph of Copertino. Pastrovicchi.
Mary, The Second Eve. Card. Newman.
The Faith of Our Fathers. Gibbons.
Manual of Practical Devotion to St. Joseph. Patrignani.
The Wonder of Guadalupe. Johnston.
The Blessed Virgin Mary. St. Alphonsus.
The Way of Divine Love. Menendez.
St. Pius V. Anderson.
Mystical City of God—Abridged. Ven. M. of Agreda.
Beyond Space—A Book About the Angels. Parente.
Dialogue of St. Catherine of Siena. Thorold.
Evidence of Satan in the Modern World. Cristiani.
Child's Bible History. Knecht.
Bible History of the Old & New Testaments. Schuster.
Apologetics. Glenn.
Magnificent Prayers. St. Bridget of Sweden.
Baltimore Catechism No. 3. Kinkead.
The Blessed Eucharist. Mueller.
Soul of the Apostolate. Chautard.
Thirty Favorite Novenas.
Devotion to the Infant Jesus of Prague.
Fundamentals of Catholic Dogma. Ott.
The Agony of Jesus. Padre Pio.
Uniformity with God's Will. St. Alphonsus.
St. Gertrude the Great.
St. Joan of Arc. Beevers.
Life of the Blessed Virgin Mary. Emmerich.
Convert's Catechism of Catholic Doctrine. Geiermann.
Canons & Decrees of the Council of Trent. Schroeder.
St. Dominic's Family. Dorcy.
Be My Son. Legere.
Sermons of St. Alphonsus Liguori.
The Catholic Answer To Jehovah's Witnesses. D'Angelo.
What Faith Really Means. Graham.
A Catechism of Modernism. Lemius.
What Catholics Believe. Lovasik.

At your bookdealer or direct from the Publisher.